The Knowing Ani

The titles in this three-part work by Raymond Tallis, and published by Edinburgh University Press, are:

The Hand: A Philosophical Inquiry into Human Being
I Am: A Philosophical Inquiry into First-Person Being
The Knowing Animal: A Philosophical Inquiry into Knowledge and Truth

The Knowing Animal

A Philosophical Inquiry into Knowledge and Truth

Raymond Tallis

Edinburgh University Press

© Raymond Tallis, 2005

Edinburgh University Press Ltd
22 George Square, Edinburgh

Typeset in Sabon
by Koinonia, Manchester, and
printed and bound in Great Britain
by Antony Rowe Ltd, Chippenham, Wilts

A CIP record for this book is available
from the British Library

ISBN 0 7486 1952 6 (hardback)
ISBN 0 7486 1953 4 (paperback)

The right of Raymond Tallis
to be identified as author of this work
has been asserted in accordance with
the Copyright, Designs and Patents Act 1988

Contents

Part 2 From Sentience to Sentences

Part 3 The Knowing Agent

Part 4 Knowledge Encounters Itself

Dedicated to Peter Rickman, true philosopher

Acknowledgements

This is the final volume of a trilogy. Without the support, enthusiasm and personal kindness of Jackie Jones at Edinburgh University Press, the three volumes would have not have reached publication. It is a pleasure, therefore, to say again how grateful I am to her, and also to her brilliant team at Edinburgh, with whom it has been delightful to work. As always, my agent Jacqueline Korn, of David Higham Associates, has provided guidance, reassurance and encouragement – for which very many thanks. Finally, it is a special pleasure to acknowledge yet again the help of Ruth Willats, whose copy-editing skills and all-round wisdom and good sense I have been lucky enough to secure for the eighth time. I have also been very fortunate in having the help of a superb indexer, Auriol Griffith-Jones, in this as in previous books. I have come to the conclusion that she would have no difficulty in producing a helpful and intelligible index of a hedge.

The dedicatee of this book is Professor Peter Rickman, emeritus professor of philosophy at City University, London, and world authority on Wilhelm Dilthey. His extraordinarily generous support of medical research through the Muriel Edith Rickman Trust, his fortitude in the face of illness and his passion for ideas make him a role-model that is difficult to emulate: a true philosopher in every sense of the word. Peter, the dedication of this book is a small thank you for many inspiring conversations.

PART ONE

KNOWLEDGE VISIBLE AND INVISIBLE

CHAPTER 1

The Assault on the Knowing Subject

Scientism is not science but a world-view that grew funguslike on the trunk of science.[1]

This is the third volume of a trilogy, *Handkind*, whose overall purpose is to try to make more visible the distinctive nature of human beings and, in support of an increasingly embattled humanism, to reawaken a sense of human possibility.

The liberation of humankind from a religious self-understanding – with its fantasies of supernatural rulers to whom homage, subservience and allegiance are owed – is far from complete. Already, however, secular thought is running into difficulties. There is a crisis of confidence in what has been called 'the Enlightenment Project' and many thinkers argue that the optimistic image of Man as first conceived in the Renaissance is set to be wiped away, 'like a face drawn in the sand at the edge of the sea'.[2] The party is over and mankind and the planet he pollutes are heading to Hell in a handcart.

The data in support of these glum assumptions are, to put it mildly, far from decisive. Such evidence as there is suggests that overall things for mankind are improving. While the many shocking things that happen in the world show how much remains to be done, this is not sufficient reason for believing that there is nothing to be done. Pessimism is often a pose, assumed out of fear that optimism might be judged shallowly Panglossian. But some intellectualised despair has deeper roots: in the assumption that humans are self-deceived when they believe they know who they are, what they are doing and why they are doing it; when, in short, they believe that they are self-conscious agents, able in some part collectively and individually to shape their future and make it better than the past. Our contemporary Panglumians argue that humans are passive instruments, the playthings of processes and forces that they are unaware of. We are sleepwalkers, ignorant alike of our own nature and of the forces that operate in the societies we have created and wish to change for the better.

The dystopian consequences of even modestly progressive ambitions will therefore seem inevitable – as the history of the twentieth century has seemed to bear out – and incremental scientific advance will simply hasten the apocalypse. If we don't know what we are doing, we can hardly be expected to predict, control or even know the overall outcomes of the actions of billions of us. We can be confident only that things are already horrible and they are going to get even worse.

These views – which I have examined at some length in an earlier book[3] – are in part the after-echo of theological images of Man as a fallen creature, whose arrogant inability to acknowledge his condition will simply amplify the inaugural disaster. This is not merely a Judaeo-Christian notion. It reaches back to the earliest phases of human self-reflection. When Prometheus stole fire from the gods, he was sooner or later going to lay waste to the entire planet. Contemporary anti-humanism, however, also draws heavily upon secular sources – ironically upon science, or the idea of it. By an even more bitter irony, it does so by extrapolating scientific ideas beyond those places where science has legitimate authority. Our image of humanity is increasingly distorted (degraded, disfigured) by *scientism*, whose deepest faith, or assumption, is that the human world can be explained entirely in terms of the laws uncovered by natural science or mechanisms that are in some way analogous to those of physics, chemistry and biology. Most bitter irony of all, such scientism had its most extreme and influential expression in the Enlightenment, when the dispassionate application of reason and science to the human world promised liberation from the oppressive hierarchies and received wisdom upheld by religion.

The 'sciences' that have been deployed in this way have not always been the most intellectually robust. In the twentieth century, some of the less well-developed of the human sciences were mobilised to attack the notion of a human being as a self-conscious moral agent. The 'physics envy' of many of these disciplines encouraged an emphasis on objective descriptions of 'social facts', 'social forces' and the like, and a devaluing of introspection: physics, after all, would not have progressed very fast if physicists had relied on the private views of pebbles about the matter of which they were composed, or the folk-science of the unsophisticated as to what made pebbles fall to the ground. What people think they think, what they believe motivates them, is to be discarded as being of little scientific relevance. What we are is concealed from us: only objective science can reveal it.

This tactical, or methodological, decision profoundly affected the beliefs, or professional beliefs, of many in the human sciences (including psychology) about the nature of human beings. Most importantly, human consciousness and self-consciousness were downplayed as forces in human affairs. Metaphysical straw men, such as the 'totally self-transparent Cartesian Ego', were mocked as being central to the illusions of a discredited humanism; instead, a variety of modes of 'The Unconscious' was installed at the heart of a 'decentred' or 'deconstructed' self. The Unconscious was put together from a selection of would-be sciences: for example, psychoanalysis (the psychological unconscious); Marxist theory (the political unconscious); and structuralism and post-structuralism (the linguistic or symbolic unconscious). Common to these diverse 'disciplines' was the belief that the reasons for which we think we do things are not the reasons for which we actually do them. More drastically, our feeling of agency is merely our awareness of the impersonal forces that are acting upon us. When I speak, for example, what I say does not originate with me: language speaks through me. As for 'me', this is merely a constellation of nodes in a system of signs, most of which are unknown to me and none of which can express what I think I mean through them.

The anti-humanist dissolution of the human subject, based upon pseudo-sciences that have mesmerised certain gullible intellectuals, notably academics in the humanities, may be becoming less influential: anti-humanist Marxism, structuralism, post-structuralism, psychoanalysis and even postmodernism are looking rather *passé*. There is, however, another form of scientism, this one based upon a real science – biology – which seems to be in the ascendant. 'Biologism' holds that humans are essentially animals and are therefore to be understood in biological terms. If you want to know what a human being is, ask a biologist. The latter, apparently, will tell you that the self, the 'I', is merely a nexus of instincts, tropisms, conditioned reflexes, etc., directly or indirectly supporting organic survival.

The river of biologistic thought has many tributaries, but the most important are Darwinism and neuroscience. Darwin showed that it was possible to understand the emergence of all species in terms of a single mechanism, albeit acting over vast stretches of time: natural selection between spontaneously occurring mutations. There is preferential survival of those variants that have an edge on the competition through being better adapted to a more or less hostile environment. Darwin made it possible to see humans as the products of the processes that had produced all living things. For some, this meant that he had exposed as a delusion the idea that humans are special and not entirely part of nature.

It does not matter that developments over the last 150 years (notably Mendelian genetics refined through molecular biology) have shifted the emphasis from survival of the organism to the survival of the genetic material expressed in the organism. The conclusion is the same. 'The selfish gene' utilises unwitting organisms as a means to ensure its continuation through replication. Crucially, this is not a conscious process. Darwin, as Samuel Butler famously said, 'banished mind from the universe'. The selfish genes are not really selfish, self-centred or self-seeking. 'Selves', in the sense of conscious agents, have nothing to do with the evolutionary process.

And this is why 150 years after *The Origin of Species* was published, the theory of evolution is no longer a liberating force. For many thinkers it justifies not only minimising the differences between humans and animals, but also marginalising the role of self-conscious agency in human affairs. Darwin's great idea has, in the hands of misguided modern interpreters, become a serious obstacle to thinking straight about mankind. Having helped us to escape the prison of a supernatural understanding of ourselves, Darwinism is now being invoked to imprison us in a no less dispiriting (and equally erroneous) naturalistic understanding. We have lost not only the theological guarantee of the exceptional nature of human beings, but also that exceptional nature itself. To assert that we are more than 'just animals' is still to be in the grip of the theological delusions that Darwin discredited.

Darwinism, in short, has been transformed into 'Darwinosis'. According to this pathological variant of Darwinism, not only are we descended from animals but we are no different from them; or at least not in those respects that most matter. Since we are beasts, we are no more free than they are. If we still believe that we are free, this is only because it is of adaptive value to be thus deluded, and to imagine, as we do, that we are rational agents. But the reasons for which we think we do things are not the reasons for which we actually do them. Indeed, reason and intention are as irrelevant to our direction of travel as the toy steering wheel attached to the dashboard on the passenger's side that gives children the feeling of being in the driving seat. Our sense of agency is merely muddled awareness of the impersonal forces operating through us. Self-consciousness is irrelevant. The 'I' is in the grip of universal material causation and is, at bottom, as third-personal as rocks, trees and monkeys.

The extension of the mindlessness of the Darwinian universe to the human world has been greatly assisted by a wild over-estimation of advances made in neuroscience and of our understanding of the basis of mental function. Numerous neuroscientists and philosophical fellow travellers such as Daniel Dennett assert categorically that the mind is identical with the neural activity of the brain. Since the brain is the most important organ for survival, our minds should be understood in Darwinian terms as an assembly of survival mechanisms. Steven Pinker's claim that the human mind 'is a system of organs of computation designed by natural selection to solve the problems faced by our evolutionary ancestors'[4] illustrates this convergence between Darwinian thought and philosophised neuroscience.

Sociobiology and evolutionary psychology are typical manifestations of Darwinosis, and their business is booming. Between them, they purport to account for most aspects of the human mind and society. E. O. Wilson, the founding father of sociobiology, claimed that 'behaviour and social structure, like all other biological phenomena, can be studied as "organs", extensions of genes that exist because of their superior adaptive value'. He added: 'It might not be too much to say that sociology and the other social sciences, as well as the humanities, are the last branches of biology.'[5] This view has enjoyed wide, uncritical acceptance. Ethical principles, political structures, human knowledge, the very idea of truth, seem ready to disappear into the voracious orifice of Darwinosis. Even where there is disagreement about the way the human mind develops – as in the celebrated battles between 'blank slaters' and those who believe in the importance of genetically determined, innate mental structures and modules – there is common ground in the assumption that the mechanisms underlying animal behaviour (genes, instinct, conditioning) also explain why humans behave as they do.

Darwinosis is a radical and comprehensive expression of the belief that human beings are driven by unconscious forces – in this case the survival tactics of genes – rather than by conscious agency. If true, this would have dire implications for human freedom and for the assumption that we know what we are doing and why. But it is not because it removes hope that Darwinosis has to be contested. For if it were actually true, it would just have to be accepted. It has to be challenged because it is simply wrong about humans and misses what is most important and interesting about us – which is also our main source of hope for continuing human progress. It is, however, very difficult to challenge Darwinotic ideas without seeming to be a closet Creationist or a deluded sentimentalist running away from the implications of what Dennett has dubbed 'Darwin's dangerous idea'.

In the previous two volumes, I have examined the fundamental ways in which humans do indeed differ from other living beings. What is more – to pre-empt the argument (prompted by the feeling that they do not fit into the Darwinian framework) that these differences are illusory – I have proposed a *biological* trigger for the increasing divergence of human beings from their nearest primate ancestors. With respect to our origins, we are indubitably a part of nature and to be understood in biological terms; but with respect to what we have become, we are to a considerable degree apart from nature and not to be understood in biological (even less physical) terms. This biological explanation as to how we have become distanced from our biological makeup and our material circumstances is, I believe, entirely compatible with Darwinian thought about our origins, though it is at odds with Darwinosis.

The first volume, *The Hand: A Philosphical Inquiry into Human Being*, explained the role of the hand in instrumentalising the human body and awakening the sense of the human subject within the animal organism. The hand, I argued, ignited a process which, over many hundreds of thousands of years – both directly, and indirectly through the tools, socialisation, the collectivisation of consciousness and the language it has inspired – took hominids from a state of nature, in which they lived much as did other organisms, to an entirely different state in which they were able actively to *lead* their lives.

The second volume, *I Am: A Philosophical Inquiry into First-Person Being*, focused in more detail on certain aspects of human being, in particular, the consequences of the Existential Intuition awoken by the hand, which distinguishes human beings from all other beasts: the emergence of personal identity and agency. *I Am* was, as much as anything, affirmative action for first-person being, reinstating first-person awareness at the heart of distinctively human life. I located the sense 'That I am this …' at the root of selfhood, and of the agency and capacity for free action that humans alone possess. As well as (I hope) clarifying the nature of personal identity, and demonstrating that it was possible for humans to act freely without having to break the laws of nature or requisition a special, esoteric kind of causation, *I Am* devoted several chapters to the complex relationship between the human subject and the human body. Embodiment proved to be much more complex, puzzling and indeed mysterious than might appear at first sight. The outstanding problems in this area are connected with one of the key intuitions behind the present volume, concerning the nature of knowledge.

The Knowing Animal: A Philosophical Inquiry into Knowledge and Truth continues the project of capturing the essence of human being by examining knowledge, which, I shall argue, sets humans apart from all other sentient creatures in nature. While it is arguable that higher primates at least have intermittent self-consciousness and may, in some very minimal sense, be regarded as agents, there is nothing corresponding to knowledge in the consciousness of any non-human creature. This may seem a vulnerable, even counter-intuitive, claim. Surely, it will be argued, monkeys – even sparrows and earthworms – know lots of things, and they use their knowledge in support of the daily challenge to stay alive. While they cannot, of course, say, write down or otherwise make explicit what they know, they have much *implicit* knowledge.

Against this, I will argue that knowledge is essentially explicit and that implicit knowledge, while it has a place side-by-side with explicit knowledge, should not be used to describe the cognitive capabilities of creatures who do not have the capacity to make their awareness explicit in the way that humans do. Connected with this is my view that the attribution of beliefs (and judgements and the ability to classify contents of the world) to animals is 'Disneyfication'; an anthropomorphism which is itself a manifestation of what I have elsewhere described as the Fallacy of Misplaced Explicitness.[6] Judgement, belief, classification and knowledge are aspects of what I shall call 'propositional awareness': awareness '*That* something is the case'. This more than anything else sets off humans from the rest of the living world. It is the root of the growing distance, the deepening gulf, between *Homo sapiens* and all other sentient creatures.

Propositional awareness is a consequence of the Existential Intuition – 'That I am this …' – which expresses a transformed relationship of the human organism to itself, and the emergence of the first-person subject within the impersonal body. As I have emphasised in previous volumes, the passage from sentience (enjoyed or endured to differing degrees by all animals) to propositional awareness and knowledge has been gradual: the Explicit Animal has been a long time in the making. Several million years of distinctively human evolution separate knowledge from the sentience of our nearest animal kin. The process has had many drivers: out of the hand came the tool; out of the tool came sociality and the collectivisation of consciousness; out of the hand-inspired and tool-enhanced self-encounter of the body came the sense of the partial scrutability of objects and the gap between sense experience and 'what is there'; out of the collectivisation of consciousness and the sense of the objectivity – the publicness and otherness – of objects came the intuition of objective knowledge, of the incompleteness of awareness and the impulse to deliberate inquiry; out of all of these came language – and literally propositional awareness – which in turn speeded up the other processes; and, in parallel with this, came the explicit notion of objective truth.

In several respects, *The Knowing Animal*, of the three volumes comprising *Handkind*, is the most direct continuation of discussions of explicitness in two of my earlier books: *The Explicit Animal*[7] and *On the Edge of Certainty*.[8] Knowledge is a mode of explicitness, of explicit-making consciousness, that is easiest to get hold of, that is itself most explicit. At the same time, *The Knowing Animal* also corrects what I believe to be a regrettable tendency, especially in *The Explicit Animal*, to merge discussion of sentience (as exemplified in basic components of consciousness such as qualia) with that of higher forms of consciousness such as knowledge.

The Explicit Animal is sub-titled 'A Defence of Human Consciousness'. The enemies it had in its sights were those who purported to naturalise our consciousness, by presenting an account of the human mind which combined biological and computational theories: the mind as a sort of natural computer. The naturalisers typically think of the mind as the sum total of the rule-governed activity of the nervous system linking sensory input with behavioural output. In *The Explicit Animal* I did not clearly separate the case against neural accounts of animal consciousness from the case against neural accounts of *specifically human* consciousness – the consciousness of the Explicit Animal. In the present book, I will be more willing to suspend judgement about the role of the nervous system in underpinning the sentience of animals. Though (as will be evident in the next chapter) I remain deeply unimpressed by neural 'explanations' of sentience, I am more concerned to rebut naturalistic accounts of specifically human consciousness. While I am dubious about finding qualia in neurones, I am absolutely certain we shall not find knowledge, facts, piety or citizens there.

Much of the apparent strength of neural – and naturalistic – accounts of the human mind comes from the strategy (which begins as a methodological decision and ends as a quasi-empirical claim about the nature of the object under investigation) of downplaying the role of explicit awareness in the human mind. Naturalisers like to tell us that the human mind is an assembly of mechanisms, of automated processes, that happen largely without our being aware of them. What we are aware of is mere froth from the industry going on beneath the surface. Emptying the mind in this way is part of a much wider trend, already noticed, of marginalising individual consciousness.

This perverse approach is not confined to neurophilosophers such as Daniel Dennett who, finding qualia (the basic elements of actual subjective experiences) difficult to accommodate in his ensemble-of-virtual-machines model of the mind, denies their existence.[9] On the contrary, it has been important, indeed pervasive, throughout analytical philosophy in the Anglo-American tradition, as we shall discuss later in this chapter. In the spirit of objective science (to which we have already referred) and of an idea of intellectual purity that refuses to countenance mysterious inner objects (which seem only to generate intractable and apparently empty philosophical problems), there has been a determination by some to avoid reference to consciousness in the treatment of human knowledge and the concept of truth. The seemingly self-evident assumption that it is not possible to understand knowledge, belief or truth without reference to human consciousness has been seen as the mark of an unreformed and unsophisticated approach untouched by the new 'scientific' spirit that has transformed the humanities.

In many respects, the present book is reactionary, criticising the conceptual revolutions that, I believe, have paved the way for scientistic (*sic*) reductions of human behaviour, diminishing the role of the conscious human agent in human affairs. More relevant to our present purposes, these revolutions in thought have made what is distinctive about human consciousness, and in particular knowledge, more difficult to see. If this volume has one overriding purpose, it is to make human knowledge *visible*.

First, however, there is a bit of 'internal' philosophical business to be transacted. We need to defend making knowledge a fundamental theme in philosophical anthropology and to justify an account of knowledge that sees it as a form of consciousness, rather than as something to be defined in terms of its formal properties; in short, to deal with a scientistic tendency to depsychologise knowledge associated with the analytical tradition.

I.2 THE ANTI-CARTESIAN REVOLUTION

Modern philosophy is usually considered to have been inaugurated by René Descartes' *Meditations*. That book conferred upon the theory of knowledge – what we know, how we come to know it and how we can be certain of the truth of what we believe we know – the status of the 'first philosophy'. In the twenty-first century, a philosophical account of human knowledge needs to take account of the anti-Cartesian revolution brought about in the twentieth century by a mighty army of philosophers, notably in the English-speaking world, influenced by Gottlob Frege – described by Michael Dummett as the twentieth-century Descartes – either directly or indirectly through Ludwig Wittgenstein, upon whom Frege had such an overwhelming impact. This revolution was best known for displacing the theory of knowledge from pole position, for its assault on scepticism-driven epistemology, and for locating the theory of meaning and the relationship between language and the world at the heart of philosophical inquiry. Its most important and lasting legacy, however, may have been hostility to 'psychologism'.

The post-Fregean assault on psychologism went beyond legitimate resistance to the reduction of logical entities – such as propositions, universals and numbers – to mental states or mental activities, and the misunderstanding of philosophy as a branch of empirical psychology. It led to a marginalisation of the contents of consciousness in areas such as verbal meaning, thoughts and truth, and ultimately (in writers as differently motivated as Gilbert Ryle and Daniel Dennett) to questioning the very idea of such contents. While Wittgenstein's *Tractatus* – which Dummett has described as 'a pure essay in the theory of meaning from which every trace of epistemological or psychological consideration has been purged'[10] – is the most extreme expression of anti-psychologism, an attitude of suspicion towards a substantive idea of consciousness was ubiquitous in much Anglo-American analytical philosophy in the first half of the twentieth century.[11] Given that 'the contents of consciousness' are particularly awkward for materialist science, their marginalisation in analytic philosophy has made the latter an accomplice (willing or unwilling) of the scientism referred to in the previous section. Much recent, and indeed current, thinking in philosophy about the nature of human beings and their minds may be seen as the joint product of scientism and the depsychologising tendencies of post-Fregean thought. The counter-revolution in the final third of the twentieth century which redirected philosophical attention from language to the mind did not entirely reverse anti-Cartesian thought. 'Syntactic', 'semantic' and 'computational' theories of mind and the identification of knowledge and truth with their formal properties are a testament to the enduring legacy of Frege and the analytical tradition he inspired.

There are obvious, as well as less obvious, grounds for the anti-Cartesian revolution that gave the theory of meaning and the philosophy of language priority over epistemology and the theory of knowledge. The obvious reason is that it is important to be clear about the terms one is using before embarking on any philosophical discussion. A certain amount of thinking about words and how they work is in order. But that is true of any scholarly enterprise; and in other enterprises getting clear about one's terms is a mere preliminary and not the real business. It is quite a jump to suggest that language is not only the medium in which philosophy is transacted but the primary object of its concern. It demands justification, not the least because the claim that examining the relationship between language and the world is what philosophy is about – or that philosophical problems are best addressed through seeing how words are used in the real world – is somewhat deflating for those of us who believe that philosophy is about trying to get a clearer idea of who and what we are.

Dummett, the pre-eminent English-language interpreter of Frege, has attempted that justification. First, any attempt to define the terms we use gets us into deeper and deeper water:

> The deeper a search for the analysis of the meaning of a word takes us, the more we shall depend upon having a correct model of the way in which language functions.[12]

For,

> When we are concerned to analyse terms which we are not accustomed to define or which are incapable of definition because their use is pre-supposed by any expressions by means of which a definition might be given, then we require, in order to know the form which an analysis must take, to appeal to some general model of meaning. (ibid., p. 669)

When 'it is clearly grasped how hard it can be to attain an adequate analysis of the meaning of an expression having the kind of generality or depth that makes it of interest to philosophers', it will become evident, he says, that the analysis of meaning is 'a primary task of philosophy' (p. 667). What is more, that analysis of meaning, at least as Frege envisaged it, would focus on the formal rules that regulated the formation of sentences out of individual words, and a logic that described, in the most general terms. the rules governing the derivation of sentences from other sentences.

The argument is not entirely persuasive. Getting stuck on the enabling works – because, for example, one has struck an aquafer when parking facilities are being built to accommodate the contractor's lorries – does not justify redefining the contract as being primarily to deliver those enabling works. The origin of philosophy is, as I will argue in section 10.6 below, the wondering encounter of knowledge with itself. While such wondering is necessarily mediated through language, it is not confined to, or about, language. It is not self-evident that articulate wonder is ultimately about articulation.

The weakness of the argument for displacing the philosophy of knowledge by a theory of meaning that is not dependent upon an analysis of knowledge or the knowing subject became increasingly evident when purely formal, 'depsychologised' accounts of meaning developed in analytical philosophy started to run into trouble. The obvious fact that the use of language is rooted in consciousness – so that it is not possible even to think about the relationship between language and the world without referring to the subjectivity of language users – was grudgingly acknowledged. The notion of a stand-alone theory of meaning, as an independent account of the rules governing the formation of meaningful sentences, looked more and more shaky, and purely formal accounts of meaning rather empty.

There were, however, good reasons for trying to limit the penetration of psychology and subjective experiences into the theory of meaning. There was the bad example of classical associationist theory of verbal meaning. This key component of 'psychologism' made the mistake of trying to find the meaning of words by appealing to particular contents of consciousness of word users, such as mental images. This was unsustainable for several reasons: mental images are unstable and private (or uncommunicable), whereas the meanings of words have to be stable and public if they are going to do the job of serving communication; not all words ('the', for example) evoke images; and words – not even excepting concrete noun-words for which there might be plausible correlative images – do not work in isolation. This last point was very complex, and ironically, far from buttressing the extreme anti-psychologism that seemed to be the goal of the analytical approach, eventually showed its inadequacy.

Yes, words made sense only as part of sentences. But more was needed: sentences conveyed meaning only when uttered, or written, in a particular context – the context of which language users were conscious of. As Wittgenstein acknowledged, 'an expression [or sentence] has meaning only in the stream of life',[13] an observation that opened more doors than a stand-alone theory of meaning could allow. Those doors proved impossible to shut when one or two obvious facts were pointed out, linking 'the stream of life' with the psychology of language users.

The first was that ordinary language could not be treated as if it were simply a pure symbolic system, like mathematics, but with impurities added. We use words to make things happen – to make people do things, feel good or ashamed, laugh, and so on. Much of the time, as in greeting, swearing, joking, thanking, kow-towing, these uses are not like anything that could be accommodated in a mathematical system or to which an analysis of a mathematical system would be relevant. Second, it was not possible to conduct even a philosophical discussion – or not a satisfactory one anyway – entirely in the aseptic discourse of logic or mathematics. This was not only because such systems had their own internal problems (as Bertrand Russell discovered they actually did and Gödel demonstrated they always would have) but because the reduction of philosophical argument to a calculus of symbols resulted not in the solution of philosophical problems but their being mislaid or bypassed. Third, not even symbolic systems were stand-alone: mathematical discourses may have the virtue of transparency, but they carry specific meaning only at the cost of contamination. Without contaminants,

$$p = \text{not not-}p$$

and

$$2 + 2 = 4$$

would carry no meaning.

The most serious assault on a stand-alone theory of meaning that would displace the theory of knowledge as the First Philosophy came from within the philosophy of language. J. L. Austin, who argued that 'The total speech act in the total speech situation is the *only actual* phenomenon which, in the last resort, we are engaged in elucidating',[14] found that understanding real language – language in use – required looking beyond language. As Wittgenstein said, 'it is our acting that lies at the bottom of the language-game'.[15]

H. P. Grice emphasised the role of language users: linguistic meaning in the real world does not reside in the behaviour of the symbols or expressions of which languages are composed – they are not located in 'the system of symbols' or its component terms – but in people who use languages to mean things, and the worlds they live in.[16] This is because the specification of linguistic meanings requires that they are *meant* (by *someone*) and that they *mean* (to *someone*). What is more, in order that I should be able to determine what you mean, I have to intuit what you mean to mean. In contrast to natural signs, which may have meaning (clouds may mean rain, spots may mean measles) without those things being (deliberately) meant, linguistic meanings have to be (deliberately) meant. As John Searle glossed it: 'In speaking, I attempt to communicate certain things to a hearer by getting him to recognize my intention to communicate just those things.'[17]

Thus is the (knowing, intending, communicating) subject reinstated at the heart of linguistic meaning. Henceforth, no philosophy of language or theory of meaning worthy of the name can ignore the speaking subject. Grice and others also reinstated the apprehended world of the speaker and the hearer; for the implications of what we say – the burden of meaning it carries – often goes beyond, or has little relation to, the meaning in the narrow logico-linguistic, or even dictionary, sense of the words we use. Our utterances are invested with, and exploit, an 'implicature'[18] in virtue of which we can always imply more than we say. Verbal meaning, in short, resides in acts performed by human beings who draw upon their knowledge of the world and make presuppositions about the knowledge possessed by their interlocutors. The theory of meaning must embrace this. Dummett's claim that the theory of meaning is 'the fundamental part of philosophy' because it is 'the only part of philosophy whose results do not depend upon those of any other part'[19] – an insight in which he believed Frege's true greatness lay – is therefore wide of the mark.

There can, in short, be no theory of meaning that does not take account of the knowing subject. The assumption that

> in order to arrive at the conception of a systematic theory of meaning, it was necessary first ... to expel psychology from logic and the philosophy of language[20]

might be correct, but it led philosophers into a cul-de-sac. This is frustrating for those philosophers for whom, like Frege, the only model of rigorous inquiry is mathematics, extended to language via a system such as the sentential calculus. For it proves that non-trivial philosophical inquiry requires us not only to deal with messy natural languages but also to embrace the things they catch in their mess. This includes our sense of what we think others mean (if we are the recipients of an utterance) or what they are likely to think we mean (if we are the utterers), and, beyond this, a wider knowledge of the world. Meaning cannot be separated from the psyche of the one who emits meaning, or from the psyche of the one who receives it. Or, indeed, the knowledge that either has. In short, meaning does not reside in systems of symbols abstracted from human consciousness but in the consciousness of Knowing Animals.

All of which is pretty obvious and it may be thought that it is unnecessary to labour the point. The paltry returns from the philosophy of language and the fact that, from the 1970s onwards, most philosophers in the analytical tradition had decided to move on, particularly in the direction of the philosophy of mind, speak for themselves.[21] It is, however, worth looking at what motivated the move from an unacceptable and absurd associationist psychologism to an equally absurd – because extreme and depsychologising – anti-psychologism, since, as we shall see, it touches on the intuitions at the heart of this book.

1.3 DEPSYCHOLOGISING THOUGHT

A clue is to be found in Frege's famous essay 'The Thought: A Logical Inquiry'.[22] In this essay, he argues that 'thoughts are neither things of the outer world nor ideas' (ibid., p. 28). Thoughts are unlike ideas, inasmuch as the latter, being contents of consciousness, need a bearer: they are had by someone. A thought, such as that expressed in Pythagoras' theorem, is by contrast

> timelessly true, true independently of whether anyone takes it to be true. It needs no bearer. It is not true for the first time when it is discovered, but is like a planet which, already before anyone has seen it, has been interacting with other planets. (ibid., p. 29)

Thought belongs to a third realm, 'neither to my inner world as an idea nor yet to an outer world of material, perceptible things'. It is is neither inside nor outside us: 'We do not have a thought as we have, say, a sense impression, but we also do not see a thought as we see, say, a star' (ibid., p. 34).

This notion of thoughts existing timelessly and independently of human consciousness is an expression of Frege's Platonism: they are there for the mind to pluck like fruit from a tree, except that this tree belongs to a timeless, non-sensible world. 'But by apprehending a thought I come into relation to it and it to me.' In this way, its strict timelessness is 'annulled'. Logic deals with the (Platonic) world of thoughts in themselves and psychology with thoughts when they have been apprehended by a bearer; when they have become contents of consciousness. Philosophy is concerned *only with the logical aspect of thought* and this is what the theory of meaning should deal with.

It should be noted that Frege here is *stipulating* what philosophy should be. The arguments in support of it are indirect; namely, that the essence of the thought is that which is communicated, and indeed, communicable and relevant to its truth. (We shall come back to this presently.) It should also be noted that it is an *assumption* that psychological contents and objective referents in thought are separable and of an entirely different character, the former participating in consciousness and the latter not, and that it is only the former that should be of interest to philosophers. In practice, the difference between them is not that the former belongs to consciousness and the latter does not, but that the former is unique to an individual consciousness at a particular moment and the latter may be had by any number of consciousnesses (or, indeed, by a single consciousness on different occasions). This distinction marks the difference, roughly, between token thought and the thought-type. What Frege influentially stipulated in 'The Thought' was that philosophy should be concerned primarily with thought-types rather than thought-tokens. The latter, however, are the only thoughts actual people have. Indeed, it is questionable whether, outside of Frege's postulated 'timeless' realm, thought-types exist. We may also question whether the timeless realm exists and whether, therefore, there are any thoughts other than token thoughts.

Accepting the existence of Frege's sub-Platonic timeless realm seems to depend on accepting the idea of thoughts that exist independently of anyone thinking. This (as we shall see) is a difficult notion. At any rate, it seems as if the realm has been postulated in order to provide *existence conditions* for thought-types, a place to hold thoughts not being thought by anyone. For the truths embodied in thoughts have existential as well as formal conditions – existence conditions in the wider sense as well as truth conditions in the narrower sense. For example, the laws of spatial geometry that make Pythagoras' theorem true once it is propounded are true independent of human consciousness; but the theorem itself does not come into existence outside of a highly sophisti-cated, distinctively human, consciousness. Likewise, the truth conditions of Newton's Laws of Motion may be said to have been in place since the universe began, though the laws themselves came into being only in seventeenth century. The actual planetary motion which suggested and conformed to these laws, however, *counted as* the truth conditions of the laws only when Newton had observed the planetary motions and propounded the laws on the basis of them. The formulation of the laws of planetary motion transformed the patterns of planetary motion into the truth conditions of those laws.

Distinguishing the truth conditions of thoughts from their existence conditions is necessary in order to draw attention to the latter as they are frequently overlooked. It is not entirely unfair to say that much of the discussion of the nature of truth in the analytical tradition focused on the truth conditions of factual assertions at the expense of the existence conditions of truths.[23] If we forget existence conditions, we can end up believing, as Frege did, that thoughts can exist (and be true), or that the truths they express can exist, without anyone thinking them:

> [Thoughts] can be true without being apprehended by a thinker and are not wholly unreal even then ... (Frege, p. 38)

This is crazy, but at least it is honest: it recognises where extreme anti-psychologism finally takes us to. As always when consciousness is expelled by philosophers from the places where it most obviously is, it ends up somewhere else: most usually in bits of the brain but here, in a Platonic heaven, built to house thoughts no one is thinking or, indeed, has ever thought.

These problems show how we cannot conduct an inquiry into thoughts without taking into account the consciousness of their bearers. There cannot be an isolated 'logical inquiry', a psychology-free inquiry of bearerless thoughts, without relocating thoughts to a 'third' realm, a sub-Platonic heaven where they can exist without being thought, and apprehended as required, plucked like ripe fruit from a tree. Differentiated, distinct thoughts require consciousness.

Frege's postulated third realm seems in part to be the product of a misunderstanding of significance of the observation that thoughts – such as 'That the sun has risen' – are not, for example, like sense impressions:

> That the sun has risen is not an object which emits rays that reach my eyes, it is not a visible thing like the sun itself. That the sun has risen is seen to be true on the basis of sense-impressions. But being true is not a material, perceptible property. (p. 20)

This should draw attention to the need to distinguish the truth conditions of a true assertion (the sense impressions that make the assertion 'The sun has risen' true) from the existence conditions of the truth 'That the sun has risen'. Unfortunately, Frege emphasises only the fact that the latter are not qualities 'that correspond with particular kinds of sense impression'. Of course, Frege is right to point out that 'That' – as in 'That the sun has risen' or, more generally, as in 'That X is the case' – is not an additional sensible property; its being made explicit as 'a fact' is not the result of a sense impression, nor does it amount to an additional or actual sense impression.

What 'that' adds is not something non-sensible that takes a piece of the material world into a timeless zone, but is psychological. 'That' is not a property of the material world; it is not part of the given. 'That it is given' does not arise out of the given *per se*, does not come bundled free with it. Contrary to Rudolf Carnap's assertion that 'the given is subjectless',[24] without the conscious subject, there is no given: 'what is' is not 'there'. What we can separate are the different (psychological) aspects of thought that permit the thought to be (objectively) true or false while at the same time marking it as *someone's* thought. This separation, underlined by 'that', belongs to what we shall characterise as 'propositional awareness', a distinctively human mode of consciousness.

We need to acknowledge both aspects of consciousness, which are particularly evident in thought: the psychological content (the processes of thinking, the content of consciousness); and the object of thought (what the thought asserts or is about). Because he was concerned primarily about truth narrowly understood as truth conditions – half-truths about truth, we might say – Frege set aside the *process* of thinking, the apprehension of a thought, which occurs in time, from the thought itself, 'which is timeless, eternal, unchangeable'. The former is inessential:

> A property of thought will be called inessential which consists in, or follows from the fact that, it is apprehended by a thinker. (p. 37)

While the contents of its consciousness may be irrelevant to the truth of the thought, they are not irrelevant to the existence of the thought – indeed, as we shall discuss presently, they are essential to the *having* of the thought; and, given that a thought cannot be true (or false) unless it exists as a token, contents of consciousness must be relevant to the existence of the truth that is thought in the thought. It is not an accidental feature of a thought that it is had by *someone* even if its being had, its being actually thought, incorporates many features – mental images, associated ideas, etc. – that are irrelevant to its truth value, are not part of its truth conditions construed in the conventional sense.

For example, the fact that when I think of Pythagoras' theorem I form an image of my first geometry teacher, or of the page of my first geometry book, or even of a laurelled thinker with sandy feet is irrelevant not only to the truth of the theorem, or even my judgement of its truth, or my sense that it is true, or even my understanding of it. And yet it is not irrelevant to my *having* the thought of the theorem and for its truth being realised. There are more things relevant to tokenisation of thought – or (since, outside of Platonism, there are no thoughts other than tokens) to thought *tout court* – than those that determine the truth values of their objects. Truths do not exist in virtue solely of the conditions that make them true and true thoughts cannot be reduced to their formal features, stripped of any conscious contents. Token thoughts have to be embedded in something (imagined symbols, etc.) none of which could be regarded as germane to their truth, their truth conditions narrowly understood, though at least some of which must be essential for them to exist – for them to be had, to be thought.

Once it is appreciated that we cannot separate truths from their being had by someone, the truth of true thoughts from their being ('tokenly') thought, then we are deprived of a principled way of separating what Frege deems 'essential' in a thought from what he deems 'inessential'; or, given that it is not possible to have unapprehended thoughts, it is equally not possible to separate what relates to the 'mere' apprehension of the thought itself.

While this is particularly obvious in the case of indexical thoughts, which contain terms such as 'I', 'here', 'now' whose reference depends upon the who, the where and the when of the thinker, it is equally true of all thoughts. This follows from the fact that all actual thoughts are token thoughts – they have to be realised as occurrent thoughts embedded in particular symbols, themselves embedded in all sorts of marginal decorations – and have to be *had*. Within token thoughts we may make a rough distinction between the psychological content or act – the content of the consciousness of the person thinking it (which may be unique, idiosyncratic, etc.) – and the object of the thought, for example, the state of affairs that it posits. Because thoughts cannot exist outside of consciousness, however, there is no such object without psychological content. We may seem to encounter token thoughts stripped of psychological contents on the printed page as in a geometry textbook; but this is only an appearance. The reader still has to make the theorem her own, otherwise there are simply dead marks on a page. The thought is actualised in her as a bearer and, as such, acquires psychological contents.

This is partly acknowledged by Frege. Towards the end of 'The Thought', there is an interesting qualification of his anti-psychologism. He reaffirms his central doctrine that 'nothing would be a greater misunderstanding of mathematics than its subordination to psychology'. But then he adds an interesting concession:

> Neither logic nor mathematics has the task of investigating minds and the contents of consciousness whose bearer is a single person. *Perhaps their task could be represented rather as the investigation of the mind, of the mind not of minds.* (p. 35; italics mine)

He is willing, it appears, to allow a kind of higher-order psychologism in which the idea (which has to have a bearer and which he set aside at the beginning of his essay) merges with the thought (which has an object); the bearer in this case is '*the* mind'. The nature of 'the mind' is a little obscure. It seems to partake of both the collective mind of humanity and the mind of God; or perhaps – as a half-way house – the mind of all possible (as well as actual) humanity. In such a bearer, the ideas and the objects of the thoughts merge and logical inquiry into the thoughts of such a bearer would be inseparable from psychological inquiry into the processes by which thoughts are apprehended. This satisfies Frege's need to separate the things which determine the truth values of thoughts (which is all philosophy should be concerned with, so far as he is concerned) from the accidental conditions under which they are conceived.

The 'mind' is a more respectable, more Platonic place for the objects of thoughts than individual minds. It is suitable accommodation for elevated, timeless things such as Pythagoras' theorem. If such thoughts are denied a Platonic heaven where they can live sufficient unto themselves, caring not at all whether they are apprehended by grubby humans, they can at least take up residence in *The* 'mind', which is equally remote from the grubby consciousnesses of individual minds, individual bearers of ideas. At the very least, this places thoughts above mere circumstances: their senses – and their referents, which form the objects of thought – are not context-dependent.

This general mind won't, however, do the work that is required of it. The concession which allows mind back into thought but requires that it should be a curiously consciousness-free mind, a depsychologised categorial mind, does not deal with difficulties that arise from separating thought from consciousness and a logical inquiry into thought from an inquiry into bearers of actual thinkings. There are many reasons for still insisting on placing conscious human beings at the centre of any inquiry – logical or otherwise – into thought.

First and foremost, the status of unapprehended thoughts, neatly separated and stacked in a putative third realm, is somewhat dubious. If, as Frege believes, 'a thought ... is the sense of a complete sentence',[25] one must assume that there are as many thoughts in that realm as there are possible meaningful sentences, all on stand-by, available to be apprehended when required. The involvement of thoughts with sentences (necessary for Frege in order to lift them out of the mêlée of individual consciousness) brings additional difficulties. For example, there will be no principled way of deciding the borders of individual thoughts or where two sentences capture the same thought or different thoughts and where a given sentence captures one or more thoughts. We are in danger of ending up with One Thought, corresponding perhaps to The True that Frege felt might be the referent of all (true) sentences.[26] Second, the timelessness of thoughts in this third realm is severely threatened, for there are some thoughts which are possible only at a particular time in history; for example, 'Jesus saved mankind' would be possible only after Jesus was born; and 'Quantum electrodynamics has proved a useful theory' would be possible only after the middle part of the twentieth century. Ditto, thoughts about Raymond Tallis's performance as a doctor. Prior to his birth such thoughts would lack a foothold;

they would be unspecifiable. Third (and in some respects as an extension of this), it is not clear that many thoughts can be considered as having any kind of discrete existence (or discrete potential existence) outside of the context in which they are had (thought, uttered) by bearers. Perhaps '2 + 2 = 4' and Pythagoras' theorem enjoy context independence, and so may seem plausible inhabitants of a Platonic or sub-Platonic timeless realm, but most thoughts seem considerably less well qualified. For example, my thought that you are not being serious when you say that you will try to spend less time at work is unlikely to find a coat-hook in Platonic space. This thought looks like a poor candidate, not only because it could hardly have antedated my existence but also because it is so embedded in the immediate circumstances, and the self, of myself the bearer. Its availablity for 'apprehension' does not seem to precede its actually being apprehended – by a conscious human being about to be its bearer.

This highlights another aspect of many thoughts that we touched on earlier: that they are steeped in indexicality. A relatively deindexicalised thought such as '2 + 2 = 4', which has a plausible timelessness, is not necessarily typical of thoughts as a whole, notwithstanding Frege's regarding them as the paradigm thoughts, the model to which all self-respecting thoughts aspired. Most actual thoughts are utterly embedded in their specific linguistic and non-linguistic context; the context-independent core is impossible to isolate. Dummett, however, has under-lined how Frege's notion of expressing a thought depends on isolating this context-independent core. For Frege, he says,

> a thought is expressed by any utterance which, in the linguistic context in which the utterance is made, has the same sense as some sentence which could, independently of linguistic context, be used to make an assertion.[27]

Such equivalence of sense could be achieved only where indexicality could be removed; since marks of indexicality are essential character-istics of bearers of thoughts, the equivalence of sense requires removal of the bearer. Frege achieves removal of the bearer only by setting aside as 'inessential' those elements that bearers bring to thoughts.

Even in those cases where it may at first sight seem to be possible to pair off the bearer-dependent elements, as for example in manifestly 'timeless' thoughts such as Pythagoras' theorem and '2 + 2 = 4', things may not be as Platonic as Frege would like. First, there is the small question of *understanding* the thought. There is no particular under-standing that is not embedded in particular features of the one who understands; and yet there is no thought without understanding. It is these necessary features that nail the thought to the thinker, to the bearer. At the level of understanding, there is no clear distinction between the ideas that the bearer has and the object of the thought. Even the abstract thoughts of geometry are compromised by the sublunary world of real, conscious people.

There is indisputably a collective, invariant element in the thought; otherwise neither the communication of thoughts nor the accumulation of truth would be possible. This collective element, however, is not held in a timeless realm, or *the* mind assumed to be static and timeless, but in the emergent collective mind – or pooled consciousness – of communities. The scale of such communities will vary: that '2 + 2 = 4' will be coterminous with all human communities after the number sense has become explicit in a number system and true for all such communities. The truth of other thoughts will be more parochial. This collective mind is not eternal and timeless: it began as we humans were separated from beasts and changes through history.

The difficulty of separating the invariant core in a thought from the variation due to psychological factors in the thinker, of divorcing Frege's 'essential' from his 'inessential' elements, points to a deeper difficulty: that of genuinely distinguishing the thought-type (which can be instantiated in an indefinite number of bearer-moments) from the token thought (which can, by definition, be instantiated only once). Apart from the obvious problem of deciding whether two thoughts represent two examples of the same thought-type or are instances of two different thought-types, there is the added difficulty, apparent throughout our discussion, of knowing what kind of ontological status the thought-types have. Frege resolved that difficulty by a kind of magic thinking in which he postulated a Platonic realm in which to house them – a cognate home. The notion of this realm – possibly identical with, or sustained by, the collective mind that he alluded to – is, as we have seen, beset with difficulties. Without such a realm it is impossible to think of the thought-type as having a clear or definite existence. Even thoughts whose content or meaning is arguably independent of context have to *occur* in order to exist. Non-occurrent existence of thought-types is perilously close to that of a thought without instantiation. The contamination that comes with instantiation is the contaminant of actuality, of actualisation.

This discussion of Frege may seem to be a digression from the main argument of the present volume. Nothing could be further from the truth. It is directly relevant to the central concern of this book – to make human consciousness, especially in the form of knowledge (thoughts, facts, etc.), visible. The differentiation between psychological contents and non-psychological objects within thoughts and other propositional attitudes, items of knowledge, etc. marks the distance between mere sentience and propositional awareness; between animal awareness and knowledge 'That [X is the case]'. For the present, we may note that a thought *is* a mental event that is capable of having a distinct content and object – and hence of seeming to have a distinct character as both token and as instance of a type. A fully formed idea – formulated in an expressed thought – has an object that is clearly distinct from itself. In thought, experience reaches out to something that is not an experience, though (if it is a declarative) it may be exposed to 'the tribunal of experience' (see section 5.3). We shall argue that the realm where the objects of thought, rather than thoughts themselves, are located is created by the pooled deindexicalised awareness of humanity – something not too remote from Frege's 'mind', though entirely without its Platonic overtones. This separation between content and object within thought is reflected, in the case of speech, by other separations – for example, between the sound (which takes place in space-time) and the meaning (which does not 'take place').

Real thoughts – actual token thoughts – must therefore take place in space and time and are events in the consciousness of real individuals. What is more, some of the psychological processes associated with thought, those which most of all Frege might be inclined to dismiss as 'inessential', are neither irrelevant noise nor mere cognitive crutches. They constitute the (psychological) material through which the thought is *had*. It is the way of making the thought *be* at a certain time and, through a link with other elements – images, memories, etc. – of making it be *mine*. They forge additional links between the object of thought and myself, the thinker – rather as the noise of one's own movement, the sound of one's breathing and the feeling of effort – in short, the hum of bodily self-presence – underline that an activity is one's own.

1.4 EMPTYING THE HUMAN SUBJECT

The displacement of the theory of knowledge by the theory of meaning was not the only assault that epistemology had to withstand in the twentieth century. There was a profound scepticism about scepticism-driven epistemology. Within the analytical tradition this took the form of questioning whether, if one suspended fundamental beliefs such as in the existence of things outside of one's thinking mind (worlds, objects, others' minds), one could still carry on as if one's words had meaning. Sceptical epistemology, in short, seemed to cut the ground from beneath its own feet.

There was also a wider scepticism about scepticism, common to analytical and existential philosophy: the suspicion that epistemological inquiry driven by Cartesian doubt was 'idle' or 'insincere'. This was shared by philosophers as disparate as G. E. Moore and Martin Heidegger.[28] And those objections still seem to be valid. A defensiveness about episte- mology, particularly where it leads to a radical revision of our view of the world, is part of the legacy of analytical thought. The most important part of this legacy – and much more destructive – has been its paving the way for empty, or rather *emptying*, theories of human consciousness.

I have discussed these at length elsewhere.[29] It is sufficient to mention here that scientist accounts of human consciousness – one aspect of which is the naturalisation of knowledge – have been given an easier passage through the philosophical world as a result of the hegemony of a way of thought in which it was possible to think of meaning (a quintessential feature of human consciousness) in purely linguistic terms and language as being primarily a system of symbols. The idea of the mind as 'a computer', 'a syntactic engine', as being 'an ensemble rule- governed process of symbol-handling' owes much to a tradition that attempted to make sense of discourse in terms of philosophical logic, a calculus of propositions, and so on. Frege's spirit lives on in compu- tational theories of the mind.

The most striking evidence of the posthumous life of the continuing effects of 'the linguistic turn' in philosophy has been the tendency to reduce knowledge and truth to their formal properties. The definition of knowledge as 'true justified belief' – which leads inescapably to the absurdities of the Gettier paradox (discussed in section 4.1) – is one example. Another is Tarski's account of truth as a relationship between sentences:

'Snow is white' is true if and only if snow is white.

Such 'subjectless' accounts of knowledge and truth – and the emphasis on secondary phenomena such as verification and truth-tables – could have seemed satisfactory rather than point-missing only within an established tradition of ignoring the knowing subject, and trying to root philosophy in a theory of meaning itself anchored in paradigms derived from unhaunted systems of symbols rather than modelled on ordinary communication where meanings are meant by people and determined as part of the lives of conscious individuals.

It is for this reason that Frege's hugely influential approach, exempli- fied in his essay 'The Thought', is of particular interest. It admits that it is a 'logical inquiry' but then, as we have seen, has emphasised the logical aspects of the thought at the expense of the psychological ones. Its 'depsychologised' account is presented as if it captured what was essential about thought and all that was of philosophical interest. Any property of thought 'which consists in, or follows from the fact that, it is apprehended by a thinker' is 'inessential'.[30] A depsychologised account of thought – *prima facie* more plausible than a depsychologised account of memory or desire – has opened the way to a depsychologised account of the mind itself. By stripping the intimate self-communion that is thinking to its logical outline, the path is opened up to a purely logical account of mind; of mind as a set of computational transactions in an otherwise empty space between perceptual inputs and motor outputs.

While psychologism is clearly wrong, an extreme anti-psychologism, which deletes the conscious subject in pursuit of a 'depsychologised' account of meaning, truth, knowledge and, indeed, of consciousness, is equally so. And there is no need to choose between these two extremes. There is a middle way, indicated in an early essay by Heidegger, written when he was still under the benign influence of Husserl:

> Fundamental for the realisation of the absurdity and barrenness of psychologism is the distinction between the psychic act and its logical content, between real thought processes occurring in time and their ideal extra-temporal identical meaning.[31]

By making this distinction and giving equal weight to 'the psychic act' and its 'logical content', to 'real thought processes' and 'their ideal extra-temporal meaning', Heidegger did not lurch from the errors of psychologism to those of extreme (or depyschologising) anti-psychologism. If only Frege had done likewise, then the history of English-speaking philosophy in the twentieth century might have been different.

These observations touch on the intuitions and arguments that lie at the heart of the present attempt to capture what is unique about human consciousness: the differentiation within it of processes and objects; its being both subjective and about objects, phenomenal and logical. The fundamental differentiation within it is that of *the elaborated intentionality* in virtue of which, to a degree unique in the animal kingdom, it has explicit objects which it is about. This differentiation between private consciousness and the public objects it entertains lies, I shall argue, at the root of our uncoupling from nature; of the propositional awareness that underpins our freedom.

The anti-psychologistic propensities of a mathematician of genius who wanted to reduce philosophy to the philosophy of language and language to an investigation of the logical relations between symbols and sentences has cast a long shadow. Most of the things that are of interest about the Knowing Animal – the preoccupation of this book – are in that shadow. So it has been important to dispel that shadow first. There was, however, another shadow waiting in the shadows.

The following passage from John Searle may be seen as an obituary for the ambitions of a stand-alone philosophy of language:

> A basic assumption behind my approach to the problems of language is that the philosophy of language is a branch of the philosophy of mind. The capacity of speech acts to represent objects and states of affairs in the world is an extension of the more biologically fundamental capacities of the mind (or brain) to relate the organism to the world by way of such mental states as belief and desire, especially through action and perception.[32]

This escape from anti-psychologism leads straight into biologism: the emergence of neurophilosophy, through the reference to 'biologically fundamental capacities' and 'the mind (or brain)'. And it takes us to the theme of the next chapter, where knowledge is defended against naturalising stories that traduce its true nature.

A NOTE ON THE DEPSYCHLOGISATION OF CONSCIOUSNESS

My use of the term 'depsychologised' in this chapter may puzzle some readers, in view of the contrast made by David J. Chalmers in his much discussed *The Conscious Mind: In Search of a Fundamental Theory* (Oxford: Oxford University Press, 1996) between 'phenomenal' and 'psychological' aspects of consciousness. The former corresponds to mind characterised in terms of what it feels (like) and the latter to what the mind does, its role as a link between sensory inputs and behavioural outputs. It might be argued that, in some respects, the depsychologisation that I am complaining of is in fact 'dephenomenalisation'. However, I do not accept Chalmers' division, for all that it has the laudable aim of reaffirming the reality of contents of consciousness such as qualia. It seems to me that separating the mind's role in linking inputs with outputs from its experienced contents is distinctly eccentric and redefines the psychological in a way that kow-tows to too much of current scientistic thinking. It also has the consequence of making actual experience purely epiphenomenal, a result that, surprisingly, Chalmers accepts with equanimity.

NOTES AND REFERENCES

1. Tzvetan Todorov, *Hope and Memory*, trans. David Bellos (London: Atlantic Books, 2004), p. 21.
2. The image comes from the last sentence of *The Order of Things: An Archaeology of the Human Sciences* (London: Tavistock, 1970, p. 387) by Michel Foucault, one of the most influential anti-humanists of the last 50 years, whose virulent attacks on the idea of progress in human affairs are curiously reminiscent of Joseph de Maistre.
3. Raymond Tallis, *Enemies of Hope. A Critique of Contemporary Pessimism. Irrationalism, Anti-Humanism and the Contemporary Counter-Enlightenment* (Basingstoke: Macmillan, 2nd edition, 1999). In this book I also examine the emptying of the knowing subject by postmodernist thinkers such as Foucault. This passage from Foucault's Foreword to the English translation says it all:
   > If there is one approach that I do reject, however, it is that (one might call it, broadly speaking, the phenomenological approach) which gives absolute priority to the observing subject ... it seems to me that the historical analysis of scientific discourse should, in the last resort, be subject, not to a theory of the knowing subject, but rather to a theory of discursive practice.

   Of course, one needs both.
4. Steven Pinker, *How the Mind Works* (London: Penguin Books, 1998), p. 21.
5. Quoted in Kenan Malik, *Man, Beast and Zombie. What Science Can and Cannot Tell Us About Human Nature* (London: Weidenfeld and Nicolson, 2000), p. 148.
6. See Raymond Tallis, 'A Critical Dictionary of Neuromythology', in *On the Edge of Certainty* (Basingstoke: Macmillan, 1999).
7. Raymond Tallis, *The Explicit Animal. A Defence of Human Consciousness* (Basingstoke: Macmillan, 2nd edition, 1999).
8. Raymond Tallis, 'Explicitness and Truth (and Falsehood)' in *On the Edge of Certainty. Philosophical Explorations* (Basingstoke: Macmillan, 1999).
9. See Daniel Dennett, *Consciousness Explained* (London: Little, Brown, 1991). For a definitive demolition, which will save the reader from ploughing through Dennett's many hundreds of pages, I would recommend John Searle's 'Consciousness Denied: Dennett's Account', in *The Mystery of Consciousness* (London: Granta, 1997). I cover the same territory, at rather greater length, in *The Explicit Animal*, and for good measure criticise Searle's own views.
10. Michael Dummett, *Frege. Philosophy of Language* (London: Duckworth, 1973), p. 684. I have presented Frege here through Dummett because Dummett has given the most comprehensive account of Frege's influence and the nature of the Fregean revolution. Not everyone agrees with Dummett's interpretation of Frege, as John Passmore points out in 'Davidson and Dummett', in *Recent Philosophers* (London: Duckworth, 1985), p. 76.
11. The pervasive anti-psychologism of the analytic tradition is set out in P. Hylton, *Russell, Idealism and the Emergence of Analytic Philosophy* (Oxford: Oxford University Press, 1990).
12. Dummett, *Frege*, p. 669.
13. Quoted in Norman Malcolm, *Ludwig Wittgenstein. A Memoir* (Oxford: Oxford University Press, 1958), p. 93.
14. J. L. Austin, *How To Do Things with Words*, Lecture XII (Oxford: Clarendon Press, 1962), p. 147.
15. Ludwig Wittgenstein, *On Certainty*, ed. G. E. M. Anscombe and G. H. von Wright,

trans. Denis Paul and G. E. M. Anscombe (Oxford: Blackwell, 1974), p. 28e. Acting cannot, of course, be separated from the psyche and circumstances of the actor.

16. See, for example, H. P. Grice, 'Meaning', *Philosophical Review* (1957), 66: 377–88. An utterance is a flower that grows out of the the soil of a self or a self-world.

17. John Searle, *Speech Acts. An Essay in the Philosophy of Language* (Cambridge: Cambridge University Press, 1969), p. 43.

18. This was a term introduced by H. P. Grice in his William James Lectures 1967/8: 'Logic and Conversation', in P. Cole and J. L. Morgan (eds), *Syntax and Semantics, 3: Speech Acts* (New York and London: Academic Press, 1975). It captures the obvious distinction between what is actually said and what is implied (but not formally entailed) in what is said. Implication in the course of ordinary conversation derives from a much wider set of conditions which determine the proper conduct of conversation and the *point* of what is said. For example, I may comment on how nice-looking a lecturer is as an indirect way of criticising the poor quality of his talk.

19. Dummett, *Frege*, p. 669. This is false even in the case of mathematics, as Edo Pivčevič has pointed out in *Husserl and Phenomenology* (London: Hutchinson, 1970), p. 31. For example, Frege's explanation of numbers – 'The number which applies to the concept F is the extension of the concept "equinumerous with the concept F"' – presupposes that we already understand what 'extension of a concept' means. It takes for granted the notion of a concept, under which objects are to fall in order to be counted (indeed, to be countable) and it takes for granted the notion of extension.

These cannot be defined within mathematics and making sense of them does involve something like reference to inner mental processes. For example, counting the number of items falling under the concept 'in this room', assumes (a) prior definition and understanding of 'in this room', (b) a decision as to what shall count as one item, and (c) something like an act of synthesis to bring them altogether as members of a single class, as a collective. This entrains a good deal of 'inner mental process'. The purely logical, mindless element can give us only definitions within mathematics understood as a closed system and cannot on its own take us as far as any mathematical process that actually engages the outside world. A theory of meaning purified of psychological content is not therefore sufficient to give us an account of how even the simplest mathematical operations gain a purchase on the most abstracted pieces of reality.

This failure to develop a stand-alone Theory of Meaning that would undercut epistemology is also evident in one of the most celebrated products of the entire analytic movement: the identification of the meaning of a sentence (assertion, proposition) with its truth conditions. This leads straight back to epistemology, as many anti-metaphysical philosophers, notably A. J. Ayer, found. For example, the logical positivists asserted that an assertion was meaningful if it was verifiable (at least in principle) by observation. But once we link observations and truth, we are taking precisely the position that epistemology challenges. Hardline logical positivists hostile to sceptical or revisionist epistemology found themselves arguing about the existence of objects.

20. Dummett, *Frege*, p. 684.

21. Particularly since, as Dummett (*Frege*, p. 98) admits, 'while most of us, including myself, would agree that the concept of meaning is a fundamental and indispensable one, we are unclear even about the surface structure of statements involving that concept' or 'what kind of sentence, of natural language, should be taken as the

characteristic form for an attribution of a particular meaning to some given word or expression'. He adds, for good measure, that 'Not only do we not know the answer to this: we do not even know whether it is the right question to ask'.

22. Gottlob Frege, 'The Thought: A Logical Inquiry', trans. A. M. and Marcelle Quinton, in *Philosophical Logic* (*Oxford Readings in Philosophy*), ed. P. F. Strawson (Oxford: Oxford University Press, 1967).
23. We shall return to this key point (which I discuss in *On the Edge of Certainty*) in Chapter 6 below.
24. Quoted in Roderick Chisholm, 'On the Observability of the Self', *Philosophy and Phenomenological Research* (1969), 30: 7–21.
25. Dummett, *Frege*, p. 371.
26. See section 6.2.4 below.
27. Dummett, *Frege*, p. 365.
28. See Raymond Tallis, *A Conversation with Martin Heidegger* (Basingstoke: Palgrave, 2002).
29. See Tallis, 'Emptying Consciousness', in *The Explicit Animal*.
30. Frege, 'The Thought', p. 37.
31. Quoted in Rudiger Safranski, *Martin Heidegger. Between Good and Evil*, trans. Ewald Osers (Cambridge, MA: Harvard University Press, 1998), p. 26.
32. John Searle, *Intentionality* (Cambridge: Cambridge University Press, 1983), p. vii.

CHAPTER 2

Naturalising Knowledge

2.1 THE EUPHORIC DREAM

Somewhere in his voluminous writings, Roland Barthes speaks of 'the euphoric dream of scientificity' through which, in the 1950s and 1960s, he passed, along with many fellow critics. This was in the heyday of structuralism, when it seemed as if literary criticism could at last be placed upon a scientific footing. The emergent science – combining stylometrics, semiotics and thematic and (cautious) historical analysis – treated as irrelevant the subjective feelings of the critic and, more disturbingly, bypassed the intentions, indeed the consciousness, of the writer. Literary works were 'textual formations' whose lexical properties were determined by many things, the least important of which was the life, talent, genius or temperament of the author.[1]

The supplanting of epistemology by the theory of meaning discussed in the previous chapter also partook of 'the euphoric dream of scientificity'. The displacement of the knowing subject from its central position in post-Cartesian thought and the predilection for reducing philosophical questions to matters of grammar that could be addressed through logico-linguistic analysis mirrored the structuralist preference for the system of signs and symbols over the conscious subject. It was a similar move towards a 'philosophy of the concept' and away from a 'philosophy of consciousness'.[2] It, too, brought rather meagre intellectual rewards. The knowing subject proved to be indispensable.

The central claims of the anti-Cartesian revolution proved untenable. The less radical claim that, in the absence of a fully worked-out theory of meaning, epistemological investigations would be premature, and the more radical claim that a fully developed theory of meaning would demonstrate the meaninglessness of most epistemology enquiry, were built on the same sand. The attempt to put epistemology in its place, and to develop a purified concept-based theory of meaning which avoided, or minimised, reference to the conscious subject, was fatally impaled on the self-evident fact that a theory of meaning cannot be developed in the absence of a theory about the knowing subject. In the final analysis, meaning can be determined only in relation to subjects who know what they are doing when they (actively) mean what they write, say or otherwise communicate, and in relation to other subjects who actively make sense of what they believe the communicant wishes to communicate. The shift from the theory of knowledge to the theory of meaning did not therefore effect a convincing escape from 'a philosophy of consciousness' to 'a philosophy of the concept'; nor did it permit philosophers to avoid awkward things like 'knowing subjects' in favour of seemingly less awkward things like systems of signification or the grammatical rules for combining their elements to create well-formed formulae. There is very little of interest – and even less of sufficient depth to address philosophical concerns – to be said about meaning, without taking account of the consciousness (knowledge, understanding, intentions, needs, etc.) of the meaners and of those for whom the meanings are meant.

While the post-Fregean dream of scientificity faded in the second half of the twentieth century, it has had a considerable posthumous influence on philosophy in the English-speaking world. When in the 1970s and 1980s the philosophy of mind finally gained ascendancy over the philosophy of language, the former was predisposed by the latter to embrace the neurocomputational theories that were emanating from the neuroscience and Artificial Intelligence communities. Such theories placed subjectless calculation at the heart of mental function. Though many post-Fregeans – most notably those influenced by Wittgenstein – would have been appalled at the scientism embraced by so many philosophers of mind in the final decades of the century, their own 'dreams of scientificity' paved the way for the capitulation to science and naturalistic, third-person accounts of the human mind.[3]

The post-Fregean disdain for the contents of consciousness, the tendency to assimilate the human subject to a grammatical one, and the belief that the philosophical problems of mind would for the most part dissolve in a linguistic analysis informed by formal logic, inadvertently created an intellectual climate particularly friendly to mindless accounts of mind: materialistic stories that could, as in the case of functionalism, empty the mind (even, in some cases, of contents such as qualia) to the point where it was simply a nexus of causal way-stations linking inputs and outputs. The notion that the theory of meaning could progress in the absence of a theory of knowledge and/or consciousness paved the way for the lexical drift that has made it possible to cross the body–mind or brain–mind barrier without doing any real work.

The near-subjectless theories of meaning developed by post-Fregean writers made it respectable to extend terms such as 'information' to material events that have nothing to do with informing conscious human beings. 'The language of neuromythology'[4] enables philosophers of mind to shuttle between first-person and third-person (or no-person) viewpoints, discourses and entities. The central idea of cognitive neurobiology – that the mind is the 'software' that runs on the 'computational hardware' of the brain – depends upon terminology that does two things. First, it 'machinises' what happens within the subject, so that the mind is an ensemble of 'mechanisms'. Second, it anthropomorphises what happens in bits of the brain so that, for example, synapses or neural ensembles 'do calculations', 'issue instructions' and 'follow rules'.

The belief that a computationalised neuroscience could solve, or at least have the last word on, epistemological issues is the current orthodoxy among philosophers of mind. Avrum Stroll, for example, at the end of his superb, even-handed historical essay on epistemology in the 1993 edition of the *Encyclopaedia Britannica*, wrote:

> There have been explosive advances in neuroscience, psychology, cognitive science, neurobiology, artificial intelligence, and computer studies. These have resulted in a new understanding of how seeing works, how the mind forms representations of the external world, how information is stored and retrieved, and the ways in which calculations, decision procedures and intellectual processes resemble and differ from the operations of sophisticated computers, especially those capable of parallel processing.
>
> The implications for epistemology of these developments are equally exciting. They promise to give philosophers new understandings of the relationship between common sense and theorizing, that is, whether some form of materialism which eliminates reference to mental phenomena is true or whether the mental–physical dualism which common sense assumes is irreducible, and they also open new avenues for dealing with the classical problem of other minds.[5]

The notion that a bit of knowledge – of how the brain functions – might explain all of knowledge and account for the framework that makes knowledge possible looks vulnerable. The passage does, however, reveal the power neurophilosophy exerts over even sophisticated philosophical minds. There could be no better instance of the displacement of the dream of philosophy as a (rigorous) science in its own right by the hope of being of some use to science which promises progress in those areas where philosophers, since time immemorial, have got stuck.

There is one philosopher who, like a Colossus, bestrides both post-Fregean analytical philosophy and the scientistic philosophy of mind: W. V. O. Quine, pre-eminent logician, philosopher of language and naturaliser of human consciousness. In many respects, he is a key adversary: someone whom I would have had to invent had he not existed without my assistance. Quine was well ahead of the recent neurophilosophers when, in the early 1960s, he developed a theory of language and of meaning which assimilated the speaking subject to the material world. For Quine, meaningful words are stimuli or responses to stimuli. Their utterance is provoked directly or indirectly by their objects and they invoke in the hearer some response appropriate to those objects. In this sense, words are proxies for bits of the world: their meaning is 'stimulus-meaning' and they are the equivalents of the objects they mean. This theory of verbal behaviour was the front door of Quine's wider ambition to naturalise knowledge. 'Epistemology', he argued, 'is best looked upon ... as an enterprise within natural science.'[6]

This has many implications, some more acceptable than others. For example, the question of how, in humans, sense experience gives rise to successful science are 'scientific questions about a species of primate' (ibid.). It will be difficult to quarrel with this – indeed, it lies at the heart of the present trilogy – so long as calling humans 'primates' is not a preliminary to eliding the profound differences between them and other primates. Among the less acceptable implications is the assimilation of science to animal awareness – redescribing it as 'a biological device for anticipating experience', which 'owes its elements to natural selection' (p. 72) – and eliminating mental life as a redundant 'intervening variable' (p. 69) linking input and output in human comportment.

We shall repeatedly allude to Quine's views, which permeate many areas of philosophy – theories of mind, knowledge, meaning, reference and truth to name a few – because he is an exemplary figure. He has taken the assimilation of humans to the natural (biological, physical) world to its limit. Most pertinently, his argument that traditional *a priori* epistemology should give way to empirical psychology or 'cognitive science' would, if true, toll the death-knell of the philosophical approach.[7]

In this chapter, I shall defend knowledge against naturalisation, prior to embarking on one of the two principal tasks of this book, which is to make knowledge *visible*. The other task is to give a plausible reconstruction of the origin of knowledge out of sentience so that I can deliver on my promise to account for human knowledge in a way that is consistent with the biological, more specifically the Darwinian, story of our origins, without minimising the extent to which we have transcended those origins. Epistogony – a theory of the genealogy of knowledge – sees it not as supernatural but as extra-natural.

2.2 TROUBLES WITH NEUROPHILOSOPHY

In this section I will build on arguments I have presented elsewhere.[8] While I will rehearse some of the key arguments of my earlier critiques of 'neurophilosophy', my present purpose is specifically to show how *knowledge* – as opposed to human consciousness in general – cannot be captured in naturalistic accounts that identify consciousness with neural activity. I show where neural theories fail to explain the layers of awareness that lead up to objective knowledge – what I call pre-indexical, indexical and deindexicalised awareness (see Glossary and Chapter 4 below) – or the community of consciousness (of factual knowledge, concepts, rules, institutions, etc.) that comes out of them. We cannot, I argue, understand these very real phenomena in terms of the activity of neural circuitry. The latter is, of course, necessary but not sufficient: whole bodies, whole environments and whole communities are also needed.

2.2.1 A Fundamental Problem: Intentionality

The most striking, indeed fundamental, deficiency in neural theories of consciousness is their failure to account for intentionality. Intentionality is 'aboutness': items that are about other items have intentionality. Intentionality is a feature of perceptions, of propositional attitudes such as beliefs and desires, and of utterances such as assertions.

It was Franz Brentano who reminded modern philosophers that psychical phenomena, unlike physical ones, are directed towards, or have within them, 'intentional objects'. The term, introduced by Scholastic philosophers, comes from the Latin verb *intendere*, 'to point (at)' or 'to extend (towards)'. Above the level of pure sensation,[9] consciousness is always consciousness *of* something other than its psychic contents: sense experience transcends the experienced moment of the experiencer. Intentionality is, of course, most manifest in visual perception and in language-mediated knowledge, examples respectively of what we shall call indexical and deindexicalised awareness. This makes it particularly relevant to our present concern with specifically human forms of awareness.

The most widely accepted neural theory of consciousness is central state materialism, which identifies the mind with neural activity in the most central parts of the nervous system. According to this theory, the

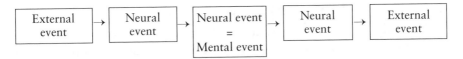

Figure 1 Central state materialism

mind is entirely wired into the causal nexus that is the material universe: mental phenomena are material effects of impingements on the nervous system.[10] They are themselves causes of material events beyond the nervous system: proximately in bodily movements and distally in the effects these movements have on the material world outside of the human organism. The causal chain passes into and out of the nervous system and nothing of ontological note happens on the way through (see Figure 1).

Central state materialism, by virtue of giving a precise location to the putative material basis of consciousness, actually makes intentionality more mysterious. Consider visual perception. I see an object 'over there'.[11] I interact with it at a distance: I may take account of it when I am navigating round a room; I may reach out for it. But my awareness of the object goes beyond my interaction with it: the object is not dissolved into me or cashed out in my behaviour with respect to it. There is something in my consciousness of it that is not reducible to immediate or delayed outputs from me: namely, my awareness of the object being there, before me; more to the point, of its being *over* there. This awareness reaches out, extends towards, the object, which retains its separateness from me, its over-thereness. This intentionality, this reaching out, has a direction opposite to that of the causal chain arising from the object and passing into my nervous system (see Figure 2). The light comes in, but the gaze looks out.

The causal relationship connecting the object with the (causally downstream) nervous system is entirely consistent with the physicalist framework; the intentional relationship, which points in the opposite direction from the nervous system to the (causally upstream) object,

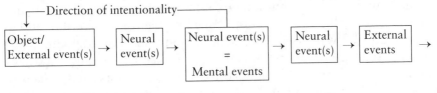

Direction of causation →

Figure 2 The mystery of intentionality

does not seem to be. It is not possible to map this 'upstream pointing' on to the kinds of phenomena – masses, fields, forces – that physicists deal in. 'Aboutness' is not a physical relation, quantity, material or substance; for, in the physical world, things interact but nothing is about anything else. Aboutness is not assimilable to the interaction between one material object and another. What is more, there is nothing in the physics of the nervous system – for example, the electrochemical events that constitute neural activity – that is sufficiently special to justify the expectation that it should give rise to something so fundamentally different from everything else seen in the material world.[12] Intentionality cannot be reduced to causal connectedness of output or input–output: the *de facto* physical connection which shapes behaviour or output is not the same as the explicit connection that is intentionality.

There are two other closely linked problems. First, there is no apparent reason why the arrow of intentionality should pause at a particular object or event – why should it have the status of being *the* seen object or the observed event? Why should intentional backtracking along the causal chain not continue until the origin of the causal chain is reached, until the Big Bang? Second, it is not clear why the causal chain should trigger the reflexive intentional arrow where it does, given that, according to central state materialism, the chain passes through the organism ontologically unmodified. What is there about the human brain that makes it the point at which this 'bounce-back' takes place? How does it 'field' what is there – in order to make it *be* there, be *over there*, be over there *for me*, the subject? There is no use invoking the notion that mind is a *special* arrangement of matter within an organism, itself a rather special form of matter, since there is nothing in the brain or the organism that is fundamentally different from arrangements of matter seen in non-conscious entities; indeed, the more complete the scientific description of organisms and nervous systems, the more completely they exemplify the general properties of matter. What is more, anything that is special in the parts of the brain that are supposed to be conscious, or to sustain consciousness, is matched in those parts of the nervous system that are not directly associated with consciousness.

The bounce-back of intentionality is massively elaborated in humans. It lies, as we shall see, at the root of the knowledge relationship and of active inquiry.[13] Whether it is present in animals is a moot point. When we sense the gaze of a beast, it is difficult to deny a 'looking out', back along the path that the light took in entering its body. Neuro-philosophers, however, would assimilate the gaze to a mere causal 'lock on' to an object that may be relevant to the creature's survival. I am content to remain agnostic here. I cannot, however, be agnostic with respect to humans, where (for reasons we shall begin to unpack in Chapter 4) there is a fully explicit intentional object, expressly other than itself, which human consciousness addresses. Bounce-back cannot, in us, be ignored.

This bounce-back presents insuperable difficulties only if one takes materialism seriously; for the human organism *qua* material object has no privileged position. Specifically, it cannot count as a terminus or a point of origin. And this brings us to a theme that will pervade this chapter: the insincerity of those who pretend to an entirely materialist viewpoint. Their insincerity – playing fast and loose with the idea of the physical world and the laws of physics that are supposed to underpin consciousness – will be evident when we consider indexicality and consciousness-as-viewpoint, and the putative basis for the unity of consciousness. Here insincerity is evident in the terms that are invoked when neurophilosophers try to avoid the problems that I have just alluded to. There is much talk of the 'representation' of objects in consciousness, of the 'modelling' of the world, of the processing of 'symbolic' markers of events, of the 'calculation' of distances. All of these are ways of trying to make materialist sense of the bounce-back of intentionality – so that consciousness reaches back up the causal chain of events that are supposed to have brought it about to (reconstruct) occurrent events or continuant objects located at some point in the chain. But they are inadmissible. Causal chains *per se* do not, of course, generate representations or replicas (literal, metaphorical, logically isomorphic) of events within themselves further downstream. They can only seem to do so if we treat the conscious organism (notably the conscious human subject) as if she were *not* a mere way-station in an ontologically uninflected causal nexus. In the physical world, there are no representations. Clouds reflected in a puddle on an unvisited planet are not represented in the puddle. At the risk of stating the obvious – or of restating it[14] – there can be no re-presentation without presentation; no second-level consciousness (such as seeing an object via a mirror or through some depiction or via symbols) without first-level consciousness.

There is another little problem that physicalists tend to overlook. If the object in perception is constructed out of perceptions, how can we make it coincide, spatio-temporally and qualitatively, with the object that caused the perceptions? According to standard materialist thought, the material object has no secondary qualities and has a spatial location. The object in perception has secondary qualities and no spatial location, other than that of the neural activity in the brain supposedly corresponding to it.[15]

2.2.2 Ineliminable Indexicality

Secondary qualities become a serious problem for neurophilosophers only when they are sincere enough about their materialism to adhere to it consistently. The same is true of indexicality which, as Colin McGinn has pointed out,[16] is a closely allied feature of 'the subjective view'. Indexicality, as McGinn says,

> is often cited as a paradigm of that which a properly objective conception of the world would exclude: the physicist ... refrains from indexical description of the world. The intuitive reason for this ... is that the use of indexicals involves treating oneself as somehow a *centre*, as a privileged coordinate; an objective description should not be thus invidious in its depiction of reality. (pp. 15–16)

And he cites Bertrand Russell:

> no egocentric particulars occur in the language of physics ... there is not, as in perception, a region which is specially warm and intimate and bright, surrounded in all directions by a gradually growing darkness.[17]

In short, not only is indexicality unavailable in the physicalist account of the world, *it should not be available*. This does not, however, discourage neurophilosophers, who purport to give physicalist accounts of consciousness, subjects, selves which are intrinsically indexical, from helping themselves to terminology that is steeped in indexicality.

It is present in the ground floor terminology used to describe what is going on in the nervous system, as well as at the higher level. For example, it is conventional to talk of the 'inputs' and 'outputs' of an organism. This makes the organism *a point of reference*, with things coming towards or entering it, and things going away from or leaving it. The contrast between inputs and outputs is necessary to make intuitive sense of the fact that a single, ontologically uninflected, causal march is differentiated into (a) sensory impulses that somehow 'bounce' back and are 'of' a world 'out there', and (b) motor impulses that lie at the origin of behaviour; that the organism is both a terminus of a sensory chain and the source of a behavioural one. A consistently physicalist account, however, would so embed the organism in its environment, and that environment in the world at large, that the distinction between inputs and outputs would be lost in a boundless causal net where an output from one place would be an input to elsewhere and nothing would count as either input or output. It would be neither a terminus nor an origin; in short, no kind of reference point. There would simply be events, as in an avalanche. An event in an avalanche would count as an input only if one took the viewpoint of a particular pebble; that is to say, adopted that viewpoint or imputed a viewpoint to the pebble.

A neurophilosopher might argue that we talk about the 'inputs' and 'outputs' of inanimate objects such as computers without imputing consciousness or selfhood to them. This only reinforces my argument: computers are machines that are subordinated to the purposes of conscious human beings. It is *from our point of view* that certain events connected with them count as inputs and others count as outputs and yet others count as neither. The argument that it is possible to discern inputs and outputs in relation to systems that are not artefacts – for example, naturally occurring thermodynamic systems – is even less compelling. Those systems are *conceptual* artefacts, deriving those boundaries with respect to which there are exits and entrances from the higher-order consciousness implicit in their being described.

The same criticism applies to the notions of 'central' and 'peripheral'. For neurophilosophers, things get more sophisticated and come closer to consciousness as one moves from the periphery to the centre of the nervous system. The states that are crucial to consciousness are those that occupy the most 'central' ensembles of neurones. These terms are, of course, steeped in borrowed indexicality. Physics does not acknowledge centres or peripheries; for, as McGinn points out, the 'centre is not just an objectively capturable location in the world but something distinctively subjective in nature'.[18] There are many other such contrasts, but the point, I think, is made: it is not possible to describe the function of the nervous system in a useful way without appealing to indexical concepts that a consistent physicalism would disallow.

Which brings us to another problem: that of accounting for the indexicality of human consciousness; the explicit sense of being 'here' and 'now'. In *I Am: A Philosophical Inquiry into First-Person Being* I argued that there was nothing in the nervous system to underpin the 'being-here' or *Fort-sein* necessary to differentiate the being-there or *Da-sein* that Heidegger had identified as the essence of human being. The body needed to be haunted by an 'I' in order for it to incarnate 'hereness'.[19] I won't revisit the arguments I set out there. Instead, I shall examine one particular attempt to find a neurological basis for 'here' and, more generally, the indexicality of experience: the self-centring of the experienced world.[20] This is the scrupulously worked-out neural theory of the 'where of awareness' by Antonio Damasio, as represented by Patricia Churchland.

Churchland begins by criticising neurophilosophical theories, based on observations of lesions in human subjects, which locate 'the where of awareness' in a particular location in the brain – for example, the intralaminar nuclei of the thalamus. These theories are consistent with the notion that awareness is based upon the rhythmic activity of coupled oscillators linking the thalamus with the cerebral cortex. This seems insufficient, Churchland argues, because

> the brain will not produce awareness unless the nervous system also generates a representation of self – a representation which carries what we would call 'a point of view'.[21]

This is counter-intuitive, inasmuch as it assumes that second-order consciousness (awareness of self or awareness of the aware self) is a necessary condition for first-order consciousness. It becomes more understandable if what she is referring to is 'indexical awareness'. This form of awareness (which I shall argue is fully developed only in human beings) is quite complex: it incorporates the sense that something is 'there' *and* that I am in relation to it; the 'there' is differentiated into an object over there and the subject who is here. At any rate, it is crucial to Damasio's hypothesis, which assumes that

> the neurobiological mechanisms for visual awareness, for example, are essentially interconnected with the mechanisms for representing oneself as a thing that has experiences, that feels, remembers and plans; as a thing occupying space and enduring through time. (Churchland, ibid., p. 52)

In short, 'awareness is related to self-representation', which in turn 'is related to body-representation'. This is the basis for the sense that one is in the sensory field that one is aware of.

Damasio argues – against, for example, Francis Crick and Christian Koch (whose theories about the unity of consciousness we will discuss, and reject, in the next section) – that synchrony of firing in visual circuits is not sufficient to generate visual awareness, though it is a necessary condition of it. What is required, in addition, is:

> *body-representation* which systematically integrates bodily-stimulation and body-state information, provides a scaffolding for *self-representation*, and self-representation is the anchor point for awareness – modality-specific and otherwise. (ibid.)

This 'neural representation of the body: the skin, muscles, joints, viscera, and so forth' is a better bet than, say, a Kantian 'transcendental unity of apperception', because it is 'reassuringly concrete' and access-ible to empirical research.

The hypothesis is mired in problems, some of which we have already discussed. For example, the assumption that the brain, or its neural activity, 'represents' anything at all, never mind 'the body' (including the brain?) or 'the self' is deeply confused. There is the additional oddness, already noted, that lower-order awareness depends upon higher-order awareness (of self). One cannot speak of the brain 'representing' anything without importing the notion of a homunculus to (or for) whom neural activity is a 'representation' – a *re*-presentation, not merely a presentation, mind you. There are, however, two particular problems with Damasio's hypothesis that touch most immediately on our present concerns.

The first is that awareness of modality-specific particulars, the higher-order awareness corresponding to self-representation and the body-state awareness that underpins self-representation are apparently fundamentally different. In neural terms, however, they are very similar. Indeed, they are indistinguishable. This deficiency is evident in other theories that Churchland alludes to. For example, the two families of 'oscillators' connecting the thalamus and the cortex – which, according to Llinás, serve the quite different functions of providing respectively the content and the integrating context ('wakeness') of sensory aware-ness – seem essentially the same.

The second specific problem is more profound and more difficult to put one's finger on. The notion of '*body-representation*, which system-atically integrates bodily-stimulation and body-state information' – that is to say, exteroceptive and proprioceptive awareness – presupposes that a lot of different sense experiences will come together of their own accord. This assumption draws upon the notion of the body as a *de facto* unified and enduring entity. But the *de facto* spatial unity and enduringness and continuity of the body, which is implicitly being drawn upon to underpin a unified and enduring self – so that this, in turn, can provide the 'where of (sensory) awareness' – does not serve itself up in and/or for consciousness. That unity *exists* only at a higher level of already established consciousness. It is a matter of *knowledge* and it cannot therefore be drawn upon to underpin the coherence of consciousness at the most basic level.

Despite these faults – and they are both deep and fatal for the theory – the Damasio hypothesis is worth discussing at this point because it illuminates (by default) what would be required of a satisfactory neural account of indexicality of consciousness – its 'hereness'. For example, it should at the very least keep apart the 'here-making' function of the body and its other functions as: a sensor; a basis for voluntary action; and as a means to its own survival. This is a neurophilosophical replication of the problem discussed in *I Am*, that the body has *too many jobs to do at once* to act as a plausible basis for the sense of 'here'.

The fundamental reason why a Damasio-like hypothesis about the basis of 'the where of awareness' will fail is that it tries to make being here both something that is derived from, or earned on the basis of, neural 'information' (a contradiction in categories) and at the same time it is assumed as a *de facto* free good in order for the neural information to be put together into a 'here', or the point of view of a sensing body or an aware self. The truth is, 'here' is inseparable from the 'sense of being-here'. To rephrase McGinn's point: there is no *objective* here. No material object is, of itself, 'here'. Physical objects – such as the body or the brain viewed through the eyes of science – belong by definition to a deindexicalised, 'hereless' (and boundless) array of material things.

Attempts to neurologise 'here' (and indexicality in general) disguise their deficiencies by helping themselves, free of charge, to those very things that they are supposed to explain: representation, point of view, etc. This is particularly evident in the neurophilosophy of 'here' which seems to depend upon the fact that the body is assumed to be (intrinsically) here – as if 'hereness' comes with the mere existence of the nerve impulses; as if, collectively, they have both being and being-here. The ultimate basis of this error, which in various guises is all-pervasive in neurophilosophy and, more widely, in materialist and physicalist thought, is the assumption, evidently false as soon as uttered, that explicitness – about a being's nature, character or circumstance – comes *gratis* with being.

This is what underpins the notion that certain nerve impulses in the brain disclose the world to us in virtue of their being self-disclosing. They would be self-disclosing, so the argument goes, because we *are* those impulses. According to Michael Lockwood, for example, we know

> certain brain events by virtue of their belonging to one's own conscious biography, knowing them, moreover, in part, *as they are in themselves* – knowing them 'from the inside', by living them, or, one might almost say, by self-reflectively *being* them.[22]

Not even Lockwood is fully confident that just being something is sufficient to make one be that thing consciously, or to afford one privileged access to its intrinsic properties. Neural impulses, he says, 'are not self-revealing; it is *awareness* that reveals them' (my italics). He has, therefore, to import, send out for, borrow, consciousness – and the inner distance required for reflection – by suggesting that there is something called 'awareness' which is different from phenomenal qualities.

As 'a first approximation', he says, 'one could think of awareness as a kind of searchlight, sweeping round an inner landscape. (Literally inner: in the brain)' (ibid., p. 163). There is, in other words, an inner light, an empty consciousness, or quality-free consciousness, picking out things in the inner landscape of neural activity. It is this, presumably, that enables the relevant neural activity to be self-disclosing – with a little help from outside (or the inside-outside). But Lockwood's sending out for 'awareness' to help nerve impulses in their task of self-disclosure betrays the difficulties faced by anyone trying to get neural activity to disclose itself.

It is clear that a theory of consciousness that has to 'send out' for awareness does not deliver what is needed. It is interesting, however, because it testifies to the intuitive attractiveness of the notion that a kind of knowledge – of what, or that, one is – comes packaged with being: that being something gives one privileged knowledge of it, access to its intrinsic nature. The notion that we get knowledge of what we are – neural impulse, whole bodies, or whatever – simply through being it actually overlooks the problems that prompted the suggestion that all we know are certain impulses in our brain: namely, that knowledge is mediated by sentience and is subject, therefore, to the doubts that mediation imposes upon knowledge. In the end, even what we get, mediated by our senses (and their echo in introspection), is rather limited. For example, we do not have the slightest knowledge of the physiological processes, and the atomic forces, that underpin our ordinary bodily functions and actions.

This lack of knowledge directly mediated by sentience should not surprise us once we get knowledge into focus. As we shall discuss in the pages to come, knowledge in its most typical form is the articulation of deindexicalised, collectivised and abstract possibility which, though it may be checked against experience, is not reducible to sentience. These various characteristics of knowledge – that it is deindexicalised, collec-tivised, abstract, about possibilities – mark its distance from immediate experience or what is given directly in introspection. What is more, the objects of knowledge are not material singulars; so knowledge of something cannot come merely as a result of being that something.[23]

2.2.3 The Unity of Consciousness

Neurophilosophers like to deny the undeniable. It serves their purposes in two ways: it gives their views a kind of respectability that comes from sharing the counter-intuitiveness of science; and it gets them out of a hole. Writers such as Daniel Dennett, for example, deny the existence of qualia – subjective experiences, first-person phenomena, and so on. There are third-person phenomena – 'stimulus inputs', 'reactive disposi- tions' and 'discriminative states' – but no 'inner feelings'.[24] There are no such things as beliefs, desires, and so on: these are imaginary entities postulated in folk psychology to make sense of the surprising, but comprehensible, behaviour of our fellow organisms. And as for selves, they are fictions – the 'narrative centres of gravity of the meme effects of the activity of the many virtual computational machines implemented in a parallel architecture'. Qualia are difficult, propositional attitudes are difficult, selves are difficult, so away they go: fictions every single one of them, because they cannot be accommodated in the third-person neuro- philosophical framework.

Dennett's deconstructed self – the 'narrative centre of gravity' – actually looks more difficult than the thing it is replacing. After all, narrative is a higher-order activity of a self; and the intuition of a centre of gravity of a larger number of independent narratives seems to be an even higher-order activity.[25] It is certainly not there *de facto* because it is (we are told) a fiction: such higher-order things do not exist in objective fact. What is more, their construction must have been motivated by something rather extraordinary, which itself does not fit comfortably into the flat plain of neural activity. Such a remedy suggests intellectual desperation; hardly surprising in view of the fact that the unity of consciousness – and the higher-level unity of the self – is impossible to understand in neural terms.

The problem is that consciousness, at many levels, is at once highly differentiated and highly integrated. At any given moment I am aware of a multitude of things that are separate and, at the same time, integrated into a unified sensory field, which itself is the seamlessly evolving background of my purposes. At any given moment, I am aware of the here-and-now and yet that moment is permeated by a multitude of memories that shape the moment-by-moment sense I make of things. I could go on,[26] but the point, I hope, is made: the nervous system has to bring together vast numbers of things that also have to be kept apart.

There have been many attempts to make sense of the unity of consciousness.[27] They all fail because they cannot overcome the conflict between keeping things apart and keeping them together. If, for example, a hierarchy of nerve cells is proposed in which neurones subserving different modalities of sensation converge, and these in turn converge with neurones that subserve memory, there is no clear reason why this should lead to integration rather than mere mushing. If, on the other hand, neural activity belonging to different phenomenal features of a given moment is kept spatially separated, the world will disintegrate into meaningless atoms unless some kind of binding mechanism is brought into play.

The most commonly proposed mechanism is one that exploits the *de facto* temporal features of neural activity; for example, it is argued that all activity taking place at a given moment *and* exhibiting the same temporal frequency will contribute to the moment of awareness. The trouble with this is that it requires an observer to bind the binding – for the synchronicity and identical frequency of the eligible neural discharges to be gathered together. For they do not gather themselves together. What is more – and this is as clear an example as one could hope for of the insincerity of neurophilosophical materialism – simultaneity is not an intrinsic feature of the material world. After Einstein, we know that only spatio-temporal coincidences are observer-independent. The selection of synchronous, resonant neural activity out of the general hurly-burly of physico-chemical activity within the brain would require an observer. Such an observer cannot, of course, be presupposed when one is trying to describe the mechanism by which observers emerge out of neural activity.

If, finally, it is suggested that neural activity is kept separate, but is at the same time unified by its relationship to some kind of inner reference point, one has to describe the nature of such a reference point. According to the Aleksander–Bartels hypothesis,[28] there is such a referent, j, which is like a tent pole supporting an entire vector space in which different sets of neural activity assume different locations within that unifying space. j is a 'sum vector' derived from a mass of neural activity associated with motor activity and sensory transducers. Unfortunately, it is not clear who or what does the 'summing' and how it is that the individual neural actions really come to self-locate with respect to the somewhat abstract space created by the summed activity.

It will be evident that unification of elements of conscious experience that are at the same time kept apart is not possible without invoking some kind of transcendent viewpoint that cannot be created within the mass of neural activity. Homunculi are unavoidable. The dispersal of the homunculus into a multitude of places and its embedding in anthropomorphic language disguises, but does not alter, its viciously regressive nature. (It would take a modern Ovid to track all the metamorphoses of the homunculus.)[29]

2.2.4 The Architecture of Everyday Consciousness

The question of the unification of consciousness is important because unification is a necessary condition of the self relating to a world, itself in some respects a whole. A genuinely unified self underpins the network of beliefs and the space of logic that will become central to our understanding of phenomena such as facts and propositional attitudes. The failure of neural activity to offer anything to establish the globalised awareness that underpins daily experience is a serious deficiency. This, and the absence of a viewpoint corresponding to that globalised awareness, are entirely predictable consequences of the physicalist framework of neurophilosophy. Physicalism cannot accommodate the central claim of neurophilosophy that there is, or can be, a set of events (such as nerve impulses) that have the capability of disclosing others events, worlds, or themselves. To press this point home, I want to look in very broad terms at the architecture, or stratification, of everyday human consciousness, the intricate structures of everyday awareness supporting ordinary deliberative behaviour (something we shall return to in Chapter 8).

We have already noted how neurophilosophy cannot reconcile the need to keep many things both together and apart: to integrate experience in the moment of consciousness, or across stretches of planned (CV, 'deposit account') life, while keeping many thousands of elements (micro-programmes of action, nascent and formed perceptions, and the frameworks that make sense of both) absolutely distinct in a nervous system in which nearly everything is ultimately connected with nearly everything else and mass activity is the name of the game. While modularity – based on spatial separation – solves the problem of keeping things tidily apart, it gets in the way of things coming together.[30]

If we accept the neural theory of consciousness, we are committed to the extraordinary idea of rather similar brain events achieving quite distinct things:

a) They enable the body to be the means by which a world, centred upon it (as the locus of the zero coordinates of egocentric space), is revealed both *by* and *to* that body.

b) In virtue of these events, the body discloses itself to itself, encounters itself as an object of a certain size, with certain properties, located at the heart of a sensory field. These give me the sense of being a particular entity in the world. They reveal the body itself – a solid, thick, warm, articulated stump of flesh – as both the (quasi-transparent) means by which a world is disclosed and as 'a thing amongst things' (Sartre). It is a self-revealed viewpoint upon the view it reveals.

c) Subsets of these events enable the body to be separately aware of different parts of itself (arm, leg, face), to be aware of its own different and successive states, and to have specific localised experiences.

They make possible different kinds of experiences: of putting one leg in front of the other; of having warm or cold hands; of toothache; or, more globally, of a feeling of bodily well-being.

d) Finally, they enable the body to have a sense of ownership, to be 'my' body, so that there is some kind of subject somehow anchored in the zero coordinates of egocentric space. This allows there to be a sense that it is *I* who am walking along – an I who is responsible in a variety of ways and who is located in, or with respect to, a biography extending through time.

In short, very similar neural events have differentially to disclose utterly and fundamentally different things: the world that surrounds the body; the body that is surrounded by the world; parts of, and events in, the body; and of the 'selved' body that is mine, or me, here-now; and of the 'selved' body.

The problem, therefore, is not simply that of intentionality – of ensuring that nerve impulses are a window beyond the brain – but of a profoundly *differentiated* or *structured* intentionality. For what is revealed in, or to, consciousness, what is supposed to be disclosed in or through brain activity, is multilayered in a way that self-disclosing neural impulses, even if the notion made sense, cannot account for. As I walk through the woods, I am aware of:

a) The material world around me accessed through my senses – the trees, the path, the air, the dogs barking and bounding, the golf course beyond the woods, the bright sky above the golf course. This world, extending in all directions to a horizon defined by obstructions to my gaze, is centred upon me: it is arranged in egocentric space, of which I – the body-subject – am the implicit centre.

b) My body in that world – this thickened stump of being, this fat, tall, clothed thumb, this 'determinately shaped, determinately sized, determinately hard or soft something',[31] this explicit and implicit centre of the field of exteroceptive awareness, which I need to know at the same time as a whole and in parts, in order to act purposively as when I walk through the woods.

c) Within the boundaries of the 'body as a whole', the specific experiences and sensations of that body – for example, the light on my eyes, the intermittent feeling of the cool air on my ears, the even more intermittent sense of my shoes on my feet and the more diffuse sense of shortness of breath, or effort or fatigue. (Not to speak of more or less alien sensations unconnected with the activity such as an aching tooth, or a sensation of bloatedness after too heavy a meal or delights more or less sinister.)

d) The sense that I, through my body, am here, now, in this place whose centre is defined by the position of my body.

Neurophilosophy requires all this to be disclosed through groups or groupings of very similar events in areas of the brain only a few milli-metres from one another. The implausibility of this layered awareness being achieved in this way does not need labouring. There is simply nothing in the differences between nerve impulses or their groupings to correspond to differences between different modes of bodily and world awareness. This problem would remain conspicuously unaddressed even if we had not already uncovered the dubiousness of the notion of nerve impulses as self-disclosing physical events. What the neural theory of consciousness requires of us is that we should believe that the further presence of the trees over there, and the nearer presence of the barking dog which I am minded to call to heel, the synthetic unity of a physical world surrounding me, the specific sensations located within my body, and the fundamental intuition that this is my body and I am here, at the centre of egocentric space, should all be disclosed in or through the same kind of events in one very narrowly defined area of the brain.

The problems faced by neurophilosophers do not end here. As I walk through the woods, I have thoughts of a more or less abstract nature. They range from reflections prompted by the events or the process of the walk, or by the proximate context of the walk – for example, the day on which the walk takes place, or the area where its trajectory is located; through irrelevant, but rather particular thoughts, such as about my chances of finishing a book by next month; to highly abstract medita-tions on the nature of consciousness. These thoughts are connected, implicitly and explicitly, in all sorts of ways with other aspects and parts of my life, and they open on to other thoughts or revert to a realisation that I am out walking; they are highly unpredictable and are subject to the lightest of overarching control, but they never decline into delirium, nor are they sealed off against a vigilant awareness of the walk and its context – so that I do not walk into a tree, allow the dogs to stray too far or forget the other things I have to do today, or the life of which the walk is a minute part. This unbroken internal monologue of commentary, fantasy, self-communing (much, though not all, of it mediated by words with rather precisely defined, if sometimes distinctly idiolectical, semantic fields) has, we are required to believe, to be carried by neural events and at the same time be clearly differentiated from the other modes of disclosure – of the things around me, of my body, its sensations, of my sense of this body as 'mine' or 'me'.

This brief description of the complex structure of the most ordinary everyday consciousness beyond simple sentience looks forward to the account of the differentiation of human consciousness into pre-indexical, indexical and deindexicalised awareness. Even if 'bare' sentience were amenable to neural explanation, these higher levels of human consciousness are not. One cannot invoke the same processes in the same object to explain (a) how objects are made visible, (b) by what they are made visible, (c) to what they are made visible, and (d) from what viewpoint. As we have had occasion to observe earlier, the brain seems to be required to do too many things at once; to fulfil too many difference kinds of role using the same material.

The passage from pre-indexical to indexical awareness – signalled by explicit intentionality, in which there is a subject related to an object seen to be 'over there' – marks the point at which neural theories lose their last shred of plausibility.

2.3 TROUBLES WITH ANTI-NEUROPHILOSOPHY

2.3.1 Taking the Brain Seriously

So much for the troubles of neurophilosophy. Anti-neurophilosophy, however, has troubles of its own. While it is easy to criticise the notion of consciousness being brewed inside the skull, we cannot ignore certain basic facts. Most basic of all is that something like a viewpoint, or a subject, is co-located with something like a body; or (if this seems easier – though it doesn't to me) that subjectivity comes to rest in specific human bodies. We cannot be worlded without being embodied. We should therefore acknowledge the intuitive attractions, and not just the weaknesses, of neurophilosophy.

It is important not to be distracted by the glamour of neuroscience. The decisive observations are the most elementary – the 'folk' observations available in everyday life – not the most sophisticated ones. No more metaphysical ice is cut by functional magnetic resonance imaging studies than by the non-glamorous folk observation that if you bang your head you become a bit odd or lose consciousness; or that decapitation is associated with a decline in IQ. Terms like 'synapse' and 'frontal lobe' only *seem* to carry greater philosophical authority than 'bang on the head' and 'behaving oddly' or 'losing consciousness'. But they take us no further into the relationship between brain function and consciousness. In this democratic spirit, therefore, let us begin not with the brain but with the whole body. (I will argue in due course that this is where we should have stayed; indeed, with the whole body engaging its surroundings.)

It is evident that the *contents* of my consciousness, the succession of my experiences, indeed the experiences that are normally possible for me, are importantly determined by the location of my body. I am, for example, experiencing a room in Bramhall, rather than a room in Cornwall, because Bramhall is where my body presently is. Indeed, I transported my body precisely in order to be aware of (and to have access to) the things in this room. My consciousness is to an important extent *of* where my body is at. As P. F. Strawson put it:

> for each person there is one body which occupies a certain *causal* position in relation to that person's perceptual experience, a causal position which in various ways is unique in relation to each of the various kinds of perceptual experience he has.[32]

Of course, the location of my body does not determine the entire contents of my consciousness. A video-link with my study in Bramhall could give me perceptual access to it from Cornwall. This, however, is a derivative form of experience and one that ultimately depends upon bodily location: I have to be near the relevant television screen in order to have the experiences mediated through it. Communication systems, however sophisticated they are, do not break the connection between bodily location and the content of experience. Even memories and abstract thoughts are ultimately linked to the history of my bodily locations.[33]

Additional ordinary observations clinch this connection: damage to the body may impact on the ability to be aware of one's surroundings. Serious injury may be associated with temporary loss of consciousness; fatal injury with permanent loss of consciousness. Although the viability of the body may outlast anything corresponding to ordinary awareness of what is going on around one, such awareness does not, so far as we know, outlast the viability of the body. Dead bodies are unaware; and people whose bodies are dead are unaware and, indeed, are no longer people.

This would be sufficient only to establish the relationship between the body as a whole and consciousness. However, there are plenty of everyday observations that seem to give overwhelming support to the conjecture – that goes all the way back to the pre-Socratic philosophers[34] – that there is an intimate relationship between the brain and conscious experience. In order for me to experience Cornwall, it is necessary for me to bring my brain there. In contrast, my mind is not necessarily where my leg is: I could leave my leg in Bramhall, and, so long as I had not bled to death, my mind could still experience things in Cornwall. So there seems to be an intimate relationship between the physical location of my *brain* and the content of my consciousness.

The central role of the brain is supported by additional low-cost observations – for which no Medical Research Council funding is required – that seem to suggest that the input of energy into my brain from the outside world determines my experiences. For example, when I cover my ears or close my eyes, that is, block the input into the organs that are connected directly with the brain, I cut off certain experiences. This seems to be consistent with the notion that experiences are in some intimate way connected with cerebral events, or with events that impinge on the brain and have effects there.

Further support comes from the many ordinary observations that indicate that the kind of 'nick' the brain – and its end organs, such as eyes and ears and touch receptors – is in and the kind of 'nick' my mind is in are closely correlated. One sort of bang on the head, with damage to the brain, may remove vision; another sort may impair memory; and a third may alter personality. These everyday observations support the notion that mental function – vision, memory, personality, whatever – everything from the most primitive buzz of sensation to the most exquisitely constructed sense of self – depends crucially on the functioning of the brain.

Subsequent, more sophisticated, observations further refine the general hypothesis. Sophisticated physiological and psychological observations have suggested that the mind is composed of discrete faculties to which are assigned distinct areas of the brain. The brain stimulation and ablation studies performed by scientists such as Gustav Theodor Fitsch, Eduard Hilzig and David Ferrier on apes, complementing the precise observation of both clinical and pathological aspects of spontaneous neurological damage in humans, strongly suggested the localisation of mental functions within different parts of the cerebral cortex. The French neurologist Paul Broca reported in 1861 the discovery at post-mortem of a discrete defect in the frontal lobe of a patient with an isolated loss of language. This seemed to demonstrate beyond doubt that even the distinctive human faculty of speech had its basis in brain function. The cerebral theory of consciousness was further supported by Hughlings Jackson's reports in the *Lancet* in 1873 of correlations between clinical syndromes and post-mortem findings in patients with disturbances of consciousness. Recent advances in medicine, which have enabled patients to survive who would previously have died, have further underlined the specific role of the brain in consciousness. Death of most of the brain, but not of any other organ, may be associated with loss of consciousness while the body itself remains viable. To be a conscious human being it is necessary not only to have a living body but also to have a functioning brain within that body.

The cerebral hypothesis of the Greeks has been further strengthened by recent data which include not only 'negative' observations showing loss of functions resulting from natural and induced lesions, but also 'positive' observations apparently revealing the mind active within the living brain: we are shown certain parts of the brain lighting up in anticipation of, or during the course of, the discharge of certain mental activities. Techniques such as functional magnetic resonance imaging, positron emission tomography, electroencephalography and other forms of brain mapping, have revealed exquisite and consistent correlations between markers of activity in certain areas of the brain, and mental function. Mental imagery is associated with activity in the same part of the brain as lights up when a real object corresponding to the mental image is seen.[35] Even more interestingly, observing an action with an intention to imitate it is associated with neural discharges in the same area as when the action is actually performed.[36] 'Purely mental' phenomena such as imagery and intention, therefore, seem to have their neural correlates just as much as gross actions do.

Everyday life and scientific observations would all seem therefore to point to this inescapable conclusion: that consciousness is due to certain activity in the brain; or that mental activity is neural activity. Anti-neurophilosophy, therefore, is in real trouble. It seems to have to fly in the face of a reasonable interpretation of an overwhelming body of evidence. Even if we deny that these observations demonstrate that consciousness is identical with brain activity, we still have to make some kind of sense of the evidently central role the brain plays in maintaining consciousness and in the determination of its contents.

2.3.2 Brain Function: Necessary but Not Sufficient

At the same time there seems to be no way of basing a satisfactory account of mental function on the activity of the brain. One way of reconciling this is to suggest that while the brain is a *necessary* condition of consciousness, it is not a *sufficient* condition of it; or, more precisely, that a certain sort of neural activity in a normally functioning (or not seriously damaged) brain is essential for normal conscious experience, but normal conscious activity is not identical with such activity.

This will be my position. There are, however, difficulties – quite apart from the challenge of specifying what it is that crosses the gap between the necessary and the sufficient conditions of consciousness. For a start, some experiments – the 'positive' observations – could be interpreted as suggesting that neural activity by itself is sufficient to create experiences. A case in point is Wilder Penfield's experiments in which subjects who receive electrical stimulation of the cortex report fully developed and often quite complex ('Proustian') memories. This would suggest that cerebral electricity alone is sufficient to constitute a full-blown content of consciousness, as opposed to a mere flash or tingle. Another, more common example is that of patients with focal epilepsies who report complex experiences associated with the abnormal electrical activity of the brain. These hallucinatory experiences correspond to what might be expected from the putative functions of the brain areas from which the seizures originate – hallucinations of music from the temporal lobes which have an auditory function; hallucinations of scenes from the occipital lobes which have a role in vision; and so on.

These findings, however, are not as decisively in favour of neuro-philosophy as they may seem. The induced memories of Penfield's patients and the hallucinations of people with focal epilepsies occur necessarily in *waking* subjects; in other words, against the background of consciousness. If the subjects were unconscious, they would not, of course, be in a position to report them. Because this background is a necessary condition of the experiences being reported, it tends to get overlooked. And yet it seriously undermines the notion of stand-alone cerebral activity producing experiences on its own account. It opens the way to another interpretation: that the electrical activity merely alters the content of an existing consciousness and does not produce consciousness off its own bat – a finding no more extraordinary than the folk observation that turning one's head or closing one's eyes alters the content of consciousness.

More fundamentally, it could be argued that the interpretation of the cerebral activity as 'experiences', and more particularly as 'experiences of something outside the subject' – a past event, a visual scene, a sound – is *parasitic* upon the interpretations that are usually deployed by this background waking consciousness. They seem to, or come to, count as experiences only because of the past (and present) of this waking consciousness having experiences in the usual way. (Just as false memories are possible only against a background of overwhelmingly predominant real memories.) The usual way is one in which the cerebral activity is part of the activity of a living body in a world of surrounding objects and a society of ideas and people. The abnormal electricity produces hallucinations that parasitise normal perception; the latter require cerebral electricity produced in the normal way, the electricity being a necessary but not a sufficient condition. The additional conditions are that of a creature who is situated in an environment and (for complex memories) has had a meaning-filled life. Bits of memory and bits of experience do not really exist in isolation: they make sense only as part of a boundless, pre-experienced whole – a world. We could put this another way: the apparent intentionality of the hallucinations, pseudo-memories, etc. is borrowed from the actual intentionality of ordinary perception and ordinary consciousness. And this intentionality cannot be explained neurally.

2.4 CONCLUSION: THE UNNATURAL NATURE OF KNOWLEDGE

I have argued that, while neural activity is necessary for human consciousness, there are many aspects of human consciousness that lie beyond any kind of neural explanation. Human consciousness, after all, is not a single thing: it can range from, say, a fleeting sensation of warmth to consciousness of looking stupid to pride in being a citizen of a country. The idea that these are all just variations on nerve impulses seems implausible: difference in brain location and the quantity of neural activity seems even less likely to capture the difference between the sensation of warmth and a feeling of national pride, than to capture the difference between orange and blue, or between the pain of toothache and the pleasure of orgasm.

In this critique of neurophilosophy, we have focused on intentionality, indexicality, unity and the complex architecture of everyday human awareness. While it is conceivable that sentience might be, more or less, a property of certain forms of material activity seen in brains – though heaven knows how[37] – it is inconceivable that *knowledge* could be found in the intra-cerebral realm of the neurophilosopher. There is a point where one passes over from 'pure' sensations (such as we might imagine could be experienced by animals)[38] to those contents of consciousness that have intentionality – so that they are both feelings in themselves (say, of green) and *of* objects (say, a green apple). At this point, consciousness slips out of the reach of neural explanation and of naturalistic thinking. The relationship of actual contents of consciousness to the objects that consciousness is *about* ranges from intimate (as in a warm feeling on the skin) to quite remote (as in national pride). It hardly seems likely that these differences could be captured in variations of location and quantity of nerve impulses.[39]

It is a particular irony that it is neural theories, which localise consciousness inside the skull of the conscious person, that make the mystery of intentionality explicit, and the non-physical character of ordinary experience particularly striking. While one might be agnostic as to whether sentience (putative primitive, unselfconscious sensations) is neurally based, it is clear that explicitly intentional consciousness – what I will call 'propositional awareness' – is not. At some point between 'feeling cold' and '*That* it is cold ...', it no longer makes sense to look to the nervous system to cast any light on consciousness.

At any rate, it is this realm marked out by intentionality, the realm of knowledge – the various allotropes of 'That' as in 'That X is ...' or 'That X is the case ...' – that we are concerned with in this book. We will not, however hard we look, find 'That', 'That X is the case ...' or, in general, *knowledge* in neurones, any more than we shall find the citizenship and the sense of justice that the old phrenologists hoped to discovery in parts of the cerebral cortex. As Simon Blackburn has pointed out, 'it is the whole person that has the psychology not bits of him'.[40] Maurice Merleau-Ponty, who of all the great twentieth-century philosophers was most versed in contemporary neuroscience, would have agreed whole-heartedly with this:

> Being a conscious subject is engaging in complex relations with objects, and these relations depend on the whole human being, not simply on the brain; a disembodied brain could not be said to have conscious experience of objects, but only to provide some of the necessary, but not sufficient, conditions for such conscious experiences.[41]

Knowledge requires not just the brain, or the body, or the engaged body, but an enworlded self.

This will become apparent to us when we look more closely at the nature of knowledge. Knowledge begins with the sense of there being something *beyond* how things appear to us: it begins with the concept of an object that is other than the self who entertains the notion of an object. Implicit in the idea of the object is the intuition of the subject contrasted with the object; more precisely, the Existential Intuition 'That I am this ...' whose nature and origin are discussed in detail in *I Am*. Object knowledge is also permeated by a sense of publicness – of a shared world – that is not available to asocial sentience or asocial neural activity. The latter precedes the steps by which awareness became first indexicalised – so that the subject was in an explicit relation to the object – and subsequently in part deindexicalised, so that awareness comes to be of things that are not in a perceptible spatio-temporal relation to the subject. Knowing animals cannot be found in neurones because their knowledge is in a complex sediment of experiences, personal interactions, institutions and artefacts that transcend the brain. Trying to find people in neurones is like trying to find the forest foliage in the seeds of the trees.

Worse. For in trying to find citizens in neurones, neurophilosophers are seeking in isolated brains the pooled activity of hominids over six million or more years, triggered by the Existential Intuition that enabled the human organism to awaken to, and out of, itself. They are trying to cram back into the present moments of individual brains the knowledge that belongs to the collectivity of billions of brains. Even if we could find sentience in the nervous system, we could not find knowledge there because, necessarily collective, knowledge does not come from necessarily isolated sentience: the science of dentistry is not to be found by adding up experiences of toothache. The collective work of many millions of nervous systems interacting in a public realm they have created will not be found by looking at the activity of nervous systems working in isolation within the darkness of the skull.[42] We cannot cram knowledge back into the brain or indeed the human body because it has escaped into extra-corporeal space, history. This is not to say that it is floating free outside of the organism, but that descriptions of neural activity cannot capture those things that have resulted from the conjoint activity of many brains, many organisms, many people over millions of years.

In the pages that follow, we shall examine the passage from the solitude of sentience to the collective work of knowledge and the creation of a shared public domain, privatised in each of us, where knowledge is at its extra-cerebral, extra-corporeal work. While it is, of course, true that all that we experience, feel, know and think has to be mediated through the brain – this remains a final pathway for all aspects of human consciousness – all but a small residue of pure sentience transcends cerebral activity. For this reason, it makes no sense to look for correlates of what we are in bits of the brain. It makes even less sense to try to map bits of what we are on to ever smaller bits of the brain; for example, to locate self-awareness in the right frontal lobe of the cerebral cortex, as the standard teaching has it.[43] Self-awareness transcends the brain; indeed, as humans have evolved, it has increasingly transcended the body. As with knowledge and abstract meaning themselves, *delocalisation*, an uncoupling from embeddedness in the material world, is of the essence.

NOTES AND REFERENCES

1. The dismal story of structuralist (and the even more dismal story of post-structuralist) theory and criticism is recounted in two books I published in the late 1980s: *Not Saussure. A Critique of Post-Saussurean Literary Theory* (Basingstoke: Macmillan, 2nd edition, 1995) and *In Defence of Realism* (London: Edward Arnold, 1988; 2nd edition, University of Nebraska Press, 1997).

2. See Raymond Tallis, 'Philosophies of Consciousness and Philosophies of the Concept, Or: Is There Any Point in Studying the Headache I Have Now?', in *Enemies of Hope. A Critique of Contemporary Pessimism* (Basingstoke: Macmillan, reprinted with new preface, 1999).

3. In many cases, they were simply unaware of what was going on. In his autobiography, *The Making of a Philosopher* (London: Scribner, 2003), Colin McGinn describes the reaction of Michael Dummett to a talk McGinn gave on the syntactic theory of mind. Dummett launched into a violent attack on McGinn's paper, rooted in his ignorance of the provenance of McGinn's argument.

4. See Raymond Tallis, 'A Critical Dictionary of Neuromythology', in *On the Edge of Certainty* (Basingstoke: Macmillan, 1999).

5. Avrum Stroll, 'Epistemology', in *Encyclopaedia Britannica* Macropaedia, Vol. 18 (15th edition 1993).

6. W. V. O. Quine, 'The Nature of Natural Knowledge', in *Mind and Language* Wolfson College Lectures 1974, ed. Samuel Guttenplan (Oxford: Clarendon Press, 1975), p. 68.

   Ironically, this may seem to represent a return to the associationist theories of verbal meaning that Frege was at such pains to demolish. In this case, however, the association is not with private, unstable, mental objects such as mental images, but with public, stable, physical objects or events. The theory, however, remains flawed for all sorts of reasons. For example, it cannot accommodate the fact that words have different kinds of functions, that they work together, that there are words such as 'the' for which there is no stimulus equivalent, and so on.

7. In *Problems of Knowledge: A Critical Introduction to Epistemology* (Oxford: Oxford University Press, 2001), Michael Williams argues that, while it is Richard Rorty who is the explicit obituarist of epistemology, having announced its death, there is little difference between him and Quine, its naturalist. I entirely agree. Stuffing human knowledge back into the material world and thereby handing it over to the physicists is not very different from killing off epistemology.

8. See, for example, Raymond Tallis, *The Explicit Animal. A Defence of Human Consciousness* (Basingstoke: Macmillan, 2nd edition, 1999); and *On the Edge of Certainty*, especially 'The Poverty of Neurophilosophy' and 'A Critical Dictionary of Neuromythology'. In these earlier critiques, I have (in common with many other writers) argued that the neural theory of consciousness is also unable to make sense of the qualitative differences between conscious experiences. For example, it offers no satisfactory way of accounting for the differences between the qualia corresponding to hearing and those corresponding to sight; between past and present experiences; or between the experiences associated with deliberate and those associated with involuntary activity. One nerve impulse seems much like another, so it is difficult to comprehend why one lot of nerve impulses should correspond to the colour yellow and another to the colour red; how one should represent or be a colour and another should represent or be a sound; and how excruciating toothache and the pleasure of an orgasm could be differentiated.

9. Whether for humans there is such a ground floor of consciousness consisting of pure sensation without intentional objects is debatable. John McDowell, in *Mind and World* (Cambridge MA: Harvard University Press, 1996) has questioned the notion of experiences that have non-conceptual content – that is to say, do not in some respect 'exceed' themselves. Merleau-Ponty also emphasised throughout his work that even the most elementary element of consciousness was charged with meaning.

10. The link between biologism and physicalism (and scientism more broadly understood) is the physical chemistry of the nervous system.

11. For philosophers such as Martin Heidegger, this kind of 'rigid staring' at an object, which produces both the sense of it as independent of the subject – itself intuited as localised – and at a distance from it, is a false intellectualisation of perception and creates the epistemological (pseudo-)problems. It is justified to take seeing an object-at-a-distance as a paradigm because: (a) the neural account locates the basis of perception within the head of the perceiver; and (b) the intuition of the object as independent of awareness and as incompletely revealed in the latter lies at the heart of the knowledge relation, as we shall discuss.

12. And difference is the point. Donald Davidson, perhaps as a way of making people more at ease with physicalist theories of the mind, has argued that there is 'no good reason for calling all identity theories "materialist"': 'if some material events are physical events, this makes them no more physical than mental. Identity is a symmetrical relation' ('Knowing One's Own Mind', *Proceedings and Addresses of the American Philosophical Association* (1987), 60: 441–58). This is not persuasive. It actually highlights the failure of the identity theory to capture the difference between conscious human beings and pebbles. Even if that difference were illusory, we may be sure that pebbles do not share in the illusion. The difference between humans that can be and pebbles that cannot be deluded remains unexplained. Nor is Donaldson's 'symmetry' at all reassuring. For the universe, right up to and including those events that are supposed to be identical with mental events, is overwhelmingly material. The material facet of the mind-brain identity is playing a home match, among its ontological kin, doing business with a material world.

13. In Chapter 4 *et seq*. Its supreme expression is, of course, deliberate activity.

14. See 'Representation (Model)'; 'Misplaced Explicitness, Fallacy of' and similar entries in Tallis, 'A Critical Dictionary of Neuromythology'. This does not stop neurophilosophers – and, indeed, neuroscientists – making assertions such as that 'Awareness results from cerebral processes that construct models of the world'. Donald T. Stuss, Terence W. Picton and Michael P. Alexander, 'Consciousness, Self-Awareness and the Frontal Lobes', in S. P. Salloway, P. F. Malloy and J. D. Duffy, *The Frontal Lobes and Psychiatric Illness* (Washington: American Psychiatric Publishing Inc, 2001), pp. 101–9.

15. This oversimplifies intentionality. As a feature of both indexical and deindexicalised awareness – being a property of perception, of propositional attitudes and of abstract thought – it has multiple manifestations.

16. Colin McGinn, *The Subjective View. Secondary Qualities and Indexical Thoughts* (Oxford: Clarendon Press, 1983).

17. Russell, *An Inquiry into Meaning and Truth*, Chapter 7, p. 102.

18. McGinn, *The Subjective View*, p. 16.

19. See 'The Existential Necessity of Embodiment: No *Da-sein* without *Fort-sein*', especially section 5.5, 'The Body Underwrites *Fort-sein*'. Sentience is 'hereless'. One could imagine an iterative process whereby a faint blush of 'selfness' awakens a tinge of 'hereness', which in turn strengthens the sense of self, and so on. This could happen, however, only in a species that passed 'hereness' from one member to another and handed down a cumulative 'hereness' embodied at least in part in the complex, multilayered cultural world.

20. A more detailed critique of another attempt to neurophilosophise being-here is contained in Raymond Tallis, 'The Metamorphoses of the Homunculus. A Critique

of the Alexander and Dunmall Extension of the Zeki-Bartels Hypothesis of a Mechanism Underlying the Unity of Sensation' submitted for publication.

21. Patricia S. Churchland, 'Can Neurobiology Teach us Anything About Consciousness?', *Proceedings of the American Philosophical Association* (1994), 67: 23–40.

22. Michael Lockwood, *Mind, Brain and Quantum* (Oxford: Basil Blackwell, 1989), p. 159, emphasis in original.

23. How little this is appreciated is reflected in the fact that philosophers such as Merleau-Ponty had to emphasise again and again that we did not need to have the slightest knowledge or understanding of the physiological processes underlying the movements of our body in order to execute complex actions. (A good thing too; for such movements are the remote and proximate precursors of any kind of scientific inquiry, including the physiological science that has recently revealed these processes!)

24. These topsy-turvy views can be found in Daniel Dennett's *Consciousness Explained* (London: Little, Brown, 1991).

25. A particularly striking example of 'the fallacy of misplaced consciousness'. When materialists deny consciousness in the places where it is normally thought to be, it has the habit of appearing in an even more complex form where it shouldn't be. See Tallis, 'Critical Dictionary of Neuromythology'.

26. See Tallis, 'The Poverty of Neurophilosophy', in *On the Edge of Certainty*, for the full story.

27. I address some of them in 'Relativity Theory, the Unity of Consciousness and Neurophilosophy', submitted for publication to *Journal of Consciousness Studies* and Tallis, 'The Metamorphoses of the Homunculus. A Critique of the Alexander and Dunmall Extension of the Zeki-Bartels Hypothesis of a Mechanism Underlying the Unity of Sensation'.

28. See Tallis, ibid.

29. One of his most interesting metamorphoses is in Andrew Duggins, 'The Mind/Brain Inequality', *BioSystems* (2001), 61: 95–108. Duggins suggests that consciousness itself – specifically, 'the global influence of a unitary mental state on depolarisation probability' (i.e. the chances of neuronal firing) – 'might be the 'binding mechanism' that synchronises firing of remote neurons'! J. G. Taylor has described consciousness as 'a global relation between functional neurobiological networks' (*The Race for Consciousness*). One has to ask: Are the networks self-globalising? If so, how? If not, who globalises them?

30. See also Tallis, 'The Poverty of Neurophilosophy'.

31. B. O'Shaughnessy, quoted in Quassim Cassam, *Self and World* (Oxford: Clarendon Press, 1997), p. 52n.

32. P. F. Strawson, *Individuals* (London: Methuen, 1959), p. 92.

33. See Raymond Tallis, 'The Logical Necessity of Embodiment', *I Am: A Philosophical Inquiry into First-Person Being* (Edinburgh: Edinburgh University Press, 2004).

34. See Raymond Tallis, 'Brains and Minds: A Brief History of Neuromythology', *Journal of Royal College of Physicians* (2000), 563–7, which covers the history alluded to in the pages that follow.

35. Stephen M. Kosslyn, Giorgio Ganis and William L. Thompson, 'Neural Foundations of Imagery', *Nature Reviews Neuroscience* (2001), 2: 635–42.

36. G. Rizzolati, L. Fogassi and V. Gallese, 'Neurophysiological Mechanisms Underlying the Understanding and Imitation of Action', Nature Reviews, *Neuroscience* (2001), 2: 661–70.

37. Even this may be too great a concession. Experience so far suggests that if *any*

element of consciousness is attributed to the isolated brain, to certain circuits, then not only is the difference between mind and matter lost – the desired outcome for neurophilosophers – but so also (not surprisingly) is the real and undeniable difference between sentient creatures and insentient pebbles. This encourages two (opposite) forms of madness: the denial of contents of consciousness – as in Dennett's attempt to eliminate awkward qualia; and the espousal of pan-psychism, which spills consciousness everywhere.

David Chalmers' extraordinary *The Conscious Mind: In Search of a Fundamental Theory* (Oxford: Oxford University Press, 1996) shows how super-soft pan-psychism lies close to hard-headed computational cerebrocentrism. Chalmers extends the notion of 'information' to 'any physical difference that makes a difference' (p. 281). He concludes that 'information processing devices' such as thermostats are conscious and that 'If there is experience associated with thermostats, there is probably experience *everywhere*: wherever there is causal interaction, there is information, and wherever there is information there is experience. One can find information states in a rock – when it expands and contracts, for example – or even in the different aspects of an electron. So ... there will be [conscious] experience associated with a rock or an electron' (p. 156). The entire universe is a gossipy, sentient being, a massive auto-pandiculation, a global bean-spilling about itself.

The language of neuromythology – in which the brain is both machinised and anthropomorphised – is a warning that just beneath the rhetoric of hard-headed science is magic thinking: mind among things; or thoughts in thing-like brains.

38. Nevertheless, I don't think an isolated nervous system would deliver sentience. Even the sentience of worms, one may suppose, is not just a few worm nerve impulses: it is those impulses-as-part-of-a-worm-in-its-burrow, *absent* even pre-inklings of self-concern.

39. At this point, people often point to encoding systems, such as the binary code used in computers, as examples of how complex ideas can be built up out of simple components. The analogy is false, primarily because codes are derivatives of languages and other manifestations of higher-order consciousness. See Tallis, 'A Critical Dictionary of Neuromythology'.

40. Simon Blackburn, 'Finding Psychology', invited introduction to *Mind, Causation and Action*, ed. Leslie Stevenson, Roger Squires and John Haldane (Oxford: Basil Blackwell, 1986).

41. Eric Matthews, *The Philosophy of Merleau-Ponty* (Montreal, Kingston and Ithaca: McGill-Queen's University Press, 2002) p. 57. The idea that an isolated brain could sustain the kinds of experiences humans have is absurd. What would it have experiences about? Experience goes beyond the brain in two ways; outwards to the entire engaged organism, and outwards to society, history and the self.

42. The fact that humans deposit much of their minds in a public world has been noted by many philosophers, from Karl Popper onwards. Andy Clarke has recently emphasised this in *Being There. Putting Brain, Body, and World Together Again* (Cambridge, MA: MIT Press, 1997): 'We use intelligence to structure our environment so that we can succeed with *less* intelligence. Our brains make the world smart so that we can be dumb in peace!'

43. See, for example, Donald T. Stuss and Michael P. Alexander, 'The Anatomical Basis of Affective Behavior, Emotion and Self-awareness: a Specific Role of the Right Frontal Lobe', in G. Hatano, N. Okada and H. Tanabe (eds), *Affective Minds* (Amsterdam: Elsevier Science, 2000).

CHAPTER 3

The Case for Epistogony

3.1 THE SCEPTICAL TRADITION

Epistemology, as we have discussed, had a rather unhappy time in the twentieth century. This was particularly true of scepticism-driven epistemology. For existentialists, scepticism seemed variously insincere or beside the point. No one could truly doubt everything – though one could pretend to do so in philosophy seminars – because one still carried on living as before, never questioning the reality of external objects or the existence of other minds. The world, after all, is not an object of knowledge or of thought, but where we live. Living goes deeper than knowledge or thought; which is why scepticism, even if apparently well founded, makes no difference. Wittgenstein argued that scepticism was *not* well founded: one cannot doubt everything because one has to have grounds for doubt. What is more, a good deal of the world has to be left undoubted if the terms in which one expresses one's doubt are to have any meaning. Scepticism is in many respects self-refuting. (This is in some ways a more generous version of the *Cogito* argument. The very fact of my doubting that I exist proves not only that I must exist – so that my doubt is existentially self-falsifying – but a good deal more besides.)

Wittgenstein sometimes had doubts about his resistance to scepticism. One philosopher who most certainly did not share such doubts was J. L. Austin. He was as impatient with the incompetence as with the insincerity of epistemological scepticism. Scepticism and the arguments thought to lead to it amounted to little more than

a mess of false analogies, definite errors, and even identifiable fallacies which had bewitched the intelligence of earlier philosophers through insufficient attention to the complexities of language and to the general conditions for the significant functioning of our actual conceptual scheme.[1]

His judgement that scepticism was deeply unserious was hugely influential in Anglo-American philosophy and, as Barry Stroud has pointed out, its influence continued long after the heyday of the linguistic philosophy with which Austin was most closely associated.

Scepticism-driven epistemology has not been without its supporters in recent decades, most notably Stroud himself.[2] Stroud has argued that one does not have to be, or pretend to be, a sceptic in order to take sceptical thinking seriously and profit from it:

> A line of thinking can be of deep significance and great importance in philosophy even if we never contemplate accepting a 'theory' that claims to express it.[3]

The 'line of thinking' that Stroud believes to be particularly fruitful is the one that has exercised philosophers since Parmenides; namely that

> our knowledge of the world is 'underdetermined' by whatever it is that we get through that source of knowledge known as 'the senses' or 'experience'.[4]

There could not be a more succinct encapsulation of the central preoccupations of Descartes, Locke, Berkeley and Hume, Kant and the Idealist philosophers he inspired: Mill, Mach, Russell and Husserl.

I too believe scepticism to be illuminating. My goal, however, will be quite different from that of the scepticism-driven epistemology which aims either to show that we know nothing or to demonstrate that our knowledge, after all, is soundly based. What I want to do is to *make the distinctive character of knowledge visible*; and offer an account of the passage from 'sense experience' (which I shall call 'sentience') to knowledge. The two aims are inseparable: describing the steps from sentience to knowledge is a way of uncovering the gap between them and, by so offsetting knowledge from sentience, making the latter's extraordinary character visible. I will not engage directly with the standard sceptical arguments.[5] Indeed, I will be assuming all sorts of things – not the least the existence of an animal kingdom from which we have partly escaped – that consistent radical sceptics should deny themselves. I hope this will not be seen as mere avoidance of the difficult and interesting problems. There are reasons, internal to my project, for not trying to justify the transition from sentience to knowledge.

The most important is that I believe that a defining characteristic of knowledge is that it is shadowed by a sense of ignorance. This is quite a complex sense. Knowledge knows that it is underdetermined: it is haunted by incompleteness, by the sense that there is more to know. Unlike sentience, it has *objects* that are other than it. In virtue of being other than the knowing subject, the object of knowledge is only partly uncovered. Knowledge has at its heart the intuition of a reality that transcends appearance. It is also, as we shall see, the site of possibility, and hence of explicit uncertainty. Finally, when our knowledge is fully 'deindexicalised', as when we are in possession of *facts*, we are aware that what we know is a small island in an infinite sea of the unknown.

Knowledge, that is to say, is *in essence* unjustifiable in the last analysis. This does not, however, warrant our concluding that nothing is truly known. There is neither justification nor the lack of it *except within knowledge*. As Quine has pointed out, 'Doubt prompts the theory of knowledge; but knowledge, also, was what prompted the doubt. Scepticism is an offshoot of science.'[6] This insight will guide our inquiry into the nature of facts, truth, thoughts, propositional attitudes, our attempt to characterise the distance between human beings and the organic world in which they are rooted, and our exploration of the impulse to transcendence that delights and torments the knowing animal. Whether or not scepticism is justified, it is a profound articulation of what lies at the core of knowledge's self-knowledge.

Since my aim is at variance with traditional epistemology, a new name is warranted to designate what I am up to. On account of the emphasis on the genesis of knowledge, I shall call my activity 'epistogony'. I shall, however, begin with something a little more conventional as an implicit defence of my 'epistogonic' turn.

3.2 REFLECTIONS ON A BENT STICK

Half a century after the lectures on which it was based, the sparkling wit of J. L. Austin's *Sense and Sensibilia* still makes the book a delight to read. In these lectures, Austin mounts a slaughterous attack on certain doctrines about sense-perception. Though still current at the time, they were at least as old as Heraclitus and certainly 'quite ancient in Plato's time':

> The general doctrine, generally stated, goes like this; we never see or otherwise perceive (or 'sense'), or anyhow we never *directly* perceive or sense, material objects (or material things), but only sense data (or our own ideas, impressions, sensa, sense-perceptions, percepts &).[7]

The reasons we get to thinking such extraordinary things – which lead us to argue, even more extraordinarily, that we are separated from the

reality of the material world by an impenetrable veil of appearance –
are

> first ... an obsession with a few particular words, the uses of which are
> over-simplified, not really understood or carefully studied or correctly
> described; and second ... an obsession with a few (and nearly always the
> same) half-studied 'facts'.[8]

One such 'half-studied' fact is the case of a straight stick that looks bent
when it is half-plunged into water. It seems a good place to begin. If we
can think straight about bent sticks, we should get a lot of other things
straight.

It is obvious that a straight stick doesn't bend when it enters water; all
that changes is how the stick looks to us. That, at least, is what we
believe. We can be confident that the stick remains straight for several
rather obvious reasons. Water is not the kind of thing that bends sticks.
More to the point, when we run our fingers down the stick, we do not
feel a kink. The stick is, from a tactile point of view, indubitably
straight. We don't, of course, usually bother to check this: we are used to
a world in which things can look different from how we know them to
be. We are confident, without checking, that the stick is straight, not
bent.

And it is a good thing, too, that we have this certainty; for if we
started checking, we would have embarked on a slippery slope leading
deeper into the mire of uncertainty. Making explicit our reasons for
being confident that the stick is not bent makes our confidence vulnerable. Better to have no reasons and rest on unquestioned assumptions.
Otherwise we might end up subscribing to all sorts of peculiar ideas. As
those philosophers singled out by Austin found, bent sticks can bend
your mind: you may end up advancing in broad daylight or at 10 p.m.,
with the assistance only of a cup of Horlicks, ideas such as that we do
not directly apprehend objects but things called sense-data (which may
or may not be in the mind); or, if sense-data are ruled out, believing that
objects are the sum total of actual or possible perceptual appearances.
At any rate, we are liable to argue that

> what is immediately given in perception is an evanescent object called an
> idea, or an impression, or a presentation, or a sense-daum, which is not
> only private to a single observer but private to a single sense.[9]

The argument that sticks don't *usually* bend when they are plunged
into water and therefore this stick cannot really be bent is vulnerable

because it is merely inductive-probabilistic. It does not rule out the possibility that on this occasion things might be different. It also raises the following, more fundamental question: How do you know – on this or any other occasion – that, despite appearances, the stick is not bent? The fact that it feels straight to touch does not prove that, contrary to visual appearances, it is straight, unless we are able to demonstrate convincingly that touch is somehow closer to the reality of the stick, has better access to its true nature, than vision does. This would require us to believe that touch is infallible, or at least less fallible; that touching is believing, or relatively more justified believing. We know, however, that touch can be deceived as to what it is that is touching – as when we rub our crossed index and middle fingers down our nose and we feel as if we have two noses. Actually, we do not have to execute party tricks to discover the limits of touch as an organ of accurate knowledge: groping in the dark is rich in misunderstandings.

Our confidence that the stick really is straight has nothing, then, to do with the intrinsic superiority of the hand as an organ of truth over the eye. Indeed, there will be occasions when the tables are turned: when the eye tells us the true nature of what it is that we have been palpating uncomprehendingly or misunderstandingly in the dark. The reason that the testimony of touch is accepted over that of hearing in the particular case of the stick in the water is that the straightness uncovered to touch is consistent with more of our future experiences of the stick than the bentness revealed to the eye. Perception may err, but it can be corrected by other perceptions: the predictions flowing from the tactile experience of the stick are consistent with more future experiences than the predictions flowing from the visual experience of the stick. Some of these experiences relate to the active use of the stick – for example, poking it down a straight channel at the bottom of the water vessel it is in, which would not be possible if it were truly bent.

For these reasons, we regard the tactile experience in this instance as revealing the true nature of the object and the visual experience as being an illusion. We say that the stick is 'really' straight, even though it 'appears' bent. Correcting one perception with another does not put us in the situation (to use Wittgenstein's witty analogy) of buying a second copy of the same newspaper to check that the news is true. In the case of the bent stick, we are checking the deliverances of the tabloid visual experience against the broadsheet tactile experience.

And that should be that. We can distinguish appearance from reality, or at least those appearances which are illusions from those which are veridical perceptions, on the basis of predictability, consistency and coherence. We can shake off this annoying and rather dull problem and move on to more interesting questions in the philosophy of knowledge.

Unfortunately, that isn't that. For a start, predictability, consistency and coherence are rather unsatisfactory, not to say fuzzy, criteria. They are not absolutes; indeed, they are graded, a matter not so much of 'yes or no' as of 'more or less'. To remain for a moment with our bent stick, the assumption that the appearance of straightness is true while that of bentness is illusory depends upon the fact that straightness predicts, or is consistent with, more future (and past) experience of the stick than is the opposite assumption. But there are certain experiences that are actually more consistent with the opposite assumption – for example, the appearance of the stick when plunged in water on future occasions.

This counter-argument may be dismissed as taking into account too narrow a range of experiences. For example, when considering the reality or otherwise of the bending of the stick when it is plunged into water, we need to range more widely in our search for consistencies and inconsistencies. We should consider all stick-like objects; or all objects with properties like sticks; or, indeed, the majority of solid objects. And we should tap into a wider range of their appearances than simply those that are evident when they are, or are about to be, or have just been, plunged into water. We need to consider their wider interactions with the rest of the world, including our own bodies. When we do this, we see that the ratio of broadsheet (non-illusory, straight-stick) to tabloid (illusory bent-stick) data – or data compatible with them – becomes astronomically large. We find that, on the whole, our experiences are more often safe guides to anticipating experiences than they are misleading.

Even granting this, we are still not out of trouble and free of the clutches of this annoying and dull argument about appearance and reality. For a large ratio, even an astronomically large ratio, is still a ratio, a matter of more or less rather than of yes or no. Moreover, as well as being graded, rather than on or off, predictability, consistency and coherence seem somewhat subjective. Predictability is related to an *ability* – to predict – and is most certaintly subjective. But so, too, are consistency and coherence: for the sense that X is consistent with Y, Z, etc. or that experiences X, Y and Z make a coherent group is very difficult to quantify against valid criteria, even though in theory one could imagine it would be possible.

It would have been so much better if we had found one objectively defined mode of perception that had authority over the others; if we had been able to say, for example, that touching is (justified) believing and everything else (hearing, seeing, etc.) should defer to its authority. But that is not how things are, as we have already noted: sometimes seeing tells touch what it, in fact, touched; and sometimes touch corrects the impressions derived from seeing.[10]

So the problem posed by the bent stick won't go away: it sticks to the mind like a burr. And this is annoying because it seems a trivial problem – a long way from concerns about the meaning and purpose of life, the nature of truth and the true nature of human beings; like an obstinate clue in a crossword puzzle and not the proper object of a serious mind trying to grapple with fundamentals. But perhaps it won't go away because, as philosophers since Heraclitus have appreciated, it opens on to something fundamental, after all. For what it tells us is not only that there are some perceptions that are erroneous, but that, ultimately, the only way of sorting out erroneous from veridical perceptions is something variously called consistency, coherence or predictability. The criteria of consistency, coherence and predictability cannot sharply demarcate those perceptions which are in error from those which are veridical: there is no objective or clear typology of broadsheet and tabloid perceptions. Moreover, when we ask ourselves the question that has been lurking in the background – How can sense experience be the basis of true knowledge? – we see something rather dispiriting: namely, that our criteria for true as opposed to false experiences are *internal* to sense experience. Predictability, coherence and consistency are about sense experiences backing up each other's stories, about corroboration between perceptions, and not about correspondence between perception and what is the case, the things that are 'really' there. By appealing to one perception to support the truth of another perception, and then to use this to separate true perceptions from false ones, we genuinely do seem to be falling into the trap of buying a second copy of the same newspaper to check whether the news is true. It is just that a cabal of newspapers gets together to confer upon itself broadsheet status and to denigrate those whose reports contradict its own as mere tabloids. In truth, the whole of perception, for all its self-corroboration, may well be sealed off against objective reality. We may be, as philosophers have argued since time immemorial, confined to a world of (false, derivative, superficial) appearance and excluded from the reality of things: their own senses fool all of the people all of the time. The fact that the consistency of perceptions extends outside of an individual perceiver – that there is intersubjective, intergenerational, international, inter-epochal reliablity – only attenuates, but does not abolish, uncertainty. The very idea of perceptual appearance damns all perception as 'appearance'.

This has led some philosophers to conclude not only that we are confined to a world of appearance – and that, since appearance differs from reality, we live in a world of illusion – we have in short, from first breath to last, got everything wrong. Such arguments are of the kind that gives philosophy a bad name. They make non-philosophers question not only its usefulness but also its seriousness, its sincerity. To say that we have got everything wrong seems absurd for two reasons. First, if we really have got *everything* wrong, we would have no benchmark against which we might conclude that we have got everything wrong. We need to get at least some things right to see that we have got most things wrong. The very assertion that we have got everything wrong presupposes all sorts of things being got right. As Ayer (p. 37) says, 'there can be times when our senses deceive us only if there are times when they do not'.[11] More encouraging still is Quine's observation, quoted earlier, that it is *knowledge* that prompts doubt. We must accept the truth of the observations that lead to our believing that we have got everything wrong if we are going to accept that we have got anything wrong: at the very least, the conflict between the perceptions that makes us aware of the illusion must be accepted as real. What is more, we must accept the validity of the arguments leading from the observation of conflict to the conclusion that one or other of the perceptions must be an illusion. Finally, we have to buy into the assumption that there is a 'we' (people rather similar to and capable of communicating with one another at a high, not to say high-abstract, level) who get things wrong.

These arguments are complemented by the existential observation that those who argue that we are confined to a world of mere appearances, and that this is a world of illusion, live like the rest of us. Perhaps they have an inner glow of hope of a future life in which we cave-dwellers would be led dazzled into the sunlight; maybe they are possessed by a hidden worm of terror that they might be led into something less attractive than sunlight. But it isn't very visible between seminars. Besides, self-proclaimed sceptics continue to distinguish between sticks that really are bent and those that merely look as if they are. They differentiate a subclass of – well, illusions within the world of illusion; of errors in this world fabricated out of error. In short, the global illusion seems to deliver for them what reality delivers the less sophisticated. If the stubbornness of the illusion that makes it seem real is a source of shame to them, they keep it well hidden.

3.3 THE FUTILE PURSUIT OF THE CORRECT SENSORY APPEARANCE

From what distance *does* an object, a cricket ball say, 'look the size it really is'? Six feet, twenty feet?[12]

The status of perceptual experiences as a source of the truth about things becomes even more problematic when we drag ourselves away from the high-profile shocks of bent sticks and the drunkards' pink rats and the headless horses of the illusionists' armamentarium and think about more ordinary experience.

The appearance of a table varies continuously, depending upon how it is viewed – from what angle, in what light, from what distance, even in what frame of mind. It is experienced differently every time it is experienced. There is no way of settling its correct look – and hence the distance, angle and lighting that would deliver its correct visual appearance – say, by touching it all over. The deliverances of touch are rather less helpful in deciding what a thing's true character is (and so what it should look like) than in deciding some particular thing about the object – such as whether the object is straight or bent. If I were to feel all the way round this table now and caress its entire surface, this would reassure me about some characteristics of the table – such that it really is rectangular – it would not constitute a definitive experience of, an authorised version of, the table. The experience would just be another (and rather unusual and not very helpful) experience of the table.

This should not be taken to prove that sense experiences are always going to be wrong. Rather, it should suggest to us that the very notion of a true experience, or accurate perceptual appearance of an object and its connection with the (reality of) the object itself, is not very clear. Philosophers have worried over what we might call the 'canonical' appearance of an object. Philosophers wanting to flaunt their common sense tell us that the 'canonical' appearance is simply what it looks like when it is not obscured by another object and is viewed in good light, from a sensible distance and at a conventional angle by someone who can be pronounced perceptually fit. The multiple vulnerability of this definition is clear: a 'good' light, a 'sensible' distance, a 'conventional' angle and perceptual 'fitness' are hardly objective terms. They are non-objective in two senses: first of all, there are no objective criteria for determining a 'good' light, a 'sensible distance', etc.; and second, these criteria have everything to do with the subject, the perceiver, and nothing to do with the object, which is, for example, at no distance from itself.

The intuition that has generated these criteria – assuming that they are not merely the fruit of impatience with pointless questions – is the feeling that appearances are most likely to coincide with reality when objects are perceived under certain 'favourable' conditions. Under such conditions objects like tables and chairs will be seen for what they truly are – what they are *in themselves*. This notion that things can be seen for what they are intrinsically when they are exhibited in 'their true light' is confused and complex, as the half-transferred epithet indicates. It is either circular or absurd. The circularity may be made explicit by recasting the claim as follows: 'the reality of an object is that which appears in conditions in which it is seen for what it really is', and those conditions are defined as 'the conditions under which the object may be perceived without distortion i.e. as it really is'.

There is clearly something deeply amiss with the idea that there are some conditions in which objects are permitted to appear as they really are, in which appearance is of reality: as if we could cancel the spell of illusion woven by experience and break through to reality by adjusting the lighting, etc.; as if better lighting were the key that unlocks the door of the prison house of illusion! One cannot rend the veil of illusion by upping the wattage of the light bulb.

Of course, those who tried to define what a canonical appearance was did not want to suggest anything so daft. They were intending not so much to show the way out of the prison house of illusion as to demonstrate that the *philosophical* distinction between (illusory) appearance and (real) reality is an illegitimate extrapolation to all experience from the ordinary distinction between illusion and reality. To describe all appearances as illusory is to empty the notion of illusion (and of the distinction between it and reality) or the notion of appearance (and the distinction between it and underlying reality) of meaning. There are conditions in which we get things right and there are conditions in which we get things wrong. Those conditions in which we most usually get things right may be regarded as the conditions in which things most often show themselves as they really are.

This common-sense view (rooted in a respect for the ordinary way of taking things and the ordinary uses of language) implicitly attacks the insincerity of those who claim to believe that perception gives us no access to how things are. It dovetails with a pragmatist account of perceptual truth: namely, that truth is what works; true assumptions are those that trigger actions that have the desired results. The fact that we are able to function in the world demonstrates that there is a real sense in which we do not get things wrong, either all of the time or even most of the time. That perception is a reliable source of knowledge is made clearer if we recognise that truth is not acquired by 'rigid staring' at objects (to use Heidegger's phrase) but by purposeful interaction with them. The truth of perception, its status as the source and foundation of (true) knowledge, is evidenced in, and guaranteed by, our successful dealings with the world. Success itself can be described independently of any presupposition about the relationship between perception and truth, as the furtherance of goals, the completion of projects, which in many cases will serve the ultimate goal of survival. The appearance of an object under good conditions must be its 'true appearance' or 'the truth about it' or 'its truth to its reality' if it enables us to engage successfully with it. It is idle to wonder whether perception, over all, gives us true knowledge of objects because there is no doubt that, for the most part, it is a successful guide to action.

There is, of course, no reason why we should accept the pragmatic theory of knowledge and truth. Nor should we accept the assumption that the very concept of knowledge (and truth) makes sense only with respect to our practical dealings with the world. Although the sceptic may be apparently insincere in questioning the truth of the deliverances of her senses, inasmuch as she behaves towards the world rather as the rest of us do, her expressed doubts are not thereby demonstrated to be illegitimate. The following argument still seems to be valid:

a) Sometimes I am deceived by the appearance of things (the bent stick in the water).
b) Even when I am not deceived, the appearance of a given thing will vary from moment to moment, depending upon its relationship to me, the lighting, etc.
c) The appearance of things to me is not securely fixed to their intrinsic reality, especially if, as Parmenides argued, that reality is, unlike appearances, unchanging.
d) All appearances – for all that they may be good enough to guide action towards success – may be incorrect in the sense of not showing forth the true, intrinsic nature of the things as they appear to me in sense perception.

This argument is reinforced by the fact that abstract scientific knowledge, which (as we shall presently discuss) bypasses most of the elements of the appearance of things (it endeavours to be non-perspectival and does without secondary qualities), is also a very successful guide to action – overall, a much more successful guide than scientifically untutored sense experience. While this abstract scientific knowledge links in with practical dealings with the world as it becomes more sophisticated, its world picture is entirely at odds with that which informs our continuing, immediate interaction with things. This seems to validate epistemological doubts; for example, about the relationship between perceptual experience and (pre-scientific as well as scientific) objective knowledge. Why, for example, is abstract scientific knowledge such an advance on pre-scientific understanding rooted in unreflective perception and practical dealings? And when, as is so often the case, scientific knowledge conflicts with the unreflective deliverance of the senses, in what sense is the former closer to the truth about the intrinsic reality of things? Is it more powerful because it is more true, rather than being counted more true because it is more powerful? And how do we – unique among the animals that also survive through effective interactions with the material world – become liberated from ordinary perception to arrive at scientific knowledge? Finally, are pragmatists justified in entirely dismissing attempts to comprehend how things are in themselves, quite separate from our immediate goals, or even from our long-term ones? Is this not the very basis and engine of science? And is it not true that in mature science, there has often been a prolonged interval between its cognitive advances and their practical application? And does not the endeavour to grasp the object independently of our local interests, even of the operation of our agency, to see it in isolation from our practical interaction with it, motivate some great art?

The attempt, favoured by ordinary language philosophers, existentialists and pragmatists, to rescue common sense and to sideline epistemological anxieties precipitated by visual illusions and the ordinary facts of non-illusory experience, is therefore unconvincing. We are still left puzzling over the fact that we cannot find a principled way of separating veridical perceptions from illusions; or a least a principle of separation which goes deep enough to dispel the uneasy feeling (however transient, and however much the academic expressions of it outlast the feeling and so become insincere) that we may be sealed off from the truth about the world 'beyond' our perceptions and be confined to a merely consistent or coherent world of experience that has nothing to do with the world of real objects outside of experience. That veridical perceptions seem to reveal the truth of things not because they in any way correspond to the reality of those things but because they simply cohere with one another.

The conclusion we may draw from our consideration of the table apparently seen under optimal conditions is more compelling than the message arising from the illusion of the bent stick. It reminds us that all perception is perception-under-certain-conditions. For example, all perception is perspectival in many senses: the table is seen from a certain angle; it is seen at a certain distance; it is exhibited in a certain light, gleaming here with a patch of light, and mottled there with a patch of darkness and tethered to a certain shadow of such and such a size and shape and at such and such an angle. Now it is obvious that the distance and the angle, with their impact on the apparent size and the apparent shape, have as little to do with the table as the pattern of light or the shape and size of the shadow. There are other features of the table that are even more clearly extrinsic to it; for example, its relationship to other objects (including the body of the perceiver); or its potential use, which is, of course, entirely relative to the purposes conceived by the perceiver. When we ask the question 'How big is the table *really?*' we run into difficulties. Close up it looks huge. From a long way off it looks tiny. Which is it then, huge or tiny? Which is its true appearance? The answer is neither. We cannot settle the question of the intrinsic size of the table through direct perception or through choosing the 'correct' perception that accesses an appearance that corresponds to the true reality of the table. This is not just because the terms in which we describe perceptions – 'huge', 'tiny' – are vague, comparative rather than absolute, relative to our conceptual schemata, and so on, but because it does not make sense to think of capturing the intrinsic properties of objects through their perspectival appearances.

We could, however, go further and argue that many seemingly intrinsic properties of the table are also extrinsic and, in some sense, perspectival. For example, its density, its hardness, its weight, its warmth or coldness are, at least as they are ordinarily and directly experienced, relative to the animal bodies that are perceiving them. The feeling of heaviness is not something that the table has, is or enjoys in and of itself. This is shown by the fact that for one person, the table might be heavy and for another it might be light. The same applies to the feeling of coldness or warmth. Cold and warmth may be set aside as already having been classified as secondary qualities, as are colour and texture: no table is dark or smooth in itself because it cannot be dark or smooth *to* itself or in the absence of an observer. In short, we may set aside those properties which have to be *experienced* in order to *be* at all. These naturally encompass all comparative properties, which, too, are perspectival. A carrot would have to experience itself as being small in order to be inherently small; ditto 'smaller than a turnip' or 'larger than a radish'. In short, no object inherently has comparative qualities; and it is surprising how many qualities are implicitly comparative, even when they sound 'positive' in the grammatical sense.

When we take away everything that is explicitly or implicitly perspectival or relational we are left with very little in the way of intrinsic properties – of properties the object has *in itself*. What properties does it still retain in itself when we remove that which it has merely for an external observer or which would require a 'for itself', a comparing self-awareness, an inner observer, to make exist within it? Remarkably few it seems.

Even primary qualities, which have been traditionally regarded as intrinsic to material objects and observer-independent, may look vulnerable. Take John Locke's list of primary qualities, common to all material bodies and mind-independent: solidity, extension, figure and mobility. Mobility is clearly not intrinsic to the table. Its figure, or shape, will depend upon the angle from which it is viewed. Likewise its extension. All that is left, in the end, is its solidity. And even this is comparative. Descartes argued that hardness was not a fundamental property of material objects for we could imagine a situation in which objects retreated as we advanced our fingers to press upon them.[13] They would not be experienced as hard, though their extendedness would remain. Hardness, it seems, depends upon an accident – a collision with a sentient being and no way to yield – and this is clearly extrinsic to the object. Of course, solidity does not boil down solely to hardness. Hardness is but one aspect of the property whereby material objects claim exclusive occupancy of a portion of space over a certain period of time and repell all other potential occupants. Let us concede this one property – solidity – as something genuinely intrinsic to the table and not apparently perspectivally dependent. This, surely, is a property it has in itself.

We have salvaged rather little for a world of perception that is indubitably true of the world of objects outside of perception. The rest of perception, even setting aside those occasions in which it is out-and-out mistaken or illusory, seems to be incorrigibly perspectival and thereby contaminated with the perceiving subject. Without perspective there is no perception: 'the view from nowhere' would be a view of nothing. Or almost nothing: perhaps we would be left with otherwise featureless solidity, which would boil down merely to 'volumes of exclusion'.[14] (These too are not absolutely clear. After all, every solid object proves penetrable to objects that are smaller than its consitutent atoms.) Beyond this, material objects (or whatever we want to call the extra-perceptual things our perceptions are of) would be inaccessible to perception.

This rather dismal conclusion, which lies at the end of a well-beaten path originating from reflections on the sometimes unreliable and always variable appearance of ordinary things like perceived tables, is a consequence of the fact that perception is not only perspectival but also inescapably interactive or mediated. We shall return to this in due course. But for the present, let us accept some of the arguments that have led us to conclude that experience may mislead us as to the true nature of the objects we perceive.

3.4 MEASUREMENT AND THE DISAPPEARANCE OF APPEARANCE

The immensely powerful belief that how things really are is captured in quantitative reports, and that the true nature of change is captured in unchanging equations correlating quantities with other quantities, including quantities of time, was expressed in Galileo's *profession de foi* (echoed by many other scientists and philosophers since) that the book of nature is written in mathematics:

> Philosophy is written in this grand book the universe, which stands continually open to our gaze. But this book cannot be understood unless one first learns to comprehend the language and to read the alphabet in which it is composed. It is written in the language of mathematics, and its characters are triangles, circles and other geometric figures without which it is humanly impossible to understand a single word of it; without these one wanders about in a dark labyrinth.[15]

How does quantification seems to offer a way out of the prison of (subjective) perception and a means of getting at the objective (true, intrinsic) nature of things? Let us return to our table. It has a different apparent shape when it is seen from different angles and yet we 'know' that it is truly, that is to say intrinsically, rectangular. By what means do we derive this solid knowledge from volatile perceptions? We measure. One could imagine a primitive scientist placing a length of wood along the sides of a square table and marking off the beginning and end of each side. He would find that the distance between the marks was the same for each of the sides. In the case of a rectangular table he would find that the distances between the marks was the same on opposite sides of the table but not on adjacent sides. He would, however, find that the ratio of the distances between the marks on adjacent sides remained unchanged. Sides a and c (opposite one another) had a ratio 1 as did sides b and d. Sides a and b (adjacent) had a ratio of 2:1 as did adjacent sides c and d. Never mind that the table looks trapezoid from this angle and rectangular from that angle, that its apparent shape for you over there is different from its apparent shape for me over here or that it varies for me depending upon my viewpoint. Irrespective of whether you measure it or I measure it, whether we measure it from this side or that, measure it today or tomorrow, we shall get the same answer.

One could imagine that the process of making these observations would be informed by an inchoate notion of 'length' – as a property which the wooden stick and the object had in common – and that, as a result of making actual measurements, the abstract idea of length would become more explicit; eventually, the abstract idea of 'the length of an object' would emerge fully formed.

Perhaps not fully formed. For these primitive observations fall short of measurement in the sense that lies at the foundation of science. The next step would be to make the notion of *ratios*, the quantitative comparison of sizes, more explicit and move towards unitisation. The standard stick becomes a unit of measure and a new sort of counting originates. Geometrical figures are digitised. This goes beyond mere counting of self-separating objects (sheep, stones, people) to the counting of sizes and distances, increasingly clearly separated as what would be later called 'parameters' or 'dimensions'. The volatile comparatives of perception – 'near to me', 'a long way away from me', 'a big table', 'a small table' – would be replaced by the seeming absolutes of stable observation: six feet away from this point; six yards away from that point; a ten foot by ten foot table; a four foot by two foot table. These measurements will remain always the same, whatever the conditions. Again and again, we shall find that the table is rectangular and has sides that are four foot by two foot. More importantly, you will find the same. And so will anyone else.[16] Quantification unites solitary perceivers into collective knowers. As W. H. Auden put it: 'Strangers were hailed as brothers by his clocks.'[17] The table is four foot by two foot when it is near us and looking big; and it is still four foot by two foot when it is far off looking tiny, and this underlines something that is central to the notion of an object: that it has properties of its own which transcend perception.

Measurement, then, is an observation that is resistant to the usual vagaries of perception. This is in part because the influence of viewpoint *factors out*. When I measure the length of the table, I am comparing one observation (that of the table) with another (that of the ruler). The ratio between the two compared with respect to length is a ratio between observations, and hence the influence of viewpoint (leaving aside the Einsteinian considerations mentioned in note 16) cancels out. We seem to have found a non-perspectival form of awareness, an objective knowledge, whose deliverances are invariant across many of the varying conditions under which perceptions vary. The penny that looks ellipsoid from the side and circular from above will always have a circumference all the points of which are equidistant from its centre and whose length is a fixed multiple of its diameter and whose volume (size) will always be the product of its (unchanging) circumference and its (fixed) depth.

Measurement seems to provide the criterion we are looking for to distinguish between false or non-canonical and true or canonical perceptions. The 'correct appearance' is the one that corresponds most closely to the shape that is revealed by the measurement. It is constant within and between observers. Any perception that tells us that the table is not rectangular with right-angled corners or that the penny is elliptical can be dismissed as, if not illusory (that is too strong a word), then distorted, even warped, by perspective. We are able to judge perceptions as if from outside of them.

Measurement can also help us to deal with out-and-out illusions. If we do not want to rely on touch to adjudicate between the visual perceptions of the stick – the ones that tell us it is straight when it is out of water and the ones that tell us that it is bent when it is in water – we can make measurements. If the stick is six inches long and its ends are six inches apart, then the stick must be straight. Measurement can take us further than this: it can generate a general description of the conditions under which illusions might be expected and predict the scale of the illusion – the degree of bending of the stick. We can, in other words, formulate a science of explicitly illusory perceptions, as when we articulate the notion of the refractive index of light through different media and develop theories in perceptual psychology.

We seem, through measurement, to have resolved the crisis precipitated by the bent stick (and the elliptical penny, etc.). We know the stick isn't (really) bent and the penny isn't (really) elliptical, not only because this does not fit in with our tactile experiences but because, when we take measurements, we find that the stick is not bent and the penny is circular. If touch has a special authority over vision in these cases, it is not simply because the deliverances of touch predict more future experiences than the deliverances of sight but because they are backed up by measurements.

All of which sounds fine until we raise the question of the origin of the authority of measurements. Surely they, too, are ultimately derived from perception and so must sit under the same cloud of suspicion. Why do we believe that measurements are more objective than other perceptions? Why, furthermore, do we believe, along with Galileo, that measurement gives us access to the inherent nature of things, and that the Book of the Universe is written in mathematics?

There are one or two inadequate reasons, based on what I have already referred to: the agreement within and between observers. Let me deal with agreement within an single observer first: that if I take the same measurement on several quite different occasions and in several different settings, I get the same answer. It might be argued that this does not distinguish measurement from ordinary fallible perception. If I perceive the object under the same circumstances (same lighting, distance, angle, and so on), the object will have the same appearance. We could explain the apparent superiority of measurement over direct perception by arguing that both of them yield the same observation under the same circumstances. The circumstances under which measurement of the size of the table is possible (e.g. good lighting and myself right up against the object) are relatively limited and always favourable. Admittedly, they are less restricted than the circumstances under which I get the same perception: for example, I can apply my measuring rod to the table from many angles and get the same result. But this is a relative not an absolute difference.

The sameness of the measurement is, in at least two respects, an artefact of the mode of observation. First, the units tend to round up; at any rate there is a limit to the precision of the observation (and hence of the range of possible observations), whereas perceptions are continuously variable and this corresponds to the fact that objects can be of any size and do not have to conform to a round number of units, however finely graded the scale. Second – and this will prove to be of great significance – quantitative observations *empty* the object of most of its contents. The table is reduced to its length and width: it is a bare $4' \times 2'$. This is desperately impoverished compared with the direct perception of the table. (When two sheep plus two sheep giving rise to four sheep is reduced to $2 + 2 = 4$, the whole bleating, meadowy business of sheep rearing is lost.) If we learn that a table top has the dimensions $4' \times 2'$, we have little or no notion of what it would look like under any circumstances.

There is, however, a further source of the authority of measurement: it is a public observation. That the table is $4' \times 2'$ is, as we would say, a *fact*. The transition from perception to observation or observed fact as it were 'freezes' perception, placing it in a public domain that is independent of individuals and their experiences. Perceptions that are expressed in any shared symbolic form – for example, verbal reports – have this authority. And this exposes observations to checking against the observations of others and to tests of agreement between observers: what we might call, using a term not in vogue until long after Galileo's time, tests of '*inter-rater reliability*'. The result I get from measurement is the same as the result you get, which is the same as anyone would get. This concordance of results validates the method of measurement and gives the individual measurement authority: it becomes a super-observation; or a perception that is given over entirely to being an objective observation. The numerical component of the measurement makes it more than simply a standardised perception under standardised conditions: the reduction of the object's properties, qualities, presence to numbers of units *de-perspectivalises* it. This process continues in the summation of measurements to laws and the linking of types of measurements in correlations expressed in equations connecting abstract parameters. F = ma or V/i = r are the antitheses of perspective-bound perceptions.[18]

Inter-rater reliability may not, however, overcome our earlier voiced suspicion that the consistency of measurement is an artefact resulting from constraints on the circumstances in which measurement can be made. In addition, there are problems in determining the circumstances under which a measurement might be rejected. If nine observers consistently report the table as being $4' \times 2'$ and a tenth reports it as being $4' \times 3'$, we will tend to reject the latter observation. This is not simply herd behaviour or the tyranny of the majority. It is because, in the case of simple measurements such as those of the length of the sides of a table, deviant findings are usually the result of faulty methodology and the latter is not defined in a circular way as being a methodology that fails to support the majority observation. At a higher level, however, when more complex measurements are being made, the demarcation between a result that differs because what is being observed is not constant and a result that differs because of methodological error is less clear.

These problems apart, there is something intuitively plausible in the suggestion that measurement liberates us from the prison house of perception, where appearances may deceive and we have no principled way of distinguishing illusions from veridical sensory experiences. The higher-level coherence of science and the huge amplification that is has afforded of our ability to control the material world is massive circumstantial evidence that it may give us access to 'the real world' beyond appearance.

The mathematised world picture, of course, has the dubious advantage of being empty of anything corresponding to sense experience. Scientists may try to recapture the world it initially excluded: smells, sounds, colours, tastes, even pains, pleasures, memories and emotions, may be subject to quantitative investigation as in, for example, psychophysics or the investigations of the physiology of perception. We may create scales to quantify anything: the sorrow of looking after one's demented husband may be digitised in a 'Caregiver Strain Scale'. But, so long as science remains within the Galilean paradigm, that world of perceptual experience will slip through its fingers. Optics and acoustics may pass through sounds en route to their own formulae; but these formulae will be colourless and silent. They will be about frequencies and amplitudes of waves, and the waves themselves will be abstractions in which are described the variations of abstract quantities with time. The culmination of all the physical sciences will be something like Schrödinger's wave equation or Einstein's e = mc^2 in which energy is not felt as warmth or brightness, mass is not experienced as heaviness or bulkiness, and the speed of light is abstracted from light and (abstraction upon abstraction) multiplied by itself.

None of this is intended to denigrate the Galilean vision or deny that is has brought humankind more blessings than the visions of all the prophets and politicians put together. I want only to clarify the distance between the world of sense experience and the world as described by quantitative science. Measurement does not contain experience; rather (in a gross simplification) it describes the general *form* of possible experiences. Just as in the case of the measurement of the table, it separates that form from its perceptual content. Does it, by this means, liberate us from the brightly painted prison house of sensory appearance? Platonists might be inclined to say yes. I am inclined to say that, *if* quantitative science liberates us from the casual illusions that surround us in everyday life, it does so by causing the virtual disappearance of appearance altogether, uncovering not reality but the mathematised ghost of appearance.

3.5 BACK IN THE PRISON HOUSE

It seems odd that measurement should have ever seemed to offer a way out of the prison house of inescapably subjective and potentially erroneous perception; that there should be qualities of objects that are accessible uniquely to measurement and, unlike other qualities, should be inherent in objects themselves; that 'objective' should carry the twin implications of 'inherent in objects' and 'not subject to the vagaries of subjectivity'; and that 'The Book of the Universe' should be written in mathematics. 'The Book of the Universe' surely is written in stars and rocks, and seas and trees, and skies and people and illusions, in aches and pains, and colours and sounds.

The story of the liberation from the cave of appearance into the sunlight of reality by science is a pretty one; and like all stories of the genesis of (implicitly true) knowledge, it begins with certain metaphysical or ontological presuppositions that need to be brought out into the open. These presuppositions play out at different levels. Take, for example, the assumption implicit in the way we link objectivity of measurement with inter-rater and intra-rater reliability: if the measurement always yields the same result, it must be objective, in the double sense of (a) 'not being subject to the vagaries of the individual', and (b) being truly about the inherent properties of the object. The jump from (a) to (b) is a huge one: (a) gives measurement intersubjective authority;

(b) gives it something more, namely, extra-subjective, even transhuman authority. We move from agreement within the human collective – albeit one extending across cultures, continents and epochs – to access from the collective viewpoint to extra-human reality.

One of the presuppositions built into this jump that is often overlooked is the presumption of the constancy of the reality that is supposed to be uncovered by objective science. The constancy of the object is a presupposition built into the size-constancy scaling evident in ordinary perception;[19] namely that, notwithstanding the variation in the appearance of the object (for example, its apparent size and shape when it is viewed from different angles and distances), it really has constant size and shape. Our objective science of measurement of size is constrained within the assumption of constancy, given that the object has not been chopped in half or squashed. The question that we have to ask is whether this assumption, imported from the world of everyday understanding (it is a rule that is sometimes mobilised to try to sort out illusion from veridical perception), can be retained without question when we reach (as we believe) outside of perception to the inherent reality of things. It may be deeply ingrained in our notion of a material object; even of a 'real thing'. Does this mean, however, that this assumption can be taken across the barrier between the world of perceptual appearance and that of the inherent reality of objects without modification or even challenge?

This is an important question, because constancy is no merely localised assumption in science. It is the ancestor of other conservation laws that have been cornerstones of scientific thought; for example, 'the law of conservation of matter', which applies not to one object but to the totality of objects. This ultimately gave way to 'the law of conservation of mass-energy' and to the conservation laws expressed in the invariants in the field equations in the General Theory of Relativity. The overall status of the conservation law now is not clear: it seems to break down at the micro-physical level (where the audit trail of causation also breaks down) and at the beginning of the universe where mass-energy has to have been created out of nothing. Nevertheless, the intuition of constancy under change lies at the heart of both our common sense and scientific understanding of the material world around us. This is in part why the repeatability of measurements – within individual observers, across observers, across continents and epochs – on successive occasions is seen as evidence of their being true to or of the reality underlying perception.

Even so, measurement and quantitative science seem to have burst through the painted veil of appearance only at the price of emptying the phenomenal world of everything but the abstract form of experience. Science does not give an account of the content of any particular here and now; but the general form of a class of heres and nows. (Therein lies its power.) Removing the content of perception in favour of its general mathematical form can seem to give us access to the inherent, non-perspectival properties of things only if we believe that the world is made up of mathematics. Hence the need repeatedly to protest this – since Pythagoras reputedly first declared that numbers were the very substance of the world.

The reason this cannot be true is very simple: nothing (whether it is an object within nature or nature itself) can be identical with the abstract form of itself. Just as, to take issue with the Pythagoreans for the moment, the world cannot be made of numbers, which are just the labels attached to classes (of classes) of things, and these classes of classes cannot displace, supersede, count as the essence or inherent nature, of their members. If we accept the starting point of sceptical thought, we are forced to concede that science does not provide an escape route from the prison house of our senses (though the prison house is greatly enlarged and made wonderfully more comfortable). Science at best gives us a story written in the prison, by a collective of generation of prisoners, about the most general characteristics of the prison.[20]

We have reached a difficult point in our discussion. We began by noting that some perceptions are illusions and, having failed to find a principled means of differentiating illusory (tabloid) perceptions from veridical (broadsheet) perceptions, we started to worry (or to argue and to pretend to worry) that all perceptions might be illusory. There seemed, at any rate, to be grounds for suspicion that we might be imprisoned in a world of appearance that would be sealed off from the intrinsic or inherent reality of the world around us. Appearances would seem real only in virtue of their mutual consistency, their coherence with one another, rather than in virtue of their corresponding to the reality of things in themselves. That was why we were particularly impressed by measurements that laid the basis for a huge consensus over a massive and growing body of observations. Even so, our perceptions would not constitute true knowledge of what is out there beyond them, only good enough indications to permit us to survive better.

One interesting spin-off of science has been to make us even more sceptical of what our senses serve up to us. While it is not quite true that (as Quine said) 'Scepticism is an offshoot of science', it certainly gives scepticism something of a boost. This is not in the slightest bit surprising. If reality is increasingly sought in the mathematical abstractions that are uncovered when phenomenal content is drained from the face of things, then it is hardly surprising that phenomenal content should be regarded with greater disdain. Phenomenal contents that cannot be reduced to numbers (as motion, size, etc. can be) are assigned the inferior status of 'secondary qualities'. While sense experience is of coloured, noisy, smelly things, the world of objects-in-themselves is colourless, silent and odourless. Left to themselves, objects would simply have certain primary qualities, such as size and shape and solidity. These in turn would seem to boil down to quantities of units. This was expressed very clearly by Galileo:

> I think that tastes, odours, colours, and so on are no more than mere names as far as the objects in which we locate them are concerned, and that they reside only in consciousness. If living creatures were removed, all these qualities would be wiped out and annihilated.[21]

In the half-millennium since then, during which time quantitative science has dramatically increased its theoretical reach and its practical effectiveness, the viewpoint that reduces reality to quantities of abstractions such as 'matter' and 'energy' has become ever more securely entrenched. There has been an increasing divergence between science that describes the world in terms of quantities, and the relations between quantities, and everyday experience – except in so far as science informs the development of the technologies that have so transformed our everyday experience. Even so, we have no good reason for believing that we have escaped from the illusions of perception into a world of objective, absolute, true-from-any-angle knowledge. For measurements, which may have looked like the super-perceptions that led the way out of fallible and even illusory perceptions to true knowledge of the world, have seemed to transcend experience only by mislaying it. Quantitative science deals either with primary qualities (which are expressed as empty abstract quantities) or with secondary qualities emptied of themselves by being reduced to quantities and the relations between quantities.

It looks, then, as if science leads us out of unreformed or ordinary perception not so much into knowledge that transcends and corrects it as into a form of awareness that occupies an empty space beside it. Measurements are less super-perceptions than non- or terminally thin perceptions. In avoiding the pitfalls of perspectival, subjective awareness, quantitative science loses not only the relativity of perspective and the vagaries of subjectivity, but also anything that feels like perception at all. The 'view from nowhere' threatens, as we move to ever higher-order equations, to become a 'view of nothing'. At any rate, progress through quantification at higher and higher levels of generalisation (reaching their present, no doubt temporary ceiling in the macro-generalisations of the General Theory of Relativity and the micro-generalisation of quantum electrodynamics) is not so much liberation from untrustworthy perception, to true and trustworthy knowledge of how things really are, as a movement to the most reliable generalisations of perceptions in a description that simply stencils their most general form or character.

Science, what is more, cannot rise without trace. Not only is it born out of perceptions, but its cognitive cash value or truth is ultimately checked against perception. As Schrödinger points out:

> While the direct sensual perception of the phenomenon [of light] tells us nothing as to its objective physical nature ... and has to be discarded from the outset as a source of information, yet the theoretical picture we obtain eventually rests entirely on a complicated array of various informations, all obtained by direct sensual perception.[22]

Measurement and generalisation – via quantification to super-observations – does not take us from the world of perceptual appearance to that of the inherent reality of things. Science is, in the end, only an ever more organised, compendious and portable account of our experiences achieved through uncovering their abstract forms cast in terms of quantities.[23]

About 2,500 years ago, Democritus pointed out the self-contradiction built into the belief that the discoveries of science undermine the truth of perception. Schrödinger[24] quotes a fragment in which Democritus imagines an argument between the intellect and the senses:

> The [intellect] says: 'Ostensibly there is colour, ostensibly sweetness, ostensibly bitterness, actually only atoms and the void', to which the senses retort: 'Poor intellect, do you hope to defeat us while from us you borrow your evidence? Your victory is your defeat'.

More recently, 'the primacy of perception' has been emphasised by Maurice Merleau-Ponty. Science, he argues, does not transcend, even less disprove, sense experience and it cannot shake off its roots in perception:

> The whole universe of science is built upon the world as directly experienced.[25]

Perception lies at the beginning and end of observation (even measurement) and the applications of science in technology are tested against experience. The audit trail of verification ends with the shared experiences of individuals. While individual perceptions may be wrong, the totality of perception cannot be so – or not *demonstrably* (empirically, existentially or even logically so anyway).

The body of knowledge that is science is not entirely abstract – a mere corpus of equations. The abstract forms of perceptions that are captured in equations make it possible to make particular predictions. This does not, however, mean that science can take one all the way back to contentful experience. The assertion that, for example, the sun is 93 million miles from the earth is such a partly abstract fact. And while astronomy may predict that one will be sunlit if one goes to a particular planet, it will not capture the experience of being bathed in sunlight. What is more, the pull of science is always in the opposite direction – to a higher level of abstraction. The accumulation of merely concrete facts is not science. At best it is mere cataloguing; in Rutherford's terms, 'butterfly collecting' rather than physics, which is counted as the paradigm science because of its generality, its links with higher-level generality and its aspiration to all-encompassing generality. Nobody would be so foolish as to believe that butterfly collecting helps one cross the boundary between appearance and reality, howsoever the exercise is subordinated to cataloguing in accordance with an internationally agreed nomenclature.

The technological success and explanatory power of modern science has given it a well-deserved authority: where its deliverances differ from those of ordinary perception, ordinary perception has to yield to its authority. It asserted this authority at the beginning of the modern era by overturning one of the most visible and unquestionable deliverances of ordinary perception: the observation that the sun circles the earth and that it moves upwards in the morning and downwards in the evening. But the basis for this revolutionary observation was another observation, available only to a few: that of the precession of the planets. Here was the archetypal example of how somebody else's observation – one available only to experts and not seen (or even entirely understood) by me – could subvert one's own. The observations that underpinned the widening divergence between the deliverances of the senses and the truth according to science became increasingly esoteric and the 'audit trail' leading away from and back to ordinary perception became increasingly long and labyrinthine. Science passes from experience to specific measurements, from specific measurements to general quantitative laws and then, via its applications, to technologies relevant to making possible particular experiences. The ultimate test of science is whether or not it works, in terms of the particular measurements it predicts, or in terms of the effectiveness of the specific technologies based upon it, though at a very high level intermediate tests, such as coherence with existing science, simplicity, elegance, etc. may be important proxies for testing and for guiding science in the right direction. As Karl Popper repeatedly pointed out, hypotheses, the necessary growing edge of science, always exceed the data; what he took less notice of was that such hypotheses often exceed what is currently testable.[26] We shall return to the significance of the fact that science 'works for us' in due course.

Given that science does not entirely liberate us from the limitations of perception, but uncovers the most general forms of perception, it may seem paradoxical that, as Schrödinger puts it, 'the scientific accounts of natural processes ... lack all sensual qualities and cannot account for the latter' (p. 163). But it is precisely because science is about the most general forms of actual and possible experience that it sheds, bypasses or builds away from *individual* experiences.[27]

3.6 WHAT HAS GONE WRONG?

We set out from one of Austin's 'half-studied facts': the illusion of the bent stick. This told us something we probably knew already; namely, that we can get things wrong. Moreover, that getting things wrong can start close to the ground floor of awareness. One doesn't have to indulge in sophisticated interpretations of the world to fall into error. Being ordinarily awake, or asleep and dreaming, is enough. Conscious beings like ourselves are susceptible to mirages, hallucinations, solid-looking rainbows, after-images, double images, and so on. For some philosophers, the fact that we are wrong some of the time and that there may be considerable delay in discovering that we are wrong – our erroneous perceptions aren't marked or labelled as such (otherwise we wouldn't fall for them) – means that we could well be wrong all the time.

There are many reason why this globally pessimistic conclusion seems dubious. First of all, scepticism does not take account of what we might call the existential inescapability of perception – or at least of sense experience. The latter is not merely a means of 'informing' us about the world: it is our being in the world. Sense experience – which encompasses our sense of embodiment as well as our sight of distant objects, our vulnerability and delight as well as our access to things seemingly beyond us, enteroception and proprioception as well as teloreception, feeling cold as well as modelling temperature thermo-dynamically – is inescapable. Genuinely questioning the overall validity of sense experience is therefore not a real option in existential terms.

And questioning its correctness is even less of an option: as innumerable critics of the Argument from Illusion have pointed out, if everyone was always wrong about everything, how would any of us even suspect it? What is more, where would the contrast between getting things right and getting them wrong arise?

Even so, some philosophers find reasons from visual illusions for being uneasy about our claims to (true) knowledge of the world. For the bent stick makes explicit something that is implicit in object perception: that it is, apparently, mediated or indirect. This leads to the intuition that there is something called an appearance, or a phenomenal appearance – of which we have direct experience – and this is distinct from the object of perception, which is only indirectly experienced or (as Hermann Helmholtz put it) *inferred*.[28] The bent appearance of the straight stick is an unusually clear manifestation of what on closer inspection turns out to be a universal fact: there is a contingent relationship between how things appear to us and how, or what, they really are. Of even greater (apparent) concern is that closer examination of seemingly veridical perception, taking place under normal conditions, leads to the inescapable conclusion that there can never be an appearance that 'matches' the intrinsic reality of the object. There is no such thing as the correct or 'canonical' appearance of an object: all perception is perspectival while the intrinsic reality of an object, whatever it is, self-evidently cannot be perspectival. More precisely, how the perceived object is perceived is in part determined by the conditions of perception. And perception – which after all is an interaction between the sensory apparatus of an embodied subject, a setting and an object – always has conditions. The conditions of perception are not an ingredient that can removed so that perception can be pure and give the uncontaminated appearance of the object. Legitimate variations in appearance (due to different angles of view) are therefore tarred with the same epistemological brush as illegitimate variations (the bending of a stick as it is plunged in the water).

It is possible to make observations that are more objective in the sense of being increasingly invariant under changing conditions, being more or less constant across different times and different observers. But the degree to which such observations – quantitative measurements – are more objective in the sense of being 'closer to the intrinsic reality of the object' is less clear. What is clear is that the passage from direct observation to measurement purchases invariance at the cost not only of phenomenal content but of pretty well all content. A table reduced to 4' × 2' has been drained of every scrap of content: not only is it no longer 'over there', it is no longer brown, heavy, solid. When the Book of Nature is rewritten in the mathematics that is supposed to capture its objective essence, it has become virtually a blank sheet upon which a few marks are inscribed. Objective science, which quantifies the world, elutes secondary qualities (though it may reintroduce them as measured quantities), leaves only primary qualities which ultimately boil down to numbers.[29] '$e = mc^2$' has the necessary invariance; but in encompassing all possible states of affairs, it designates none of them. The everything it says evaporates to nothing.

There are several ways out of this impasse. Here are three of the most popular. The first is to conclude that we shall never pierce the veil of appearance and, in so far as sense experience is our only access to the world, the latter's intrinsic reality will be forever hidden from us. We shall never know what there is in itself, only what it is for us. The second is to agree that, yes, reality is hidden behind sense experience but, given that sense experience is the sum total of experience, the hiddenness of what is hidden will make no difference. If the sum total of reality is different from the sum total of appearance, this is a difference that cannot possibly make a difference. For example, as Barry Stroud has put it: 'We could perceive what we perceive now even if there were no material world at all.'[30] The third is to deny that there is anything beyond what sense experience reveals to us collectively. Objects, such as they are, are simply the sum total of the actual and possible experiences of conscious creatures.[31] This last response – phenomenalism – can arm itself against counter-attack not only by asserting that the world is the sum total of what is experienced and/or experiencable but also by saying that, since the truth conditions of any assertion are observations, and since the meaning of a sentence is the sum total of its truth conditions, any appeal to the notion of realities beyond the observable is meaningless.[32]

All three responses are unsatisfactory for different reasons which have been extensively explored by philosophers. And this in part accounts for the low standing of arguments such as the Argument from Illusion and the exhilarating impatience of writers such as Austin with scepticism-driven (or worry-driven) epistemology. Austin's advice, 'to dismantle the entire doctrine [of the difference between immediate data of sensation and the material objects which we perceive through them] before it gets off the ground', seems sound.[33] After all, scepticism can get off the ground only by not doubting the existence of many things – for example, misleading sense organs, the interactions between our perceiving bodies and perceived objects in perception – not to speak of higher-order pieces of knowledge (for example, the whopping assumption that 'Perception is the basis of all the knowledge all human beings have'). Philosophers can be sceptical, or present grounds for being sceptical, only when they have taken a vast number of things for granted. Sceptical arguments have to be pitched on the ground of some pretty solid knowledge.

This suggests another, more positive, response to sceptical epistemology, along the general lines suggested by Stroud: to use it as a tool for making the general nature of knowledge visible and for exploring the links between our most fundamental beliefs about the world. We should not, for example, take the scientific critique of ordinary experience as a given: that critique *presupposes* things that are ultimately rooted in ordinary experience. We must be as critical of science (and of other sources of scepticism) as of everyday perception. And, as Merleau-Ponty has argued:

> if we want to subject science itself to rigorous scrutiny and arrive at a precise assessment of its meaning and scope, we must begin by reawakening the basic experience of the world of which science is the second-order expression.[34]

This seems pretty obvious. So how did our inquiry – much of it along the standard epistemological trail – go wrong? Essentially because it accepted the Parmenidean intuition that has driven epistemology since the beginning. We shall return to Parmenides in the final chapter when we consider his overwhelming influence on the philosophical response to knowledge's encounter with itself. For the present we note that he and his successors have picked up on something that goes to the very heart of knowledge: an intuition that there is something there – the object of knowledge – that lies beyond current experience; that experience is *of* something other than itself. This 'other' lies beyond current experience and, given that it is different from experience, it may lie beyond all possible experience.

The pre-Socratics arrived at conclusions about the way in which the object of knowledge differed from that which was disclosed to experience, by gaining access to those objects via a means other than sense experience: abstract argument, a rational intuition uncontaminated by sense experience. They agreed on some things; for example, that experience shows us a world of things that are comparatively unchanging and of things that are comparatively labile: the sensible universe is a mixture of beings and becomings. They disgreed profoundly on other things. For Heraclitus the fundamental error of sense experience was the appearance of stability. There were no stable things: all reality was endless becoming. For Parmenides, the fundamental error of those who were beguiled by their senses was to believe the appearance of *in*stability: all reality was immobile, unchanging, undifferentiated being. Both shared the intuition that there was knowledge that went beyond sense experience; that knowledge could be disencumbered by sense experience, when it would show clearly the truth about how things were, the reality behind sensory appearance.

This, as we shall discuss in section 10.6, was a decisive encounter of knowledge with itself; a reflection of the fundamental intuition at the heart of knowledge. The nature of this intuition, which they had in common, is more important than the fact that they had opposing views as to how reality differed from appearance. The Parmenidean vision seems to have won – not only in the metaphysics of substance and in the scientific notions of equilibrium, conservation and uniformity, in the hunt for invariants as the key to reality (general laws that are unvarying bases for variation) and the preference for the stasis of mathematics (the stasis in particular of equations as an account of what is there), but also in pumping the intuitions as to the nature of the reality behind appearance. The bent stick, the wobbly penny, the unstable table are an outrage to philosophers because they seem to defy the intuited stability of the object. The stick cannot be both bent and straight because that would be at odds with its necessary identity with itself; or rather, with the notion of something that is intuited to be identical with itself; that is to say, to be itself over time marked out in successive appearances. Without the idea of an invariant object, made of matter and independent of the senses, there would be no basis for concern about changing appearances.

This intuition at the heart of knowledge – that there is more to what is there than what is revealed, and that what is there will differ in certain general ways from how it appears – will be a central theme of the chapters to come. The pre-Socratics, who articulated this intuition with incomparable brilliance, also unfortunately placed the philosophical inquiry into knowledge on a path in which it became tangled up with speculations about the true nature of the object beyond sense experience – ontological questions about what kinds of things there truly are – and conflicting judgements about the relative legitimacy of sense experience and the knowledge that goes beyond it. In what follows, I will take a different path. The theory of knowledge – or at least trying to get straight about knowledge, or to see it more clearly for what it is – will remain central. I will not, however, attempt to explain how we know the things that we know, or debate the comparative truth of knowledge and sense experience.

Instead, I will try to make sense of the fact that humans are knowing animals; that is to say, that they subscribe to an ontology which includes (physical and abstract) objects that transcend their own, individual sentience. This, the most primitive manifestation of the intuition of a reality hidden behind appearance, is connected with the notion of objective truth – of truth lying beyond the experiences of the perceiving subject.[35] This intuition opens up forms of awareness – which I will call indexical and deindexicalised awareness – unique to humans. In short, instead of arguing for or against the reality hidden in objects, I will focus on the origin of the idea of such a reality in the passage from animal sentience to human knowledge. I will offer a reconstruction of the emergence of the sense of an inscrutable, or only partly scrutable, outside world and argue that this, and its attendant sense of ignorance, is what most characterises knowledge; in particular that an object of knowledge is something that, *by definition*, transcends its appearances at any time and that no finite number of appearances will exhaust its intrinsic nature. If knowledge is a leap beyond sentience, shadowed by ignorance, uncertainty, error, it also creates that which is there to be ignorant of, uncertain about, in error over.[36]

Exploring the manifold consequences of the intuition underlying knowledge, the sense that there is more than I am sensing – itself a consequence of the Existential Intuition that was the subject of *I Am*, Volume 2 of this trilogy – will be the substance of the 'epistogonic' inquiry in the chapters to come. Whether or not it is a prolegomenon to a future more traditional epistemology, or whether, in fact, it forecloses on the possible outcomes of such an epistemological inquiry, will remain unresolved.

NOTES AND REFERENCES

1. Barry Stroud, 'Taking Scepticism Seriously', in *Understanding Human Knowledge. Philosophical Essays* (Oxford: Oxford University Press, 2000), p. 37.
2. A respect for scepticism is, of course, implicit in the work of descriptive metaphysicians such as P. F. Strawson (at least until recently) and the many philosophers within the analytic tradition influenced by him – Gareth Evans, John MacDowell, Quassim Cassam and Mark Sacks to name a handful at random.
3. 'Scepticism and the Possibility of Knowledge', in Stroud, *Understanding Human Knowledge*, p. 1.
4. Ibid., p. 6.
5. No argument can. As I have argued in *I Am* (especially Chapter 2), the sceptic's starter pack always includes a good deal more than his arguments allow him to have. The assertion that we often get things wrong, for example, assumes a gold standard by which we might be corrected. It also presupposes the truth of the belief that we often get things wrong. The formulation of the argument itself presupposes the existence of a community of other minds who sustain the meanings of the words in which the sceptic thinks out loud for our benefit, as Wittgenstein pointed out.

The sceptical position cannot be stated, therefore, without self-contradiction. Sometimes this is quite profound. One of the most interesting expressions of the belief that perception is only a source of illusions is Schopenhauer's denial of the truth of experiences – a product of a fusion of Kantian idealism and Eastern philosophy – which goes deeper than almost any other in Western philosophy.

For Schopenhauer, the errors of perception are rooted in the *principium individuationis* which results from our organising the world of appearance under the rubric of space and time. The world as will, as it is in itself, is not differentiated into perceptible individuals set out in, and distinguished within, space and time. As Michael Tanner expresses it, in 'Nietzsche', *German Philosophers: Kant, Hegel, Schopenhauer, Nietzsche* (Oxford: Oxford University Press, 1997), p. 354, Schopenhauer had located the principle of individuation 'as the major error that we suffer from epistemologically – we perceive and conceive of the world in terms of separate objects, including separate persons. As beings with sense organs and conceptual apparatus, we cannot avoid this fundamentally erroneous way of viewing the world; and for Schopenhauer it is responsible for many of our most painful illusions.'

One doesn't have to think too long to appreciate that, if the principle of individuation really were an illusion, it must also be an illusion that there are separate individuals. There can therefore be no individuals, with their sense organs and conceptual apparatus, to be bearers of such illusions. (For there to be illusions, the bearers of illusions must exist. 'I's' cannot get things wrong if there are, in truth, no 'I's'. As Descartes pointed out, I cannot be mistaken when I believe that I am.) It is difficult to imagine how anyone could commit the error of individuation without being an individual.

What is more, individual viewpoints presuppose the existence of material objects in order that they should be individuated. There is no viewpoint without a material standpoint to support it; more particularly, there is no 'there' without 'here' and no here without a body; in short, no body, no there (see *I Am*, Chapters 4 and 5).

The assumption that sense experience is intrinsically erroneous because it is 'of' things that are localised in space goes deeper than the assumption that experience is bound to be erroneous because it is perspectival. It avoids the objection that experience is necessarily perspectival but ends up more deeply mired in self-contradiction. Individual things, it says, would not exist if there were no individual subjects. But, given that these subjects are real enough to divide the world into entities, including themselves, which they fail to notice are in themselves really all one undivided thing, it seems as if they are real enough.

There is an analogy between Schopenhauer's self-contradictions and that of philosophers who say that 'perception is questionably true because it is mediated through the body, the brain, etc.'. If we are so uncertain about the truth of perception, on what grounds do we accept that our perceptions *are* mediated through the body, the brain, etc.? Why should we be especially confident of the truth of those perceptions that have led us to the conclusion that our perceptions are mediated through a biological apparatus?

6. W. V. O. Quine, 'The Nature of Natural Knowledge', in *Mind and Language*, Wolfson College Lectures 1974, ed. Samuel Guttenplan (Oxford: Clarendon Press, 1975), p. 67.

7. J. L. Austin, *Sense and Sensibilia*, reconstructed from manuscript notes by G. J. Warnock (Oxford: Clarendon Press, 1962), p. 2.

8. Ibid., p. 3.

9. A. J. Ayer, *The Problem of Knowledge* (London: Penguin Books, 1956), p. 85.

10. If touch often seems to have more authority and to be less prone to illusion, this is because: (a) it is less likely to jump to conclusions as it typically discloses objects gradually as opposed to all at once – it has a built-in modesty; (b) we are more directly exposed to the thing in touch – touch is reciprocated – I am touched by that which I touched; (c) it gives a more consistent account of things because there is a sharply limited range from which things can be touched and, more important, touched-and-seen, so there is also a limited range of visual experiences which are associated with touch.

11. Or, as Gilbert Ryle said, 'there can be false coins only where there are coins made of the proper materials by the proper authorities' (quoted in Ayer, *The Problem of Knowledge*, p. 37).

12. Austin, *Sense and Sensibilia*, p. 46.

13. See *Principles of Philosophy*, Second Part, Principle 4, trans. Elizabeth Haldane and G. R. T. Ross (Cambridge: Cambridge University Press, 1967), pp. 255–6.

14. See Howard Robinson, *Matter and Sense* (Cambridge: Cambridge University Press, 1982), in particular, his final chapter, which 'turns the tables' on matter, for a powerful critique of the notion of material physical objects. These latter, as he shows, are reduced to 'volumes of impenetrability' en route to being reduced to 'a nameless residue'.

15. Quoted in Stillman Drake, *Discoveries and Opinions of Galileo* (New York: Doubleday, 1957), pp. 237–8.

16. This may seem to be naively pre-Einsteinian. However, I am talking about the world of everyday observation which, even as it intersects with science, *is* naively pre-Einsteinian. The variability of the length of objects and the replacement of invariance of spatial and temporal size with invariance of spatio-temporal size matters only as we approach the speed of light. It is only under such circumstances that the role of the observer and the viewpoint of the observer in determining the outcome of the measurement of something seemingly as objective and object-intrinsic as length become significant. What is more, the Theory of Relativity – in which, for example, there is no true length of an object, only an observed length which will be viewpoint-dependent – is itself built upon many layers of science in which objectivity has been taken for granted. Moreover, even the General Theory of Relativity does not relativise all measures: there are invariants – space-time coincidence, for example – which are observer-independent. The Theory of Relativity has not simply found new variability and observer-dependency; it has also discovered the principles that govern the observer-dependency and hence revealed deeper invariants.

17. W. H. Auden, *Sonnets from China*.

18. What we are describing here is the move from individual, indexical awareness to collectivised deindexicalised awareness which will be central to the arguments of this book.

19. A receding object normally looks the same size over a wide range of distances, despite the fact that its retinal image will shrink as the object recedes. This is due to a perceptual compensation called 'size constancy scaling' which reflects the assumption that objects don't shrink just because they are moving away from us; and the assumption is translated into compensation for the shrinking image under the guidance of a variety of 'distance cues': convergence of the eyes, geometrical perspective, and the graded texture and falling sharpness which are all associated

with the increasing distance of the viewed object. See the editor's excellent short entry on 'Emmert's Law' in Richard L. Gregory (ed.), *The Oxford Companion to the Mind* (Oxford: Oxford University Press, 1987). It shows how deep the intuition of the independent reality of objects lies in us: we automatically adjust appearances to 'save reality' – the opposite, of course, to 'saving appearances'.

20. I am not aligning myself here with those who would wish to sociologise science and relativise scientific truth to 'interpretive communities'. It has often been pointed out – for example, by Rom Harré, 'Some Narrative Conventions of Scientific Discourse', in Cristoper Nash (ed.), *Narrative and Culture* (London: Routledge, 1990) – that much of a scientist's training is in learning how to get the apparatus to work and this is not clearly differentiated from learning how to get the results everyone else gets. What is more, scientists are often selective in publishing those measurements that fit their theories. Neither of these observations undermines the claims of science to give us new truths about the natural world, as I have argued elsewhere. See Raymond Tallis, *Newton's Sleep: Two Cultures and Two Kingdoms* (Basingstoke: Macmillan, 1995). They do, however, underline the difficulty of accounting for the difference between intersubjective or herd truths and objective truths. Perhaps the difference between herd truths and objective truths shrinks as the herd expands to be coterminous with all of humanity: when the 'epistemic community' transcends the boundaries of all other communities, as is so often true with respect to scientific truths.

21. Quoted in Drake, *Discoveries and Opinions of Galileo*, p. 274. Interestingly, Newton accepted this but was unworried by it. Writing about our sensations of colours in his *Opticks* (1704) he agreed with Locke about the secondary nature of colours. 'Red', he said, is not itself red but 'red-making' and in light rays there is 'nothing else than a certain power and disposition to stir up the sensation of this or that colour. For as sound in a bell or musical string ... is nothing but a trembling motion' (quoted in Gregory, *The Oxford Companion to the Mind*, p. 599). Importantly, as Drake emphasises, '[Galileo's] science required simultaneously sensible experience and necessary demonstration; [he] did not accord greater "reality" to one than to the other, nor did he regard sensation as nonexistent or less important than external physical phenomena' (*Galileo: A Very Short Introduction* (Oxford: Oxford University Press, 1980, reissued 2001), p. 85). He did not, that is to say, buy all of the Pythagorean vision.

22. Erwin Schrödinger, *What is Life?* with *Mind and Matter* and *Autobiographical Sketches* (Cambridge: Cambridge University Press, 1992), pp. 162–3.

23. This must not be interpreted to imply that knowledge – scientific or everyday – is merely heaped up sense experience or compressed sentience, a point we shall make clear in due course.

24. Schrödinger, *What is Life?*, p. 163.

25. Maurice Merleau-Ponty, *The Phenomenology of Perception*, trans. Colin Smith (London: Routledge & Kegan Paul, 1962), p. viii.

26. Superstring theory is a striking case in point. The fact that it may never be testable accounts for its currently questionable status as a scientific theory. For some it is merely a mathematical exercise.

27. It could be said that science continues the process that begins with the transition from sensation to perception to propositional factual knowledge. Sense perception, as Aristotle said, gives the form of the object without its substance. This emptying of the sensory content from experience in science is connected with the purification of

the experimental situation – the removal or ignoring of additional variables, such as friction, and the analysis of idealised situations such objects being placed in a vacuum. T. L. S. Sprigge's observation that the scientific notion of the physical world 'can characterise the world only in structural terms' is very much to the point here (see 'Consciousness', *Synthese* (1994), 98: 79–93).

28. A founding intuition of the psychology of perception and the representational theory of mind. See Raymond Tallis, 'Unconscious Consciousness', in *Enemies of Hope. A Critique of Contemporary Pessimism* (Basingstoke: Macmillan, reprinted with new preface, 1999), pp. 290–302.

29. Which justifies Russell's poignant observation that our account of the world is cast in mathematical form not because we know so much, but because we know so little.

30. Stroud, *Understanding Human Knowledge*, p. 102. We could put this another way: the way things appear to us would be the same irrespective of whether there were things, beyond appearance, underpinning appearance. This is, of course, a truism.

31. Variations on this theme – that, for example, material objects are logical constructions out of sense experiences – simply emphasise its problems. The key one is that there is no basis for the organisation of sense experiences into objects. If a range of experiences does not originate from a particular object, what grounds can there be for posting them all to the same object? This problem is the inevitable consequence of trying to ground the transcendence of sentience in object knowledge directly in sentience.

32. Ironically, this position marks the half-way point between a tough materialist empiricism and a fluffy idealism, for the conclusion of the journey prompts a revisiting of the starting point. Physical objects become constructs out of the experiences that are supposed to have been caused by them. The experiences cause (the positing of) the objects that (are supposed to) have caused the experiences.

33. Austin, *Sense and Sensibilia*, p. 142.

34. Merleau-Ponty, *The Phenomenology of Perception*, p. viii.

35. The obverse of this is something we have already noted: there is no such thing as the intrinsic appearance, or the canonical appearance, of the object.

36. That is why it makes no sense to argue whether knowledge brings us nearer to the truth of things than sense experience. Truth (and falsehood) emerge only when we have gone beyond sense experience; when, as I will argue, 'That' appears on the scene. The assertion 'That I have toothache' is neither more nor less true than the experience of toothache. 'Pure' sense experiences are incorrigible because they cannot be either correct or incorrect.

PART TWO

FROM SENTIENCE TO SENTENCES

CHAPTER 4

An Outline of Epistogony

There can be no doubt that all our knowledge begins with experience ... But though all our knowledge begins with experience, it does not follow that it all arises out of experience.[1]

We are the species that discovered doubt.[2]

4.1 WHAT IS KNOWLEDGE?

Many philosophers have abandoned the attempt to define knowledge. Timothy Williamson, for example, denies that knowledge can be 'factorized' into a set of non-circular necessary conditions.[3] The after-shocks of the blow delivered by Edmund Gettier, in his brief paper published 40 years ago against the standard and seemingly unassailable definition of knowledge as 'justified, true, belief', are still being felt. He persuaded the philosophical community that he had found cases where someone could have a justified true belief and yet not know something.[4]

One of Gettier's examples is as follows. Smith believes – and for whatever reason, is justified in believing – the false proposition p that (i) Jones owns a Ford. On the basis of p, Smith infers, and and is therefore justified in believing, that either (ii) Jones owns a Ford or (q) Brown is in Barcelona. (The logical basis for this is that 'p' implies 'either p or q'.) As it happens, Brown *is* in Barcelona, but Smith does not know this. Smith therefore is in the curious situation of having the justified true belief that q, while not actually knowing q.

This absurd conclusion is a consequence of reducing knowledge to a set of *criteria* for separating knowledge from inferior material. It identifies those features which contrast a privileged subset of beliefs with a much larger, underprivileged class of beliefs: those that are either unjustified, untrue or both, separating knowledge from inferior contents of consciousness. This results in a rather empty conception of knowledge as well as one vulnerable to ingenious attack from logicians such as Gettier. Knowledge consists not only in what distinguishes it from false beliefs but also in what it has in common with false beliefs, just as a virtuous man is not just a piece of virtue but also a man with many other characteristics that are neither virtuous nor vicious. In common with many vicious men, he has kidneys, children and a salary. We could express this another way by saying that the Gettier problem is the result of reducing knowledge to certain formal properties which differentiate it from other propositional attitudes. Being justified and true are necessary conditions for making something a matter of knowledge but they are not sufficient; for the latter it has in addition to be *believed*. The 'thin criterial' account of knowledge also empties belief. Jones can apparently have a belief – a consequence of a belief that he is aware of having – without being aware of believing it.

I make these obvious points in order to rescue knowledge from a post-Fregean formalism that depsychologises it; that, in other words, minimises its character as a subjective state and virtually eliminates the knowing subject. Of course, being in a certain psychological state, while it is sufficient to have a belief, isn't sufficient for knowledge. Nevertheless, the psychological state cannot be ignored. Beliefs do not lose their psychological content simply in virtue of being true and justified. In the Gettier example, Smith apparently is allowed to have a justified belief that he is unaware of. Knowledge, being logicised, falls victim to logic.[5] Any account of knowledge has to be rooted in an account of belief: justification and truth rest on this ground floor. Belief cannot be separated from the psyche of the believer. At the heart of belief is a sense of possibility, of a world that lies beyond sense experience that has features independent of the believer, and, as an obvious correlative of these, a sense of ignorance. To this we shall return. For the present we note that we can meet the criteria for knowing something without actually knowing it only if we remove consciousness from knowledge.

First, we need to note another attempt to attenuate knowledge: Heidegger's assault on the notion of the subject–object relation in knowledge, and his merging of the knower and the known. For Heidegger, the philosophical belief in the primacy of the knowing self and the known world is the product of reading back, into our primordial mode of being-in-the-world, the intellectualised view of the world we adopt when we are approaching it in the course of a formal (e.g. scientific) inquiry. In reality, he says,

> Self and world belong together in the single entity *Da-sein*. Self and world
> are not two beings, like subject and object ... [instead], self and world are
> the basic determination of Dasein in the unity of the structure of being-in-
> the-world.[6]

Unfortunately, as already discussed[7] there cannot be a differentiated
being-there without a differentiating being-here: no *Da-sein* without
Fort-sein. This, it appears after all, requires the real separation of a
physically differentiated knower (or embodied self) and the known
object.[8] Heidegger's dissolution of the epistemological problem by
collapsing the distance between the knower and the known fails
precisely because this distance is of the very essence of knowledge. It is,
what is more, central to the human condition. While it corresponds to a
profound schism in human consciousness, a 'wound' that we shall
discuss in Chapter 10, the gap is the condition not only of knowledge
but also of facts, truth, active inquiry, freedom, thoughts and desires.

The account of knowledge to be developed in this chapter will be
remote from the depsychologising formalisations that have characterised much discussion of knowledge in the analytical tradition. It will be
equally distanced from the naturalisations that we discussed in Chapter
2, which aim to minimise the difference between knowledge and the
sentience of the engaged organism immersed in everyday life.

4.2 THE EXISTENTIAL INTUITION AND THE AWAKENING TO KNOWLEDGE

The account that follows of the passage from the sentience enjoyed by
organisms to the knowledge unique to human beings begins with the
Existential Intuition 'That I am this ...'. I have described the nature of
the Intuition and its origin in the previous volumes.[9] A brief résumé will
have to suffice here.

The Existential Intuition, the sense of my own being, is unique to
human beings. Ultimately, it owes its origin to a relatively minor difference between hominids and other higher primates. Humans have full-
blown hands (most notably with an opposable thumb) and adopt the
upright position that enables these hands to be exploited to the full.
Hands have two features that make them *proto-tools*: meta-fingering,
whereby the fingers finger each other during manipulative activity; and
constrained manipulative indeterminacy, arising out of the fact that, at
any given time, there is a range of grips that may be employed to a
particular end. The emergence of the hand as a proto-tool sets in train a
series of self-reinforcing developments that amplify a minor difference

into a widening gulf between hominid and the rest of the animal kingdom. The tool-like status of the hand retroactively instrumentalises the body and, at the same time, makes the hominid a subject within its own body. The animal awakens to sustained self-consciousness: 'That I am this ...' is a continuous, not an intermittent, awareness of its own being.

The awoken self is an agentive self and the scope of its agency is extended by another consequence of the hand-tool: it becomes the prototype of non-bodily tools. The latter not only extend agency directly but also become signs of need and, indeed, of agency. They are visible signs of one's own consciousness and that of fellow hominids. Shared tools thus become a means by which consciousness – solitary in sentient beasts – is partly collectivised. Being shared, they form the foundation for pooled agency and awareness, the seeds of a social world. This latter is the forum for genuine cooperative behaviour, which is quite different from the pre-programmed dovetailing activity, based upon stereotyped resposes to stimuli, that characterises the seemingly social behaviour of animals and may, as in the case of ants, be very highly developed, resulting in extraordinary monuments of collective endeavour.

Tools, as abstract, general signs of invisible states such as needs, are proto-linguistic. In the discussion of human tool-use, I set out detailed reasons for differentiating it from the apparently analogous use of tools by other higher animals. The most important difference was that, when humans use tools, the latter are not entirely assimilated into the body schema. This is because the body schema in humans is already differentiated into a hierarchy of agents and patients, subjects and instruments, as a result of the 'toolness' of the hand. Hominid tools are therefore explicitly extra-corporeal, and hence explicitly what they are. They are manifestly signs of themselves and consequently are ripe to be *used* as signs. Hence their aptness to be precursors of language.

Each of these factors – the direct instrumentalisation of the body by the hand; the enhancement of actual agency and of the sense of it by tools; and the collectivisation of solitary sentience into explicit social awareness through tools as the agents of agents and as proto-linguistic signs – interacts with and drives the development of the others. The awakening of the Existential Intuition was a gradual process, with ever more complex elaboration of the sense of self and of agency.

The key development for our present concerns is the emergence of the subject within the body. As self-consciousness is increasingly sustained (being upheld both from within and also from without, as the self-consciousness of others impinge upon an increasingly socialised individual), so the sense 'That I am this ...' becomes ever more emphatic. The 'this' that 'I' am is not entirely transparent. At its most primitive and least complex, it is the engaged body; and the relation of the inchoate 'I' to the body that it feels itself to be is extraordinarily complex.

I examined the multilayered and indeed multimodal ways in which we 'exist' our own bodies in *I Am*.[10] A few glimpses into the miasma of embodiment will be sufficient for our present purposes. When I touch my cold shoulder with my warm fingertip, I feel *that* my shoulder is cold with my finger and my shoulder feels *that* my finger is warm. I am two subjects – the finger experiencing the shoulder and the shoulder experiencing the finger – and two objects – the fingered shoulder and shouldered finger. There is an obvious asymmetry, reflected in the awkwardness of the phrase 'shouldered finger', which ensures that the two subject–object relations do not cancel out. Within the body there may be a complex hierarchy of agents and their tools: in the course of a particular complex voluntary action such as tying a shoelace, different components of the limb may be used to transport the fingers to the right place, to stabilise the hand and the object, and to carry out the necessary manipulations. At a given time, a particular part of my body may be something that I seem to be, something that I suffer, something that I possess, something that I use or something that I seem to know, in differing proportions.

At the heart of all this fluctuating awareness is the sense that I *am* something *that is incompletely disclosed to me*. This is the crucial point for our understanding of the origin of knowledge out of sentience: our body, as well as being the seat of our subjectivity, is the first fully-fledged *object* that I encounter. For the embodied self is aware of something that he is but which in part at least lies beyond his awareness. This, I want to argue, is the root intuition underpinning human knowledge, the awakening of sentience out of its own repleteness, to a sense of its incompleteness.

It is necessary, however, to get something out of the way first. When we discussed the neural theory of consciousness we noted the common misconception that 'being something' gives one privileged access to its nature. That what you are is self-disclosing because you are it. That you know its true nature, as if from within. One of the most striking examples of this misconception is Schopenhauer's claim that we know the noumenal world, the in-itself through the instance of it that is ourselves, through our own being: 'the will reveals itself to everyone directly as the in-itself of his own phenomenal being'. That which we know is our bodies, and 'the whole body is nothing but objectified will, i.e. will become idea'.[11] Our investigations in *I Am*, however, seemed to suggest the opposite: there is no part of our body with which we are completely identified. Even those parts which seem to be most ourselves continue to surprise us. The object with which I am most identified remains for the most part a *terra incognita*. This awakens us to the sense of the inscrutability, or part-inscrutability, of things. The body is the first object in our world and, since it is also the embodiment of our subjectivity (as it is not in the case of non-human organisms), it makes us aware of the otherness of objects. The object is disclosed *as* other. We could thus turn Schopenhauer on his head: it is the very fact of our being something that we also feel lies beyond us – a body expropriated as ourselves in the Existential Intuition – that underpins the sense that there are objects that lie beyond our sense experience.

Kant argued unassailably that, if we are to derive knowledge from experience, we must also have some input that is, in his words, 'independent of all experience'. The input – I do not use the words 'knowledge' or 'experience' here – is the intuition of something that lies beyond sentience. This input is the feeling of ignorance (available only to a formed subject), the sense that what is there transcends our sense experience of it. This outside-of-sentience begins with ourselves as embodied subjects. Awakening to self and awakening out of sentience to objects that exceed sentience – and hence to the undisclosed, to the possibility beyond actuality – are inseparable.[12]

4.3 OBJECTS, OBJECTHOOD AND OBJECTIVITY

Barry Stroud's observation, cited earlier, that 'our knowledge of the world is "underdetermined" by whatever it is that we get through that source of knowledge known as "the senses" or "experience"'[13] therefore touches on a fundamental truth about the nature of knowledge: that it exceeds what is available through immediate awareness, through the sentience that we might imagine humans share with beasts. The objects of knowledge, as it were *ex officio*, lie beyond, transcend, the deliverances of the senses. It is of the very nature of knowledge to exceed what is available through sense experience. This sense of something existing in itself, beyond what we are aware of, has originated from the inscrutability of our own bodies, made explicit because the Existential Intuition appropriates them, or tries to appropriate them, as ourselves. It is this that lays the foundation for our progressively elaborated sense of the difference, or distance, between how things are and how they appear. Such a difference could not arise without this sense of ourselves as embodied subjects, being and not being the bodies that they animate.

The manifest objectivity of the object, the explicit sense that it is different from ourself – itself rooted in a robust sense of self – is inseparable from the intuition of its being incompletely known. With object knowledge comes the intuition of the yet-to-be-known, of ignorance. This is the stimulus to active inquiry. At its simplest, this may take the form of consciously scrutinising a visual field, or cross-modal checking of a visual appearance against tactile ones ('touching is believing'). Ultimately, it leads to the active, knowledge-led, verbally guided, methodologically powerful investigations that characterise science. This journey we shall examine in section 7.3. Suffice it for the moment to note that the acknowledgement of the possibility of a better, more accurate appearance – ranging from giving credence to subsequent appearances of an object over earlier appearances, to allowing that there is such a thing as (to use Bernard Williams' phrase) 'positional advantage'[14] which may be enjoyed by one's self at a future time or by another self, to systematic inquiry – could not arise *within* sentience.

It is important to appreciate that this sense that 'there is more to know [about the object]' – if, for example, one assumes a different position, finds better lighting, simply waits around – is explicit, even at the most everyday, informal level in humans. For this reason, it should not be assimilated to the driver to animal 'inquiries'; for example, a hawk hovering in the air, scanning a field for its prey; or a dog working a field in pursuit of game. A dog following a trail has not embarked on a true inquiry. The most obvious reason for saying this is that successive sensations are not related to a second-order consciousness, a consciousness of self extended over time. The next most obvious reason for upholding the difference between human inquiries and animal pseudo-inquiries is that the animal does not have an explicit idea of the object of its inquiry. The root of the difference, however, is that the dog does not have a self that can entertain the sense of another entity with intrinsic properties of its own that may or may not be disclosed.

Let us make this a little clearer. A living organism, such as a dog, is not an embodied subject in the way that a human being is. It does not appropriate its engaged body as itself. Lacking a sense of being its self, it has at best an attenuated sense of things (other than itself) being in-themselves, located outside of itself. More specifically, it is not located in its own sensory field: it is not an item in a world that is correlated with, or is the internal accusative of, itself. The transformation of the body from a sentient organism to an embodied subject makes the organism's implicit location within the environment an explicit relation-ship to a sensory field and, beyond that, to a world composed of physical objects and undisclosed things related to its self. Mere sentience does not sustain an obtrusive or ontologically dense sense of the subject as self. Which is why, although animals interact with the material world as humans do, they are not surrounded by space or by objects located in space.

The intuition of partly disclosed, partly scrutable, objects is the cornerstone of the 'natural attitude' which Husserl saw as the starting point of his phenomenological inquiries: the belief

> in the existence of an external material reality that is extended in space, that persists through time, and that contains objects that interact causally with one another.[15]

This is natural to (extra-natural) humans but not to animals. Humans are alone in entertaining the sense of the disclosed separated from the disclosing, of the discloser separated from the disclosed.[16]

Unlike the sentient animal organism, the embodied subject, in virtue of intuiting objects that exist in themselves, independent of its self, can also intuit that they are available to other subjects also located with respect to them. Objects are multiply accessible; they are public. In this way they are doubly dissociated from the vagaries, the 'fugitive impressions' (to use Hume's evocative phrase) of individual experience: they are enduring beyond the moments of perception; and they are outside the consciousness of one particular individual, being accessible to others. This is the link between object status and objectivity, between the knowledge of objects and the objectivity of knowledge, in the sense of an ideal agreement about the 'what' of the object, in which there is concordance between an indefinite number of embodied subjects.

The intuition that there is more to the object than meets, or has met, or will ever meet, the eye (or other senses) is due to the fact that what does the meeting is more than an eye. It is an embodied 'I'. This sense of 'more than meets the eye', coagulated into the explicit notion of a public object, has on its lower slopes the intuition of 'the not-yet', 'the no-longer', 'the round-the-corner' – in short, *possible* experiences. There is, that is to say, the sense of *sources* of experiences – objects, the unfolding external world – that transcend actual experiences. The object, and the world in which it is located, is sensed as 'the permanent possibility of experience' (to borrow J. S. Mill's famous phrase). The positing of objects, with their not-yet, their no-longer, their hidden as well as their disclosed, their reality transcending what is now understood as 'mere' appearance, opens possibility within the sensorium. Knowledge, the sense of possibility and the permanent feeling of ignorance emerge together.

This already suggests an entirely different approach from the data invoked by scepticism-driven epistemology. Consider, for example, the Argument from Illusion. Unmasking an illusion – such as that the seemingly bent stick is actually straight – is not just the result of a quarrel with someone else; it is a quarrel with one's self. Indeed, the quarrel with another could cut no ice if one did not already have the sense that one might be mistaken and that appearances might mislead. The idea that there are misleading and non-misleading appearances is inseparable from the notion of an underlying something (reality, object, state of affairs) that (a) is independent of one's impressions; (b) is continuous, the same, stable, across appearances to one's self and to others; and (c) may be more correctly revealed in certain appearances compared with others. In other words, illusions presuppose a world in which there are enduring selves and enduring objects that are not reducible to a mere succession of sensations. Such a world would not be comprehensible within, or accommodated by, phenomenalism, where both the object and the subject dissolve into a stream of impressions and the barrier between the two fades; or in the world of pure, unfolding sentience, such as is available to animals. As Quine has put it, 'Illusions [such as mirages] are illusions only relative to a prior acceptance of genuine bodies with which to contrast them'.[17] This shows how scepticism, based upon, say, the Argument from Illusion, about our knowing an external world, requires the assumption that there is such a world – something whose essence is to be beyond experience.

The very notion of an object is rooted in the intuition of something that lies beyond, and can be different from, how we perceive it – not only how we perceive it at any particular time, but how we could perceive it at any time. That is why we may never have sense experiences that give us a 'super-canonical' appearance that is true to the intrinsic nature of the object conceived of in itself. The pursuit of the 'correct appearance' is an attempt to find the constitutive in the epistemic while, at the same time, maintaining the difference between them.[18]

The passage from sentience to object knowledge should not be seen as a 'leap' of *inference*. The foundationalist idea, in accordance with which sense experience is a kind of ground floor, where the search for evidence comes to a halt, is itself ill-founded; the notion that an external world 'must be inferred or derived from prior knowledge of the deliverance of sense experiences alone which themselves imply nothing about such an independent world' is self-defeating.[19] If it really were an inference, it would be an invalid one, as so many sceptical philosophers have pointed out; for there cannot be valid ontological or existential (as opposed to logical) inferences, to the beliefs that steer us through our daily life.

Indeed, as soon as object knowledge is presented as an inference, the insufficiency of the grounds for it becomes evident.

The passage from sentience to object-intuition is both the opened-up gap and the leap across it. It is more like a global awakening than an inference. (Our awakening to our bedroom from sleep is not an inference.) As for the question as to whether objects do or do not really exist, this is truly unaskable. For there is no fact of this matter since objective truths – ontological or otherwise – exist only after objects have been brought into the frame.[20] We cannot sensibly ask whether objects objectively exist.[21]

The story I have set out is not without philosophical ancestry. It overlaps, for example, with some features of post-Kantian thought.[22] The notion that our experiences *are* 'experiences' of things they are not, of things that are their causes – namely, the objects of which they are the appearances – transforms our interaction with the natural world into a confrontation. This casts a striking sidelight on the bounce-back that we spoke of with respect to intentionality in section 2.2.1. In object knowledge, intentionality is fully emergent. A distance is crossed between the object 'over there' and 'me here'. As Knowing Animals, we are (to use Schelling's beautiful phrase) that 'in which nature opens her eyes and sees that she exists' and man reveals his status as 'a counter-throw of nature'.[23] This is the awakening of 'that' in 'That it is the case' – as the consequence of the 'that' in 'That I am this ...'. It is the moment at which consciousness differentiates into experiences and objects of experience, separating content and its objects, the experiencing subject and the object of experience.

This way of understanding the nature of the subject–object relationship in knowledge (and, more generally, in what we shall call 'propositional awareness') is remote from the depsychologised post-Fregean account that would reduce this to a formality, the shadow of the grammar of the language in which we think of ourselves. This grammar is universal because it reflects a universal feature of human consciousness. To put this another way, grammar is explained by the structure of human consciousness; it is not that which explains its apparent structure.[24]

4.4 INDEXICAL AWARENESS

I have so far talked about object-knowledge as if it were homogeneous; as if, that is to say, there were only a single mode of awareness available to the hominid once it has awoken out of sentience. This is obviously not the case. Distinctively human consciousness – which for reasons that will become apparent in Chapter 5 will also be called 'propositional awareness' – is rich and varied. For the present, I will divide it into 'indexical' and 'deindexicalised' awareness. (Sentience in humans, if it exists in a pure state, is 'pre-indexicalised' or 'pre-indexical'; in animals, which never awaken out of sentience, it is 'anindexical'.) This is a gross simplification, but it will help to make clear certain things that are central to the story I want to tell about human consciousness.

It will be recalled from section 2.2.1, where we identified the fundamental problems with neural accounts of consciousness, that we singled out intentionality as the most intractable. Intentionality is the 'aboutness' of consciousness. 'Aboutness' becomes fully apparent, or unignorably real, in our consciousness of material objects. There is a clear-cut gap to be crossed (but not closed) between consciousness – the consciousness of the subject – and its object. Neural theories of consciousness, which locate the basis of consciousness inside the skull of the subject, make that distance a literal one; the awareness is located over here (inside my head) and the object is located over there. But we need not subscribe to a physicalist account of mind to accept the reality of the intentional relation.

It is easiest to think of the intentionality of perception with respect to vision. The intentional relation is less clear (though no less real) in the case of the other major distance receptor – hearing – where the object may not be evident but only inferred. Sight seems to give objects directly. In the case of smell – a proximate sense as regards its immediate content and a distance receptor as regards its (remote) source – the relation to any object is usually inferential. Until it is seen, or touched, the object is only general; the internal accusative of a surmise. It should not be concluded from this that all visual awareness is intentional. An undifferentiated sensation of brightness, or darkness, or colouredness would not have explicit intentionality. Intentionality is fully developed, or explicit, only in relation to visual *perception*. Sentience is not enough: there has to be an explicit relation between a subject ('here') and an object ('there').

This may be relevant to a putative role played by vision in the emergence of distinctively human consciousness. The assumption of the upright position by hominids when they left the safety of the forest for the open savannas had three important consequences. First, the hand was liberated from the demands of locomotion; this allowed unobstructed development of manipulative skills. We have already discussed the overwhelming importance of this. Second, the role of the eyes as visual warning and forewarning systems was greatly enhanced. Third, the hand was brought within the visual field. This meant not only that its manipulative capacity could be improved by visual control but also that more of it, and indeed of the body, fell within the hominid's own visual field. Together, these developments conspired to intensify – perhaps to *thicken* – the individual's presence to itself within its own sensory field. Explicit intentionality – the relation between the object over there and the subject over here – is underlined by the italicisation of the subjective, or proximal, end of the intentional relation. This relation is fully developed only so long as there is a fully developed proximal end in the form of a partly objectified subject. Under such circumstances, we are the warm hub of our own sensory field. We are the present centre of our visual field.

Hume spoke of the mind having a propensity to spread itself over things; and Sartre described the for-itself (his version of consciousness as nothingness arising within being) as 'sacrificing' itself to the things it is of.[25] These are important and illuminating half-truths. For what they describe is not distinctively human consciousness but sentience, where there is no knowing subject but simply the awareness that is lost in its own sensory field. In the case of subject–object consciousness, something of the subject is held back in order that there should be an explicit relationship with the object; in order that there can be two to tango. Actually, she does not hold herself back entirely; she is inescapably an object – or a subject–object – within her sensory field.[26]

This, then, is the nature of indexical awareness: not only is the object granted independent existence in its own right; in addition, that independent existence is underlined by the independent, objective existence of the subject in her own right. Subject and object are clearly and explicitly differentiated as opposite poles of an intentional relationship. I describe this form of consciousness as 'indexical' because it is a relationhip defined at least in part by the location of the subject: the 'I–It' relationship is also a 'here–there' or 'over here–over there' relationship. The object exists as an object in a spatio-temporal relation to myself partly objectified in my body. And the subject is there, 'in the frame', the explicit centre, of her sensory field.

There are other reasons in the lexical hinterland for my choice of terminology here. 'Indexical' was a term introduced by C. S. Peirce to refer to words that relate utterances to the spatio-temporal co-ordinates of the act of utterance. They would include demonstratives such as 'this' and 'that' and words such as 'here' and 'there' and 'now' and 'then' and, of course, 'I' and 'you'. 'Indexical' means pointing – as with the index finger. 'Intentionality', as was noted earlier, comes from the Latin verb *intendere*, 'to point (at)' or 'to extend (towards)'. Within indexical awareness, there is a distinction between the content of consciousness and the object towards which it points; a distinction within the subject between her awareness and that of which it is aware, a distinction that is replicated in that between herself and the world of objects by which she is surrounded.

Indexical awareness has an object separate from itself but related to it by means of a relationship of which it is aware. Not only do I see the object but I am capable of seeing that I see the object. This awareness points back to myself. This second-order awareness is present as a constant background, a frame around vision, though it may become more obtrusive, as when I am conscious of problems in seeing what I am trying to see; or when seeing is the result of active scrutinising, peering, or such like. This 'seeing that I am seeing' makes indexical awareness not merely implicitly perspectival as sentience is; it incorporates in addition awareness of the perspective from which seeing is had. The Existential Intuition makes us a thick presence at the centre of our field. Our bodies have 'cognitive obstance' – the model, as we have discussed, for the obstance of objects. Indexical awareness, unlike the implicit perspective of sentience, points to the subject, which is not merely implicit in the sensory field. It is an explicit subject related to an explicit object. Object awareness is 'indexed' to the knowing subject.

Let me make the reason for the choice of the term 'indexical' a little more explicit. Indexical awareness is an awareness that locates the aware subject among that which it is aware of. It is *an awareness that, as it were, points to itself, or points to its own source*, if not directly, at least indirectly, through its explicit relation to the objects of which it is aware. I – the embodied, present subject – am next to the object and the object is next to me. I am a sensed sensor, a touched toucher and, above all, a seen seer.

This second-order awareness – seeing that I am seeing – is linked with the central element of object knowledge discussed in the previous section: the intuition that the object is independent of my awareness of it and hence is incompletely disclosed to me; that it has a reality that goes beyond its appearances to me; that there is a 'disclosed' separate from the disclosing, a discloser separate from the disclosed. I know, for example, that at any given time I am aware of this object only from a certain angle. It could be seen from other angles, whence it would present different appearances. This implies not only that my awareness of it is incomplete and (given that the number of angles, variety of lightings, etc. are unlimited) *uncompletable*, but also that any given experience of the object has components that are not intrinsic to it. Not only do I in fact see the object in a certain light, but I am aware that I am seeing it in a certain light. The changes of the object that take place as a result of my own changes – as when I blink, look to one side, crane my neck, turn round or walk away – underline the 'me-ness' of the experiences over and against the 'it-ness' of the object.[27]

On the other hand, the sense that the object has intrinsic properties brings with it the notion that some appearances to me are more true to that nature than others. No appearance is purely of the object; but some are closer than others. The criterion for discriminating between true and false appearings is coherence. The bent stick in the water is an illusion rather than just another appearance of the stick to be treated with the same respect as its straight appearance because being bent fits with fewer of the other appearances of the stick, predicts fewer future experiences, than straight appearances. The purpose of saying this is not to point to some hard-and-fast criterion for discriminating true from false appearances, or even to make a psychological claim about the criteria we use in practice, but to underline how coherence (or otherwise) between our experiences is invoked to say something about it, the object, rather than about ourselves. In saying this, we come from a different angle upon Quine's earlier quoted observation that 'Illusions are illusions only relative to a prior acceptance of genuine bodies with which to contrast them'.[28] The notion that something cannot be both bent and straight without some intervening events is rooted in the idea of some *thing* – an enduring object, a keeper of constraints on change, on the succession of events.

In addition to being committed to a folk ontology of continuing, independent objects, indexical awareness is associated with at least an inchoate sense of a continuing self. The successive experiences of the same object must imply successive experiences by the same subject. A mere succession of experiences could not, without the idea of some kind of restraint on possibility imposed by the embodied subject continuing (in a literal spatio-temporal sense), generate the notion of an illusion or of the contrast between illusory and veridical experiences. The mutual correction of successive perceptions – as when we take the stick out of the water and realise that it is, after all, straight – is a self-correction of the perceiver, which reinforces her awareness of herself as being positioned with respect to, and having a viewpoint upon, what is there. Constancy of object and sameness of subject are inextricably linked in indexical awareness. There has to be some kind of ontological parity between the embodied subject 'over here' and the stable object 'over there'. Just as the idea of an only partly disclosed reality of the object comes from the Existential Intuition of this body which I am and am not – which is disclosed to and hidden from me – so the notion of object constancy is a projection of the perceived, constructed or postulated constancy of the embodied subject.

Many people will be rightly uneasy with this notion of the emergence of object-knowledge and the emphasis a few pages back on vision. For some it may bring object-experience too close to the 'disinterested beholding' that Heidegger criticised the Greeks for valuing above other forms of engagement with the world. He disgreed in particular with their implicit assumption that disengaged observation would reveal the deeper truth about the world around us. The truth of the world was the existential truth emerging from everyday existence. He took even greater exception to the notion that the model of distant beholding – as in vision – was closer to the truth about the way we related to that world. The world, he argued, did not consist of 'objective presences' that were offset from localised subjects who observed the world as if from the hideouts of their bodies. The world is an interactive reality. Its primordial objects are things that are *ready-to-hand* – tools and the like that exist only as parts of a nexus of signification – rather than 'objective presences', bits of matter, and so on. Our primordial mode of being, *Da-sein* or being there, is being-in-the-world in which we are inseparable from the world. It is only the intellectualising gaze, a 'rigid staring' at 'something merely objectively present',[29] which reads back into everyday awareness what science subsequently uncovers through its tenacious detachment, that sees it thus.

Yes and no. Of course, we do not interact with 'bits of matter' in our everyday lives, in what H. L. Dreyfus characterised as 'absorbed coping'.[30] The world does not sit at the distal end of our gaze: we are immersed, engulfed, 'thrown'. All of this is true, but so is something else: we are not drowned, even less dissolved, in the world we inhabit. Even at the level of indexical awareness, we are at a distance from our habitat; we are (to anticipate the discussion in Chapter 7) 'uncoupled' from the world. Placing the world at the distal end of our (multi-sensory) gaze is central to this uncoupling and, indeed, to our special potency. What Heidegger sees as the central error of the Greeks – evident almost at the beginning with Parmenides (though he later acquitted him and shifted the blame to the later Greek philosophers) – that they 'overlooked the world' of everyday life in their over-valuing of 'disinterested beholding', is no such thing. It is worth pausing to look at this.

In his discussion of 'seeing' – in the context of a rather hostile account of [idle] 'curiosity' – Heidegger notes that even in the early stages of Greek philosophy, cognition was 'conceived in terms of the "desire to see"' (ibid., p. 160). He notes that 'the treatise which stands first in the collection of Aristotle's treatises on ontology begins with the sentence ... "The care for seeing is essential to the being of human being"' (ibid.):

This Greek interpretation of the existential genesis of science is not a matter of chance. It brings to an explicit understanding what was prefigured in a statement of Parmenides ... Being is what shows itself in pure, intuitive perception, and only this seeing discovers being. Primordial and genuine truth lies in pure intuition. This thesis henceforth remains the foundation of Western philosophy. (ibid., p. 160)

What lay behind this root intuition of Greek philosophy – and it is connected with what Gabriel Marcel refers to as the 'hegemony' of vision in Greek thought (and in their thought about thought) – was the sense that vision was a model for distinctively human awareness, that form of awareness that has so empowered us and liberated us from the state of nature. Human vision, which, in the context of the Existential Intuition and the developed sense of ourselves as embodied subjects, is the paradigm of that form of awareness which is *disenmired* from nature. It is not only a metaphor or a model of human cognition, but a primordial instance of it.

While Heidegger is right in some important respects about our everyday being-in-the-world – this world is not something we deal with at arm's or glance's length – he is wrong in other respects that are equally important. If we were as absorbed into the world as he argues we are, we would not have built the human world we actually inhabit. We would be like beasts. He overlooks what has made our profoundly and uniquely human mode of everyday life. The character of our absorbed coping is utterly transformed by the non-absorbed, disinterested beholding that is first adumbrated in indexical awareness and strikingly illustrated by the seeing subject consciously gazing at the seen object at an explicit distance from itself.[31]

There are other reasons why my account of indexical awareness may seem seriously inadequate. The most important, it seems to me, is that it may give the impression that object-awareness is static, one-off and passive. Of course, it is none of these things. Our relationship to objects is interactive. We manipulate, avoid, use objects and these are equally valid ways of tasting their objectness, their independence from us, their having a nature that is hidden from us. We encounter them from different angles, and indeed move in order to do so. We walk past, peer round, look behind, shelter beneath objects. The difference between the apparent movement of an object when we move our bodies or parts of them and the real movement of bodies when they are displaced is as profound a way of encountering their objectivity as seeing them at the distal end of a gaze. These are different aspects of a double dissociation between myself and the object that reinforces both my sense of myself and my sense of the objectness of the object: that I may change in certain respects while in those respects it remains unchanged; and it may change in certain respects while in those respects I remain unchanged. My sense of agency also differentiates between things that seem to fall directly under the control of my will and those that fall only indirectly, or not at all. Moving myself, causing bits of my body to move and moving objects all contribute to the elaboration of object–subject relations. This is the kind of awareness which is fostered at the distal end of a gaze that makes our walking past, peering round, looking behind and sheltering beneath the object, ways of elaborating an awareness that is not available to animals doing superficially similar things. The sense of the object over there is radically transformed by, indeed deeply implicated with, my sense of myself over here: object and subject are correlative.[32]

One final observation. It might be felt that I am traducing indexical awareness by the 'object-talk' through which I have introduced the concept. It would suggest an atomised world that is the correlative of an atomised consciousness.[33] Worlds, as Heidegger was at pains to emphasise, are not simply jumbles or heaps or arrays of independent elements. They cohere. Wittgenstein made the same point when in *Tractatus Logico-Philosophicus* he described the world as a totality of facts set out in logical space. At any given time, each item is part of an unfolding scene which has a multitude of evolving, nascent and developed meanings. The cat is the purring centre of a room; a cup is handy; a piece of paper is part of clutter; a carpet colours the space to the door; the same carpet is scuffed, clashes with the curtains, is a disgrace; a meadow is part of a lovely country walk or of a long and weary walk home. Objects are glimpsed, inspected, ignored, stumbled over, absorbed into general impressions, contribute to 'hard going' or an obstructed view, etc. We see all sorts of non-localisable things: the lateness of the hour, the emptiness of the house, the messiness of the garden. All of this is true but irrelevant. While localised objects-in-themselves are islands of indexical awareness emerging from the ocean of sentience, they are important islands. They are stepping stones to something even more distinctive: deindexicalised awareness, to which we now turn our attention.

4.5 DEINDEXICALISED AWARENESS

In our reconstruction of the path from sentience to knowledge, we have identified perception, as exemplified in visual perception (where we not only see but also see that we see), as a half-way stage. Of itself, vision gives knowledge only of particulars tethered to a particular spatio-

temporal context. Even so, it is a striking awakening out of sentience –
to sentience and to the idea of a world beyond sentience.

The position of visual perception may be presented as follows:

SENSATION ──────────► PERCEPTION ──────────► KNOWLEDGE

　　　　　　Sentience　　　　　　　　Propositional Awareness

PRE-INDEXICAL　　　　　INDEXICAL　　　　　　DEINDEXICALISED

　AWARENESS　　　　　　AWARENESS　　　　　　　AWARENESS

Thus presented, it is midway between exposure and understanding. In
conjunction with the manual prehension delivering the sense of self,
visual perception lifts the subject clearer of the bath of sentience, beyond
the glue, the continuum of awareness, that links the focal objects of
knowledge. The visual subject is in part liberated not only from the
object of sight but from the scene in which it is located. My subjectivity,
incarnate in my body and made present in the hum of background
carnal awareness, makes me more than a mere implicit viewpoint that
discloses the view.

Visual perception is special – and a particularly apt, as well as an
inescapable metaphor of cognition – not only because we can see
ourselves seeing while we cannot (for example) hear ourselves hearing.
What is more, we can see our relation to the seen object while we cannot
smell our relationship to the smelt object.[34] Vision is special because,
more than any of the other senses, it corresponds most clearly to
Aristotle's notion of perception as 'the capacity to receive the sensible
forms without the matter'.[35] In contrast to touch or taste, or even smell,
the exposure of the creature compared with the awareness gained is
minimal. That, in the case of non-human animals, is where it would stop.
In the case of humans for whom the object has an independent existence,
this awareness-at-a-distance, which keeps the object at a distance, this
'receipt of the form without the matter', is the beginning of several things.

It is the first step towards abstraction and the disappearance of
appearance. The object is presented in outline. It is possible to represent
that outline separately from the object. Such representation will be
encouraged by naturally occurring 're-presentations' – reflections and
natural abstractions such as shadows. Where that outline changes, due
to altering the angle of view, the underlying constancy of the object is
reaffirmed by direct tactile experience. Touch confirms the egg as having
an unchanging egg shape. The changing shadows cast by the same
object play with the idea of that shape: it makes explicit the notion that
there is something constant that withstands change.

This constancy of form underlying changing visual appearances opens on to a second abstraction: the invisible form that corresponds to the intrinsic nature of the object. This in turns underpins the notion of classification: if one thing can be not the same and yet the same, then two different things may be, in one sense at least, the same. They are different members (examples, instances) of the same type. Types are yet more abstract forms. The abstraction of form from 'matter', or content, in vision is also the first step towards measurement and is the continuing essence of measurement, as we noted in Chapter 3.

None of these successive revelations would be possible without the firm idea of something unchanging beneath changing appearances, transcending sensory experience which does not change in step with it, which has its own properties and propensities. Animals live in the same world of shadows and reflections as we do, the same universe of change and stability as we do; but they do not have the *fundamental intuition* derived from the Existential Intuition of constant objects, independent of the ocean of sentience in which they are immersed.[36] We may illustrate this with the example of classification.

It has often been suggested that animals classify the contents of their world on the grounds that they show discriminative behaviour towards its different components. The emptiness of this criterion for classificatory behaviour is easily dealt with by pointing out that spiders, thermostats and pebbles also behave differently, and in a predictable way, towards different types of elements of nature. Pebbles, for example, remain still when they are placed on firm ground but sink when they are placed on water. Whether favoured species such as squids (supposed to be able to sort and so classify shapes such as triangles and squares) and chimpanzees have a better claim to be classifiers of their worlds must therefore depend upon some other criterion.

I have elsewhere argued that classification should be *explicit* and this should require the ability to *re*classify objects as well as place them in a particular box defined by patterns of reaction to them.[37] Why *re*classify objects? Because the ability to move an item from one class to another indicates not only an explicit and sophisticated sense of that class but also a sense of the continuity of the object beneath its different relations to one's self. To see that something is both the same and not the same is to have fully grasped the notion of an object; to be equipped with the essential ontological precursor to knowledge – to objective knowledge that resists dissolving the object into our awareness of it.

Which brings us to another feature of vision: that it is a highly public domain of awareness. We not only see objects and see that we see them; we also see that (or whether) others see them and that they can see that (or whether) we can see them. If you see the back of an object and I see the front of it, then together we can see the entire object. (Such an addition, it need hardly be repeated, is predicated on the idea of an object that transcends experience.) From this originates the intuition of what Bernard Williams called 'Purely Positional Advantage'. This is

> implicit in the idea of what one can come to know by observation. If someone has this idea, for instance, of a person's coming to know something by looking and seeing, then he has the idea of things that this person, so placed, could not come to know by looking and seeing.[38]

This passage reminds us not only of what Williams calls the possibility of an 'epistemic division of labour', but also of something that is central to the ideas we are developing: that knowledge is haunted by ignorance. The explicit viewpoint carries with it the notion of its own incompleteness and, as a corollary of that, another viewpoint where more may be seen; for every vantage-point there is a disadvantage-point. And since no experience exhausts the object, all vantage-points are disadvantage-points relative to some ideal of comprehensive awareness.

Indexical awareness is thus linked in different ways with individual consciousness. The rear of the horse, the interior of the cave, that which is round the corner which that man over there can see (and I can't), the thing that is going to come into view in a minute – these are the near reaches of the invisible, of that which lies beyond my present awareness. They are still spatio-temporally tethered, in so far as they have one foot in the particular here-and-now and one foot in the general, or indeterminate, elsewhere. To put out from spatio-temporal location altogether and pass from indexical to deindexicalised awareness it is necessary to lift both feet off the ground of particularity and part company from objects that have a specific, perspectival relation to the conscious individual.

A first step would be something like pointing. Pointing is a uniquely human activity.[39] It depends upon many things, the most important being a sense of the other person's cognitive deficit relative to one's self; my being able to see, for example, that you cannot see something and what that something is. It is a means of directing attention and so is a primitive pedagogic act. (It is not for nothing that learning by ostension has played such an important part in the mythology of language acquisition.) The directing of attention is based upon a visible analogue of directed visual attention: my pointing arm replicates the line of a directed gaze. When I point to an object, my arm or finger replicates the proximal part of the intentional link between my eyes and the object. Pointing, in short, is targeted intentionality made visible. To understand what is being pointed at or out, one has, in addition, to put one's self in the position of the pointer and, under the guidance of their gesture, look at what they are looking at. One has, in other words, to displace one's self from one's own viewpoint and assume a position at the proximal end of their gaze.

This is a dramatic shift, a profound decentring of one's awareness;[40] but it is only the very first step in the deindexicalisation of awareness. The object pointed to is still a particular and, once identified, it stands in a specific spatio-temporal relationship to my body: I see it 'over there'. The next step is when someone has a positional advantage that arises not from being in a different position, or from being in a different attentional state, in a largely overlapping visual field, but from having an almost totally different visual field – as when, for example, you are in a 'lookout' position, at the centre of a visual field of which I can see very little. Under such circumstances, your pointing is to what is for me only a general possibility. The out-of-sight object has entered my awareness but it has no precise location and no determinate characteristics. My relationship to it is not spatio-temporal. Pointing points beyond a particular neck of space-time to something more general: a space of possibilities. 'Round the corner', 'out of sight' are blank sheets on which only expectancy is written, expectation that is differentiated into specific surmise.

This space of possibilities is of especial significance. At the primitive level we have just described, it is the space of objects that exist for someone (you) but not for me. My awareness of your awareness of the object that I am not directly experiencing is a further development of the intuition of the object as transcending my experience of it – what we might call the 'de-Berkeleyanising' of the object – and it links the notion of an object with that of objectivity. An object is (objectively) real if someone can see it when another person points it out. Outside of collective delusions, more-than-one-seeing is justified believing. The unreality of the dagger seen by Macbeth, already suspect because daggers don't usually appear of their own accord unattached to owners, is confirmed by the fact that others cannot see it. An object is something that is accessible to all right-perceiving members of the public. Object-hood and consensus are deeply linked. So too are the collectivisation of consciousness and the maintenance of the space of possibility. We collectively keep this space – of the not-here, the not-yet, the no-longer – open for all. The not-yet may be of particular interest to me, but it belongs to everyone.

The space of possibility can be extended further, beyond that opened up by pointing, in many directions and by many means. For example, you might draw my attention to your own pointing by a cry or call. Such a cry need not be linguistic or even proto-linguistic. It is sufficient that it is used to make me look and see *that* you are pointing and what you are pointing at. My relationship to the object of which you have made me aware is, until I join you to look at it, further deindexicalised: it is mediated by signs that make of it a general possibility.

Since the cry is *not* linguistic, it is tempting to think of this kind of information sharing – and the deindexicalised awareness that begins here – as the sort of thing that animals participate in. After all, it might be argued, the outermost member of a herd may act as a lookout and warn the others of an oncoming predator. It is *not*, however, the same, because deindexicalisation must lift off from a base of indexical awareness and the latter in turn is rooted in the Existential Intuition, which is unique to humans. When one member of the herd warns the other of a predator in the vicinity, this is not information sharing. It is not strictly 'warning', either. The transmission of behaviour – moving from the predator or its putative location and calls associated with fear – from one to the other is more like the spread of an infection than the passing on of information.[41]

Likewise, the indeterminacy of that which is being pointed to (because it is invisible to me) would not alone be sufficient to make it an abstract object or an occupant in the space of possibility. A consciousness cannot entertain abstract objects if it does not also entertain concrete ones. This means that we do not have to conclude that a horse communicating a general terror to another horse by whinneying was invoking an abstract object. Abstract objects, differentiated possibilities, higher-order generalities, can arise only against the background of subjects confronted with real objects. There is no deindexicalised awareness without prior indexical awareness.

The key to further deindexicalisation of awareness beyond what is achieved through, say, pointing must, of course, be language or, at least, a proto-linguistic precursor.[42] This is a huge topic which I am not competent to address. I just want to say enough here to bring the notion of 'fully deindexicalised awareness' into broad daylight. In *The Hand: A Philosophical Inquiry into Human Being*, I argued that, for a variety of reasons, tools could be important precursors of language: they are the external expression of internal needs; they are stable; and they are had in common. In short, they enable the needs that in animals are locked in the privacy of sentience to be made visible, to enter the public domain, and consequently start a process of pooling or collectivisation of awareness. From the point of view of our immediate concerns, the most important feature of tool-signs is that they are *general*: they are the concrete expression of general possibility. As such, they 'point' beyond themselves to an invisible – indeed supersensible – world of *possibility*. Like uttered words, they are both themselves and other than themselves. In addition, however, since (unlike animal quasi-tools that are assimilated to the body schema[43]) they are explicitly extra-corporeal, they are manifestly signs of themselves. They are ripe to be *used* as signs. Hence their aptness to be precursors of distinctively human communication systems, of language in the true sense.

This is worth unpacking further. One of the most fundamental differences between human language and animal communication is evident even in a child at the stage of using only single-symbol utterances: this is the non-situation-specificity of words:

> The word *kitty* may be used by the baby to draw attention to a cat, to inquire about the whereabouts of the cat, to summon the cat, to remark that something resembles a cat, and so forth. Other primates' calls do not have this property. A food call is used when food is discovered (or imminently anticipated) but not to suggest that food be sought. A leopard alarm call can report the sighting of a leopard, but cannot be used to ask if anyone has seen a leopard recently.[44]

This highlights how words are used explicitly as tools, rather than merely being relays in a causal chain linking a stimulus (e.g. a predator) with a response (predator warning-cry) which stimulates behaviour, in conspecifics, appropriate to the imminence of a predator. Words, being explicit signs, deal with explicit, general possibilities; likewise their precursors, explicit tools. Explicitness enables them to prefigure the transmission of *meant meaning*, the positing of possibilities which, by their nature, are locationless, deindexicalised, though they may then be referred to a location where the possibilities are realised.[45]

The realm of possibility opened up to and by deindexicalised awareness – and greatly expanded and elaborated by language – is not divided up in the way that the realm of spatio-temporal objects is. The occupants of the space of possibility are not related to the body in the way that material objects relate to the body. They are the objects of *knowledge* rather than being revealed in sense experience. Such objects of knowledge are not 'next to my body', 'near to me', 'over there'. They are in an invisible realm. Which is not to say that all objects of knowledge are solely in that realm or that they are purely general. Human knowledge, at its most basic, is of (domestic) particulars; or of possibilities that are realised in particulars – particular objects, particular events. But even a realised possibility – this shoe I have been looking for, which is now next to me – occupies two spaces: the space of more or less general possibility in which its existence was entertained; and the physical space of actuality in which, when it is found, is before me, or next to me, or 'over there'. It never fully abandons the space of possibility: an actualised possibility never becomes merely actual; a piece of matter, say, confined to its niche in space-time. It is never fully re-indexicalised because its point of origin is non-indexical space. That sugar bowl I have been looking for is discovered to be over there; but because it came into my visual field as it were 'meaning-first', it is never totally 'plugged into' over there. We could put this another way by saying that meaning is not localised and its not being localised becomes explicit when it is instantiated in a meaningful object – either a material object that happens to have meaning and its meaning is captured in a classification (see below); or an object (such as a symbol) that has been manufactured in order to carry meaning. Such local expressions of meaning point to a non-spatial elsewhere where the meanings are 'located'.

That the human world is one of realised possibilities becomes more completely true as it is increasingly composed of realised anticipations. Anticipations, at the most basic level, may be seen as the product of spatial and non-spatial pointings, indicating at different levels of generality what I might expect next: the things that will happen in my vicinity or to me, the things I will encounter. Non-spatial pointings are fastened to their targets by signs – images, words, images prompted by words – which differentiate general expectancy into more or less specific expectations. This is as true of the object of a quest for a missing shoe as of what is sought in a holiday visit to another country. In each case, that which is actualised exists in its own right with a multitude of features that were not laid down in the specification of the possibility they realise; but they remain, none the less, instantiations of what was anticipated or sought.

We have entered a boundless territory and I will confine myself to reiterating the one or two points that are most relevant to the present inquiry. The objects of knowledge are not located in space and time, in the sense of being related to the body of the subject. When the object of knowledge is not a mere possibility but a material particular and one, what is more, that is right here next to me, it is none the less still located in the space of possibility – of sense, of general meaning – because it is incompletely separated from the general sign that designated it. This cup next to my hand is, as Heidegger pointed out, not merely an isolated object[46] (though it is, of course, literally isolable and has literal spatial boundaries); it is part of a nexus of signification. In the case of a cup, it is maintained in this dual state for two reasons. First, the cup is an artefact: it wears its general character on its sleeve. Second, it has a second handle: the word that names it. It is kept in a state of classification, of being an actualisation of general possibility, because it makes (general) sense.

The relevance of this to our examination of human consciousness is as follows. We have so far separated indexical from deindexicalised awareness. It is, however, an artificial distinction. Deindexicalised awareness contaminates everything. There is no recovery of innocence. In humans knowledge routs sentience. There are no aconceptual percepts and it is difficult to imagine even a sensation which is not haunted by general possibility. That is why, although pure indexical awareness would not count as full-blown knowledge – no one is going to be deemed 'knowledgeable' simply by virtue of seeing what is in front of them, simply because they have a visual field – one can have knowledge of what is before one; know that there is a cup in front of one and know that cup as an instance of a general 'what'.

There are circumstances under which such awareness counts as full-blown knowledge; namely, when someone (myself or another) is uncertain as to the whereabouts of the cup or the nature of the object in question. Where the location of the cup is the answer to a question, its being in front of one counts as a piece of knowledge. By making the type-identity of the cup the answer to a question, one isolates a piece of indexical awareness as an item of knowledge. (This is one of the many ways in which knowledge is linked with ignorance: uncertainty can make even the present object of indexical awareness – located in space and time – an object of knowledge, located in the space of possibility, a *fact*.)

Earlier, we observed how acknowledging the privileged awareness of others – for example, someone who is pointing out something that we cannot yet see – displaces us from the centre of the field of indexical awareness. This is something of an exaggeration. After all, the person who is obliging us in this way is still located in our sensory field. What is true is that the new space that is opened up, the space of possibilities, does not have us at its centre. While the possibilities are (most importantly for me) possibilities for me, they are also possibilities for others in a similar situation to mine. That situation may be very general, so the others may constitute a boundless crowd. There is another sense in which the space of possibilities is polycentric to the point of being centreless. When I am part of a large group, the pointings out may not be from just one individual at a time; and that which is pointed to may not be a singular possibility. This will most particularly apply to an established community in which there is language. Under such circumstances, the source of the pointings – a heritage of beliefs – will not be localised. While it will on any given occasion originate from persons and be directed to persons, this will merely be an instantiation of the transmissions throughout the culture – from everyone (or anyone) to everyone (or anyone) else. Both what is pointed out and the pointing will be decentred. This will be particularly true when what is transmitted is a consensus, the received wisdom, that belongs to no one and is not rooted in any particular individual's experience. It is not something that either the pointer or the recipient of the pointing has, or could, experience for herself. The communication may have important personal components (you are being helpful, bossy, boring, boasting, patient), but the elements that are communicated get their authority because they are not personal.

We have a situation, therefore, where how things are and how they appear are even further adrift. The knowledge that extends, confirms or corrects experience is not, centrally, another experience had by the same person. Indeed, knowledge is often about realities that have never appeared directly to the individual in question. This will be most obviously true of general factual knowledge (to which we shall return in the next chapter), but it is equally true of particular items of knowledge, such as the age of the cat or the earlier whereabouts of a lost item that has now been returned to me. The sentient individual cuts a smaller and smaller figure in the sum total of her own consciousness as awareness arising from direct sensory experience is dwarfed by awareness mediated by signs. As a knower, she is increasingly dis-located from the centre of her field of awareness. Indeed, knowledge does not form such a continuous, unified field, let alone one centred on the field of the knower. The world in which the self is situated is composed less and less of the things surrounding one's body, though the body is always enclosed, surrounded, by a world disclosed to its senses. An 'inner' world of information and preoccupation, of planning and possibility, partly occludes the world in which the body is located.

Even those things that do surround the body are – inasmuch as they are known rather than merely sensed (as when I know that this cat is called Felix and it is seventeen years old and has certain needs) – are not there in a merely indexical sense of being, for example, next-to-me. Deindexicalised knowledge transforms even the seemingly indexical core of experience surrounding the embodied subject. The objects that fill the sensory field are not only credited with a reality that goes beyond their sensory appearance, but are invested with a significance that goes beyond their individual reality, a significance they merely instantiate.

In summary, the knowing subject is not located at the centre of her field of sapience in the way that she is located in the centre of the field of indexical awareness. The objects of knowledge are not arrayed around her as, say, the objects of 'pure' perception might be envisaged as being. Her relationship to what she knows is not perspectival (or not in the primary sense). The de-location of the object, which began when one person pointed out an object to another who could not see it, and the dis-location of the embodied subject that resulted, had momentous consequences. The surrounding world never quite recovered its full indexicality; for its objects took on the character of realised possibilities and, ultimately, of referents. With the tool-inspired birth of language, the proliferation of de-located objects and the dis-location of the subject from the explicit centre of things, so that she was no longer the hub of her world, became an unstoppable trend. In the last few thousand years, with the advent of writing – the untethering of communication from the mouth of a speaker, from the human body, or indeed from any localised conscious source – this centrifugal trend has gathered an unimaginable speed.

This said, it cannot be emphasised too strongly that deindexicalised awareness is *not* a regression to pre-indexical awareness; it is *post*-indexical in the sense of being available to a creature that owns its own body. This means that, however wide the field of deindexicalised awareness, the individual who is de-centred in it is not de-centred in the sense much talked about by post-structuralists and other post-modernist writers. The Knowing Animal is not dissolved in knowledge, even less in a system of signs or any of the other modes of collective unconscious that are so often invoked when the self is discussed in postmodern circles.[47] For her knowledge is tokenised in an individual centred on her own body, which in turns lies at the centre of a field of indexical awareness.

4.6 RETROSPECT AND PROSPECT

We have traced the barest outline of the passage from the sentience possessed by all animals (including humans) to the knowledge that humans alone enjoy. My main purpose has been to *make knowledge visible* and thereby to reaffirm the distances between sentient beasts and sentient and sapient humans.[48] There are numerous reasons why the reader might be dissatisfied with my account. I have skated over many things – most notably the role of language and pre-linguistic signs – and though I will return to some of them, my treatment will remain sketchy. I have treated, as if it were a series of steps, a process that, in the prehistory of hominids and in the cognitive development of individual human beings, will not be sequential: at the very least, it will be iterative and interactive. For example, the sense that one is an embodied subject which lies at the root of object-sense will itself be reinforced and transformed by dealings with objects. And the displacement from the centre of a field of indexicalised awareness will not only always be incomplete but will be differently elaborated as one develops cognitively. Accepting the authority of a playmate who is pointing at something just outside of one's visual field is clearly quite different from accepting the authority of someone who is giving you key dates in history, thus formatting a collective past of which you have only the slightest inkling. If the story I have told were intended to describe *successive stages* of development of humanity or individual humans, it would be wrong. It is perfectly obvious that pre-indexical, indexical and deindexicalised awareness are not successive phases of human consciousness; nor do they exist merely side by side. They interpenetrate and are interdependent. For example, an individual receiving a piece of information does so through the receipt of acoustic or visual tokens. He has to be placed in such a (physical) position as to be able to experience them. The informational core of the communication may be impersonal and decentred, or centreless, but the recipient will have his own angle upon, his own realisation of, it. What is more, he will be in the centre of a field of indexical awareness and will be so located through the preindexical hum of sentience that makes him explicitly *in* that field. We do not, even in the most sophisticated settings, entirely evaporate into sentences. Finally, notwithstanding a nod in the direction of agency, I have done little justice to the fact that object knowledge and all that flows from it is at least in part the result of active engagement with the materials of the world, in pursuit of specific goals, as well as the passive receipt of input from without.

This final deficiency I will attempt to remedy in my 'Inquiry into Inquiry' in section 7.3. For the present, I want to focus on a yet more fundamental problem with the story I have been telling: an ambiguity as to what the story is intended to do. Is it meant to be an empirical account of successive steps in the acquisition of knowledge by the human (replicated by each generation of newcomers)? Or is it a rational reconstruction of the steps that must have been taken to get from sentience to sapience? It is not quite either. Likewise, as an 'account' of the awakening out of sentience, it wobbles between being a description, an explanation, and some assertions that are not quite either. Like the reader, I don't quite know what it is. What I do know is that any attempt to generate a theory of how knowledge came about must depend upon a lot of knowledge and for this reason must be somewhat dubious. We cannot look beyond knowledge to find out what is underneath it; or look over the entirety of knowledge to arrive at a piece of knowledge about what, in general, knowledge is. I can hope only that the reader will recognise some important truths – intuitive, logical or empirical – in the things I have been saying about the relationship between sentience and knowledge.

The vulnerability of my account as an empirical hypothesis will be particularly evident. Hominid pre-history is, by definition, hidden from us and the tape cannot be run twice – with and without hands, with and without the Existential Intuition, with and without vision – to see whether the same outcome – Knowing Animals – results. An obvious place to look for confirmatory evidence might be the development of individual humans from sentient infants to knowing adults. Unfortunately, the maturation of individual humans is unlikely to recapitulate the history of human cognitive evolution since hominids parted company from pongids because, unlike the first humans, contemporary infants are surrounded from Day One by language, facts and artefacts. Nobody talked to the first hominids or handed them any facts or instructive toys. They were not given lumps of pre-formed worlds off the shelf. It is only in a very limited sense that contemporary children replicate in their twenty years of cognitive growth the achievements of six million years of hominid development, by building up the world of knowledge out of sense experience. From the moment it is born, the child is exposed to factual knowledge as well as sensing the world directly. The voices round the crib bear news of a universe that is quite distinct from that which is reported directly by its senses. By the age of three, a child will have a concept such as 'Africa' which could not possibly have been built up out of sensings. However crazily distorted that concept is, it will be a first draft open to endless revision.[49]

This is a reminder of something that we shall examine in the next chapter and which I hope will have become evident in the preceding pages: that not only is knowledge not built up out of personal experiences, out of sentience; it is not built up out of experiences at all. It begins in sentience but is not bound by it or tied down to it. The key insight that knowledge is 'underdetermined' by sentience has many facets: sense experiences do not add up to knowledge; even less is knowledge condensed or compressed sentience. This observation – a radicalisation of Popper's famous point about the systematic inadequacy of the support provided by experiences for general statements supposedly founded upon them – is a reiteration of the difference between animal and human consciousness.

The fundamental purpose of my Just-So story has been, as I have said, to make the *distance* between sentience and knowledge evident. This in turn is intended to discourage a wider tendency to close the gap between human beings and other animals and so assimilate humans to the natural world and, through this, to the material world described by physics. By showing just how distinctive human beings are, I hope to make it less easy to conflate human and animal behaviour, the knowing existence of humans who lead their lives and the organic existence of animals that just live.

It is easy to fancy that a dog following a trail is propelled by a sense of incomplete knowledge, of an appearance (the scent) that falls short of reality (the prey that left the scent). This description is permitted only if we allow that dogs have the explicit sense of objects outside of themselves. A fully developed object sense, however, must rest upon a sense of being an embodied subject, an identity with something that one knows only incompletely. This is not available to non-human animals that lack the Existential Intuition. It is not a knowledge-based sense of ignorance but instinct that drives the dog along the trail of scent. To anticipate the discussion in Chapter 8, it is cause-pushed and not reason-pulled.

Here is another example, which we have already touched on. A herd of deer is grazing peacefully. One of the herd, located in a favourable spot, senses a predator. It starts running away, bellows or otherwise communicates its terror. The remainder of the herd takes flight. Is this not an example of one animal informing others of a fact that it has acquired through its positional advantage? Of a piece of knowledge being transmitted? No; it is not *a fact* that is communicated; or, rather, what is communicated becomes a fact only under a description formulated by a human observer. The transmission of the privileged animal's terror is not mediated through abstract discourse rooted in de-indexicalised awareness. The latter is not available to the beast because it requires a prior indexicalised awareness; the latter is available only to embodied subjects, not to mere organisms. Relationships of positional advantage and disadvantage cannot be the basis of deindexicalised awareness – facts, knowledge, truth – for a creatures whose conscious-ness is pre-indexical.

These examples, as well as showing how little of human con-sciousness can be assimilated to animal consciousness, also point to the work that has to be done to get a clear idea of notions such as 'beliefs', 'facts' and 'truths'. That such work is worth doing is justified by the role that the ascription of beliefs and other propositional attitudes to animals plays in supporting scientistic accounts of humanity that try to narrow the gap between ourselves and beasts. In making knowledge visible, I am trying to show the distance between sensing and knowing-that.

More specifically, I am trying to get hold of the 'That ...' which lies at the heart of human knowledge 'That such-and-such is the case'. 'That' is awoken with indexical awareness: 'That over there ...' With deindexicalisation, it is transformed into full-blown explicitness: 'That it is ...' 'That' is the essential precursor to facts, truths, inquiries, reasons, causes, desires and many other things that humans uniquely have access to, deal in, deploy, hold or harbour; to all the things that make man The Explicit Animal.

One last preliminary observation about the nature of the 'epistogonic' enterprise upon which we are embarked. Self-evidently, it belongs to the genetic or genealogical rather than the justificatory approach to epistemology. While many philosophers, for example Locke, were concerned with the origin of our knowledge, they did implicitly appeal to the genesis of our beliefs as justification of them. Hume showed that this was not possible: the objects of knowledge (material objects, causal connections, etc.) lay beyond the reach of the sense impressions that were supposed to underpin our access to such objects.

Kant and many others since have seen this as a challenge – in particular to find something other than sense experience to transport us safely to certain knowledge. Our present inquiry is informed by the belief that once we have identified a *genealogy* of our knowledge – and see it as either natural or extra-natural but not transcendent or super-national in origin – we can't justify it. The belief, dear to physicalist thinkers, that you can justify knowledge because it is caused by that which is known, is invalid. Apart from the obvious difficulty of checking the universal claim that our knowledge is caused by its objects, there is the additional problem that knowledge is of deindexicalised objects. These are clearly not causes in the physical sense. Nor (as we shall discuss in section 5.4) is knowledge simply totted up or compressed sentience. Even if this were true, the assumption that sentience is caused by the things that are known would make the status of sentience as *effects* uncertain, given that causes belong to the world of knowledge, as do objects/events separate from sentience. Knowlege is of facts and they are quite unlike impacting objects, energies or forces.

Which is why epistogony will attempt to be epistemologically agnostic. And why, too, it will not entirely succeed in this respect.

NOTES AND REFERENCES

1. Immanuel Kant, *Critique of Pure Reason*, trans. Norman Kemp Smith (London: Macmillan, 1964), p. 41.
2. Daniel C. Dennett, *Freedom Evolves* (London: Penguin Books, 2003), p. 165.
3. Timothy Williamson, *Knowledge and its Limits* (Oxford: Oxford University Press, 2002).
4. Edmund Gettier, 'Is Justified True Belief Knowledge?', *Analysis* 23(6) (1963): 121–3.
5. A similar error motors the Frege–Gödel Sling-Shot argument against the Correspondence Theory of Truth. We shall return to it in section 6.2.4.

Of course one can know (be knowing) a fact – have a piece of knowledge – without being continuously aware of it, while one cannot have (or be having) a sensation without being aware of it, if only subliminally. Likewise, one can have a belief of which one is fully aware only when it is challenged by one's self (when one discovers that it is wrong) or by someone else. Even so, knowledge cannot be entirely separated from consciousness. While it would be absurd to suggest that I have been continuously conscious of the piece of knowledge that 'The Battle of Waterloo took place in 1815' since the middle 1950s when I first learned of this fact, it would be equally absurd to suggest that I could know it without *at any time* having been conscious of it. Suggestions like this, when taken seriously, lead quickly to the lunacy of taking literally the notion of information 'stored' outside of the consciousness of individuals.

Not all Gettier examples necessarily involve ascribing beliefs to individuals who are not conscious of them and reducing knowledge to putative formal characteristics. Supposing Harry has a twin brother, Charlie, who is to all intents and purposes indistinguishable from him. I am acquainted only with Harry and am unaware that he has a twin brother. I see Charlie driving a Porsche at 5 p.m. on 12 December 2004 and, thinking I am seeing Harry, conclude that Harry was driving a Porsche at 5 p.m. on 12 December 2004. It so happens that Harry *was* driving a Porsche at 5 p.m. on 12 December 2004. My belief about Harry was true and apparently justified and yet it feels wrong to say that I know what Harry was doing at 5 p.m.

The problem this example illustrates is not that we are attributing beliefs in the absence of psychological contents. The problem is that my conclusion qualifies as knowledge on the grounds of being a belief that is (a) true and (b) justified. In practice, the belief, while it is certainly true, is only *apparently* justified. Some philosophers would say, the belief does not amount to knowledge because it does not have 'the right kind of cause' – it is caused by the sight of Charlie driving a Porsche when it should be caused by the sight of Harry driving a Porsche. The notion of causation of belief, and beliefs being caused by their intentional objects, however, is one that we should treat with suspicion.

(I am very grateful to Lawrence Tallis for both the above points, and the Gettier example that illustrates it.)

One could see the Gettier paradox as the result of treating belief from an externalist viewpoint and yet still attributing it to an individual person. A person cannot have a justified true belief, if he does do not have that belief; and he cannot be said to have a belief, if he does not have it explicitly. Failure to see these obvious things is the result of shifting the focus of attention on knowledge to the narrowly logical issue of justification of a (true) belief and away from the having of a belief.

6. Martin Heidegger, *The Basic Problems of Phenomenology*, trans. A Hofstadter (Bloomington: IN: Indiana University University Press, 1982), p. 297.

7. See *I Am: A Philosophical Inquiry into First-Person Being* (Edinburgh: Edinburgh University Press, 2004), Chapter 5.

8. The non-separation of the subject and its world is the condition of mere sentience, as we shall discuss presently. This is the condition of beasts who do not have *Da-sein*, explicit being-there.

9. For a detailed account of the origin and consequences of the Existential Intuition, see *The Hand: A Philosophical Inquiry into Human Being* (Edinburgh: Edinburgh University Press, 2003), especially 'Towards Chiro-Philosophy' (Chapters 10 and 11) and *I Am*, especially section 1.2.

10. See *I Am*, Chapter 6, 'Reports from Embodiment: On Being, Suffering, Having, Using and Knowing a Body'.

11. Patrick Gardiner, *Schopenhauer* (Harmondsworth: Penguin Books, 1963), pp. 58, 57.

12. Quassim Cassam, *Self and World* (Oxford: Clarendon Press, 1997), p. 52n. Cassam's central argument that self-consciousness requires that we conceive of ourselves as 'an object in the weighty sense' – an object that exists when it is not being perceived or thought of – is very much to our point. The residual inscrutability of the body with which we identify ourselves is, for Cassam, essential for it to deliver what is required of it.
  One might even argue that the sense of an object's being essentially unchanged – being *the same object* despite surface changes – is rooted in the sense of one's own continuity in the face of change. Consider this famous passage from Thomas Reid:
  > The identity of ships and trees is not perfect identity; it is rather something which, for the conveniency of speech, we call identity. It admits of a great change of the subject, providing the change is gradual; sometimes, even of a total change. And the changes which in common language are made consistent with identity differ from those that are thought to destroy it, not in kind, but in number and degree. *Identity* has no fixed nature when applied to bodies; and questions about the identity of a body are very often questions about words. But identity when applied to persons, has no ambiguity, and admits not of degrees, or of more or less. It is the foundation of all rights and obligations, and of all accountableness; and the notion of it is fixed and precise. (quoted in Derek Parfit, *Reasons and Persons* (Oxford: Clarendon Press, 1987), p. 323)

  This is compatible with the view developed in this book that the sense of the continuing identity of objects is rooted in the sense of the continuing identity of one's self as an embodied subject.

13. Barry Stroud, *Understanding Human Knowledge. Philosophical Essays* (Oxford: Oxford University Press, 2000), p. 6.

14. Bernard Williams, *Truth and Truthfulness* (New Haven, CT: Yale University Press, 2002), passim.

15. David Bell, *Husserl* (London: Routledge, 1991), p. 164.

16. In a fascinating paper, to which we shall return more than once, Lewis Wolpert has argued that not only are causal beliefs unique in humans but that such beliefs are 'primitives'. They arise so early not only because of 'the explanatory drive' which 'is at the core of a child's development' but also because children from a very early age (a few months old) 'already perceive the world as composed of cohesive solid bodies' which links with the notions of mechanical force and their controllability

and of the idea that 'a moving object – a ball – can make another move on impact'. 'It is', Wolpert concludes, 'this key concept of mechanics which may be the key brain property that originally evolved in early humans.' 'Causal Beliefs and the Origins of Technology', *Philosophical Transactions of the Royal Society Lond* A (2003), 361: 1709–19.

17. W. V. O. Quine, 'The Nature of Natural Knowledge', in *Mind and Language*, Wolfson College Lectures 1974, ed. Samuel Guttenplan (Oxford: Clarendon Press, 1975), p. 67.

18. Knowledge is haunted by the sense of the constitutive beyond the epistemic. In the case of mere sentience, the epistemic is the constitutive; more precisely, the contrast cannot be sustained. That is why the difference between phenomenal experiences and nerve impulses, which is a difference in ways of knowing, is a difference in the things themselves. On this score Saul Kripke was quite correct. See Raymond Tallis, *The Explicit Animal. A Defence of Human Consciousness* (Basingstoke: Macmillan, 2nd edition, 1991, 1999), pp. 65–6.

19. Stroud, *Understanding Human Knowledge*, p. 126.

20. The reader may not be convinced by this epistemological agnosticism. It is still possible to ask: 'Does the intuition of objecthood uncover something that was already there? Were objects – stable entities, occupying space and enduring over time, and existing independently of sense experience – always there to be discovered?' If they were not, their gradual emergence in human inquiry would not be useful, never mind true. My biogenetic standpoint supposes objects, etc. are there … So my seemingly purely phenomenological approach to the gap between sentience and (object) knowledge is certainly not ontologically agnostic.

But then neither is ordinary scepticism-driven epistemology, as we have already noted. The assumed priority of 'experiential knowledge' over knowledge of objects is itself something that is based on evidence. How, without evidence, could we come to the conclusion that sensory experience is unreliable and it does not give us the objective account of objects that we ordinarily believe it does?

One could be more ontologically decisive by saying that, if there are subjects, there must be objects. Given that we cannot be wrong about being subjects, we cannot be wrong about there being objects. What are objects other than things that subjects have to take account of in their lives? This, however, seems to reduce objects to the internal accusative of subjects and in no way clarifies their intrinsic nature, whether they have independent reality, etc.

Interestingly, this problem illustrates a general principle: as soon as knowledge is given a cause or basis, it seems to be compromised: genesis becomes aetiology. One cannot avoid the aetiological problem by arguing that the concept of the cause of an experience is reducible to the concepts of the experiences that it causes. There may not therefore be such a clear difference between epistogony and epistemology. At any rate, epistogony can evade epistemology only by (a) showing that it can get off the ground without assuming all sorts of things it questions, and (b) overlooking the fact that this account of the origin of all knowledge is based upon some (rather large-scale) knowledge. Neither (a) nor (b) is true. This does for Quine's idea of a 'naturalised epistemology': a theory of knowledge rooted in science is not the same as a scientific epistemology because the latter would have to account for the higher-order knowledge made available through science.

21. Just as the Existential Intuition cannot be factually in error because it is the prior condition of there being facts.

22. For example, the metaphysical thinking of J. G. Fichte.
23. Quoted in Rudiger Safranski, *Martin Heidegger. Between Good and Evil*, trans. Ewald Osers (Cambridge, MA: Harvard University Press, 1998), p. 26.
24. See also *I Am*, section 2.12 '"I": From Philosophical Grammar to Existential Grammar'; and Raymond Tallis, *In Defence of Realism* (2nd edition, Lincoln, NB: Nebraska University Press, 1998), chapter 5.
25. In a famous and now somewhat politically incorrect poem, Henry Reed says that 'the idiot greens the meadow': his consciousness is inseparable from that of which he is conscious. Hume and Sartre would seem to believe that this is the condition of humanity. Hume speaks of the 'propensity of the mind' to spread itself upon things and Sartre of the way the 'for-itself' sacrifices itself to the appearances which are revealed through it.
26. And a rather complex object, too. The sight of an arm, a feeling of weightiness, a cup of tea in the hand, a sensation in the gut, a preoccuption or two flaking off into scattered thoughts. Such are the elements that go to make the 'hum of hereness' that we examined in *I Am* (see Chapter 5).
27. This makes clear why the idea of the correct appearance of an object is self-contradictory. The very concept of an object is of something that has a reality beyond its appearances and it emerges at the level of indexical awareness which is precisely aware that it is perspectival (condition-dependent, etc.). To try to find 'the correct appearance' of an object is to try to rediscover the epistemic in the constitutive – and at the very point at which the two are separated.
28. Guttenplan (ed.), *Mind and Language*, p. 67.
29. Martin Heidegger, *Being and Time*, trans. Joan Stambaugh (New York: State University of New York Press, 1996), p. 57.
30. H. L. Dreyfus, *Being-in-the-World. A Commentary on Heidegger's Being and Time Division I* (Cambridge, MA: MIT Press, 1991).
31. We could make this point in more Heideggerian terms by reiterating the argument from *I Am*: there can be no *Da-sein* (being-there) without *Fort-sein* (being-here). The force of this argument is seen more clearly when we think about indexical (and later deindexicalised) awareness. This *always* takes off from and refers back and relates to our indexicalised bodily being. We need a fully developed 'me-here' to have a fully developed 'that-there'. The indexicality of specifically human awareness places beyond doubt that *Da-sein* cannot replace body and mind. It cannot encompass both poles of the relationship, both 'that-there' and 'me-here'. Point and counterpoint need each other.

   What Heidegger dismissed as 'rigid staring' – the intellectualising gaze that reduces the world to an ensemble of physical presences – in fact makes the fully-fledged intentionality of human consciousness explicit. It also makes evident the undissolved residue – the hiddenness, the otherness, the reality beyond appearance – of the object. This residue stands for a possible future (and a past) which opens up the present moment beyond the present, a necessary condition of the 'disenmire-ment' of human consciousness.
32. I cannot, of course, rule out the possibility that animals have fleeting indexical aware-ness, particularly as certain primates show evidence of fleeting self-consciousness. This is not sufficient to sustain a particular world-picture, an ontology of a world of stable, independent, inscrutable objects.
33. It is arguable that, in order for sentience to be broken up into individual sensations, or clusters of sensations, it is necessary for there to be a putative intentional object –

a thing out-there it is about, a place in-here, or a significance located nowhere in particular. Animal sentience is individuated only by spatio-temporal separation, as in the case of an itch lasting for a particular time located at a particular place in the body. There is also the question of whether sentience is or is not aconceptual. John McDowell argues, against Gareth Evans, in *Mind and World* (Cambridge, MA: Harvard University Press, 1994) that no experience is non-conceptual. There is no way of checking this – least of all by introspection from the inescapable standpoint of the 'knowing animal'; it seems reasonable, however, to distinguish within sense experience between aconceptual sensation, which belongs to pure sentience, and human perception which, having intentional objects, is conceptual.

34. Though there will be considerable cross-sensory mutual assistance – for example, looking for where the sound comes from, touching the seen object to check out its nature. Even so, vision retains its primacy. You can see yourself sniffing, listening out, groping, but can't, for example, hear yourself looking.

35. W. D. Ross (ed.), *Aristotelis 'De Anima'* (Oxford: Clarendon Press, 1959), 424a17–19. This beautifully captures how the perceived object remains over there while the perception of it is 'here' – the de-distancing that Heidegger spoke of.

36. It is difficult to imagine their being puzzled by the visual illusions that worry philosophers and fascinate small children. It is no coincidence, by the way, that it is the visual sense that is so rich in illusions: mirages, dreams, after-images, etc.

37. See Tallis, *The Explicit Animal*, pp. 186–8.

38. Williams, *Truth and Truthfulness*, p. 51.

39. See *The Hand*, section 6.3. A recent study has confirmed that not even apes appreciate pointing in the way that human infants do from before one year of age. See Daniel J. Povinelli, Jess M. Bering and Steve Giambrone, 'Towards a Science of Other Minds: Escaping the Argument by Analogy', *Cognitive Science* (2000), 24: 509–42.

40. Helmuth Plessner, in *The Steps of the Organic and Man*, defines man in terms of his 'eccentric' position. He does not, like animals, live 'from his middle into his middle'. Quoted in Safranski, *Martin Heidegger*, p. 159.

41. We shall return to this point in section 5.5, when we consider the nature of 'propositional attitudes' and whether or not animals have them.

42. The characteristics of such a proto-language are discussed in Ray Jackendoff's reconstruction of the incremental evolutionary steps leading to language in *Foundations of Language. Brain, Meaning, Grammar, Evolution* (Oxford: Oxford University Press, 2002), Chapter 8.

43. This point is made by Wolfgang Kohler. See Peter Reynolds, in Kathleen Gibson and Tim Ingold (eds), *Tools, Langauge and Cognition in Human Evolution* (Cambridge: Cambridge University Press, 1993) p. 8.

44. Jackendoff, *Foundations of Language*, p. 239.

45. The explicitness of signs *as* signs is reflected in the fact that, quite early on, children use words metalinguistically – refer to them, play with them, indulge in play using them in a non-serious way, and so on. See Tallis, *The Explicit Animal,* especially pp. 188–94.

46. For Heidegger, 'there "is" no such thing as *a* useful thing. There always belongs to the being of a useful thing a totality of useful things in which this useful thing can be what it is ... A totality of useful things is always already discovered *before* the individual useful thing' (*Being and Time*, p. 64). It seems as if, for him, the entire human world is either tools, or tools-in-waiting, discarded tools, tools out of use or

negative tools (things that lie between us and the realisation of our projects; things that are in the way, distances to be crossed, etc.).

47. See Raymond Tallis, *Enemies of Hope. A Critique of Contemporary Pessimism* (Basingstoke: Macmillan, reprinted with new preface, 1999).

48. I owe this pairing to Michael Williams, *Problems of Knowledge. A Critical Introduction to Epistemology* (Oxford: Oxford University Press, 2001). I have not adopted it more generally because 'sapience' carries the implication of wisdom and I don't think I know what wisdom is, though I am familiar with the idea of it.

49. 'I am going to leave this family and go to Africa' one of our children informed us at the age of three, following a disagreement about whose turn it was to bat during beach cricket. The faltering first drafts of large-scale concepts are beautifully captured in A. A. Milne's stories. The child's induction into the human world is an extraordinary crash course.

CHAPTER 5

Aspects of Propositional Awareness

5.1 THE HUMAN WORLD

The human world is fundamentally different from the habitats of all other animals. There are surface differences and there are deep ones.

Most of the surface differences can be gathered up in the familiar observation that, uniquely among living creatures, man *creates* the greater part of his *Umwelt*. For most of the time he is surrounded by, and interacting with, artefacts (focal, like tools; or global, like cities) or their effects, such as the warmth and light that artefacts create on dark, cold nights.

There are other, perhaps deeper, differences. Man pursues his goals indirectly – often so indirectly that the link between behaviour and any basic (for example, organic) need is all but lost. His behaviour is governed by a multitude of explicit and implicit culturally-determined rules; he works for and in institutions; he has a range of roles; and, linked with all these things, he engages in cooperative activities of huge complexity and variety. And at the deepest level, the way in which humans are conscious of their world is utterly different from the way animals sense their environments.

This difference is reflected in the vastly different scale of the world available at any given instant to individual humans compared with that which is open to beasts. The contrast between the spatio-temporal and conceptual realms that constitute the world to which we relate in our everyday lives – which we are aware of, take account of, are deployed in – and the successive, non-additive environment-moments, scoped by instantaneous sensory fields, that an animal occupies is extraordinary. In the light of this comparison, truly animals are exposed as being (to use Heidegger's phrase) 'world-poor'.[1]

Like animals, we can be in only one place at a time; and our bodies are smaller than those of many beasts. What is more, the sensory field that surrounds us is little greater than that of many other creatures, though whether anindexical animals synthesise their successive sensations into a sensory field which they possess is questionable. At any rate, our hugely inflated world is the result not of increased sensory range but of the distinctive way we are conscious of what surrounds us and of how we accumulate, individually and collectively, those surroundings. Our surroundings have semantic, temporal and cultural depth. As Ungaretti said in his famous brief poem:

M'illumino
d'immenso.

I examined some of the features unique to human consciousness of the world in the last chapter. I described how humans have woken out of the sentience that would simply dissolve them into their immediate environment to explicit awareness of that environment and to a highly differentiated idea of what lies behind and beyond it. I suggested that we first intuited objects being 'out there', confronting us, and having a reality that exceeds what is revealed of them to us. This first awakening was to an indexical awareness which included consciousness of ourselves as embodied subjects located in the sensory field. Beyond indexical awareness of the contents of our sensory field, there was a boundless territory, marked out by a sense of possibility, of happenings and beings beyond those of which we are aware; of realities beyond those putatively underpinning the objects presented to us in our sensory field. This expansion into an unlimited field of deindexicalised awareness was linked with the sharing, pooling or collectivisation of consciousness, both directly through sharing positional advantages and indirectly through the embodiment of general possibilities in tools and other artefacts (notably and ultimately words) taking on a symbolic function. The moments of our contemporary human world – steeped in the past, directed towards a complexly differentiated future, enclosed in a multitude of interlocking, sense-making frames of reference – are fathomless. We look forward, we look back and we look sideways, into immensities that surround and engage us and in which we are deployed.

The world to which we relate is not simply a large collection of material objects. While we have intentional relations to such arrays in indexical awareness, the deindexicalised awareness that underpins the (shared) human world is not tethered to our particular location, or indeed to any location.[2] We connect with the world through our projects, expectations, thoughts, beliefs, imaginings, desires, and so on. They are intentional states but not confined to material objects or clearly delineated volumes of space-time. They appropriate sectors of the space of possibility that inflates the spatio-temporal moment, beyond the material bounds of the organism and its sensory field, into a world. The bounds of the world, the constraints on possibility, are not material; they cannot be specified through, say, a description of an array of material objects. What, then, does make up the (human) world?

In the the famous opening of his oracular *Tractatus Logico-Philosophicus*, Wittgenstein made the seemingly unexceptionable assertion that 'The world is all that is the case'.[3] He then proceeded to make the more contestable assertion that 'The world is the totality of facts, not of things'. One might think that things have a better claim than facts to being the more basic, not to say more solid, components of the world that surrounds and invades us. In the light of what has just been said, however, there seems to be a deep truth in Wittgenstein's assertion – possibly not quite the one that he wished to convey. It is that the *human* world is a totality of facts, rather than material things. More particularly, since animal experiences do not add up to worlds – as animals do not have selves, to create and house worlds, or pool their consciousness to have worlds in common – *all* worlds are nexuses of facts rather than constellations of interacting material things. We may think of the world in which we live, the world bound together in the moments of our lives, as the correlative of our distinctive human awareness, and not as being composed of the kinds of things that we imagine interacting with merely sentient organisms.

This human awareness I would like to characterise as 'propositional awareness'. The notion of propositional awareness encompasses both deindexicalised and indexical states of consciousness. The propositional form of deindexicalised awareness is 'That X is the case ...'. It is less easy to see this in indexical awareness of a particular object, which might be expressed as 'That-X-over-there'. However, as we noted in the previous chapter, much seemingly indexical awareness is of objects that have been picked out by deindexicalised awareness; actual objects that are the realisation of general possibilities proposed in deindexical awareness. The cup in front of me does not belong entirely to material space: it belongs, too, to the space of possibilities, as the realisation of one such possibility, and explicitly connected with a nexus of possibilities.

The use of the term 'propositional awareness' is not meant to imply that human consciousness is made up entirely of propositions, so that the stream of human consciousness would amount to, say, a stream of sentences (though in its most developed form, quite a lot of human consciousness is propositional in the literal sense). It is intended to draw attention to certain things. First, that human awareness above mere sentience *proposes* possibilities. Such assertions of possible existents or states of affairs may be cast in the form 'That X is the case ...' without too much distortion or 'reading into'. Against this background of possibility, even present objects and actual events are re-presented as (realised) possibilities.[4] Such awareness has the inchoate form of a subject (the proposer) related to an explicit object (that which is proposed). So, while not consisting solely of propositions in the full-blown sense, deindexicalised – and to a certain degree indexical – awareness is 'apt or meet to be propositionalised'.

Propositional awareness encompasses all those forms of consciousness that may, without misplaced explicitness, be cast in propositional form. The term therefore encompasses (a) propositional attitudes, such as the belief 'That X is the case ...'; and (b) full-blown propositions, most notably those that propose states of affairs in factual assertions. These are the two chief forms into which the seamless flow of propositional awareness – often represented, with incomplete fidelity as a stream of words – may segment. We shall say something about propositional attitudes in sections 5.5 and 9.1. For the present, I want to focus on facts.

5.2 FACTS, POSSIBILITIES AND LOGICAL SPACE

Although, according to Wittgenstein, the world is 'a totality of facts', that totality is not an indivisible whole: 'the world divides into [individual] facts' (*Tractatus*, 1.2). Each of these individuals is 'the existence of a state of affairs' (2). A state of affairs 'is a combination of objects' (2.01). Here Wittgenstein runs into difficulties, mainly because he cannot decide what objects are. He has some difficulty in coming clean about this. Objects are 'simple' (2.02) – that is to say, unstructured and not susceptible to breaking down any further – and they are 'unalterable and subsistent' (2.0271). Beyond that, they are so ill-defined that commentators have found it possible to identify them with entities as different as material particles and individual sense data.[5]

While it is therefore difficult to accept Wittgenstein's rather simplistic (and as we shall see) erroneous account of the constituents of facts, and hence of the world, his emphasis on the constitutive role of facts in the human world points to something very important. So too does his observation that the facts are 'in logical space' (1.13). This captures the relationship between facts and possibilities: a fact is a possibility that happens to be realised. Two possibilities can be compatible or incompatible. Compatibility is determined not by the availability of physical space, but by the constraints of logical space. We may think of 'p' as a possibility – a proposed reality – occupying a particular point in logical space and 'not-p' as occupying the same point. The law of non-contradiction is a generalisation to the effect that the same point in logical space cannot be doubly occupied.[6]

Spelling this out underlines the attractiveness of what, after all, is a only metaphor: 'logical space'. The veto on double occupancy in logical space – 'not both p and not-p' – makes intuitive sense in part because of the law against the double occupancy of points in physical space, captured in the minimalist notion of matter as 'a volume of exclusion or impenetrability'.[7] What is more, there are points of intersection between the two spaces. For example, it is impossible for a given physical object at a particular time to be green all over and red all over. This is apparently a spatial and a logical impossibility *de re* and *de dicto*: the exclusion is both (literally) physical and (metaphorically) conceptual. The modes of exclusion seem to meet on a single plane. This, however, raises the possibility of turning the hierarchy – metaphorical logical space, literal physical space – on its head. The impossibility of having an object that cannot simultaneously be red all over and green all over may be seen primarily as a logical impossibility and only secondarily as a spatial one because impossibilities – which by definition do not exist – cannot be thought of as located in physical space. And this applies also to possibilities: they are locationless (except perhaps inasmuch as, in some sense, they share the location of the person entertaining them). The primary space of the human world is therefore that of (logical) possibility.

There are two reasons for supporting this somewhat counter-intuitive conclusion. The first is that the only direct, physical experience of 'volumes of exclusion' is touch and this could not of itself give rise to the purely spatial notion of the impossibility of an object being both red all over and green all over. Direct interaction of the material body with the material world does not open up a space of possibilities, or a space in which impossibilities can be made explicit as being impossible. The second concerns the nature of space, that is to say of the abstract or pure 'extendedness' in which (extended) objects are to compete for locations. While we may accept that both matter and space are primitives and precede human consciousness (indeed, they designate the setting in the broadest sense in which life, and human life, emerges), we may still see the construction or re-construction of physical space within human consciousness, and its becoming *a space where some things are possible and others are not*, as a late manifestation of deindexicalised awareness.

We could put this another way, as follows. The notion of space as the sum total of all locations, as boundless, as available emptiness, is of a kind of locationless location. To the deindexicalisation of consciousness there corresponds the de-location of location into the abstract idea of space. The fully developed notion of space is the preserve of a decentred consciousness. One can, in other words, remain agnostic as to the priority of, say, physical and human space, while at the same time seeing the space of possibility as a late entry into human consciousness and mutual physical exclusion as a small sub-group of logical incompatibilities arising within that space of possibility, the logical space in which the objects of deindexicalised awareness are located.

We may think of facts as 'realised possibilities in logical space'. What does this mean? What is the nature of a fact?

5.3 A THEORY OF FACTS

It will be useful first to clarify, as far as possible, certain terms – proposition, sentence, statement (assertion), fact – in order to establish the relationhips between them. This will be little more than a gesture in the direction of a forlorn task. Each of these terms has evolved, has done so independently of the others and has both formal or technical meanings, core meanings and colloquial connotations. To vary Kant: 'of the crooked timber of human discourse, no straight thing was ever made'. A full and coherent account of these words and their relationships is simply not achievable. My remarks are intended only to serve the narrow purpose of clarifying the argument that follows.

Let us start with a 'proposition' – a 'very troublesome' term as the linguist John Lyons describes it.[8] A *proposition* is something that might be proposed. It has this general form: That ... [X is the case].[9] We could summarise the totality of propositions in the single word 'That', which captures the explicitness that characterises propositional awareness. That which is proposed and the proposing – or the use of the means by which proposing might take place – are different things. Propositions are typically, or most fully, expressed in sentences: I use a sentence to propose a proposition. Whether propositions are individuated prior to being expressed in sentences – indeed, whether they *are* 'they' – is a matter, of course, of venerable concern.

It is not even clear what kind of issue this is. Is it about the relationship between thought and language (and whether the latter precedes the former)? The assumption that it is such a question has not gone unchallenged. After all, some philosophers have denied that propositions have a particularly intimate relation with thoughts, at least in so far as the latter are understood as psychological entities. Russell, for example, argued that a proposition consists of 'the entities indicated by words' and included among such entities 'A man, a moment, a number, a class, a relation, or anything else that can be mentioned'.[10] Propositions, that is to say, contain things-in-the-world and so cannot be psychological entities. As Richard Gaskell has put it:

> Russellian propositions are meanings of declarative sentences, and are composed in some way of the worldly entities introduced by the semantically significant parts of those sentences, centrally objects and properties.[11]

Russell did not seem to be certain whether propositions were individuated by sentences or whether they actually existed independently of sentences, being only *expressed*, or made manifest, or picked out or up, through them. In the latter case, sentences would merely draw a line round, and present, some worldly state of affairs. This suggestion is not as perspicuous as it might be because it is not clear that one can maintain a sharp distinction between expressing and individuating a proposition; or between expressing a proposition and bringing a proposition into existence. Do unexpressed propositions actually exist? If they do exist, what are they composed of? Bits of the world? Mixtures of concrete objects, abstract objects and relationships between them? This, I suspect, is one of those cases where there is simply *no fact of the matter* – at least in part because of the aforementioned crookedness of the discursive timber. The notion that declarative sentences express propositions, and that propositions are the meanings of declarative sentences, while consistent seems circular and, because of this, takes us no further. Certainly, to make a proposition *the meaning of a sentence* seems to empty it of worldly contents, unless one has the rather odd notion that meanings are scattered over the world.

It is tempting to leave the status of propositions unsettled and simply stand by the notion that they are expressed in declarative sentences. But this would be to lose the point of the wider notion of propositional awareness; specifically to lose the link between the kinds of propositions that seem to be expressed in sentences (such as facts) and propositional attitudes; the common root – beneath language – between propositional discourse and propositional attitudes; more importantly to lose what is indicated by the form 'That X is the case'. I would like therefore to hold to the notion of a form of consciousness that is an undifferentiated mass of propositional awareness which can be sliced into individual propositions. These are individuated when sentences – or some other form of expression – do the slicing.[12] The enduring status of a proposition, its objectivity, is most easily captured in the notion of the meaning-content common to all the tokens or instances of a particular sentence-type. While the question of the degree of independence of propositions from the language in which they are expressed remains unclear, we can leave this unresolved because our ultimate quarry is not 'the proposition' but a cardinal manifestation of propositional awareness, 'the fact', to which we shall come presently.

Sentences, compared with propositions, seem fairly straightforward. Or they do, once we have distinguished token sentences from type sentences; the sentence as something uttered on a particular occasion from the sentence as an abstract, theoretical entity in the linguist's model of the language-system; and the declarative sentence mobilised in making a particular assertion (the actual string of tokens – sounds, marks on the page – being used) from the string of tokens used to mention, or signify, their types. After that, all should be plain sailing. Nevertheless, we are still in difficulty, because the notion of a sentence *expressing* a proposition is still obscure and would remain so, even if we had sorted out the nature of propositions and settled the question of their independence or otherwise from sentences individuating them. Even so, let us stick to the notion that a proposition is something that is typically expressed in a declarative sentence and pretend that we know what we are talking about.

A statement (or assertion) is made by the utterance of a sentence (or proxy for a sentence) on a particular occasion. This is also not as easy as it looks at first sight. For what is asserted will depend not only upon the words that are strung together, but upon the context in the widest sense: what has been said before, the spatio-temporal location of the speaker and hearer, what has happened before, including what has passed between speaker and hearer, and what is deemed relevant. Assertions acquire a determinate meaning only in the context of the lives of speakers and listeners. My understanding what you are saying presupposes that I have, for all sorts of reasons, some general idea of what you are getting at.

Let us, nevertheless, press on. We come at last to facts – the building bricks, according to the *Tractatus*, of the world. It is important to note, first of all, the singular: 'the world'. This is an idealised totality; the asymptote of the convergence of the worlds of individual conscious beings; at any rate, the world experienced in common, not experienced singly and separately; the world as the opposite pole to the multiple solitary sensory fields of sentient creatures. Facts, as the building blocks of this world, belong to deindexicalised awareness. The world is (early) Wittgensteinian in proportion as it is purely the object of deindexicalised awareness.

This is not to suggest that facts are in some sense mental, that they are constructs of consciousness, bits of deindexicalised awareness. So what are they? Facts, like propositions, are slippery entities and, like propositions, they slip back and forth across the boundaries of language. They are characteristically formulated in sentences and seem inseparable from them. The fact that the Battle of Hastings took place in 1066 is difficult to separate from the sentence 'The Battle of Hastings took place in 1066', or one of its synonyms. It is easy to sympathise with David Armstrong's dismissal of facts as non-entities – as mere 'tautological accusatives' of true propositions, notwithstanding that it is *sentences* rather than propositions that seem to be the source of the accusatives in question.[13] Sympathy is in order not simply because it is impossible to pick out individual facts – so that we can identify or discuss them – except by means of sentences structured in that way but also because there are difficulties in the way of anyone (such as early Wittgenstein) who thinks of the world 'out there' as consisting of facts, as opposed to objects and their arrangements and the events and processes that take place in them.

For a start, we cannot literally *point* to facts (with our index fingers), though, once the facts have been articulated, we may seem to be able to do so. A group of objects and their arrangements may 'realise' a fact in the sense of meeting the truth condition of a factual statement to the effect that this arrangement obtains. (We shall return to the notion of 'truth conditions' when we discuss the Correspondence Theory of Truth in the next chapter.) It becomes equally evident that the facts are not 'out there' in a simple sense when we ask a question such as 'How many facts are there in this room?' There is no answer to this because the number of facts depends upon the number of types of sentences that are articulating those facts. Indeed, the facts seem to be articulated and generated in the same breath. The facts of the room, after all, could include not only obvious facts, such as 'There is a cat in the room', but also less obvious ones such as:

a) There is a cat making its sixth appearance in the room.
b) There is a cat 18 inches from my keyboard.
c) The line drawn between the cat and the keyboard is at right angles to the shadow cast by the window frame and at an angle of 10 degrees to the meridian line drawn on the atlas open in the room next door.
d) The cat's presence in the room is annoying to a person like me who is trying to concentrate.

In short, there is no limit to the number of facts that could be articulated with respect to the contents of the room.

Now it could be argued that the unanswerable question as to how many facts are in the room is no different from the unanswerable question as to how many objects there are in the room. Even if we leave aside abstract or semi-abstract objects (such as 'the cat's breathing pattern') and confine ourselves to what may be roughly called material objects, the question cannot be answered simply by inspecting the room and counting its contents. We shall need a ruling as to what counts as *one* object. Is the cat one object or is it a collection of objects – paw, whiskers, etc. – to be separately counted? Is the computer one object or does it consist of a keyboard plus a processor plus a screen, etc.? Is a ream of paper one object or 400? There is no way of determining in a consistent fashion what counts as a single object so that even the most conscientious attempt to enumerate all the objects in the room would be bound to fail because of the description-dependency of the boundaries of 'an' object. The number of objects depends upon the acuity of linguistic discrimination.

There is a deep connection between our inability to say how many facts there are in a room and our inability to say how many objects there are. What counts as 'one' is in each case language-dependent.[14] In neither case, however, does this mean that the answer to the question lies *entirely within* language. In the case of objects, what needs to be settled is a definition of the objects to be counted; after that, the answer is determined extra-linguistically. If this cannot be determined, then there is no answer. Linguistic relativity, in other words, is brought to an end *within* language by clarifying what it is to be counted. Once the question is settled, then the answer lies 'out there'. I can linguistically manipulate the answer to the question 'How many things are there in the room?' but not the answer to the question 'How many cats are there in the room?' or 'How many articles of clothing are there in the room?' (if we make clear in advance what is to count as an article of clothing). The answers, then, lie not within language but within the room.

Language, in other words, legislates over the question but not over the answer. Where language seems to legislate over the answer, the question is not only unanswerable intra-linguistically but unanswerable period – or not without further clarification. This is an important point of difference between the question 'How many objects are there are in the room?' and the question 'How many facts are there in the room?' We cannot in the latter case so clarify the question as to separate the contribution of language to the answer from the contribution of the external world. Any attempt to clarify what we are asking by further specifying the kind of facts that are to be counted would be unhelpful. 'How many facts of a certain size are there in the room?' is clearly an unhelpful qualification. But it is equally unhelpful to qualify the question as follows: 'How many facts about the cat are there in the room?'[15] The truth is that there is no fact of the matter as to how many facts there are in a particular quarter of 'out there'.

Matters of fact cannot be extricated from the language in which they are expressed. They do not exist 'out there' in the world. To put this rather dramatically: matter does not secrete facts and arrangements of matter do not of themselves form facts. Facts are *facta*: they are made. They are made in articulate (and consequently collectivised) human consciousness. Facts exist only in so far as they are picked out and they can be picked out only linguistically. An expression of a fact in a declarative sentence gives it distinct existence, gives it boundaries, makes it count as 'one fact'. Sentences, as has often been pointed out, individuate facts.

Facts are not, however, mere 'tautological accusatives' of propositions, sentences or assertions. While they are made, they are *not* made up. While sentence-making human consciousness is necessary for there to be discrete facts – i.e. facts period – it does not create the truth conditions of facts. There are no facts in or about the room in the absence of articulate human consciousness, but this does not give me, the current inhabitant of the room, a licence to print whatever facts I like. For example, the following are *not* present facts in the room:

a) There is a cat making its first appearance in the room.
b) There is a cat 19 inches from my keyboard.
c) The line drawn between the cat and the keyboard is at 45 degrees to the shadow of cast by the window frame and at an angle of 11 degrees to the meridian line drawn on the atlas open in the room next door.
d) The cat's presence in the room is not annoying to a person like me who is trying to concentrate.

Although I created these counterfactuals, these unrealised possibilities, and they are very much rooted in my present situation, there is an important point at which I cede control over them – namely, when they appear before the tribunal of experience. Then they are denied the status of facts. (This is not, of course, altered by the further, higher-order fact that I can bring some of them about – that, for example, I can place a cat 19 inches from my keyboard.) I can, of course, *propose* what I believe to be facts: this is merely an articulate mode of entertaining possibilities. But my proposing them cuts no ice 'out there'.

We may see facts as the result of the interaction between articulate human consciousness and an encountered state of affairs 'out there' –

between what Kant called the 'spontaneous' and the 'receptive' powers of the mind. 'The facts' lie neither wholly 'out there' in the extra-linguistic or the extra-conscious material world nor wholly 'in here' in articulate human consciousness. Three objects in a room do not themselves bear within them the fact '*That* there are three objects in the room'. The cat, the laptop and the chair do not join together of their own accord into a group of three things seen as exemplars of the single kind 'objects'. If they were really able to establish a grouping of their own, there is no reason why the laptop and the chair should not join forces as 'two inanimate objects in a room'. If they *were* self-presenting as components as facts, they would be faced with a dilemma as to how to choose between an indefinite number of facts to join. Nor do they relate themselves to the room they are in. After all, they could equally well relate themselves to the house they are in, the country they are in, or the century they are in.

States of affairs have to be picked out by a conscious human being that puts them together. This in itself requires the 'That' that picks out part of what is there and makes it be *there* and makes it *factually* the case. This is the fundamental character of propositional awareness. The picking out and the articulation occur almost at the same time and it is difficult to separate the two, especially when one wants to refer to what it is that has been picked out. This is why it is so easy to make either of two opposite errors: that of overlooking the role of language in the making of facts; and that of exaggerating the role of language in the making of facts.[16] And that is why the concept of a proposition proved so 'troublesome': it resisted being located entirely within and entirely outside language and yet it wasn't ready for the 'third realm' we have identified for facts. To think of a proposition as being made up of the kinds of 'worldly entities' Russell spoke of creates all sorts of interesting difficulties, not the least being those created by false propositions.[17] To think of a proposition being made up of linguistic terms poses a different kind of problem – namely, that of differentiating propositions from the sentences in which they are said to be expressed. Expression would simply boil down to the realisation in a token sentence (or, more precisely, a token utterance) of a sentence-type. Even so, this would seem to render the notion of a proposition redundant. We are best, therefore, leaving the notion of a proposition to its troubles and deal with that of a fact, where things are sufficiently well developed for analysis to be more than mere speculation about customary use or, alternatively, definition by stipulation. There is, that is to say, no answer to the question of what a proposition is, though I hope none the less that 'propositional awareness' – awareness 'That' [X is the case] – is sufficient, despite the crookedness of the discursive company the word 'proposition' keeps.

Fully-fledged facts, then, arise out of the interaction of three components: human consciousness; the system of language; and the way things are 'out there'. They are not internal to human consciousness; nor are they intra-linguistic; nor are they inherent in the material world. They may be seen as aspects of what is there, lifted up from that reality and given independent existence through being formulated in language, so that they can be made available on a page or broadcast in the air. The reality from which they are extracted is not, of course, the world of objective material presences but a world of significances, constrained in part by objective material presences. Facts are dissected-out parts of the sense things make to us, or of things in so far as they are significant or intelligible. 'The cat is in the room' does not capture the entirety of, does not exhaust, the material objects in question. The designation of a particular piece of living matter as 'a cat' connects it with a whole system of classification under which many different kinds of living creatures may be classified. The fact that one sense does not exhaust the entirety of the cat and no sense at all touches something we may call the-cat-in-itself is clear from the fact that we may secure reference to it by other terms – for example, 'that lazy lump' – that have quite different senses. And we may encounter it in many different ways, as, for example, when we stroke it, respond to its demand to be fed or trip over it in the dark.

Individual words – even those words that seem to capture the 'canonical' sense of the object and call it by its 'correct' name (as when we refer to the cat as a 'cat') – materialise only one sense which is a minute part of the totality of possible senses inherent in the object. The notion of a 'canonical sense' of a material object is as vacuous as that of the 'canonical appearance' of the object, which we criticised in section 3.3, and for the same reason. Material objects are precisely those things which exceed the senses that can be extracted from them. This is connected with the fact that there is a multitude of ways they may be experienced; indeed, it is inherent in the intuition of objects that they exceed all sense experiences of them.

While material objects are a convenient point of mental repair, a refuge of stability in a conceptual quicksand, this is probably the wrong place to start when we think about facts, if only because factual knowledge (especially where it is articulated in sentences) is a sophisticated, quite late expression of deindexicalised awareness. Nevertheless, starting here gives us a foothold on some rather complex and elusive ideas. We may think of a material object – an inexhaustable source of appearances, endlessly re-classifiable – as having a nimbus of sense around it. The sense is as it were 'tethered' to the object and the possibilities that the object holds out for the subject. The nimbus cannot be separated from the object and cannot be spatially divided from it. To put this very awkwardly (because we have to use language, and rather explicit meta-linguistic thought, to get hold of something that is intrinsically pre-linguistic, and we cannot bypass language by pointing to it directly[18]), it is not possible, outside of language, to separate the qualities or properties from the object that has them. The black colour cannot be separated from the fur of the cat. The annoyingness of the cat's presence – 'The fact that its presence is annoying' – cannot, without language, be separated from its presence, any more than the presence of the cat can be separated from the cat itself. The senses that are, through language, materialised independently of the cat – variously the classes under which it falls, the significance it may have, the possibilities the speaker has in mind – cannot exist by themselves except as part of a fact expressed linguistically. Language slices up the nimbus of sense and materialises slices in terms that have a general meaning. The following very crude diagram captures this notion in its most simplified form:

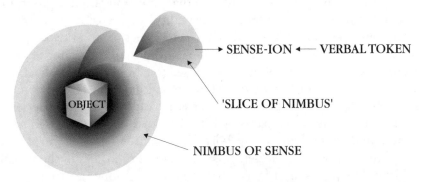

I have, in a previous presentation, called the slices 'sense-ions', by analogy with chemical ions such as H^+ which cannot exist by themselves and have to be joined up into molecules.[19] These, I believe, are the 'objects' that Wittgenstein was looking for or the 'entities' that Russell believed to be the substance of propositions. They are senses in the Fregean sense, inasmuch as they give linguistic access to extra-linguistic entities such as cats and splashes of colour and cities. Language makes it possible for them to exist independently of the objects with which, in the extra-linguistic world, they are inextricably associated.

Appropriately joined up, they form the facts that are expressed – individuated, brought to independent being – in sentences to make assertions. The connections between words in a sentence merge these

sense-ions, these part-senses, in the realisation, or materialisation, of
one potential relationship between them. The factual assertion captures
– pulls a thread out of – the interpenetrating aura of significance or
intelligibility of a world of things. This is as true of simple factual
assertions such as 'The cat is in the room' or 'That bloody animal is in
the warmest place in the house' as in more complex factual assertions
such as 'The acceleration of an object is proportional to the force
applied and inversely proportional to its mass'. In each case, the fact is
synthesised out of components whose sense is *identical*[20] to the part-
senses that make up the state of affairs the sentence picks out:

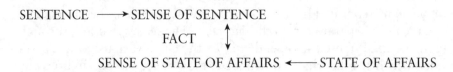

SENTENCE ⟶ SENSE OF SENTENCE

FACT

SENSE OF STATE OF AFFAIRS ⟵ STATE OF AFFAIRS

The fact is the identity between the sense of sentences and the sense of
the state of affairs. It is not to be found either in a sentence or the state of
affairs.

Thus, the reality picked out by a factual assertion is not a miserable
internal accusative of a sentence: that reality, a state of affairs, has an
existence independent of the sentence – of its structure and the occasions
of its utterance – and, indeed, this is the condition of the sentence being
used to make a statement of fact as opposed to a false assertion. Facts are
made, but they are not *made up*. They are neither internal to language
nor are they merely sweated out by matter in response to our experience
or our gaze – even our collective gaze. They have to be expressed to be
individuated, and hence to exist. Facts are between proposed
possibilities individuated in sentences and states of affairs in the world.

This middle position of facts – between propositional awareness and
the world – is important to the conception of truth. As we shall discuss
in the next chapter, truth requires explicit consciousness (as the primary
'existence condition' of truth), language (as the subsidiary existence
condition of truth – the condition of individuated assertion) and the
relevant state of affairs which will determine whether what is asserted
actually is true. Truth, as we shall see, is not 'correspondence to facts'
but, at least in part, the correspondence which facts constitute.

It is important not to anchor our discussion to a narrow notion of
factual reality as being composed of arrays of present, particular
material objects, such as the cup being next to me as I type. We have
already mentioned one, fundamental reason for not doing so: facts
belong to deindexicalised awareness and, contrary to what might be

thought, this is as true of the facts about my immediate surroundings as it is of facts about remote events of which I have had no experience myself, such as the Battle of Agincourt. All facts are equidistant from me because they are neither located, nor located with respect to my body. Wittgenstein's observation that a

> Complex is not like fact. For I can e.g. say of a complex that it moves from one place to another, but not of a fact.[21]

underlines the 'locationlessness' of facts. And his next sentence identifies the source of that locationlessness:

> But *that* this complex is now situated here is a fact. (italics mine)

The de-location lies in the 'that' – the propositional awareness that is the background out of which specific factual knowledge crystallises with the help of language. De-location encompasses not only manifestly locationless entities, such as the fact that the Battle of Agincourt took place in 1415, but also facts about things that are here and now. This underlines how facts are neither things that are 'on the surface of the globe' nor are they in the minds of individuals, nor, in some mysterious way, inside language.[22]

This is worth pressing a little further. The cat is certainly in the room, but the fact that the cat is in the room, or (more simply) 'That the cat is in the room', is not in the room. The sentence 'The cat is in the room' – as both token and type – belongs to language. The fact expressed in the sentence does not; otherwise every grammatical sentence (and perhaps a few ungrammatical ones) would express a fact. These obvious points are often concealed by the sloppy way in which we use the word 'facts' to mean both the state of affairs expressed in a sentence and the expression of that state of affairs. The former may be on the surface of the globe but it is not a fact; and the latter is a fact but is not on the surface of the globe. A failure to grasp this has got some distinguished minds into a mess. Take this passage from J. L. Austin:

> Phenomena, events, situations, states of affairs are commonly supposed to be genuinely in-the-world, and even Strawson admits events are so. Yet surely we can say that they *are facts*. The collapse of the Germans is an event and is a fact – was an event and was a fact.[23]

Of course, if facts were 'things on the surface of the globe', there could be neither negative facts such as 'the absence of X', nor abstract facts.

Sentences expressing facts are about objects but, even in those cases where the object in question is a particular and actually present, the object is accessed through general senses as a (realised) possibility, and is therefore, as a piece of factual reality, locationless. As an object of discourse it is abstracted.[24] Facts do not belong to the space of the material world surrounding the embodied subject asserting, or acknowledging, them. They are not related to one another in physical space: the fact that the cat is sitting on the windowsill is not next to the fact that the windowsill is being sat on by the cat or the fact that the windowsill is under the cat. Facts are, as Wittgenstein said, set out in the logical space that is the world. 'The world' is meant here in the sense adopted earlier: an idealised totality of deindexicalised awareness. It is a shared space, a shared product, contributed to by all humanity, though the available world – available, that is, to particular individuals – will be only a portion (a very small portion) of that.

The coherence of facts is not that of a spatial array but a logical one in 'a space of general possibility'. Facts are possibilities that have been realised. The sum total of all facts is the sum total of all possibilities that could be realised in the history of the world. If certain facts obtain at a particular time, other facts cannot. One realised possibility makes another possibility unrealisable.

Given that the space of possibility, the human world, is a collective product, the facts, too, will be a collective product. Facts are the paradigm items of human knowledge and their collective status is reflected in Davidson's observation that the basis of knowledge is 'a community of minds'.[25] We examined the early stages of the communalisation of minds in section 4.5, when we discussed pointing. Communalisation, while vastly extended, and made immeasurably more dense by language, must precede language. We identified tools and artefacts as key linguistic precursors: pre-facts on the ground. They intensify the sense of the inner reality of others, and so deepen the awareness of them as being like ourselves, both knowing and ignorant.

All of this will underline the complexity of ordinary declarative knowledge and its distance – in its most straightforward form of factual knowledge – from animal sensing. Written down facts – even seemingly simple ones such as 'The cat is in the room' – belong to a very late stage of deindexicalised awareness: a long, collective journey of humanity separates the first inklings of propositional awareness from the inkings that now dominate human lives. Much has changed. But, as I hope will have been clear, something hasn't.[26]

5.4 FACTS, KNOWLEDGE, EXPERIENCES, THE TRIBUNAL OF EXPERIENCE, THE EVIDENCE OF THE SENSES

The world of facts is a shared world. Facts are the most developed and copious fruit of the deindexicalisation of awareness; they are the paradigm item or atom of knowledge. They are objective in a cluster of linked senses. First of all, they are available to everyone, if the circumstances are right. A fact that only one person could ever know hardly warrants the status of fact. (This is connected with the disdain with which *ex officio* first-person authority is held.) Facts are up for checking. If I assert that a cat is in the room, I can look in the room to check that my belief is correct, and so can anyone else. This is one aspect of the separation of the fact – realised in my awareness of it, as part of my articulate awareness – from my subjectivity, from the totality of my sense experience. The fact is anyone's, everyone's and no one's. Second, a fact is part of a body of knowledge – a world – that is internally connected in a way that is quite different from my connectedness with myself, from, say, my sequence of sense experiences.

Facts do not boil down to sense experiences. When I check my factual assertion that there is a cat in my room by 'having a look', what I see is both more and less than what is in my assertion. I see more than the content of my assertion, inasmuch as I do not see a mere instantiation of the general concepts of a 'cat' and 'being in my room'. I see a cat with many features over and above what has been asserted. The cat is in a specific position, is in a definite posture, has a sheen on its coat, is in a particular state, none of which is relevant to the fact that I am checking. Actuality always exceeds what is asserted of it because no finite set of assertions could exhaust a piece of reality. This is well-trodden territory. Of more interest is the observation, much commented on in Anglo-American philosophy of the last few decades, that what I see falls short of what I have asserted.

While my observation is adequate confirmation of the assertion I have made, that assertion, given that it is composed of general terms, points to a network of potential assertions, and the beliefs that might prompt them, that are not confirmed by a quick glance in my room. The assertion that what is in my room is a cat seems to some philosophers to commit me to all sorts of things that I may not have meant but I have said none the less. These include further facts; information about cats (some of which I may not know), so that my assertion amounts to the claim that (say) 'There is an animal in my room which metabolises food using a particular enzymic pathway'. And they include further consequences, so that, if the cat is in my room, it is not in another room; it is in my room at 2.15 p.m. on 20 August 2004; it is 93,000,001 miles from the sun; and so on. (This is a version of the sling-shot argument which I will deal with in section 6.4.)

Whether one accepts that I have committed myself to all these additional things, it cannot be doubted that any given fact is part of a nexus of facts, belonging, as Wittgenstein said, to a logical space – realised possibilities, of compatible or incompatible concepts. No fact is an island – or an atom. And in accepting that, we go beyond the obvious point that when we say what is the case, we also imply that the opposite is not the case; that when we assert that 'p', we also assert that 'not not-p' and that 'not not not not-p', and so on.

What are the consequences of the observation that the experiences we seek out to confirm, or refute, factual assertions both exceed and fall short of the asserted content? It reminds us just how complex the relationship is between sense experience and knowledge. In particular, it demonstrates the fatuity of the notion that knowledge is heaped-up experience, condensed sentience, or a mind-portable summary of actual or possible sense impressions. Popper, of course, famously made this point against the reduction of knowledge – and in particular universal general statements (such as 'All swans are white') – to the summation of experience. His particular target was the identification of the meaning of general factual statements with either a state of affairs that would verify them or with the means by which they might be verified (operationalism).[27] No general statement, he argued, could be proof against the future discovery of counter-instances that would overturn it. He replaced verifiability with falsifiability as the criterion for a genuinely contentful assertion.

The position I wish to advance here regarding the relationship between (true) knowledge and sense experience is even more radically hostile to naive positivism than Popper's. Of course the battle-lines have become more ragged since the heroic days of the conflict between verificationism and falsificationism. Those philosophers who believe in a close connection between the meaning of factual assertions and the conditions that would make them true do not, for the most part, subscribe to the idea of a simple cashing out of such assertions into a set of sense experiences. It is acknowledged that a fact also occupies a place in a network of other facts, beliefs and concepts. Facts are objective not only in the sense that they can be confirmed by the experiences of others but also in the sense that they belong to the pooled awareness, the 'community of minds', that Davidson spoke of. When we check the truth of a fact by, for example, going to see or listen or touch or to sniff for ourselves, we do not re-enter the solitude of the sentient beast. Under such circumstances, where experience becomes confirmatory evidence, even sensations are deeply social and riddled with those abstract concepts that belong to 'the community of minds'. While the audit trail may lead from time to time to our immediate experiences, we do not as auditors regain beastly innocence.

The profound difference between knowledge and 'summed experience' has been emphasised by those many writers (such as Davidson) who have pointed out that beliefs, even factual ones, are not directly exposed to what Quine called 'the tribunal of experience'. This can be seen most clearly in the case of science, where at the cutting edge are tentative hypotheses that are very vulnerable to the outcome of observation and in the core are basic conceptions that will take an earthquake to shift. Our everyday understanding of the world also has its exposed outworks – where there are beliefs that fall at the first contrary observation – and its root convictions stored in the innermost keep. The most robust beliefs are those that are interwoven with many others. Contrary observations are going to have a hard time overthrowing them and may themselves be discredited. If I see my cat flying without support I am more likely to doubt my eyesight or sanity than to adopt the belief that cats can levitate and the laws of gravity are waived for their convenience.

Science, as Quine said, 'is a linguistic structure that is keyed to observation at some points'.[28] Unfortunately, this does not lead him (and many philosophers influenced by him) to the right conclusion. Science, he argues,

> like the animal's simple induction over innate similarities, is still a biological device for anticipating experience.[29]

The linguistic structure that distances the body of scientific knowledge from the lability of daily experience and creates enduring (or comparatively enduring) truths is composed of terms that, by association, stand proxy for experience.

> Mastery of the term 'red' is the acquisition of the habit of assenting when the term is queried in the presence of red and only in the presence of red.[30]

The link between animal induction (similar, appropriate, survival-favouring responses to similar stimuli) and science is, for Quine, language – whose terms carry their charge of meaning through their power to stimulate verbal behaviour.

This is wrong and, with respect to our present concerns, importantly so.[31] Knowledge goes beyond induction from experience – or conditioned response to experience – in several respects. First, it is a collective product: it has lost its roots in the individual sentient creature. Deindexicalised awareness is decentred, deorganismal – remote from sense experience. It is therefore cut off from anything that could be called a 'stimulus' – at least in the biological sense. This hardly needs reiteration. (The implication that, at this level, awareness is also modulated into active inquiry, beyond energetic trail following, will be examined in section 7.3.) Second, and more fundamentally, knowledge *originates* with the intuition that there is something beyond sense experience: the object of knowledge (indeed, any object) by definition exceeds the appearances it has to the knower. It is, as Stroud put it, 'underdetermined' by whatever we get through our senses: this, as we have already pointed out, is not a a critique of knowledge but a revelation of its essential nature. The known is surrounded by, or permeated with, the sense of the unknown. Since no experiences could exhaust the known object, no number of experiences could legitimately extinguish uncertainty.

This shows that Popper was right in principle; unfortunately, he was not radical enough. Our radicalisation of Popper extends his observations to everyday life. Life is full of random events and our 'devices for anticipating experience' are imperfect. Knowledge, unlike sentience, knows this. The attempts to improve our anticipations of experience through identifying the laws that govern change – the interactions between things, the unfolding of events – result in very powerful predictive tools but they are not omnipotent. Science gives us only better and better odds. What is more, things never turn out quite as expected. Even when, as usually happens, things occur as planned – the bus turns up on time, the technology works, the friend reacts in the amicable way we have been accustomed to expect – there will still be an infinitude of details that were not foreseen. Our anticipations do not encompass all the *tissues* of any event. What happens is at best the partly expected.

While it is true that factual knowledge – or knowledge claims – are judged in 'the tribunal of experience', we need to look beyond this to think about the occasions for, and the nature of, the sittings of this tribunal. Only under certain conditions – that of inquiry and explicit uncertainty in response to claims, the entertainment of possibilities, the proposals advanced by propositional awareness – is experience 'tribunalised' and broken up into sittings. In general, we may describe these conditions as being typically when lower-level knowledge is presented as 'evidence' of a higher-level claim. For example, I might check the assertion that all European swans are white by having a look at a few swans. At a more homely level, I might confirm my belief that the cat is in the room by popping my head round the door and experiencing a cat-in-the-room scenario. Even at this lowest level, we do not return to mere sense impressions. Experience-as-evidence, as evidential support for knowledge claims, is denatured: it is cut up into fragments of sentence that, if they are not sentence-shaped or at least sentenceable, are at the least fact-shaped. Fact-shaped experience is not mere sentence. So while we may move up and down the levels of knowledge, we cannot reach back from a putative 'lowest level' of knowledge to wordless sentence. Experience as evidence is still collectivised and in many respects belongs to a space of logic.[32]

This must not be understood to imply that experience is intermittent, that we merely enjoy what John McDowell called 'bits of experiential intake'.[33] Experience is in bits and counts as 'intake' only in relation to an evidence-seeking activity, as when I am making specific observations to support an assertion. Even then, it is not as 'bitty' as the intermittency of the sittings of the tribunal suggests. When, for example, I am looking round for an object that someone says is in the room, the 'looking' round does not break down to a countable number of discrete observations, though, when I have found the object, I may report my experience of finding it as a sentence-shaped, discrete observation. What is more, the sitting of the tribunal may not always be convened in order to judge – that is to say to check – particular assertions with their implicit or explicit claims to knowledge. I may just be vaguely 'on the lookout', as when I make myself uncommittedly available for something valuable that might be found or something nice that might turn up. The tribunal of experience might be even less formal than this: its inquiry might be so open that it has no clear question.

What is more, the tribunal has to sit on, or in, something: its court-rooms are built out of those experiences that are not relevant to the question at issue. Our experience does not break up into knowledge or the observation/evidence that is sought in tribunals. We are more exposed than this. Even the scientist in the laboratory testing a claim about the fundamental nature of matter is a sentient creature in receipt of, enclosed by, even immersed in, a multitude of merged experiences that amount to being in that place at a particular time. Just as knowledge does not boil down to compressed sense experience, so sense experience does not amount narrowly to a set of claims, or the internal accusative of a set of potential claims, which are vulnerable to refutation. Experience is not (primarily) evidence.

We do not, for the most part, 'visit' experience or 'requisition' it merely to verify claims. There is bodily being-there that is a necessary background to the act of checking the higher-level abstract contents of our knowledge. This, in turn, is a necessary condition of our knowing what we know. The knower has to exist as a sentient being and knowledge exists only as it is instantiated in such beings. Knowledge, in short, requires bearers. If we fail to notice this, then we shall be in danger of repeating the fallacies of anti-psychologism, denying the psychological contents of knowledge and propositional attitudes such as beliefs. Though much of our life consists in dealing with facts, and that 'The facts in logical space are the world' (*Tractatus* 1.13), that is to say the ideal totality of a common world, we are nevertheless individuals in that common world and we do not dissolve without residue into our commonality. We are individual beings who have token thoughts, and our own realisations of facts, our own take on bits of logical space. As token beings, we are embodied, surrounded by things that are not facts, albeit they may become so as soon as we specify or individuate them, that is to say, articulate them.

The key point is that knowledge cannot reach down to the sentience of individuals, in the sense of being entirely cashed out as sense experience, and equally the sentient creatures we are cannot evaporate into impersonal knowledge.[34] As the gulf between knowledge and sentience gets wider and deeper, so we humans who remain sentient creatures even as we become ever more knowing animals are increasingly deeply divided within ourselves and increasingly lost in the ever-expanding space of possibility within which we live our lives. This division began with the Existential Intuition when we became aware that we were, and were not, our bodies. It amounts to the opening of a wound whose healing is a fundamental preoccupation of humankind, as we shall discuss in Chapter 10.

5.5 PROPOSITIONAL ATTITUDES

Propositional awareness has two main manifestations: formal propositions expressed in sentences that, at their most developed, assert facts; and propositional attitudes, such as beliefs, desires, expectations and thoughts. Propositional attitudes separate us as much from animals as the higher-order fact that we relate to a collective world that, unlike the *Umwelt* of a beast, is comprised of facts set out in logical space.

Sufferers from Darwinosis, who want to narrow the gap between human beings and animals, have a choice of strategies: to deny that humans have propositional attitudes; or to assert that animals do have them, just like humans. Neurophilosophers typically choose the first strategy, arguing that propositional attitudes belong to a pre-scientific or 'folk psychology'. I will not contest this view here because I have, I think satisfactorily, dealt with the assault on so-called 'folk psychology' elsewhere.[35] Instead, I will focus on the idea, in my view mistaken, that animals have propositional attitudes – notably beliefs, which, as Davidson has pointed out, play a central role among propositional attitudes.

One of the strongest reasons against ascribing beliefs to animals is that any given belief has to be part of a complex network of beliefs. One cannot have a single belief. Consider the example first discussed by Norman Malcolm of a dog chasing a cat. The cat races up a tree. The dog waits at the base of another tree, barking. It is tempting to think of the dog as barking up the wrong tree because it is 'in the grip of a mistaken belief'; namely, 'That the cat is hiding in this tree …' The temptation should be avoided because any formulation of the cat's belief involves concepts – 'tree', 'cat', 'hiding' – themselves rooted in general beliefs that no dog could have. For example, the concept of a cat is very complex indeed and incorporates a good deal of knowledge that it would be absurd to attribute to a dog. The same is true for tree and hiding. Beliefs can be individuated only within a dense network of related beliefs: each belief requires a world of further beliefs to give it content and identity.

This argument – whose classical expression is in Donaldson's 1984 paper[36] – is entirely sound, but vulnerable to a counter-argument. When a dog believes that a cat is up a tree, it doesn't have to be in possession of all of the components of the belief network that Davidson has suggested. After all, when *I* believe a cat is up a tree, there are many things I do not know about cats in general or this cat in particular. I know very little about the genealogy or the metabolism of cats, or the number of hairs they typically have. As for the particular cat, I might well be unaware of the identity of its owner, its sex, its location in the tree, and so on. There is no principled way of separating those parts of the belief–knowledge–concept network I need to have in order to entertain a belief about a cat and those that are quite unnecessary. It is not possible, therefore, to identify a point at which belief vanishes and we have only inputs of stimuli and outputs of behaviour.[37]

It is better, therefore, to think that Davidson's point is that it is impossible to attribute one belief to a dog without attributing to the dog a whole network of beliefs, many of which it could not possibly entertain. As he himself says:

> there may be no fixed list of beliefs on which any particular thought depends. Nevertheless much true belief is necessary. Some beliefs of the sort required are general … Some are logical … To have a single propositional

attitude is to have a largely correct logic, in the sense of having a pattern of beliefs that logically cohere.[38]

Another counter-argument would be that one is loading the dice against animals by expressing the propositional attitudes in question in linguistic form – though this is of course necessary in order to individuate the beliefs and get the argument off the ground. It is obvious that the dog does not have the *explicit*, individuated belief 'That cat is up this tree'. But if we refrained from formulating the belief in question in human language, which is heavy with knowledge and concepts, all of which belongs to a logical space that extends infinitely in all directions, then we might ascribe it to the dog without running into problems of attributing undoggish concepts, etc. to it.

This counter-argument is actually both more alarming and less impressive. For it leads rapidly to the notion that dogs, and other animals, have *implicit* beliefs that are active, real and individuated, and yet not available to language. Once we concede the notion of implicit beliefs, then we are on the edge of a slippery slope, at the bottom which lies a good deal of lunacy. It becomes possible to attributes beliefs (and other propositional attitudes) to all sentient creatures; for example, to argue that the spider spins a web in the belief, expectation or knowledge that this will trap flies. There is no defensible point of cut-off between belief-expressing behaviour and simple behaviour.

The belief-everywhere view actually joins hands with the belief-nowhere view. Functionalist (anti-folk psychology) philosophers argue that, since the same piece of behaviour could be explained equally well by invoking causal relations between input and output as by invoking causal relations between input and output *plus* a propositional attitude in the middle, the principle of economy demands that we should dispense with the middle man, the propositional attitude. This argument fails on two counts. First, it has not yet proved possible to explain very complex (i.e. ordinary everyday) human behaviour without resort to propositional attitudes such as beliefs, knowings, thoughts and purposes. Second, and more importantly, there is introspective evidence that we have propositional attitudes and we are able, for the most part, when challenged to say what they are, for the most part accurately. (The claim that they are purely epiphenomenal and that they are not causally efficacious does not dispose of their phenomenal reality. What is more, it is only a claim and one, what is more, that leaves them entirely unexplained.)

These arguments are operating at too superficial a level. Let us remind ourselves of the circumstances under which we attribute beliefs and other propositional attitudes to animals. It is when they do something like barking up the wrong tree; when there is a discrepancy between expected and observed behaviour. We are less inclined to say of a dog barking up the right tree that it is in the grip of a belief: it is just chasing a cat. It might be argued that it is only when the dog barks up the wrong tree that we become aware of something that is the case all the time; namely that whenever it barks up any tree, it is being steered by a belief. The wrong tree situation simply makes explicit what is present all the time – namely, that it is always acting on beliefs. The omnipresence of belief throughout the dog's behaviour – when it is chasing a cat as well as when it is barking up right and wrong trees – of course delivers too much. The animal would then be in a permanent state of wall-to-wall, unindividuated belief – knowledge – thought – disbelief – expectation.

It is evident that propositional attitudes have to be differentiated as to kind, and individuated as to type, truly to be present as guides, steers or motivators. But it is equally evident that they have to be 'held' or 'entertained' as something different from the behaviour which they are supposed to shape. This is phenomenologically obvious in humans: we have beliefs of which we are aware that are not cashed into any kind of action, or not immediately anyway. And this is even more obviously true of knowledge – for example, my knowledge of history or world affairs. This explicitness and their being disconnected from the here-and-now in which I am immersed is what opens them up for correction. The dog barking up the wrong tree may eventually bark up the right tree but that would be a sequence of behaviours, and not the acknowledgement of the incorrectness of the belief that had motivated the earlier behaviour. The behaviour – not a belief expressed in the behaviour – would be corrected in the eyes of the observer, not of the dog.

How can we be *sure* that the dog does not have a belief that is corrected? We have already indicated that it appears that the dog has no medium in which the belief can be held, challenged and then modified. We could put this as follows: an animal could not entertain a belief because there isn't sufficient self to be an entertainer, to be the subject of a complex, segmented, mediated psychological state. It isn't offset from its environment in the way that embodied subjects, inwardly lit by the Existential Intuition, are. What is more, there isn't sufficient pooling of sentience for beliefs, which interact with general knowledge, to be formed. The dog doesn't have the necessary 'toolkit' to put beliefs together. The inability of dogs to have beliefs is not simply because they do not have language in which to individuate and express them. Their aphasia and their lack of beliefs and other propositional attitiudes come from their lacking the broader conditions which are necessary for both.

This in turn links back to the earlier discussed point that it is impossible to think of beliefs without connecting them with other beliefs and, more importantly, with knowledge. The objects of knowledge are in the realm of deindexicalised awareness. In order to be privy to (abstract, general) objects of knowledge, animals must have passed through and have reached the other side of indexical awareness. For reasons given in earlier sections, we cannot attribute indexical awareness to non-human animals. Beliefs, knowledge, etc. are the paradigm forms of 'That X is the case ...'. It is not possible to arrive at 'That X is the case' without (a) 'That I am this' – which gives indexicalised awareness; and (b) symbols to materialise and individuate the possibility corresponding to beliefs. One cannot have a second floor (propositional attitudes, deindexicalised awareness) without a first floor (indexical awareness) or a ground floor (the Existential Intuition).[39]

Propositional attitudes are modes of consciousness whose intentional object is something – a proposition – that does not exist at a particular point in space or a particular point in time. It is important to emphasise that they are modes of consciousness because even those philosophers who agree that they exist and that they are unique to humans are likely seriously to misunderstand them. For writers in the analytical tradition, the very fact that propositional attitudes are rooted in a collectivised consciousness, a logical space – and that they are communicable – lifts them away from the individual person and hence out of consciousness. In Chapter 1 we discussed how Frege, who emphasised the essential communicability of propositional attitudes, was hugely influential in this radical depsychologisation. The following passage from an interview with Michael Dummett, his foremost interpreter in the English-speaking world, illustrates this:

> The fundamental idea for Frege was that the contents of what are now called propositional attitudes – that is, things that are believed or known – which he called 'thoughts', are not *mental* contents. They are not ingredients of the stream of consciousness. Such ingredients are things that are purely subjective: mental images, sensations, feelings, and so forth. By 'thoughts' Frege means not particular acts of thinking but the contents of those acts; and these contents are objective, that is, common to all. One person can think, or consider, or deny just that very same thought which somebody else asserts. Frege made a sharp division between the subjective, which cannot be fully communicated, and the objective which, being independent of any particular mind nust, Frege believed, exist independently of being grasped or thought about. [40]

Ditto for beliefs, items of knowledge, and so on.

This is, of course, wrong and it is based upon a confusion between the type and the token; between the general propositional attitude and the bearer of it. Propositional attitudes have to be realised in individuals. They are re-indexicalised as they are instantiated in tokens – beliefs, thoughts, desires – in order that they can inform and shape behaviour. This is also necessary for them to relate to particular objects, themselves interacting with our bodies in behaviour.[41] Which is not, of course, to deny that they belong to an internally coherent space of possibilities (Davidson's belief networks, etc.). In this sense, they are about things that are not located in space, which are not available to dogs any more than they are to the trees, rightly or wrongly, they bark up. The difference between the appropriate behaviour and the inappropriate behaviour in the case of the dog is supposed to betray the dog's implicit belief; but all it shows is that it responds to one stimulus as if it were like another.[42] A failure of discrimination between a cat-bearing and a cat-free tree is not evidence of the holding of a belief.

NOTES AND REFERENCES

1. Martin Heidegger, quoted in Rudiger Safranski, *Martin Heidegger. Between Good and Evil*, trans. Ewald Osers (Cambridge, MA: Harvard University Press, 1998), p. 199. The discussion around this passage is of immense interest. One could argue that animals are not even 'worlded' in the way that humans are. The environment, the *Umring*, of non-human animals does not amount to a world in the full sense. Objects are located, animals are environed and humans are worlded. (See also section 14 of *Being and Time*. 'The Idea of the Worldliness of the World in General'.)
2. Helmut Plessner (quoted in Safranski, *Heidegger*, p. 159) put this rather dramatically: 'As the I, which enables the complete return of the living system to itself, Man no longer stands in the "Here-Now", but behind it, behind himself, unlocalized in nothingness ... His existence is truly placed upon Nothing.'
3. Ludwig Wittgenstein, *Tractatus Logico-Philosophicus*, trans. D. F. Pears and B. F. McGuinness (London: Routledge & Kegan Paul, 1963), p. 1. I say *seemingly* unexceptionable. He speaks of *the* world, as if there were a single totality. This removes the concept from the consciousness of individuals, to something brought together in a compendious viewpoint outside of the world. Unfortunately, under such circumstances there would not be any that *is the case*. For 'what is' does not of itself become 'what is the case', does not make itself as *what is the case*. In addition, if the world were the sum total of the worlds of all individuals, then it would have to include quite a lot of what is not the case; for we all populate our worlds with non-existent possibilities, the intentional objects of false beliefs. In what follows, we accept the notion of the world as an idealised totality, as that which is bounded by the horizon of all actual and possible human consciousnesses.
4. As W. V. O. Quine famously put it (though with a quite different intention), 'to be is to be the value of a variable'. Cited and discussed in 'Universals', in P. F. Strawson, *Entity and Inentity and Other Essays* (Oxford: Oxford University Press, 1997), p. 54.

5. See David Pears, *Bertrand Russell and the British Tradition in Philosophy* (London: Fontana, 2nd edition 1972), pp. 138–9.

Such problems always occur when anyone tries to specify the ultimate constituents of the world. At this level of sophistication, it is impossible to separate linguistic from extra- or pre-linguistic contributions to individuation. The notion of, say, an atom is both that of an absolute primitive, there before there was life, never mind human consciousness, and of the internal accusative of a highly sophisticated way of thinking about the world. This was particularly difficult for Wittgenstein in the *Tractatus* whose fundamental project was to determine the logical conditions for language to be connected with the world. One is left, as he himself acknowledged, trying to see both sides of the relation through the lens of language, which is one side. The very notion of the relationship between language and world is a highly sophisticated, and very late, manifestion of language.

6. The link between impossibility (logical non-possibility) and possibilities that happen (contingently) not to be actualised is that the contingent realisation of a possibility places constraints upon other possibilities.

7. This is in fact incoherent, as Howard Robinson demonstrated in *Matter and Sense* (Cambridge: Cambridge University Press, 1982), see especially pp. 108–23 and the discussion in section 3.3. Nevertheless, it has a powerful intuitive attractiveness in both everyday and philosophically sophisticated discourse. The influence of the analogy between physical and logical space occupancy for Wittgenstein is reflected in this passage: '(A proposition, a picture, or a model is, in the negative sense, like a solid body that restricts the freedom of movement of others, and, in the positive sense, like a space bounded by solid substance in which there is room for a body)' (*Tractatus Logico-Philosophicus*, 4.463).

8. Lyons describes some of the trouble it causes: 'Some authors think of propositions as purely abstract, but as in some sense objective, entities; others regard them as subjective or psychological; and there are certain logicians who avoid the term entirely because they do not wish to adopt either of these alternatives ... some writers identify propositions with (declarative) sentences, and others with the meanings of (declarative) sentences. (John Lyons, *Semantics*, Volume 1 (Cambridge: Cambridge University Press, 1981) p. 142).

9. For Wittgenstein, the general propositional form is 'This is how things are' (*Tractatus*, 4.5).

10. Quoted in Richard Gaskin, 'Proposition and World', Introduction to *Grammar in Early Twentieth-Century Philosophy*, ed. R. Gaskin (London: Routledge, 2001), p. 1. This is a painstaking, beautifully argued paper to the effect that propositions are located at the level of reference, that is to say in the world, but in a world construed in a transcendentally idealistic sense.

11. Ibid., p. 2.

12. That propositions do have some kind of existence prior to individuation through sentences seems to be supported by the fact that one can indicate a proposed reality by other means than full or part, unpacked or elliptical, sentences. However, one can do that only against the background of a good deal of prior discourse that may have contributed to individuating the proposed reality. (Just as ostension is able to pick out the referents of words only because other words have indicated what kind of thing is being pointed out.)

13. D. A. Armstrong, *A World of States of Affairs* (Cambridge: Cambridge University Press, 1997), p. 19. One could put the boot on the other foot and call propositions

tautological accusatives of sentences, as the earlier discussion suggested.

14. Russell defined the 'entities indicated by words' in propositions as (among other things) whatever 'can be counted as *one*'. Cited Gaskin, *Grammar in Early Twentieth-Century Philosophy.*

15. Where the question cannot be clarified – as with Sorites-type questions – we are right to say that there is simply 'No fact of the case'.

16. The classic expression of the former error is Wittgenstein's picture theory of language, in which language simply mirrors states of affairs and its role in making them visible, in picking them out, in shaping what is expressed, is overlooked. The latter error – in accordance with which words shapes the world of things, and human consciousness was bypassed or in thrall to the system of language – was the key notion of the post-Saussurean (structuralist and post-structuralist) thought that was so dominant in the second half of the twentieth century. I have discussed this in *Not Saussure. A Critique of Post-Saussurean Literary Theory* (Basingstoke: Macmillan, 2nd edition, 1995).

17. Russell's mistake here may be seen as that of importing into the proposition those referents picked out only when the proposition has been expressed in a particular situation and when, with the aid of all sorts of anaphoric and deictic props, a speech act has particular referents.

18. As Wittgenstein, says, 'It is impossible to describe the fact that corresponds to (is the translation of) a sentence without simply repeating the sentence' (*Culture and Value*, extracted in 'Philosophical Extracts', *Truth, Oxford Readings in Philosophy* (Oxford: Oxford University Press, 1999), p. 110). This does not, however, excuse non-substantive accounts of truth, such as Tarski's non-rescue of the correspondence theory, as we shall discuss in the next chapter.

19. For a more detailed discussion of this concept and its relevance to a theory of reference, see Tallis, *Not Saussure*, pp. 107–11.

20. It is important to appreciate that we are talking about *identity* and not some kind of isomorphism between the sense of the sentence and the sense of the situation. Early Wittgenstein, along with many others, appealed to the notion of an isomorphism between expressions and their referents in order to explain how one could mean the other and the fact that the former means the latter could be seen without further explanation. Such a transparent relationship (of self-evident representation) seemed to be necessary (and sufficient) to bring the regress of interpretation to an end.

   In practice, isomorphism does not (as Wittgenstein eventually appreciated) bring the regress to an end. More importantly, there are no forms – of the sense of the sentence and the sense of the state of affairs expressed in it – to be matched. The relationship discussed here is not one of representation. Senses do not have shapes, so they could not have matching shapes (even if that did explain *anything*!). Only identity can bring the regress to an end.

   I will discuss the nature of this identity further in Chapter 6. The reader might also wish to read a more detailed account of some aspects of this theory of facts in 'Statements, Facts, and the Correspondence Theory of Truth', in Tallis, *Not Saussure*, pp. 235–50.

21. Wittgenstein, in Blackburn and Simmons, *Truth*, p. 110.

22. Facts are locationless and general, like an object's general significance, which is realised in the object but not located in it, being part of its relation to a general space of possibility.

23. J. L. Austin, 'Unfair to Facts', in *Philosophical Papers*, ed. J. O. Urmson and G. J.

Warnock (Oxford: Oxford University Press, 2nd edition, 1970), p. 156.

24. This explains the complex nature of reference, which remains, even when the referent is as seemingly straightforward as an object that is present to me now. As Ray Jackendoff has said, 'reference is ... a relationship between linguistic expressions and the world as it is conceptualised by the language user' (*Foundations of Language. Brain, Meaning, Grammar, Evolution*, Oxford: Oxford University Press, 2002, p. xvi).

25. Quoted in Barry Stroud, *Understanding Human Knowledge. Philosophical Essays* (Oxford: Oxford University Press, 2000), p. 202.

26. That is why John Searle's retention of the distinction between 'brute' and 'institutional' facts remains, despite his redrawing the boundaries to extend the realm of brute facts, incorrect – though instructively so.

    In *Speech Acts. An Essay in the Philosophy of Language* (Cambridge: Cambridge University Press, 1969) Searle argues that there are brute facts, 'such as the fact that I weigh 160 lbs' (p. 51). While 'they require certain conventions of measuring weight and certain linguistic institutions in order to be stated in a language' they are brute in the sense that they are rooted in 'simple empirical observations recording sense experiences' (p. 50). It will now be evident that facts are remote from 'simple empirical observations recording sense experiences', belonging as they do to the realm of deindexicalised awareness.

27. Logical positivists dined very well off the belief that all factual propositions can be reduced to basic propositions that are somehow directly connected with sense experience.

28. W. V. O. Quine, 'The Nature of Natural Knowledge', in *Mind and Language. Wolfson College Lectures 1974* (Oxford: Oxford University Press, 1975), p. 72.

29. Ibid., p. 72

30. Ibid., p. 73.

31. Indeed, one might say, ideally so. To have someone of Quine's genius saying the things one might have had to put in the mouth of a straw man is a once-in-a-lifetime opportunity. I am, perhaps, being unfair to Quine, given that in many places in his writings he has argued that a meaningful statement is *not* a construction out of immediate experience. If only he had had the courage of his conviction and recognised that an experience mediated in the way that is necessary to get statements is no longer in touch with the biology of the organism.

32. It is important not to think of knowledge as being narrowed to evidence, as Timothy Williamson does in *Knowledge and Its Limits* (Oxford: Oxford University Press, 2002). Knowledge becomes evidence only under certain circumstances – one's own or someone else's doubt. But doubt, or potential doubt, always stalks knowledge, so Williamson is not far off the mark.

33. John McDowell, *Mind and World* (Cambridge, MA: Harvard University Press, 1996), p. 4.

34. It will be evident that I could not disagree more with McDowell's claim – central to his entire argument – that 'experiential intake' is 'not a bare getting of an extra-conceptual Given, but as a kind of occurrence or state that already has conceptual content. In experience, one takes in, for instance sees, *that things are thus and so*' (ibid., p. 9). This is how it is with awareness above the level of sentience; but not with all levels of awareness. The problem is, it is not possible to focus on pure sentience because doing so brings with it its own impurities – language individuating it into bits of experience, for example. Wall-to-wall conceptualisation is a necessary

consequence of looking at consciousness through the sophisticated lens of intro-spection.

35. In Raymond Tallis, *The Explicit Animal. A Defence of Human Consciousness* (Basingstoke: Macmillan, 2nd edition, 1999), pp. 116–18.

36. Donald Davidson, 'Rational Animals', *Dialectica* (1982); 36: 318–27.

37. A similar point is made by George Graham, 'Mind and Belief in Animals', in *Philosophy of Mind* (Oxford: Basil Blackwell, 2nd edition, 1998), pp. 65–86.

38. Davidson, 'Rational Animals', p. 477.

39. This is the opposite position to Graham, who asserts that 'wants, like beliefs, possess aboutness; and, since they possess aboutness, they are fused to a point of view' ('Mind and Belief in Animals', p. 77). This is true of the aboutness of indexical awareness but not of the aboutness of deindexicalised awareness.

40. Michael Dummett, in *Key Philosophers in Conversation: The Cogito Interviews*, ed. Andrew Pyle (Routledge: London and New York, 1999), p. 2.

41. Propositional attitudes are, of course, linked with emotions which are necessarily had by individuals. They are a particularly highly developed form of propositional attitude, where content and object are clearly heterologous. The content is infused with physiological experiences – e.g. tachycardia – and so is explicitly rooted in the body; while the object (e.g. next week's lecture) is locationless. This is one of the things that makes emotions world-transforming: they infuse the body through which the world is refracted.

42. This, incidentally, is why a propositional attitude could not be just a mental state correlated with neural impulses. It is realised in a succession of mental states, but while its tokens are individual, private, first-person singular, that which informs, shapes the succession of mental states that make them up is borrowed from the collective. Beliefs are rooted in systems of understanding, typically expressed in language.

CHAPTER 6

Some Truths about Truth

Truth had rather a tough time in the twentieth century and the going looks to be getting no easier. The assaults have come from many directions.[1]

Humanist intellectualists, once the self-styled guardians of objective truth, dismiss belief in it as the mark of an unreflective, or at least politically naive, mind. Truth is relative to the perspective from which things are seen.[2] What you believe to be true depends upon where you are standing. This in turn depends, in the deepest sense, upon who you are. The truth from one angle will be different from the truth as seen from another angle. The appeal to 'the facts' is empty: interpretation determines the identification, the citation and the synthesis of facts. The truth will differ for the oppressed and the oppressors, for the rich and the poor, for men and women. There is no disinterested account of what is the case: truth, public truth, what is said to be 'out there', is relative to communities of discourse (or cultural, social and historical 'matrices') that reflect the values and interests of those who predominate within them.[3] What is held to be true by the community – the official, public truth – will depend upon who is in charge. 'Objective' truth is simply truth according to the most powerful: the rulers' truth in society; the victors' truth in history; the professionals' truth in science. Even those who accept that there are intrinsic standards of truthfulness believe that, since what counts as true evolves over time, the notion of truly objective truth is self-defeating. The perpetual revolutions of science, for example, undermine the very notion of truth as its asymptote or regulative idea.[4]

Much of this onslaught is, leaving aside its insincerity, a deeply boring mix of truths, half-truths and falsehoods. For this reason, and because I have addressed it at length elsewhere,[5] I will not take issue with it here, except to note that all relativisers and sceptics bolster their case by appealing to certain facts, often of a very large kind, which one assumes they accept as being true.

There is another, perhaps more profound, though no less mistaken – and self-contradictory – attack on the idea of objective truth, originating from the Darwinisation of human being, which is close to the central theme of this book. This assimilates the notion of truth to that of adaptive behaviour necessary to ensure the survival of the organism. It will be discussed in the next chapter.

The third type of assault on truth denies that the notion has any essential or substantive content. This will be our starting point. Davidson, famously, spoke of 'The Folly of Trying to Define Truth',[6] and argued that 'the concept of truth has no application to, or interest for, our mundane concerns, nor … does it have any content at all'. This deflationist account of truth is part of a flourishing twentieth-century tradition, whose source is usually traced to Frank Ramsay's observation that to assert 'p is true' is the same as to assert 'p'; consequently, the notion of truth is redundant or empty: 'there is no problem of truth but merely a linguistic muddle'.[7] The muddle is to think of 'being true' as a property and 'is true' as a predicate.

Now, one can accept (as I do) that truth is neither a property nor a predicate, and equally (to address another assault) that it is not any kind of 'substance' found in beliefs, propositions, statements or in the material world, without having to conclude either that it is nothing, or that there is nothing to be said about it – or at least nothing interesting. Austin's assertion that 'the theory of truth is a set of truisms' is wrong.[8] It is also, I believe, importantly wrong, as I will explain presently.

Nevertheless, one should in fairness acknowledge that emptying truth to the point where all that can be salvaged is the notion of 'the norm of inquiry' – though this is no small thing, as a proper examination of the notion of a 'norm' and of 'inquiry' (see section 7.2) will show – is driven by some good intuitions as well as by some that are not so good.[9] For a start, it does not make sense to consider truth as a property (like green), or as a kind of substance (like God knows what), or as a predicate that denotes some such property or substance. Equally, the immemorial hope of finding some means by which particular truths can be found to converge in some unity called '*The* Truth' has – outside of its partial realisation in the natural sciences – done mankind little good and considerable harm. Deflating such notions can only be welcome.

Less welcome is the claim that truth is nothing at all or, yet more radically, that it has no defining characteristics. This overlooks something

central to Man, the Truth-bearing (and Falsehood-bearing) Animal –
closely linked with Man the Knowing Animal. Minimalist theories of
truth tend to overlook how it is that, for example, true assertions are
possible. In doing so, they miss many things that are unique to humans,
thereby making it easier to assimilate humankind to the natural world.
If, as we noted in Chapter 2, naturalisation makes knowledge virtually
invisible, rendering truth slim to the point of invisibility also renders it
more vulnerable to naturalisation. At any rate, arguing that truth is a
redundant notion, and denying 'robust' theories such as correspondence
theories, helps clear the way for a form of pragmatism in which truth is
assimilated to usefulness with the latter relating ultimately to survival.
This, one of the paths to Darwinosis, threatens to close the gap between
humans and animals by assimilating knowledge to sentience or discri-
minatory behaviour. Deflationary theories of truth, in other words,
overlook the long journey from sentience to knowledge (set out in
Chapter 4), which uncoupled human consciousness from its original
centredness on the human body. It is only a short step from there, via a
stimulus theory of the meaning of sentences, to the notion that, for
example, the truth of observation statements lies in 'the conditioning of
strings of words to sensory stimulation'.[10]

I want to reflate truth by seeing it as a relationship between propositional awareness and that which it proposes. That which is proposed
may or may not exist – possibilities may or may not be realised: truth
and falsehood, like knowledge and the intuition of ignorance, are twins
and evolve together. Truth is the relationship between a proposed state
of affairs and that state of affairs if it exists; falsehood is the relationship
between a proposed state of affairs and the non-existence of that state of
affairs. We cannot comprehend truth separately from falsehood even
though the falsehood relation as we have just described it seems less real
than the truth relation, if only because the two relata do not have quite
the same standing in the case of the falsehood.

The twin birth of truth and falsehood is the reason why we should
not reduce the notion of truth to, say, a criterion for separating that
which is true from that which is false. Truth includes that which it has in
common with falsehood: the conditions under which both exist.
Therein lies the substance of truth and the basis for a non-deflationary
account of what it means for something to be true. To use a distinction I
have made earlier, we must separate the existence conditions of entities
such as assertions that may be true or false from their truth (or falsity)
conditions.[11] It is the former that gives substance to the notion of truth.

To grasp the nature of truth, we must not take it too much for
granted, as a finished product. We must see that it has, as it were, to

come about. We cannot separate a theory of truth – as opposed to a theory for the abstract criteria of truth – from a theory of the context in which issues of truth arise; a theory of the origin of that context. In short, a theory of truth will be empty (and inadequate) so long as it ignores its origins and in an extreme case confines itself to formal features.

Bernard Williams attempted 'a genealogy of truth' in his final book.[12] Just how difficult – and substantive – a task this is was indicated by the reservations Simon Blackburn registered, at the beginning of his largely laudatory review, about the extent to which Williams delivered on his aim:

> a theory of the origins of truth must not imagine up-and-running notions of belief, judgement or representation, since each of these is integrally connected with the idea of getting something right. This leaves it quite hard to see just what is legitimately allowed at the beginning of the story. Some kind of distinction between being right and being wrong, whether we are making an observation or an inference, is so firmly embedded in our thinking that it is hard to imagine starting yet further back. It would be at a point in human life at which there is no distinction between something appearing to be so and it being so, which is sufficiently far from us to be unrecognizable as human life in the first place. At the very least, it would have to be one about the emergence of self-consciousness itself ...[13]

Deflationary accounts of truth overlook all of this; indeed, overlook all that goes into making what is the case into '[That] X is the case', all that is encompassed in the journey from sentience to knowledge.

While a theory of truth that takes nothing for granted would be remote from the deflationary accounts of truth that philosophers have constructed in the wake of Ramsay's suggestion that 'is true' is a redundant predicate, it need not run into making truth a predicate, a property, a substance, or the final point of convergence of all 'correct' human consciousness or of all cognitive endeavour. Nevertheless, we need, as Pascal Engel has pointed out, an *inflationist* account of things like meaning and belief – or of the context, origin and background of truth – in order to secure 'deflationist' truth.[14] We can develop such an inflationist account without filling the concept of truth with gas.

6.2.1 The Need for an External Relational Account of Truth

While there has, over the centuries, been much difference of opinion amongst those who have subscribed to correspondence theories of truth, as to what (propositions, thoughts, perceptions, sentences, assertions) corresponds to what (states of affairs, facts, events, the world, etc.),[15] there has been agreement that the correspondence is a *relation* between two types of elements separated by some kind of space and linked by that space. Therein lies the central attraction of such theories: they acknowledge a special *distance* between individual awareness and what is the case. It is not a literal spatial distance. It is a gap between subjects and their worlds, the enhanced form of intentionality or aboutness that is evident in mediated interaction with reality. That which is true is true *of* or *to* something: the prepositions mark the distance. Without such a distance, it is not possible to understand the nature of assertion, consent, assent, dissent, claim, counterclaim, and so forth. Correspondence theories posit an *uncoupling* between the truth-sayer and, say, the material world of which he is a part. (This will be the theme of the next chapter.)

Such uncoupling is necessary for something as simple as 'checking whether it is true that the cat is in the room' as much as for something rather more complex, as in making a scientific observation. Which is precisely why causal theories of meaning, reference and truth – such as those suggested by Quine – are inadequate. Accepting an assertion as true on the strength of observation is remote from 'the conditioning of strings of words to sensory stimulation'.

6.2.2 False (Internal) Correspondence

A correspondence theory has this general form:

  X is true if and only if X corresponds to what is the case

If this formulation is to capture the distance inherent in knowledge (even in the stunted sense of 'justified true belief'), the relation between the correspondent entities must be external rather than internal. It is no good if the relata are the same kind of thing, so that the object of truth seems like, for example, a mere 'internal accusative' of that which is asserted. The requirement that the relationship should be external rules out two very popular – perhaps the most popular – versions of the correspondence theory: Tarski's semantic theory; and the version according to which (e.g.) assertions correspond to *facts*. Let us dispose of these first.

Tarski's so-called Semantic Theory of Truth has this form:

'X' is true, if and only if X

To take the standard example:

'Snow is white' is true if and only if snow is white

While this definition has solved a few problems in philosophical logic, it otherwise offers meagre rewards. It looks tautologous or circular. It is neither of these, of course, because the first instance of 'snow is white' is a *mention* of the sentence in question and the second instance is a *use* of it; the first belongs to a meta-language and the second to an object language. Even so, the disappointment is palpable and Austin's dismissal of the theory of truth as 'a set of truisms' seems not entirely unfair. It seems also to justify Ramsay's observation:

> For a proposition to be true is for things to be as someone who utters thereby says they are … this is a correspondence account in a sense, but I would call it a correspondence platitude or truism rather than a theory.[16]

All that Tarski's definition does is offer the same sentence twice, first in quotation marks and then out of them. To put this another way, the assertion and what it asserts are individuated by means of two tokens of the same sentence-type, mentioned in one instance and used in the other. Attributing truth to the sentence mentioned in quotation marks just involves cancelling the quotation marks. Truth, which lies in the passage from the first to the second instance of the same sentence, is *dis*quotation.

Quine, who is particularly associated with the disquotational interpretation of Tarski's Semantic Theory, admits that there are circumstances in which truth is a genuine predicate and that, while the disquotational account in a sense *defines* truth, it does not eliminate it.[17] And a good thing, too. For what is missing in Tarski's theory – once it is stripped down to its essential operation of disquotation – is anything outside of language. The piece of language and the piece of the world it is about are grasped through instances of the same sentence. The quotation marks are merely a pair of tweezers to pick up a sentence-type through one of its tokens and, through that sentence, to pick up the piece of reality to which it refers and which can be asserted through it. The theory, therefore, places truth on the near-side of the language–

world barrier. Truth is a relation, yes, but the relation is an internal distance within language, the distance between first- and second-order language. To redescribe this in terms that connect more closely with our wider preoccupations, the theory is simply a movement between a first and second floor of propositional awareness that has no ground floor at all. We have no explanation of how the quotes got there in the first place. If they (and much else that comes with them) are passed on the nod, then no wonder the resulting theory of truth seems trivial.[18]

There is another way of internalising the correspondence theory – and hence of creating a trivial or point-missing account of truth. This is by describing it as 'correspondence to or with the facts'. To describe it thus is almost standard. For example, Simon Blackburn and Keith Simmons, in their Introduction to *Truth*, say that 'for a proposition to be true is for it to correspond with the facts', adding that 'this is a platitude that nobody denies'.[19] (As will become apparent, I am that nobody.) And Engel[20] characterises the correspondence theory as follows:

X is true if and only if X corresponds to the facts

When, additionally, facts are understood as an 'internal accusative' of the sentences that individuate them, then platitude looms. The correspondence of an assertion to the facts becomes the (rigged) correspondence between a sentence and its internal accusative. The relation becomes an internal one and the distance it holds open proves to be illusory. In summary, when truth is billed as correspondence to facts and facts are assimilated into language, truth threatens to become a relation between items of language.

6.2.3 True (External) Correspondence: Factual Truth

In what follows, I am going to focus on factual truth. Not all truth boils down to facts, of course: truth is not exhaustively articulated in sentences. There are existential truths; there is something called 'living in [the] truth' and that does not mean somehow inhabiting a nest woven out of facts. But this is too difficult, in part because it is too vague. Besides, factual truth seems close to the essence of truth. At any rate, there does appear to be a profound link between truth and facts as captured in sentences. Clarifying that link may tell us something central about truth.

It is necessary first of all to have a clear idea of facts. More particularly to appreciate that, as was argued in section 5.3, facts are neither internal to language nor 'on the surface of the earth'. When we tear up a sheet of paper, we do not tear up the facts that are recorded on it; when we shoo the cat out of the room, we do not displace 'That the cat is in the room'. Facts straddle language and a reality which, *with respect to that piece of language*, is extra-linguistic. The qualification 'with respect to that piece of language' is important. It acknowledges that, at the present late stage in human consciousness (which began about 100,000 years ago), the boundary between what is inside and what is outside language is not straight, nor is it continuous, or complete. What has already been said (and what a long already it has been) informs the shape 'reality' presents to us as much as 'reality' justifies what is said. The important thing is to recognise that at no time is language calling all the shots.[21]

We captured this intermediate, and intermediary, status of facts when we argued that they subsisted in an identity of the sense of a proposition expressed in, say, a sentence and of a state of affairs which, at its most basic, will consist of something on the surface of the earth. The correspondence theory of factual truth is not, therefore:

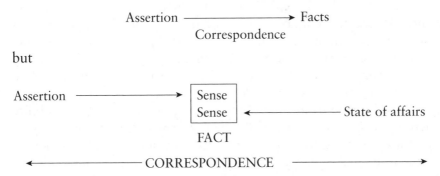

but

Far from truth being a relation to facts, facts are the tissues of truth. Truth is realised in the fact that such-and-such is the case. A fact is an identity between the sense of an assertion (a declarative sentence used on a particular occasion) and the sense of an actual state of affairs. An assertion (more precisely a person making an assertion) uses a sentence to express a proposition. This is how the proposed reality gets proposed. Because proposed realities may not actually exist, because general possibilities may not be actualised, there are false assertions as well as true ones. An assertion may be factual or counterfactual.

We may depict a counterfactual assertion as follows:

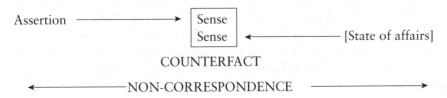

This is the 'failure-of-correspondence' theory of falsehood. Counter-factuals are single-parent progeny that lead one to expect the missing parent: they parasitise the expectations awoken by 'factuals'. The sense of the assertion carries through to a non-existent state of affairs. A state of affairs which has the sense of the assertion may have obtained on some occasion or in some world. On this occasion – the occasion implicit in the assertion – it does not, however, exist, though it could have done. One way in which the onward projection of the sense of the assertion to a putative reality is secured, even though nothing real corresponds to it, may be because the proposed state of affairs combines entities (properties, qualities, objects, times and places) that have existed even if they do not do so in that combination. Wings and horses exist, but not winged horses. Meaningful falsehoods parasitise the sense of actual states of affairs; counterfactuals trade on their being a massive background of facts, as counterfeit coins depend upon an overwhelming predominance of legal coins. In the case of both true facts and false counterfactuals the relationship is one of correspondence. A state of affairs is proposed: in the former it also exists; in the latter it does not.

This version of the correspondence theory may seem unsatisfactory and dissatisfaction will focus on the key term 'sense'. It will seem unacceptably vague or simply wrong. I have tried to clarify it in section 5.3. There I linked it, in the broadest sense, with a general possibility which is a central outcome of the deindexicalisation of awareness. It does not have the narrow meaning that it has in philosophical logic in the wake of Frege's distinction between sense and reference. It does, however, have some overlap with it. For Frege, sense was that aspect of the meaning of a sentence 'which is relevant to determining its truth or falsity'.[22] This might suggest that my version of the correspondence theory has a hidden internality. But I believe that it is acceptable to think also of the non-sentential sense of states of affairs: something like their significance, their relevance, connected with those features that are salient at a particular moment.[23]

The suggestion that what sentences offer is sense, not reference, may seem simply wrong to some. After all, factual assertions are most typically about singular situations which cannot be fully grasped through general senses, or even combinations thereof. This is perfectly true; but what takes a sentence down as it were from general senses to particular referents is nothing within it, nothing linguistic, but the circumstances within which it is uttered. When I say 'The cat is in the room', it is not what is intrinsic to this sentence that enables it to refer to a particular cat in a particular room. Deixis, either directly, or indirectly through anaphora (reference to what has just been said), is necessary to bring the sentence down to the earth where particular referents are to be found. Referents are outside language, which is why the *combination* of a sentence and the circumstances of its use are both necessary to pick out the referent. The sense is realised in the assertion but the referent lies outside of it. Apparent reference to non-existent objects – for example, 'the square circle' – which seem intra-linguistic, as they do not exist anywhere, is apparent only. If the case for the purely 'intra-linguistic' existence of 'the golden mountain' seems compelling, this is only because comparable linguistic formations have actual referents. Square circles and winged horses parasitise actual referents rather as bent sticks and mirages parasitise veridical perception (just as unrealised possibilities seem possible – i.e. possibilities – because there are realised ones).

The version of the correspondence theory that is on offer here makes truth an *external* relation and between *radically different kinds of things* – assertions and states of affairs in the world. This is necessary in order to do justice to the distances built into truth-telling and the uncoupling of the truth-teller from, say, the material world. The reason why such obvious theories are unpopular is precisely because some philosophers have argued that such radically different things could not be in any kind of relationship, least of all a truth-relationship. Frege, for example, under the impression that perfect correspondence required for truth 'can only be perfect *if* the corresponding things coincide and are, therefore, not distinct things at all',[24] rejected the theory. Since a sentence could not be like a bit of reality, it could not be true of it. Correspondence merely in 'a certain respect' would not, he argued, be enough, even if one could specify that respect, because it would then be essential to determine whether the relata corresponded in those 'laid-down' respects. Heidegger, too, dismissed the correspondence theory for an almost identical reason: it depended upon the notion of 'agreement' between things, such as knowledge and its object. How, he asked, could such disparate things agree?[25] The attractions of internalised forms of the correspondence theory – as in Tarski's semantic theory – is that the same sorts of things (sentences) are on both sides of the putative correspondence. Triviality, or a deflationary account of truth, is an acceptable, or necessary, price to pay for upholding the correspondence theory. But I have already argued that heterology of the elements at either end of the corres-pondence, true externality between the relata, is essential if the *distance* implicit in the concept of truth – true *of*, true *to* – is to be captured.

The present version of the correspondence theory overcomes the apparent problem that heterologous elements – for example, a sentence and a state of affairs 'out there' – cannot be in a correspondence relation because they are not like one another. At the heart of the theory is not

similarity – for example, in respect of certain material characteristics –
but *identity of sense* between, say, that of an assertion and of a state of
affairs. The sense is not intrinsic either to the assertion or to the state of
affairs. The assertion has the sense it has not in virtue of its material
properties but in virtue of the linguistic conventions governing the use
of the words of which it is composed and the deictic and anaphoric
circumstances in which it is used. The state of affairs, likewise, does not
intrinsically have just this sense (there is no canonical, or purely
intrinsic, sense of the states of affairs): it is normally dissolved into a
fluctuating nimbus of significance that is the world. An aspect of its
significance is linguistically frozen. Both relata, therefore, are 'playing
an away match'.

The identity is what 'being true of' consists in. This echoes, in a way
that he might not have liked, Heidegger's observation that '*Confirmation* means *the being's showing itself in self-sameness*'.[26] It is not an
(impossible) 'agreeing of knowing with its object, still less something
psychical with something physical' but neither is it 'an agreement
between "the contents of consciousness"'. The senses – or two ways of
materialising one sense – are public: even where the state of affairs is
before me, it transcends my awareness of it and the sentence that
captures it does so through an agreed convention and locates it in a
deindexicalised realm. (Facts are not located 'with respect to me'. I am
next to the chair but not next to the fact that I am next to the chair.)
Facts are not anywhere in particular; nor are they nowhere; nor is the
identity of sense a kind of isomorphic relation. Assertions are 'true to'
bits of how things are – those aspects that relate to the sense in question.
They do not have the kind of verisimilitude that pictures have, a truth
based on likeness, on replication of material properties.[27]

The keys to the nature of truth are explicitness, partly propositionalised awareness, knowledge. Saying this falls short of a full
characterisation of truth. On the other hand, overlooking it will result
in minimalist, or deflationary – in short, point-missing – theories of
truth. The foundation stone of truth is the passage from X to 'That X is
the case'. This passage is not to be equated with the passage into and out
of quotation marks. The trajectories of Quine's semantic elevator do not
capture the journey between being and truth, which takes in *both* 'that'
and things such as quotation marks. For this one needs a full-blown
correspondence theory, with sufficiently different relata at either end of
the correspondence to prevent them collapsing towards one another.
They have to relate through an identity that does not favour one over
the other. Nothing less than this can capture the difference between X
and 'That X is the case': a theory of truth that captures 'That ...' and the

individuation of that. Correspondence may or may not be an irreducible 'truth primitive'; but it is certainly necessary if we are going to capture the nature of truth; and of Man, the uncoupled truth-bearing animal.

6.2.4 No Free Gifts

The necessary link between truth and explicitness – or making explicit – means that truth does not supervene from being of its own accord, like steam rising from a dish. Facts, as we have noted, have to be made, even though (by definition) they are not literally 'made up'. What is more, facts are not what true assertions correspond to; they *are* the correspondence. We can use these two observations to deal with the Frege–Gödel 'sling-shot' argument against the correspondence theory.

If facts really were what made propositions true and the former were defined in terms of the latter, then it would be impossible to separate the individuation of facts from the individuation of propositions. What is more, it would be very difficult to delimit the facts that correspond to true assertions. If, for example, in virtue of asserting that Liverpool is 36 miles from Manchester, it would seem to follow that I was also asserting the fact that Manchester is 36 miles from Liverpool, that a northern city 200 miles north of London is 36 miles from Liverpool, that the birth-place of the Beatles and the birthplace of the members of Oasis are both 200 miles from London, and so on. There is no way of separating the 'personal' fact that corresponds to the original assertion from a bound-less network of equivalent facts. We are in danger, it seems, of arriving at Frege's position, whereby all true propositions are simply different names for the True and have only one truth-maker 'the Great Fact that is the World itself'.[28]

The version of the correspondence theory I have suggested does not run into this problem. First, truth is not about correspondence *to* facts; facts *are* the correspondence. This means that they do not exist merely by courtesy of the assertions that identify them. Nor, of course, do they exist on the surface of the earth. They are generated by an interaction between a state of affairs and an assertion. Facts do not exist without being asserted, though the states of affairs that are picked out by assertions exist independently of being asserted. This is the necessary condition of assertions being 'true of'. Thus facts, truth and assertions can be linked without the first two being swallowed up into assertions: facts are not (as they are too often described) mere internal accusatives of propositions, sentences or sentences used to assert or propose propositions. They are dual-, not single-, parent entities.

The fact that Manchester is 36 miles from Liverpool does not give birth to the fact that 'the birthplace of the Beatles and the birthplace of Oasis are both 200 miles from London' of its own accord: all the intermediate steps have to be made explicit. Additional explicitness does not come free of charge. This is true even with respect to purely logical consequences. While p implies not not-p, it has to be made explicit in an additional assertion. While it follows from the fact that Liverpool is 36 miles west of Manchester that Manchester is 36 miles from Liverpool, the first fact does not parthenogenetically breed the second. One person may know the first and not realise the second. Just as my knowing that Liverpool is 36 miles from Manchester does not mean that I bring to birth the facts that Liverpool is not 35 miles from Manchester, not 36,000 miles from Manchester, not the square root of 2,376 miles from Manchester, and so on.

The logical consequences of facts, that is to say, do not come free of charge, otherwise being in possession of one fact would put one in possession of an infinity of facts – and even if the world is logically coherent, the Great Fact of the World. Facts have to be made explicit by someone to exist for anyone and they do not exist in themselves. Someone has to be conscious of them and articulate them. When one fact is picked out, it does not follow that all the other facts that are logically connected with it – that have the same truth conditions – are also picked out. The reason why these very obvious points are not put into play in discussion of truth lies in the tendency, already noted with respect to thoughts (Chapter 1) and knowledge (Chapter 4), to de-psychologise truth, separating it from making-explicit. While psychology is irrelevant to the truth conditions of an assertion (neither are the conventions which make certain sounds the assertion of a particular state of affairs), the conditions under which the assertion is made, those conditions under which states of affairs in the world *are* turned into truth conditions, has everything to do with psychology, even though the psychological contents in question are tokenisations of impersonal deindexicalised awareness.

The tendency to displace psychology by logic when dealing with truth comes from the fact that one is inside language when one is *talking* about truth and entities such as propositions, sentences and facts and events such as assertions. Truth looks like a relationship between one bit of language and another, and hence to belong to the logical structure of the system of language. This explains the tendency noted in section 6.2.2 for correspondence theories to drift towards internal correspondence; to become intra-linguistic theories, which in turn, as Quine has shown, can be minimalist. In philosophical discussion, both sides of the correspondence have to be picked up with language. When we talk about facts, we talk about them from the side of sentences, propositions and assertions. That is how we name them when we are talking about them, and this mode of individuation (a second-order individuation) seems to show what they are. The tendency to name facts by reiterating the sentence used to individuate them not only makes facts seem internal to language but the correspondence, supposed to be between facts and assertions, seem rather empty of everything – including consciousness.[29]

6.3 CORRESPONDENCE IS NOT ENOUGH

I have defended correspondence as a necessary, indeed the most fundamental, constituent of truth. The correspondence theory I have advanced proposes a genuine external relationship between different kinds of relata without running into problems arising out of the heterology of the relata – thought and reality or assertion and that which is asserted. Crucially, a truly external correspondence theory affirms the distance between a human being and a putative natural world that makes assertion, affirmation, dissent, consent, argument and inquiry possible. But it is not sufficient in itself to capture all features of truth. Though more substantive than many of the theories currently on offer, it still seems thin or impoverished.

While correspondence is fundamental, beyond a certain imagined primitive level, something like coherence comes into play in the formulation and evaluation of truths. As we discussed in section 5.4, many statements are not directly tied to, assessable against, particular pieces of extra-linguistic evidence: they are remote from the tribunal of experience, being linked to the latter only notionally by an audit trail. At higher levels of generality, as in science, the criterion of truth – and the means of confirming or refuting assertions – seems more often to take the form of checking their consistency with other truths that may in turn have been validated by their consistency with yet further truths. It seems, that is to say, that there is no simple correspondence with things outside the realm of discourse, even though there is ultimately and intermittently a connection, through something like the logical positivists' 'basic' or 'protocol' statements, with extra-linguistic reality. The inadequacy of simple correspondence as a complete account of truth is even more evident if we consider the holism of our beliefs and the internal connectedness of the concepts and terms that are mobilised in discourse. Facts, after all, are linked with language, with the collective (they are impersonal), and with each other. They belong to a space of possibility, a logical space, a space of reason. Even so, if truth is to remain on the gold standard, it has to touch base with extra-linguistic reality. Just as the truth of the assertion that 'The dog is in the room' can be assessed directly by popping one's head round the appropriate door, so the truth of the assertion that 'Gravity is a bending of space-time' has ultimately to be checked against readings on machines that are looked at by someone.

I can of course rely on coherence to support my belief that the dog is in that room rather than observing the correspondent state of affairs directly. I can argue that he must be in the room because I locked him in there a moment ago and it would be inconsistent with all sorts of other truths I know about the dog to believe that he had got out – by picking the lock and opening the door, for example. And the pointer reading that confirms the correctness of Einstein's claims about space-time is still only a pinpoint on a pyramid of coherent truths, ranging from truths concerned with the validity of the readings from the machine (and the theoretical basis behind them) to the network of theoretical understanding that Einstein's theory was built upon.

Correspondence and coherence are interwoven at every level, from the homely at which we expect coherence between what you tell me and what I tell you, to the inter-theoretic relations of Grand Science. Above a certain level, it is impossible to have correspondence except against a background of coherence. The very idea of 'correspondence to reality' becomes deeply impregnated with notions of reality that demand coherence at quite abstract levels: what counts as the justification for a belief may come chiefly from the network of beliefs to which it belongs. A single fact makes sense only as part of a body of knowledge – local, general, personal, communal – which then forms the background against which it sticks out, the cognitive and cultural soil on which it stands. Even so, correspondence remains fundamental: coherence is simply the context whose ultimate underpinning is correspondence.[30]

The importance of coherence long antedates the absolute idealist philosophy with which it is particularly associated. In his attempt to find a criterion for differentiating between waking truths and dreaming falsehoods, Descartes (in common with many others since) offered 'coherence' between one truth and another as the mark of truth:

> I ought to set aside ... that very common uncertainty respecting sleep ...; for ... I find a very notable difference between the two, inasmuch as our memory can never connect our dreams with one another, or with the whole course of our lives, as it unites events which happen to us while we are awake.[31]

Such coherence, however, counts as a mark of the 'truth' of the experiences we have when we are awake only when we have the notion of truth in place; when, that is to say, we have the notion of a correspondence between (say) a belief and a state of affairs. There is a fundamental difference between coherence of truths and the mere continuity of awareness, whereby (say) one moment seems to follow on from another without gaps or jumps. Coherence of truths is found on the hither side of the gap between knowledge and awareness, a gap crossed by correspondence.

Nor can we ignore what might be called the pragmatic dimension of truth. This becomes prominent within human institutions such as politics and religion, where correspondence and coherence cannot easily be applied, and 'what works' and 'what prevails' become criteria of truth. This is, however, a secondary development: it is parasitic on the notion of truth as established through correspondence. It cannot, therefore, be extended to encompass all truth as pragmatists, postmodernists and evolutionary epistemologists would have us believe. The pragmatist position that 'the truth' is simply a belief that works cannot explain why some beliefs work better than others – unless it is because they are true. Postmodernists cannot explain why truth claims matter and why things that prevail seem like prevalent truth. Evolutionary epistemologists – the ultimate pragmatisers of truth – cannot explain why one needs any middle terms. If truth is about survival, and survival is unmediated by a conscious and independently accurate account of how things are, then there is no point in having truth: all that is required is that we should be more snuggly coupled into our habitat.

At the root of pragmatism is a tendency to put things back to front. To reduce the true to beliefs that work is to miss the point that the most likely reason that beliefs work is that they are true. To suggest that truth conditions can be reduced to meaning and that meaning can be found by attention to practical consequences is also to put things the wrong way round. The practical consequences are determined by what is there, by whether or not what corresponds to an assertion really is the case. The truth of the assertion 'There is a dog in the room' resides in there being a dog in the room, irrespective of the practical consequences. (The claim, *presumably based upon empirical observation*, that truth tends to be what works, and what works is what promotes survival, is itself offered as a large truth. Is this truth about truth assumed to be true because it works, because it promotes survival?)

Pragmatism, as already noted, contributes most impressively to defining what is true when what is in question is remote from observation, when there is no other tribunal than the authority of collective belief or individual say so to appeal to. Our sense of what is 'true' is, under such circumstances, a product of 'the will to believe'. The will to believe is a complicated matter. At its most benign, it is trusting the authority of others. And, of course, our sense of what is 'out there' must always be, to an overwhelming extent, based on the say so of others. In some cases, this is not a matter of assent but of thoughtless conformity, or kow-towing, to majority opinion. This comes close to Nietzsche's notion of truth as 'a mobile army of metaphors' and of truthfulness as accepting 'the obligation to lie according to a fixed convention, to lie herd-like in a style obligatory for all'.[32] At this point, however, the pragmatic theory of truth – supposedly the final truth about truth – runs into its own contradictions. As an account of certain kinds of truth – for example, ideological, religious truth – however, it is perceptive. As a global criterion for distinguishing true from false beliefs, as in the 'teleosemantic' version that equates those beliefs that are true with those that tend to be beneficial for a species, it fails dismally. There was little initial benefit in scientific theories of planetary motion; and yet the true ones ultimately led, via the Newtonian mechanics they inspired, to the entire fabric of physical science and the technology that flowed from that.

The upshot of this discussion is that we need a richer account of truth than can be provided by the correspondence theory alone. Correspondence, coherence and practical consequences as features of truth and criteria for differentiating truth from falsehood are each insufficient. Coherence and pragmatist theories are not rivals to the correspondence theories but essential supplements to the latter's fundamental description of the nature of truth. At times, the truth of assertions will seem purely correspondent, at other times coherent, and at yet other times to reside in practical consequences – just as space-time sometimes seems space-like and sometimes time-like. Correspondence, however, remains fundamental.

6.4 TRUTH, EXPLICITNESS AND LANGUAGE

Discussion of correspondence theories often begins by quoting Aristotle's superficially uninspiring definition of truth:

> To say of what is that it is, or of what is not that it is not, is true.[33]

Interestingly, Engel (in *Truth*, p. 6) cites this as the first minimalist conception of truth. Such accounts of correspondence theories of truth will always look thin or minimalist, so long as the key word in them is overlooked: 'That'.

A theory of truth ultimately must be a theory of 'That' as in 'That X is the case'; the transformation of what is to 'That it is ...' or 'That it is the case'. It is this that points up the roots of truth in something wider and deeper: the propositional awareness that is unique to humans. This opens up the space of possibility in which existents (entities, states of affairs, events, trends) can be proposed and asserted to be the case.

A theory of truth, then, is a theory of the differentiation of explicitness. Since language is the supreme means by which we differentiate explicitness – and, indeed, make explicitness itself explicit, as something that is public and held in common – it is not surprising that such theories tend to become intra-linguistic as they deflate towards minimalism. This is why Tarski's semantic theory looked like a theory of truth, and one that made the correspondence theory respectable again. Unfortunately, both relata were linguistic and a minimalist interpretation was not long in coming. If you start a theory of truth within language, it is difficult to get outside of language. Attempts to do so tend to have rather unrewarding results. No wonder Davidson was driven to conclude that 'nothing can usefully and intelligibly be said to correspond to a sentence'.[34] It is impossible to access the (general) referent of a sentence, even less its sense, except via the sentence: there is no extra-linguistic backdoor. Pointing, for example, has neither the requisite generality nor the requisite singularity: it cannot point specifically at the glossiness of the cat's fur without linguistic help or connect that glossiness with other instances of glossiness.[35] All we can *say* is another 'said'; say the same thing again, in other words. If you start with sentences, you are stuck with them;[36] you can't talk your way out of talk.

How then did Tarski's theory seem like a satisfying theory of truth? This becomes apparent when its essential nature is exposed, as in Quine's deflationary analysis. Disquotation is actually two processes: quotation *plus* removal of quote marks. It therefore makes explicitness explicit and so captures (without perhaps intending to) the connection between truth and explicitness. Tarski's theory is a way, therefore, of making a crucial aspect of truth explicit. It makes the upper surface of the 'That ...' in 'That X is the case' visible. Tarski's theory leads to a deflationary theory of truth if one removes all the underpinnings that are required for explicitness to be realised. Tarski's theory takes for granted everything that makes the quotation mark tweezers possible and so reduces truth to the application and removal of quotation marks; it reduces truth to its formal characteristics, to the criteria for differentiating (under certain very special, easy, protected, circumstances) spoken or written truth from spoken or written falsehood.

What it overlooks is all that is entailed in proceeding from, say, my headache, to 'my having a headache' to 'I have a headache'. For Quine, this is merely semantic elevation – the passage from first- to second-order language. But the lift has to be created and fuelled. Aches don't articulate themselves; they don't self-separate; even less do they speak. Tarski's semantic version of the correspondence theory, by starting too far down the track, is ripe to be deflated. We have to see the entire journey; and for that we need a more substantive correspondence theory, such as has been offered here. Correspondence is fundamental because it is closest to the intentionality, the crossed gap, that lies at the root of explicitness, of propositional awareness, of object sense, which characterises human knowledge.

Once the journey leading up to the advanced explicitness expressed in sentences is forgotten, a reduction of truth to its formal features – mere disquotation or a redundant predicate that at most passes judgement on assertions and other surface features – is inevitable. As redundancy theorists from Ramsay onwards have pointed out, nothing is added to the content of an assertion by adding that it is true. An adequate theory of truth will be substantive because it will take its rise from the deindexicalisation of human consciousness. This brings with it a danger of its own: that of an idealist, coherent theory of truth. When I claim that the relata in the correspondence theory – for example, the assertion and the state of affairs – are related in virtue of instantiating the same general sense, I may seem to be suggesting that truth lies in the correspondence between two contents of consciousness. The sense, however, is a communal one: the awareness is deindexicalised, impersonalised. I do not exist in a personal relation to facts in the way that I do to particular objects, which, not altogether accidentally, brings us to something that we discussed, and bypassed, at the outset: the relativisation of truth in fashionable contemporary perspectivism.

It will be recalled how the notion of an object was of something underlying variable experiences; of something that lay beyond my awareness; of a reality that, by contrast, made my experience be that of 'mere' appearances. The notion of the object, that is to say, creates the background against which my actual experiences can be criticised as inadequate, partial or misleading. It is this sense of ignorance that uncovers experience as partial, or incomplete knowledge, as a mixture of truth and falsehood. It enables me to see my viewpoint *as* a viewpoint; indexical awareness as indexical, perspectival. It postulates a ('higher') level of awareness from which the present level will be seen as partial, biased, even mistaken. This is where the sense of truth – as something independent of me – dawns. When we get to such deindexicalised forms of awareness as factual knowledge – objects that I do not approach from a literal angle and are lifted up from literal location and from myself – we move to a higher perspective. There is an important sense in which I do not have a personal angle on facts. 'The cat is in the room' is perspectival only from the point of view of a greater degree of deindexicalisation. (Residual indexicality is signified by the way the definite article is used, indexing the assertion to a limited universe defined anaphorically or deictically.) The personal angle, at a higher level yet, comes in the noticing, invoking and the selection of facts; as seen from a higher level of deindexicalised awareness.

The point is this: truth is perspectival only from the standpoint of a more encompassing truth, ultimately from some postulated point of convergence called 'the truth'. This anticipation of a higher-level viewpoint, and their reliance upon it, is what undermines the modern sophists who assert that truth is purely a matter of perspective and *the* truth is the perspective of those who have the most power. This claim itself depends upon observations that are not perspectival in the sense suggested.

A theory of truth needs to be rooted in a theory of 'That [X is the case]'. The misconception that the formal or formalisable features of truth account for it in its entirety, that truth has no constitutive properties or 'underlying nature',[37] will recur, so long as truth is uprooted from explicitness and from those consequences of explicitness – belief, assertion, doubt, all forms of meant meaning, and inquiry – that characterise human consciousness. It is in these things that the substance of truth is to be found. Paul Horwich's claim that truth is 'metaphysically trivial – nothing more than a device of generalisation' – seems persuasive only so far as everything that goes into making truth (and falsehood) possible is overlooked. Such overlooking takes us far from the truth about truth. The fact that there are assertions, the fact that there are facts, the fact that the senses of pieces of reality can be realised in assertions – alternative pieces of reality that express them through the independent materialisation of sense-ions – what could be less trivial or more extraordinary?[38]

NOTES AND REFERENCES

1. For an excellent, comprehensive account of the humanist assaults on truth, see Jeremy Campbell, *The Liar's Tale. A History of Falsehood* (New York: W. W. Norton, 2001). Inevitably, because it is sympathetic to these assaults and purports to describe them accurately (and, so far as I can tell, succeeds in doing so) – that is to say, accepts their truth – his book is riddled with pragmatic self-refutation. See Raymond Tallis, 'The Truth about Lies. Foucault, Nietzsche and the Cretan Paradox', *Times Literary Supplement* (21 December 2001), 3–4.

2. We can accept the persectival nature of truth, without having to abandon the notion

of making progress towards greater objectivity. One blind man reports that the elephant has a trunk, another that it has a tail. This is the first step towards the recognition that the elephant has a trunk and a tail and that there are people who will from one perspective report that it has a tail and those from another who will report that it has a trunk. The next – crucial – step is (as we discussed in Chapter 3) quantitative: the reduction of the element to, say, its weight or its length; that is to say, its unitisation. Even this is not absolute: the apparent length of an elephant is dependent upon the relative motion of the frames of reference of the elephant and the observer; the measured and the measuring system. But even then one can, as Einstein did, observe this relativity and so discover new absolutes. Moreover, Einsteinian relativities are remote from the relativities of culture and of individual viewpoints. The ultimate, objective invariance is when quantity is lifted out and we have pure numbers – for example, 2×2.

Perspectivalism takes the notion of 'angles of view' with respect to knowledge too literally. In a very important sense, knowledge does not have angles. It is deindex-icalised awareness. The sense that indexical awareness is 'only indexical' is the first step towards the knowledge. (Perspectivalism is discussed further at the end of the present chapter.)

3. This claim is in part based upon confusion between neutrality and objectivity. Our values may direct our attention to the areas that are of interest to us, but they do not determine our findings. As Robert Proctor notes, geologists know a lot more about oil-bearing shales than about other rocks, for very obvious political and economic reasons, but they do know *objectively* about oil-bearing shales. That is why their knowledge serves their interests. What is more, what they learn about those shales can be generalised to other, less favoured rocks. (I owe this example to Daniel Dennett's excellent 'Postmodernism and Truth', a paper given to the 1998 World Congress of Philosophy.)

4. Of course, the history of science is littered with abandoned laws, falsified theories and discredited substances such as phlogiston. This does not mean that the truths of science are only temporary, imposed by charismatic leaders supported by a praetorian guard of disciples and trained professionals. First, many of the laws that have been abandoned still look more accurate as accounts of the way things were than the rivals at the time. Second, successive laws, such as Einstein's theory as a successor to Newton, have often (a) been built on the earlier laws; (b) have been somewhat more accurate, though the earlier ones were good enough for most purposes; and (c) are simply more general in their range. Third, there is a cumulative body of knowledge which is not discredited by subsequent developments: some things that Archimedes and Galileo discovered are as true now as when they were discovered. This is true of both empirical findings and conceptual developments.

5. See Raymond Tallis, *Enemies of Hope. A Critique of Contemporary Pessimism* (Basingstoke: Macmillan, 2nd edition, 1999); *In Defence of Realism* (Lincoln, NB: University of Nebraska Press, 2nd edition, 1995); *On the Edge of Certainty* (Basingstoke: Macmillan, 1999).

6. Donald Davidson, 'The Folly of Trying to Define Truth', *Journal of Philosophy* (1996), 93(6). Bernard Williams, in *Truth and Truthfulness. An Essay in Genealogy* (New Haven, CT: Yale University Press, 2001), urged resistance against 'any demand for the *definition* of truth, because truth belongs to a ramifying set of notions, such as meaning, reference, belief and so on, and we are better employed in exploring the relations between these notions than in trying to treat some of them as

the basis of others' (p. 74). I still think there is something substantive to be said about truth, although it is not precisely definitional.

7. F. P. Ramsay, 'On Facts and Propositions', *The Foundations of Mathematics*, ed. R. B. Braithwaite (London: Routledge & Kegan Paul, 1931).

8. J. L. Austin, 'Truth', in *Philosophical Papers*, ed. J. O. Urmson and G. J. Warnock (Oxford: Oxford University Press, 2nd edition, 1970), p. 121. The 'truism' he selects to illustrate this claim – 'That a statement is true when it corresponds to the facts' – is also wrong, or seriously and interestingly misleading, as I will discuss.

9. The drive towards minimalist and deflationary accounts of truth is brilliantly summarised in Pascal Engel, *Truth* (Chesham: Acumen, 2002).

10. W. V. O. Quine, 'Truth', in *Quiddities. An Intermittently Philosophical Dictionary* (London: Penguin Books, 1990), p. 214.

11. 'Explicitness and Truth (and Falsehood)', in Tallis, *On the Edge of Certainty*.

12. Williams, *Truth and Truthfulness*.

13. Simon Blackburn, 'Where the Tiger Went. And Other True Stories from a Master of the Art', review of Bernard Williams, *Truth and Truthfulness*, *Times Literary Supplement* 18 October 2002, pp. 6–7.

14. Engel, *Truth*, p. 52. Heidegger, too, emphasised how, while we tend to attach the notion of truth to entities such as propositions, sentences and assertions, their truth or falsity presupposes a more fundamental 'disclosure' or 'uncovering' which has a stronger entitlement to be regarded as the essence of truth. *Da-sein*'s disclosure of the world is the precondition of there being any particular truth or falsehood.

   The influence of Heidegger throughout this present book will be evident. However, I believe that Heidegger fails to notice, or at least to overcome, this problem: the link between disclosedness and truth and the definition of *Da-sein* as disclosedness, makes it difficult to understand where falsity, partial knowledge and the sense of a reality beyond what is disclosed, come from. Truth as 'disclosure' is not sufficiently localised; it does not permit truth to be segmented into truths. See Raymond Tallis, *A Conversation with Martin Heidegger* (Basingstoke: Palgrave, 2002).

15. This is not the result of sloppiness among truth theorists but merely a reflection of the fact that, once a certain level of consciousness is reached, the notion of truth is emergent over a broad front – hence the inadequacy of Tarski's semantic theory (see below) – though it emerged fully only with respect to propositions expressed in sentences, thoughts and utterances.

16. This I believe is quoted by P. F. Strawson. Alas I cannot remember where.

17. See Quine, 'Truth', p. 214.

18. Anthony Quinton put this very well:

   There can be no doubt that if 'p' is an assertion, 'p' and 'p is true' mean the same thing. But what is an assertion? It is a sentence uttered as true. If this is accepted, the formula reduces to the vacuous triviality that if 'p' is a sentence uttered as true, to utter it is to do no more than to say that it is true. The point is that the formula does not really show the dispensability of the predicate 'is true' for in its reliance on the concept of an assertion, brought out explicitly above, it presumes that the concept of truth is already understood. (*The Nature of Things*, London: Routledge & Kegan Paul, 1973, p. 142)

   If, as Bernard Williams has pointed out, 'truth has an internal connexion with belief and assertion', then one cannot take the quotation marks, which assert assertion, or assert the idea of assertion, for granted. It is important, however, not to make the opposite error of assimilating truth to assertion.

19. *Oxford Readings in Philosophy* (Oxford: Oxford University Press, 1999), p. 1.

20. Engel, *Truth*, p. 14. A recent review in the *Times Literary Supplement* by P. F. Strawson ('Usefully True', 7 May 2004, p. 7) describes the notion of truth being a relation to facts as 'undeniably the most popular' account of the truth.

21. For more on this, see Raymond Tallis, *Not Saussure. A Critique of Post-Saussurean Literary Theory* (Basingstoke: Macmillan, 2nd edition, 1995), Chapter 3 'The Illusion of Reference'.

22. Michael Dummett, *Frege. Philosophy of Language* (London: Duckworth, 1973), p. 2.

23. It might be queried whether sense has a token or a type-identity. In the case of sense, which is about possibility lifted up from actual material objects, there cannot be anything corresponding to this contrast, which relies implicitly on the contrast between particular and general.

24. Gottlob Frege, 'The Thought. A Logical Inquiry', trans. A. M. and Marcelle Quinton, *Mind* (1956), 65: 289–311. Reprinted in *Philosophical Logic. Oxford Readings in Philosophy* (Oxford: Oxford University Press, 1967), pp. 18–19.

25. See Tallis, *A Conversation with Martin Heidegger*, pp. 78 et seq.

26. Martin Heidegger, *Being and Time*, trans. Joan Stambaugh (New York: State University of New York Press, 1996), p. 201.

27. Wittgenstein recognised this even when he was in the grip of his 'picture theory of propositions'. The picture was not a literal picture but a 'logical one'. The isomorphism was an identity of logical not of spatial, or some other material, form. The problem, which Wittgenstein did not solve, so that he abandoned the theory, was that of specifying what he mean by 'logical form'.

28. I owe this account of the slingshot argument to Engel, *Truth*, pp. 20–1. Interestingly, Richard Gaskin, in 'Proposition and World', Introduction to *Grammar in Early Twentieth-Century Philosophy*, ed. R. Gaskin (London: Routledge, 2001), p. 23, points out that the slingshot argument (at least in the version offered by Davidson) is based upon the assumption that logically equivalent sentences (e.g. 'Manchester is 36 miles east of Liverpool' and 'Liverpool is 36 miles west of Manchester') have identical referents. This assumption is clearly invalid. 'The distance from Liverpool to Manchester' and 'the distance from Manchester to Liverpool' may be identical in terms of mileage, but they are clearly not the same thing, any more than two journeys in opposite directions are the same things. This strengthens my own argument that you don't get, free of charge, all the logical consequences of a fact, especially where those facts are captured in sentences with different senses, so that even if they had identical 'underlying' referents (e.g. 'the distance between Manchester and Liverpool') this would not necessarily be apparent to a particular individual, for whom identity would be obscured by referential opacity.

29. This problem affects truth-bearer/truth-maker versions of the correspondence theory. The truth-bearer (e.g. an assertion made at a particular moment) and the truth-maker are both identified by the same sentence. In one case, it names the sentence – 'Snow is white' – and on the other occasion it names that which would make it true – the whiteness of snow.

30. For more on the interaction between coherence and correspondence in truth, see Raymond Tallis, 'Correspondence and Coherence Theories', in *On the Edge of Certainty*, pp. 17–32.

One could argue that coherence is 'sideways' or 'up-down' correspondence between truth-bearers. And, indeed, there are circumstances where, as Davidson once argued (though he later distanced himself from any theories of truth at all), 'coherence yields correspondence'. Donald Davidson, 'A Coherence Theory of Truth and Knowledge', in *Reading Rorty. Critical Responses to Philosophy and the Mirror of Nature (and Beyond)*, ed. Alan Malachowski (Oxford: Basil Blackwell, 1987), p. 121.

31. René Descartes, *Meditations on First Philosophy*, in *The Philosophical Works of Descartes*, Volume 1, trans. Elizabeth Haldane and G. R. T. Ross (Cambridge: Cambridge University Press, 1967), pp. 198–9.

32. Friedrich Nietzsche, 'In Truth and Lie in an Extra-moral Sense', a posthumously published manuscript. Available in *The Portable Nietzsche*, trans. Walter Kaufmann (New York: The Viking Press, 1954), pp. 42–7.

33. *Metaphysics*, Gamma 7.27, trans. Christopher Kirwan (Oxford: Oxford University Press, 1993), quoted in Blackburn and Simmons, *Truth*, p. 1.

34. Donald Davidson, self-citation, in 'A Coherence Theory of Truth and Knowledge'. Afterthoughts 1987, in *Reading Rorty. Critical Responses to Philosophy and the Mirror of Nature (and Beyond)* ed. Alan Malachowski (Oxford: Basil Blackwell, 1987), p. 135.

35. Pointing to a visible object is too early in the journey from sentience to deindexicalised awareness to capture what is captured in language.

36. And you end up (as Frege did) with making rather dispiritingly airless observation such as that 'The thought expressed in the words "that sea water is salt" coincides with the sense of the sentence "that sea water is salt"' (quoted in Engel, *Truth*, p. 42), which is not far off saying that the sense expressed in a sentence is the sense expressed in a sentence.

37. Paul Horwich, 'The Minimalist Conception of Truth', reprinted in *Truth. Oxford Readings in Philosophy* (Oxford: Oxford University Press, 1999), p. 262.

38. It may be worthwhile here linking back to the discussion in Chapter 4 on genesis of indexical and deindexicalised awareness. The fact that pointing may take place in the absence of pointees, in order to induce incorrect beliefs in the consumer, connects pointing with the elaboration of truth and falsehood. In the world of the actual, there is neither truth nor falsehood. That which is, is – and that is the end of it.

Truth and falsehood require the entertaining of *possibility* by a individual who has a sense of actuality that goes beyond mere sentience. This is already bundled in with object sense: objects are an inexhaustible source of as yet unexperienced experiences. Judgement and indexical awareness co-awaken. The judgement that an object is of such and such a nature, connected with expectations one has of it, lies at the root of the categories of the true and the false. With indexical awareness of objects, arise the possibility of error. Object awareness, unlike mere sentience (sensations of warmth and cold, say), is *corrigible*.

Within indexical awareness, truth and falsehood, however, remain embryonic, incompletely explicit. They develop fully only within the common world postulated in the realm of deindexicalised awareness. Within that realm, we have not only possibilities attached to actual objects, but possibilities attached to objects that are *themselves* only possibilities – truly free-floating possibilities – that are shared between individuals. In this realm, the division between possibilities that are realised and those that are not cuts deeper and the distinction between truth and falsehood, and consequently the reality of each, is sharper.

PART THREE

THE KNOWING AGENT

CHAPTER 7

The Uncoupled Animal

7.1 THE GAP BETWEEN MAN AND BEAST, MAN AND NATURE

According to Paul Churchland, intelligence is a means of ensuring that organisms are 'more intricately coupled to the environment':

> If the possession of information can be understood as the possession of some internal physical order that bears some systematic relationship to the environment, then the operations of intelligence, abstractly conceived, turn out to be just a high-grade version of the operations characteristic of life, save that they are even more intricately coupled to the environment.[1]

We humans, with our uniquely developed intelligence, should therefore be the most snugly coupled of all living creatures. In fact, the reverse is true. It will be evident from what we have said so far that we are the most uncoupled of all creatures, living at a distance from our material environment, and this is due to our special mode of awareness (one aspect of which is intelligence). And a good thing too; for our uncoupled condition permits us to engage with nature on our own terms, which are more favourable than those granted to any other animal.

All animals sense their environments. Humans not only sense their environments but also know a common world. They interact with it not only, and certainly never purely, through the senses but also through knowledge. Their world is, as much as anything, a totality of facts and the objects of other ingredients of propositional awareness. It is a space of possibilities, all of them general (though many have singular realisations), and many of them at a very high level of generality. What animals experience is not a world at all; it is a surroundingness from which they are not extricated; it is factless, being comprised of wall-to-wall sensation. They are *immersed* in what exists for them. What exists does not have a reality transcending their experience of it. Just as there are no independent partially scrutable objects, there are no unknowns. Such world as the beast has is the field of the immediately sensible. The not-yet and the no-longer, like other spaces of possibility, do not exist for them. The pauseless succession of experiences, the one damn-thing-after-another that is animal life is embedded in an environment but is worldless.

Animal emotions are not propositional attitudes but merely physiological reactions that energise and direct behaviour. Human emotions, by contrast, transform an entire landscape of possibility, illuminating certain facts and extinguishing others, making some glow and others fade. The terror the animal can feel when directly confronted with a biologically legitimate object of terror such as a predator may be experienced by a human at the thought of giving a lecture in a fortnight's time. The sight or smell that makes the beast salivate is the internal accusative of an appetite that is locked into what it immediately there. Salivation is a small part of my anticipation of food. At least as much time may be spent in adjusting my tie, checking the clock, shopping, finding the restaurant, worrying about whether my guest will be happy, and so on.

My appetites, transformed into desires, are unlocked from my immediate surroundings. Even something as seemingly primitive as greed is transformed. (To attribute 'greed' to an animal is, anyway, a gross anthropomorphism, importing moral judgements into the world of physiologically-driven instinctive behaviours.) It is mediated through abstract institutions – currency, barter, property, and so on. The purposeful activity of my body may be many steps away from the purpose to which that activity is ultimately related. Not uncommonly, I may be separated even from that intermediary purposeful activity of my body: my outer occupations give no clue to my preoccupations. After all, I can relate not only to facts that are about things that are out of sight; I can also relate facts about the past and know that they are explicitly in the past; that is to say, I can brood over tensed facts.

The point is, I think, sufficiently made. Deindexicalised awareness, our being individually in a relationship to a shared world much of which is not directly visible or even in any sense perceptible (and this applies not just to highly abstract behaviour, as when I sell my shares on account of an expected downturn in the economy), has uncoupled humans from the biological environment. This has 'de-located' us: at any rate our physical locations, or biological surroundings, are only a small part of where we are 'at'. It is facts, steering us through the human world, as much as the multitude of artefacts that make the material fabric of that world, which separate us from nature. We run because we know that the train is due to leave at six o'clock and that it is now a quarter to six, and therefore that we have 15 minutes to get to the station if we are going to catch the train. Our hurry, our worry, our scurry, is energised and guided by such facts and by such calculations. We are at least as much fact- as event-driven, certainly as far as our overarching actions are concerned. Our tranquillity and our joy are likewise abstractly inspired. Possibilities more often prey on our minds than predators on our bodies; we are fuelled at least as much by hopes, ideas and ambitions as by food. Most importantly, we spend much of our lives sorting, among the possibilities we entertain, those that are true from those that are false.

Uncoupling goes right to the heart of what we are: it is the difference between seeing X and seeing *That X is the case*, between (say) sensing a predator and seeing *that* there is a predator of a certain type in a certain place with respect to me. The latter is a piece of knowledge which is not reducible to a sample of the former, for reasons that will be evident from earlier discussion. It is the difference between sensing a red spot and observing that a spot is red; between feeling cold and knowing *That I am cold*. It is the difference between hearing the wind and hearing 'The wind' – that is to say, moving air, that has a probable character and probable effects. Facts are not reducible to sense experience, though factual beliefs may be audited against deliberately sought sense experiences.

This profound difference underpins *inquiry* which is peculiar to humans (and which will be the theme of the final section of this chapter). Because we deal in explicit possibilities, we move in a bath of complex expectations. The surface area of human expectation is infinitely elaborated. Language is a prime source of its million folds. The production of talk is not the result of stimuli in a biological sense and the effect on us of others' talk is not that of a stimulus. We judge what happens and we judge whether to express what happens and we judge whether or not to respond to what others say. In this sense, language is, as Noam Chomsky said, 'stimulus-free'. We measure verbal or non-verbal happenings, what we think has happened and the validity of what we think has happened, against norms. We are sufficiently unimmersed in what we encounter to judge it against our expectations. That is why we are the only objects in the universe to laugh at other objects in the universe. As Hazlitt said:

Man is the only animal that ... is struck with the difference between what things are, and what they ought to be.[2]

He is the only beast, that is to say, who deals in possibilities and has norms – based on experience (his own and that of others) – and explicit expectations (personal and collective) against which actuality can be judged. Man is the normative animal who is sufficiently outside the flow of events to pronounce upon, predict and argue about what happens.

Uncoupled indeed.[3]

7.2 DENYING THE GAP: EVOLUTIONARY EPISTEMOLOGY

The refusal fully to acknowledge our uncoupled state – and the extent to which we interact with the material world and each other through intermediaries, abstract symbols and facts, as well as through tools and other artefacts – has a venerable history. In comparatively recent times, Darwin's influence seems to have made it almost a mark of honesty, of being undeceived, that one refuses to acknowledge any true discontinuity between man and nature and, consequently, any profound difference in the relationship humans have to nature compared with beasts. An early Darwinian empiricist, the great physicist Ernst Mach, argued that even scientific knowledge was not fundamentally different from animal sentience: conditioned reflexes were 'rudimentary concepts':

> there is no difference between ordinary experience accessible to any being endowed with a nervous system and scientifically organised experiment. There is no break and continuity between science ... and modes of behaviour characteristic of the entire animal world.[4]

This must be the most radical challenge to the notion that we are uncoupled from nature in virtue of the special character of our consciousness. Mach assimilates knowledge at its most general and complex, at its most dispassionate, to conditioned reflexes. And yet he would nowadays be one of many thousands of evolutionary psychologists and epistemologists reinserting man into nature, or at least the (unnatural) idea of man into the (unnatural) idea of nature. Amongst the most distinguished is Quine, whose mission to naturalise knowledge and epistemology we discussed in Chapter 2.

Quine attempts to assimilate knowledge to sentience by assimilating evidence to sensory causes. While the tribunal of (basic sensory) experience is not in permanent session, and knowledge (or belief) not always in the dock, it is true that this is the ultimate place of appeal:

> The stimulation of his sensory receptors is all the evidence anybody has had to go on, ultimately, in arriving at his picture of a world ... Whatever

evidence there is for science *is* sensory experience ... and all inculcation of meanings of words, must ultimately rest on sensory evidence.[5]

Whether or not that does lead to naturalisation of knowledge, and in particular, scientific knowledge, depends on the force of 'ultimately'. A 'hard-line' naturaliser such as Mach would argue that science comes out of the shaping of behaviour patterns by smells, sights, sounds, etc. that condition expectations. Ascribing the status of a 'concept' to something like a conditioned reflex reinserts concepts, which seem public, into solitary sentient creatures, placing them in the natural world rather than in the communal space of possibilities. Quine is more ambiguous. The beliefs that form the corpus of science are not atomic; they are parts of networks. Moreover, they relate with different degrees of directness to sensory experience; and, as a consequence of this, are exposed to a variable extent to confirmation or falsification by sense experience. We are not always in the realm of his 'ultimately'. Even so, Quine is a through-and-through biologiser.

In common with many other philosophers, and indeed psychologists, of a behaviourist persuasion of the twentieth century, he argued that 'we must study language as a system of dispositions to verbal behaviour'[6] – dispositions which ultimately boil down to physiological mechanisms. The meaning of an utterance is to be understood not in terms of ideas and other mentalistic notions but in its power to evoke a response: its 'stimulus-meaning'. This is quite a complex notion, as it has to take account not only of utterances as stimuli but of utterances generated *in order to act as stimuli*. The stimulus-meaning of an utterance is a class of events consisting of the kind of stimuli which would prompt a person to assent to an utterance. In the case of 'Car!' this is the sound of a horn, dust rising from the road, the squeal of brakes, the visible presence of a natural object of a certain size. There are numerous problems with this and other behaviourist attempts to reinsert verbal meaning into the natural order – the flow of cause and effect biologised as the chain of stimuli and responses passing through the human organism. For example, it is not clear how the principle determining membership of the class of stimuli would be evident. The elements I have just listed do not actually mean 'car', as the words I have chosen to describe them indicate clearly. Moreover, it is not possible to think of a set of effects that would mean 'car' and only 'car'. Quite apart from this, there is the problem that words have different functions, work together in complex ways and derive their meaning at least in part from the system of language to which they belong.

In short, this attempt to cash out the highest mode of propositional awareness – speech – as if it were responses to stimuli, thereby reducing knowledge to sentience or, via language, to expectation of portions of sentience does not work. It shows how far one has to traduce human characteristics, such as speech, in order to reinsert humans into the natural world; and that it proves impossible to jettison everything that locates us outside of the natural world. Quine, for example, assumes that humans communicate with one another at quite a high level: a collectivisation of consciousness which already takes us beyond the world of 'stimuli' and other biological phenomena that belong to the isolated organism.

This is evident when we consider the seemingly most primitive form of linguistic behaviour: assenting to what somebody says and, possibly, acting on it. This depends upon many things that go far beyond the material characteristics of the utterance as stimulus, conditioned by association with a particular event or state of affairs. In order to assent to what someone says, we need (for starters) to know what he means to mean, what he wants us to believe, and *that* he wants us to believe it. Communication is not merely the transmission of verbal stimuli through brains: it draws on complex conventions of utterance and requires of us that we understand not only those conventions but also something about the utterer – as to whether he is trying to tell us something that is the case, or merely entertaining possibilities, or carrying out some other speech act. (Irony, for example, has no place in the natural world, in a network of stimuli and responses.) We also give or withhold our assent on the basis of our background knowledge and beliefs and our circumstances; and this will influence whether or not we decide assent has to be translated into some kind of response or action.

Consider this sequence:

a) The utterer associates a verbal event with a particular class of events impinging on him. This is the result of his teacher inculcating this association.[7]
b) The utterer emits the verbal event when an instance of the relevant class of events occurs in the vicinity.
c) The recipient hears this verbal event.
d) The recipient, who has received identical training to the utterer and so makes the same associations, comes to believe that there is an event of the relevant class occurring in the vicinity.

What is most striking in this story is the passivity, indeed the innocence, of both parties. Utterer and recipient are merely way-stations in a chain of stimuli and responses, or causes and effects. Nothing in the sequence captures the *meant meaning* that permeates all communication and which has to be ascribed to the utterer for the recipient even to guess at what is meant. It is precisely because I see your utterance as a piece of meant meaning that I can decide whether or not to assent to it. I make a judgement as to your fallibility or unreliability as a source. This is not the way of an organism responding to a stimulus. A causal chain being relayed from the world, to a teacher-become-utterer, and thence to a recipient bypasses meant meaning and the judgement of the recipient.

More important for our present concerns is that it loses the 'That ...' in 'That X is the case ...' and the stocking up of non-active knowledge, of deindexicalised awareness disconnected from particular spatio-temporal occasions, and unrelated to particular sensory experiences. Quine does seem to have a go at accommodating this kind of awareness – disconnected from the immediate surroundings – in his distinction between 'observation sentences' and 'standing sentences'.[8] Observation sentences are triggered by observations – such as the assertion 'It is raining' when it is in fact raining. A 'standing sentence' would be something like 'Rain at Heathrow 1600 G.M.T. 23 February 1974'. It is 'a standing report' rather than 'an occasion sentence'. What is more, 'it gives lasting information, dependent no longer on the vicissitudes of tense or indicator words such as "here"' (Quine, *Mind and Logic*, p. 75). It is 'ready for filing in the archives of science' (ibid.).

What Quine is describing in the passage from 'observation sentences' to 'standing sentences' is nothing other than deindexicalisation. It is very difficult to see how this can be understood in a theory of linguistic meaning that reduces it to a set of dispositions to utter certain things in response to the appropriate stimuli, or to accept someone else's utterances as true in the presence of the correct stimuli. It seems totally inadequate as a means of separating mere ejaculations that are supposed to draw attention to things that are present from, for example, 'cool' descriptions that have more remote purposes and do not draw attention to anything localised. It relies, what is more, on 'queries', 'assent' and 'dissent' which seem too *active* to be assimilated into his biologistic framework. This is obvious, at least in the case of Quine's 'standing sentences'. But it is equally true of his 'observation sentences'. First, the observations one makes are highly selective: humans are not in the grip of ejaculatory pandiculation in which they impose a total transcript of their immediate surroundings on their fellow humans beings who are, of course, doing the same. Describing the constraints that prevent them from doing this would be very difficult without employing such 'mentalistic' notions as 'having an idea of what the other person would like to know/needs to know/would like to hear'. Second, even 'observation sentences' express deindexicalised awareness. The rain at Heathrow is presented linguistically as an instantiation of a general possibility. The assertion 'It is raining' is not merely an ejaculation in response to a stimulus, like 'Ouch!' It is segmented, it specifies the nature of the stimulus in terms that are at arm's length from behaviour.[9] 'Observation sentences', while not as manifestly uncoupled from the environment of the speaker, are uncoupled none the less.

The wider aim of biologising knowledge and other mental functions requires giving a biological account of both its origin and its role. In order to make biologistic accounts even transiently plausible, it is necessary to do certain things:

a) reduce knowledge to the correlative of bits of behaviour or dispositions to such behaviour non-circularly defined;
b) connect behaviour with survival;
c) deny deliberation guided by knowledge;
d) incorporate language into a causal net by inserting meaning and reference into a causal net alongside sensory stimuli.

It will be obvious why none of these will work; most obviously because they presuppose a solitary, unselfconscious creature, without propositional awareness.

Since Quine's pioneering attempts from the 1950s onwards to naturalise knowledge (and, indeed, the human mind), evolutionary psychology and evolutionary epistemology have achieved an extraordinary ascendency. Expressing what is now the standard view, Steven Pinker asserts that our minds are 'organs of computation' that are 'a product of natural selection' and that they are 'designed to solve the kinds of problems our ancestors faced in their foraging way of life'?[10] Though Pinker admits that 'Three hundred thousand generations are enough to revamp a mind considerably' (p. 41), he is still committed to narrowing the gap between humans and animals: both parties have computational minds composed of modules that serve biological purposes. All the significant features of human being are phenotypical expressions of those genes that survive because they produce, and are carried by, those organisms most fitted to survive to reproduce. To reiterate the passage we quoted from E. O. Wilson in Chapter 1: 'Behaviour and social structure, like all other biological phenomena, can be studied as "organs", extensions of the genes that exist because of their superior adaptive value.'[11]

According to the doctrines of 'evolutionary psychology', the mind is innately pre-structured to enable it to make the most of the data it is given. These innate structures or modules, universal to mankind, are analogous to organs or tools with different functions – the so-called

Swiss knife theory of the mind.[12] The modules, or mental organs, are as universal in Man as other organs and are genetically determined. Despite the fact that human life even over the last 500 years has changed out of all recognition, humans have hardly changed since they parted company with the beasts. This is because the genes shaping the mental modules have not changed.[13] According to John Tooby, 'Our modern skulls house Stone Age minds', which serve us poorly in the civilised world in which we humans now live.[14] Thus a Grand Synthesis of genetics, evolutionary theory, cognitive science, neurophysiology, computational theory and anthropology supported a pessimistic, biologically determinist account of human nature and closes the gap between man and beasts. The characteristic and seemingly unique manifestations of human consciousness – intelligent behaviour, practical reasoning and abstract thought – are no different from the manifestations which humans share with animals, such as sensing. They are mediated by cerebral activity; and they are there because they promote survival by enabling the creature to fit more snugly into its ecological niche. If human knowledge and human truths are more effective organisers of behaviour than animal sense experience, it is because they are more closely coupled to the environment in ways that will ensure the right energy exchanges between the knower of truths and its environment.[15]

This view is beautifully expressed in the passage from Paul Churchland quoted at the beginning of section 7.1. Churchland goes on to say that 'Intelligent life is just life, with a high thermodynamic intensity and an especially close coupling between internal order and external circumstance'.[16] This represents the final point of convergence within physicalist thought of cognitive science, neurobiology, evolutionary theory and physics. The animalisation of humans is but the first step in their reduction to matter. Knowledge, like sentience, is a form of thermodynamic exchange. The relationship between a human being and her world is assimilated to the relationship between any closed system and *its* 'outside'.[17] The point of consciousness, of knowledge, of reason, of deliberateness, of agency is to plug the organism – human or subhuman it matters not – more snugly into its context so that its self-maintenance, its continuation, its survival is better assured.

The fundamental error of evolutionary epistemology and, indeed, all neurobiologically and biologically-based accounts of human cognition is that it denies the gap between the knower and the known. Because it denies this gap, it cannot accommodate the notion of 'truth' which, as we have seen, is most typically about a correspondence between one entity (for example, a sentence) and another (for example, a state of affairs) achieved through an identity of senses. Closer coupling achieved

by the fit between neural activity and the exigencies of the environment
– so that the one triggers the other – does not constitute a truth or
knowledge relation. Without the gap, the *un*coupling, these relationships collapse into one of mere causation.

The causal interaction between organism and environment – howsoever finely tuned to ensure the immediate and long-term needs of the
organism – does not amount to a truth relation, a knowing relation, or
even a sensing relation. At no stage does the causal chain:

$$\ldots \; E/C_1 \rightarrow E/C_2 \rightarrow E/C_3 \rightarrow E/C_4 \ldots \; .$$

entrain a truth relation, such that (for example) 'E/C_2' is true *of* 'E/C_3' or
E_3 is true *of* C_2. Neurophilosophy, by embedding organisms in the
material world, hopes to make the organism itself somehow true of or
true to that world in virtue of its being part of that world. But the
category of knowledge and of truth cannot arise without disengagement
and uncoupling, without the world being encountered through possibility (that may or may not be actualised) and generality (that may or
may not be instantiated). 'Part of' does not deliver 'knowing that' or
'true to/of' or 'in possession of the truths about'. Causal chains do not,
as we have discussed, generate even the faintest hint of 'That ...'.

Which, from the point of view of (materialist) evolution, is no great
loss. For if it is survival that you are after, unconscious mechanisms are
the better bet. Actions informed by knowledge tested to be true after
deliberation seem a cumbersome method of interacting with the
environment to promote survival. A gene that is really 'selfish' and
really does know its business is hardly likely to requisition for its survival
an organism that engages with the environment in this ponderous way –
or not in the first instance, or for the first few million years anyway.
After all, it is only in recent centuries, too late for evolutionary
mechanisms to have had a hand in it, that knowledge, and actions
informed by declarative knowledge, have greatly extended our power to
make the world safe for ourselves. From the evolutionary point of view,
knowledge (and agency and deliberateness) are as useful as a hole in the
head. Not only, then, does materialist evolutionary theory fail to deliver
knowledge, truth, deliberateness and agency, but they are of little or no
evolutionary value. As I have remarked elsewhere previously,[18] if you
were serious about survival, which would you choose, an errorless
mechanism or knowledge-mediated activity, with all its room for error
at the inception of knowledge and technology?

Freedom, deliberateness of action, etc., therefore, make *absolutely no
sense* within the evolutionary framework – not just because of the

latter's materialism but because mechanisms are more reliably and more perfectly coupled to needs (seen in the wider sense) than are free actions. Mechanisms, by definition, cause things to happen more efficiently, smoothly and reliably than actions can bring them about and there are things that are 'achieved' by mechanisms – most things, including amazing *tours de force* such as building a human brain *in utero* – that no deliberate action can begin to match. Even though it is comparative advantage we are talking about, we could imagine that more comparative advantage could accrue to a beast with better mechanisms (including instincts) than to a creature encumbered with self-consciousness.[19] The progressive fine-tuning of instincts would seem to be a more effective strategy than an increasingly persuasive illusion of free action.

Truth, agency, knowledge, therefore, have no place in the Darwinian scheme; the very fact that we now elude the survival of the fittest – or that fitness is being redescribed in all sorts of unbiological ways that make no sense in nature – shows how unDarwinian we are. The emptiness of evolutionary epistemology, with its reduction of the criteria of truth to survival, lies in the fact that distinctively human knowledge began to deliver on the Darwinian imperative of survival only long after humans had parted company with the natural world. Knowledge works only for an animal uncoupled by knowledge from nature. This is the animal that operates less with what is before her than with possibilities and for whom what is actually before her is a realisation of general possibilities, and a source of future possibilities. Knowing humans are connected to the world through possibilities, which do not exist in nature (since nature is composed entirely of actualities), not just through energy exchanges.[20]

The most striking flaw of the neo-Darwinian accounts of human beings is that it overlooks the discontinuity between Man and nature that is written into the very structure of knowledge. The Knowing Animal confronts nature as something that is before him, set over and against him. And out of this confrontation, and the connected collectivisation of consciousness, comes a second nature, a human world created within the biological universe. Evolutionary epistemology fails to see that knowledge is an awakening out of the immersed condition of beasts; from their conditions of being coupled mechanisms. We humans uniquely wake out of and *to* nature. As Schelling put it: 'Nature opens its eyes within man and notices that it exists.'[21]

After an initial period of excitement in which it was believed that 'the selfish gene', requisitioning organisms to provide shelter for its replication and so ensure its survival, dictated most aspects of human behaviour, there has been a certain amount of retrenchment. For example, Richard Dawkins, who first described genes as 'selfish', points out that 'to force a naive Darwinian interpretation on everything we do in our everyday lives would be an error':

> We are totally surrounded by artefacts of our own civilization. The environment in which we now live has especially little to do with that in which we were naturally selected. We can still make a simple Darwinian interpretation of things like hunger and sex drives, but for most of our questions we have to employ re-writing rules.[22]

This actually takes back too little. The expression of sex drives and even of hunger is remote from animal behaviour, as we shall discuss in Chapter 10. Even defaecation is far from the animal dropping of animal droppings: the importance humans place on privacy, potty training, toilet paper, porcelain, sewage systems and public health issues, each a tip of a cultural iceberg, marks just how far. What is more, the transformation of the environment to which Dawkins refers was not something that merely happened: it was painstakingly brought about by a huge collective physical and cognitive effort. It is the roots of this effort that I want to examine.

There seems to be an essential passivity in sentience, a pure receptivity, a mere exposure or suffering. The awareness of the knowing animal is more active: humans manipulate the conditions under which they are conscious and so deliberately shape the contents of their consciousness. There is an obvious sense in which this is true: we have in large part created the environment in which we live our lives. But there is a more intimate and profound sense: we *control* our experiences in complex ways and seek out experiences of a prescribed kind. This active regulation of experience is rooted in the very nature of knowledge, extends knowledge and drives the widening of the gap between humans and their nearest animal kin. I am referring to *inquiry*.

To get hold of the essence of inquiry, it will help to remind ourselves of what stands at the root of knowledge, at the very origin of propositional awareness. If we go back to indexical awareness, there are two things that already set human consciousness apart from animal awareness. One is the intuition of objects that have a reality that transcends their appearances to us. This intuition – the result of the sense of being an embodied subject combined with being able to perceive at a distance – opens up the sense of possibility and is shadowed by a sense of ignorance, of the 'yet to be found out'. This is where the explicit cleavage between consciousness and its objects, the epistemic and the constitutive, originates. The other (which is of course intimately connected) is a condition of being explicitly unimmersed, of being located in the sensory field but not dissolved into it, of being set off from it. The archetypal form of indexical awareness is vision and it is here that human awareness becomes most readily active. The unimmersed organism, aware of something lying behind or beyond what it senses, passes from seeing to looking; from looking to scanning and scrutinising; and ultimately from scrutinising to testing and measuring. Looking that sees not only its object but also itself looking is the point at which the surrounding world ceases to be a source of mere stimuli and humankind the passive recipient of experiences. It is here that humans embark on their unique path to science – the most unnatural manifestation of man's unnatural knowledge.

The seeming continuum between suffering what one's senses serve up, unfocused staring and, say, deliberate observation is misleading. The transition from passive gawping to active scrutinising, and hence to everything that lies beyond this, is driven by an intuition of the otherness of the world in which one is sensorily immersed, but not drowned, even less dissolved, and a correlative intuition of one's self as a particular thing located in the field opened up by one's senses.

Behind inquiry is a sense of the incomplete scrutability of a confronted object. This is quite different from the stimulus-driven 'investigations' of an animal following a trail. Without the explicit intuition of an object, there is no clear distinction between the occasion (the scent or its gradient) of the search and that which is being searched for. That is why such a 'search' is not truly a search. Describing an animal as 'investigating' its environment and as being 'inquisitive' is unwarranted anthropomorphism. An animal following a scent in pursuit of its prey may be objectively uncertain but is not subjectively so, in the sense of formulating the gap between what it knows and what it needs to know. The trail-following, what is more, is stimulus-driven: menu-driven in more senses than one.

For animals, there is no path from objective uncertainty to ever more active, ever more complex, ever more abstract, ever more systematic, ever more collective, ever more institutionalised uncertainty because there is no springboard of self, with its intuitions of the substantive otherness of objects, to drive that uncertainty. Animals lack the fundamental sense that there is more to what is experienced than is revealed in the experience – my experience, your experience, anyone's direct experiences, anyone's assisted experiences.

With progressive deindexicalisation of awareness – the separation of the sense of what is 'out there' from experience of objects and from individual consciousness – uncertainty, and the inquiries it prompts, are progressively uprooted from the immediate circumstances of the moment. The agenda of inquiry is uncoupled, that is to say, from the agenda of the moment. A man who enters a laboratory is not detained by most of the material of the laboratory, only by certain items used and experienced in a pre-planned way, in accordance with a purpose whose definition would take many pages to define and many thousands of pages to get to the bottom of. The human inquirer is exemplified in a man thinking to himself on a train, during the course of a journey which has thousands of components, most of which make sense only with respect to an abstract frame of reference (as we shall discuss in Chapter 9), about matters that have little to do with the sensibilia surrounding him. This is entirely different from an animal following its nose or working a field or even one assuming a vantage point in order to look out for prey. The drivers to inquiry in humans are increasingly abstract, indirect and internal to the individual or the community of which he is a part.

A key ingredient of inquiry is the differentiated sense of possibility which generates hunches, guesses and, eventually, formal hypotheses. These prompt the requisitioning of experience. Such requisitioned experience is the basis of (deliberate) *observation*. Observations may require only disciplined attention. Very often much more is needed: self-positioning (ranging from popping one's head round the door, to going to the top of a hill to travelling to another place); the authority of others to assist the directing of one's attention; instrumentation; or a body of theory. Scientific observation typically requires all of these things. The investigator goes to a particular place where equipment and materials are available so that, under the direct or indirect (textual) guidance of a collective of peers, he tests a particular consequence of the most exposed part of a corpus of beliefs. The sensory experiences that form the content of the observation are the mere tip of a huge iceberg of collective, deindexicalised awareness. Beyond a very primitive level even seemingly direct seeing is informed by theory, experience is informed by general knowledge: the visual field is a continuum of significance in which visible surfaces and invisible meanings, actualities steeped in general possibilities, are inseparable.

The cognitive itch driving incessant inquiry, curiosity, looking about, is awoken early in humans and hardly at all in beasts. While chimpanzees of all ages seem remarkably uninterested in their environment except in so far as it directly stimulates them, 'an explanatory drive is at the core of a child's development'.[23] Infants point at things in the spirit of inquiry (and knowledge-sharing) and this is soon followed by the delightful (and wearying) question: 'Wazzat? Wazzat?' Such questioning, and the explanatory drive, bears witness to two things: the sense that there is an incompleteness in sense; and a faith that it will be closed, either by verbal inquiry or by direct exploration. Even the animal activity that appears most akin to human inquiry – hunting for prey – is nothing of the kind. Human hunting is qualitatively different from hunting by other animals. According to Wolpert,

> Unlike most animals, which either sit and wait to ambush prey or use stealth and pursuit techniques, human hunters use a wealth of information to make context-specific decisions, both during and after prey is encountered.[24]

The explanation-seeking human is also a fact-finding creature and (as we shall discuss in section 9.3) a cause-bearing one. The envisaged goal of inquiry is not localised, although it may be reached as a result of an encounter with something localised. When I see the change in the pointer readings that tell me that the metal I am seeking is near, the observation does not point to a localised object. When I unearth the missing item, it is localised, but the possibility that it realises is not. The object of inquiry is as deindexicalised when it is encountered as when it is sought; when it is an object, as when it is a fact, a solution or a theory.

As inquiry develops and is enhanced in the way we have described in the previous paragraph, the sense of ignorance grows and occupies a wider and wider realm. The sea of human uncertainty extends ever further beyond the basic human needs – food, safety, etc. – that were its first objects. The world that is known to exist beyond the here and now grows in a multitude of directions – spatially, temporally, conceptually, socially. Local uncertainties – I do not know what lies ahead or is just round the spatial corner, or round the spatio-temporal corner where what is out of sight is yet to occur – are lavishly supplemented by locationless uncertainties, a personal factual ignorance or a collective ignorance of the not-yet or of 'the true nature' of things. The suspicion that I might be wrong widens from the first encounter with an illusion that is unmasked. The preparedness for the unexpected and the counter-intuitive remain undiminished as knowledge pushes further away from the territory where the expected usually happens into the more consistently counter-intuitive realm of science, a realm where even (ordinary) knowledge is surrounded by the sense of error and uncertainty.

These observations about active inquiry and the pursuit of location-less goals of knowledge – of facts, concepts, of new methods and new skills – make clear just how far knowledge is from being compressed or summarised sentience. To try to connect knowledge with (say) events in 'sensory endings' and so naturalise it, does no justice to distances that have been travelled to arrive at it. It is (to steal Jonathan Swift's analogy) like trying to find the sunbeams that went into the cucumber.

As inquiry extends in all directions, so the gap between human and animal nature widens, and humans build a second world within the material one. The point where the passivity of a stimulus-receiving, or driven, life passes over into active inquisition of the surroundings, the platform from which active inquiry is possible, is the Existential Intuition. This platform, that permits 'bounce-back' (see sections 2.2.1 and 4.2) and makes intentionality explicit and allows intentional objects to be transformed into objects of knowledge, grows more and more solid. The fundamental break is not between science and ordinary inquiry but between inquiry and passive, stimulus-driven behaviour. Inquiry reaches into the roots of indexical awareness. The fundamental difference between science and 'general looking round' in active scrutiny is the greater body of explicit communal knowledge upon which particular scientific observations sit. Once inquiry is started, the distance between it and the aconceptual gawping and sniffing of animals becomes ever greater. The creature that experiences its body as being both itself and not-itself, and so discovers its toes in a way that no other animal discovers any part of the organism it is, extends its inquiries into infinite space and eventually discovers Alpha centauri.

NOTES AND REFERENCES

1. Paul M. Churchland, *Matter and Consciousness. A Contemporary Introduction to the Philosophy of Mind* (Cambridge, MA: MIT Press, revised edition 1988), p. 174.
2. William Hazlitt, *Lectures on the English Comic Writers* (London: Dent, 1906), p. 1.
3. Not entirely uncoupled, of course. Perception is not detached awareness, though of course knowledge that is detached grows out of perception.
4. Leszek Kolakowski, *Positivist Philosophy: From Hume to the Vienna Circle*, trans. Norbert Guterman (London: Penguin Books, 1972), pp. 146–7.

    Mach at least took Darwinosis to its logical conclusion. As did Nietzsche, turning it upon his own thought. For Nietzsche, as Michael Tanner, one of his more sympathetic commentators, points out:

    The conscious thoughts of philosophers, are dictated by their inclinations, 'valuations, or more clearly physiological demands for the preservation of a certain kind of life. (*Beyond Good and Evil*, 1.4; *Nietzsche* in *German Philosophers* (Oxford: Oxford University Press, 1994, p. 413)

Hence 'untruth is a condition of life'. Darwin himself entertained similarly sceptical thoughts:

> Can the mind of man, which has, I fully believe, been developed from a mind as low as that possessed by the lowest animal, be trusted when it draws grand conclusions? (*Autobiography*, ed. Nora Barlow (Norton: New York, 1993), p. 93)

It scarcely needs saying that this thought undermines 'grand conclusions', such as the Theory of Evolution, as much as it undermines the more flattering accounts of human beings, their origins and their nature, Darwin had in his sights.

5. W. V. O. Quine, *Ontological Relativity* (New York: Columbia University Press, 1969), p. 75. Quine's position illustrates the aptness of Bernard Williams' warning not to

> suppose ... that at every point of cultural elaboration, there is (or ought rationally to be) a reductive route back to the primitive basis. That is simply false of human historical and cultural development, and it is a virtue, as I have already said, of a genealogical method that it helps to remind us of this, by not confusing explanation with reduction. (*Truth and Truthfulness. An Essay in Genealogy* (New Haven, CT: Yale University Press, 2002), p. 147)

Likewise, we should not think of knowledge as piled-up sense experiences.

6. 'Mind and Verbal Dispositions', in *Mind and Language. Wolfson College Lectures 1974*, ed. Samuel Guttenplan (Oxford: Oxford University Press, 1975), p. 91.

7. Quine invites us to imagine language being acquired as follows:

> Consider the case where we teach the infant a word by reinforcing his random babbling on some appropriate occasion. His chance utterances bears a chance resemblance to a word appropriate to the occasion, and we reward him. The occasion must be some object or some stimulus sources that we as well as the child are in a position to notice. (*Ontological Relativity*, pp. 83–4)

8. Quine, 'The Nature of Natural Knowledge', in *Mind and Language*.

9. To suggest that asserting 'It is raining' is the behaviour appropriate to the experience of rain is circular and, what is more, takes no account of the selectivity of the occasions under which, seeing rain, we report it.

10. Steven Pinker, *How the Mind Works* (London: Penguin Books, 1998), pp. 36, 21.

11. Quoted in Kenan Malik, *Man, Beast and Zombie. What Science Can and Cannot Tell us about Human Nature* (London: Weidenfeld and Nicolson, 2000), p. 148.

12. For a brief account of the origins of evolutionary psychology, see Raymond Tallis, 'Against Dr. Panglum', *Prospect* (2000), pp. 24–9. This is based on Malik, *Man, Beast and Zombie*. There have been robust arguments over how many of these cognitive organs there are. Is there a general 'Find-a-Mate' module or is there a whole cluster of task-specific modules, such as 'Go-to-a-Disco' module? There have been disagreements, too, over how much mental activity is mediated by task-specific modules and how much is given over to relatively undifferentiated central processing in the brain.

These arguments will always be inconclusive because of the essential error of the modular theory: it is based on the daft notion that human being-in-the-world can be broken up into a series of types of tasks to be handled by modules. It is easy to do this in the case of animals, if only because we do not know them from within and moreover, they do not have our elaborated 'within' (so far as we can tell). Human behaviour, which we *do* know from within, evidently has a complexity that no finite number of modules could generate.

Moreover, as I hope the discussion in the next chapter will make clear, even simple behaviours – such as going to London for a meeting – draw upon a world of such depth and extensity that no module, or parley of modules, could manufacture. The problem, ultimately, with modules is that they are mechanisms; but in order to do what we do do, we have to know what we are doing; we have to *do* it and this cannot consist of simply hosting the activity of a series of mechanisms.

13. In the 1960s, Konrad Lorenz, an evolutionary psychologist *avant la lettre*, was much listened to for his notion that civilisation was degrading to Man *because* men were like animals. Domesticated animals became decadent under domestication. Man, too, therefore would decay under domestication.

14. Which makes it rather difficult to understand how civilisation got going in the first place and how it has kept going for so long. The fact that the distinguishing mark of Man since he parted company with the pongids has been that he has increasingly adapted his own environment, rather than survived through adaptation to a given environment, seems to have escaped the notice of many evolutionary psychologists. (Richard Dawkins is a partial exception.)

15. Of course, the notion of 'coupling' to the environment, of embeddedness in nature, is anyway a revealingly ambiguous one. Being assimilated into the environment is the most complete way of being coupled with it. It might be argued that being eaten, rotted, etc. hardly counts because it is not compatible with survival. Consider, however, a pebble. It is totally at one with its environment and nothing could be better coupled than a pebble with its gravitational field. As for survival, it will live to bury us all.

Someone might say that I am missing the point of evolutionary theory which is about comparative advantages for survival to reproduce in the context of competition for scarce resources or threats from predators. The point, however, of my 'absurd' comparison is that the emergence of organisms is about *un*coupling from what becomes more explicitly differentiated *as* the environment and, in the case of humans, as his or her world. A consistent physicalism makes it difficult to retain the very notion of the differentiation between entity and environment: there is only matter. (A pebble, of course, is not only 'world-less' but also 'environment-less': it does not interact with the rest of the world even from across a membrane.)

16. Churchland, *Matter and Consciousness*, p. 174.

17. The fact that the 'outside' does not exist for a thermodynamic system – a stone is 'world-less', though is has a *de facto* outside – is overlooked.

18. See Raymond Tallis, *The Explicit Animal. A Defence of Human Consciousness* (Basingstoke: Macmillan, 2nd edition, 1999), pp. 23–9 for the argument against the notion that consciousness has a positive survival value.

One could cite a large number of philosophers and other writers who have seen human consciousness as positively disabling. Among them Thomas Hardy must be awarded the palm for pessimism and succinctness:

A time there was when, we may guess,
Things went well before the birth of Consciousness
The Dynasts

19. This is further evidence against those who would subsume the notion of truth under that of power. The direct link between knowledge and immediate action is uncoupled for the sake of a future better link between knowledge and more effective

action. Truth and power reconnect in technology and its uses but the distance remains. Truth does not dissolve in power. Moreover, truth is arrived at collectively by the pooling of resources; of all the human enterprises, the pursuit of scientific truth involves the widest cooperation – across disciplines, human groups and epochs. People build on other people's findings and, although there is much in-fighting en route, self-assertion has to be tempered by the necessity to accept others' ideas and to submit one's own findings to criteria of methodological validity. The technological gains for mankind and the social gains for individual scientists are postponed. The neo-Darwinian account of the acquisition of knowledge is thus empirically untrue as well as self-refuting.

20. This difference has one of its most striking expressions in the fact that (as Popper expressed it) the growth of our knowledge 'is the result of a process closely resembling ... "natural selection"; that is, *the natural selection of hypotheses*' (*Objective Knowledge: An Evolutionary Approach*, Oxford: Clarendon, 1972, p. 261, emphasis in original). If one sets aside Popper's evolutionary epistemology, we can accept the essential point: humans put their ideas, not their bodies, on the line by entertaining possibilities rather than stumbling about among actualities.

21. Quoted in Rudiger Safranski, *Martin Heidegger. Between Good and Evil*, trans. Ewald Osers (Cambridge, MA: Harvard University Press, 1998), p. 200. Such noticing arrives at an astonishing climax in Darwin's own theory.

22. Richard Dawkins, in *Key Philosophers in Conversation. The Cogito Interviews*, ed. Andrew Pyle (London and New York: Routledge, 1991).

23. Lewis Wolpert, 'Causal Belief and the Origins of Technology', *Philosophical Transactions of the Royal Society of London* A (2003), 361: 1709–19, p. 1713.

24. Ibid., p. 1717. This difference is apparent even in simpler situations. The dog looking for a ball has an inchoate sense of something-to-be-found. He is driven by a sense of lack. But what he seeks is the ball; whereas what a human seeks may be characterised correctly as 'the location of the ball'. The dog seeks the ball, the human seeks knowledge of the ball's location. The dog tries to find, the human tries to find out. In the human there is a distance from the seeking body and its goal, which is not merely the objective distance between the two bodies. What the human lacks is not merely the ball but knowledge of where the ball is, the truth about the ball's location. His search is therefore hypothesis-driven whereas the animal's search is cue-driven, perhaps scent-driven. The animal's search is conducted entirely within the realm of the senses, the humans search from outside, from a realm of general possibility applied to a particular situation. This is the difference between finding and finding out; and between trying to find and trying to find out. The animal returns with a ball in its mouth and the human returns with the ball in its hand and with a fact located in his consciousness – the location of the ball. As seeking becomes more complex the abstract reward – the fact – becomes more important than any concrete one.

Connected with this is the very distinctive expression in humans of curiosity: an appetite for stories. A story is a withheld fact combined with the means for creating an appetite for it; that is to say, the means of awakening the sense of something worthwhile to be found out. The enjoyment of stories is about the passage from a felt lack of knowledge to that knowledge. Someone may say, 'Oh, but that's only the plot. What really matters is the realisation of character, caressing the details of a scene, making things present, analysing the general nature of humankind.' Yes, but that's still all about revelation – of a world; moreover, the plot is what energises most novels and motivates their readers to read them. This is true even of a novel such as *Moby Dick* where the first 132 out of 135 chapters are preliminary, often purely descriptive and even more often seemingly digressive; of *Ulysses* where the plot is as much as anything a passage from early morning to the depths of the night – where the overarching story is the story of a day – and everything else is mere sub-plot.

What the knowing human finds is not a set of sense experiences. This fits with something that Wilfred Sellars 2said, when he attacked 'The Myth of the Given': 'In characterizing an episode or a state as that of *knowing*, we are not giving an empirical description of that episode or state; we are placing it in the logical space of reasons, of justifying and being able to justify what one says.' 'Empiricism and the Philosophy of Mind', in Herbert Feigl and Michael Scrivens (eds), *Minnesota Studies in the Philosophy of Science*, vol. 1 (Minneapolis: University of Minnesota Press, 1956), pp. 253–329, quoted in John McDowell, *Mind and World*, with a new Introduction by the author (Cambridge, MA: Harvard University Press, 1996), p. xx.

The Rational Agent

8.1 SOME GENERAL OBSERVATIONS ON HUMAN AGENCY

'Responsiveness to reasons' is a good gloss on the notion of freedom.

When Kant describes the understanding as a faculty of spontaneity, that reflects his view of the relation between reason and freedom: rational necessitation is not just compatible with freedom but constitutive of it. In a slogan, the space of reasons is the realm of freedom.[1]

We have discussed how the passive receptivity of the senses is supplemented by active inquiry. Active inquiry is rooted in the bounce-back based on the Existential Intuition and with the intuition, arising out of it, of objects which transcend their appearances in consciousness. Object intuition not only awoke a sense of ignorance, but opened up a space of possibility. This space is the theatre of human action, where uncoupled awareness trades with the natural world on ever more favourable terms. The knowledge that comes from inquiry guides increasingly deliberate action. The acquisition of knowledge is itself active. Often a quite complex series of actions will be necessary to make an observation. Craning one's neck to see something that someone is trying to draw to my attention, manufacturing or acquiring some instrument to enhance my senses, are all variations on the uniquely human activity of 'inquiry'. Contrariwise, continuous observation is necessary to ensure that action remains on the path leading from the first step to a more or less distant goal. Separating the awareness of the Knowing Animal from his special status as an agent is therefore somewhat artificial. The focus here will, however, be on agency. I want to pick up some business left over from the final chapter of *I Am: A Philosophical Inquiry into First-Person Being*, where I discussed how true agency could arise and develop in the hominid organism.

The key to agency is first-person being: the Existential Intuition 'That I am [this] ...' growing out of the primordial self-consciousness made possible by the hand. Itself a proto-tool, the hand instrument-alised the body and made the hominid organism a subject within its body. This in turn inspired literal tools that not only enhanced agency but also raised the agent to a higher level of self-consciousness. Tools were signs: they placed markers of human needs and human intentions outside of the body. This broke down the solitude of sentience; human consciousness began to be collectivised. A feedforward mechanism, involving the hand, the brain, tools (and other artefacts) and language, was set in motion. Several hundred thousand generations later, a universe parallel to nature has been established: a human place of artefacts, institutions, rules, rituals and customs, jobs, languages, histories, stories, and so on.[2]

In the previous volume, I discussed the way in which the 'am-ground' or 'am-soil' of the self created a platform from which true actions could arise. The self was a new point of origin or departure in the material world. This agentive self has, in the several million years since the awakening of the Existential Intuition, acquired an impressive toolkit to support its free actions: artefacts, institutions, inherited know-how and know-that, and language. The primary driver to the expansion of 'am' and the co-expansion of agency was the tool-directed, tool-inspired over-reaching of the agentive self. The tool, set out in space as the bodily agent's external agent, awakens the possibility of action that goes beyond what is currently achievable. The tool holds open a space of possibility of reaching beyond grasp. When the area of over-reaching is occupied by action, the expanded agency forms the new baseline. The tool is particularly apt for driving agency because it is attached to the body and yet explicitly corporeal, is concrete and yet a sign of a general need. Its status as a sign, and as something had in common, makes it a crucial driver of the collectivisation of consciousness which permits higher levels of cooperation. Powers and understanding are pooled so that the socialisation of humans can go beyond the stereotyped dove-tailing actions of so-called 'social' animals.

One of the issues left unresolved in *I Am* was this: whether, given that the roads to human freedom have been collective, individual humans have bought liberation from physical determinism at the price of being psycho-socially or culturally determined. It is difficult to doubt our collective liberation from physical determination. There is abundant evidence to support the notion that, collectively, humans have deflected the course of nature, filling it with things that only humans could have created and subordinated it to their own use. But does this species-freedom to change things imply that we are, individually, free? I want to argue here that while the collective capacity of humanity to distance itself from nature creates the 'outside-of-nature' from which it is free to manipulate nature to its own ends, the freedom of individual humans is not simply a passive reflection of the freedom of the collective. We have personal, as well as collective, freedom. Individual freedom is guaranteed by the fact that participation in actions that have collective meaning is made possible only through that special relationship to the bodies that made us free in the first place. Individual freedom, rooted in the Existential Intuition 'That I am this ...', is a necessary condition for full participation in the collective activity that expressed the species freedom of humanity. Individuals cannot contribute to the collective if they are entirely dissolved in it. Persons, I shall argue, are unique points of departure not only because they enter the collective from different starting points, each being objectively unique, but also because they have to appropriate a singular portion of the collective (defined by their location and, in the widest sense, their history) and that appropriation is in the final analysis mediated by a body that is itself appropriated by the individual. It is this body that is the ultimate basis for the integrated consciousness that unites the elements of an individual's awareness into an instantaneous totality and the successive phases of that totality over time.

We participate in the collective effort in so far as we make sense of it and it dovetails with our singular purposes whose uniqueness is guaranteed by the uniqueness of our history – the sum total of the encounters resulting from our trajectory through the world – and our present circumstances. This uniqueness is in turn underwritten by the uniqueness of the body that is the internal accusative, the complement, of the Existential Intuition. While the collective – culture, society, language, technology, abstract ideas – guarantees our distance from nature, our bodies are the guarantors of our distance from the collective. The embodied subject with her complex relationship to her body is the indissoluble bolus in every culture, the point from which its novel future may be created, the enduring point of origin.[3]

It is this double point of reference, therefore, that guarantees our freedom: our culturally sustained distance from our body holds open the space between ourselves and nature; and the anchoring of self-consciousness and the Existential Intuition in our bodies (with their unique locations and trajectories) keeps us at a distance from the collective. Deindexicalised awareness – whose convergence creates the culture of which we are a part, and whose idealised totality is 'the world' – has always to be realised in a located individual, with her immediate context of material objects and preceding and succeeding events.[4]

Humans are individually, as well as collectively, free in other words because they are both indexically related to an immediate environment, at whose centre they lie, and deindexically aware of a (personal) subset of the collective world. This dual allegiance is evident at every turn, even in those archetypal situations where individuals appear to be almost entirely possessed by the collective. Consider a group of soldiers on parade. Their uniforms, their actions, the constraints within which they operate are identical: they look like a platoon of tokens instantiating the same type. That, indeed, is the point of drill: to emphasise the subordination of the individual soldier to the collective. The pathway each soldier takes to and from this drill, the invisible lives in the hinterland of their collective marching, are, however, unique to each; and that uniqueness is guaranteed even during the drill. Each has a personal relationship to the drill underwritten by a body with its own experiences, self-expropriated in its own way. What is more, obedience to the commands depends upon an active understanding of what is barked out, its meaning and its relationship to a vast nexus of possibilities.

The supreme agent for collectivisation of consciousness is, of course, language. Much of what we say to one another is both conventional and almost automatic. Our comments about the weather, the government, the railway system, seem like conditioned reflexes. Sometimes it is as if words happen on our lips rather than being used by us to express what we, individually, feel. Some have even suggested that 'language speaks us' (rather than vice versa) even in our most personal or calculated or effortful or complex communications; that utterances are simply nodes in the network of the communicable whose scope and origin lie beyond our grasp. We don't really know what we are saying because utterances belong to systems that are largely hidden from us. Since we do not know what we say, our speaking selves (ourselves at our apparently most deliberate and free), passively reflect cultural forces that are operating through us. Language, the most compelling expression of our distance from nature, demonstrates, it seems, that we have acquired freedom from material forces only to be imprisoned by social and cultural ones.

This is a mistake. It overlooks the difference between types of utterances and utterances on particular occasions. Learning how and when to use even the most conventional utterances involves high-level self-consciousness. Even when the rules have been internalised, there is still plenty of scope for individual decision. Deciding whether and when to say something as utterly conventional as 'Hello' to someone in a particular situation, and in what tone of voice, and whether and how to follow it up, can be very complex indeed and draw deeply on many *arrondissements* of the self.[5] We are individuals even when we conform to conventions: they are painfully acquired and, in many cases, deliberately applied. We don't have to *break* conventions in order to be individuals, though we may do so (at a certain stage in history, and our own history) in order to *signal* our individuality. There is a general principle here: the fact that we are not the utterly 'pure' source of our socially meaningful actions does not discredit the notion that we are independent points of departure.

One final example. Many of our thoughts are of a highly general nature. Indeed, we may think of thinking as potentially the most developed form of deindexicalised awareness. This has led some philosophers to deindexicalise thoughts completely; indeed, as we have seen, to depsychologise them. For Frege, and those many philosophers influenced by him, the 'essential' contents of a thought are not psychological contents because the latter are irrelevant to its meaning or truth:

> A property of thought will be called inessential which consists in, or follows from the fact that, it is apprehended by a thinker.[6]

They are irrelevant to the meaning of a thought because the latter is essentially communicable while psychological contents are incommunicable. They are irrelevant to the truth of the thought because mental contents such as hearing one's self think the words and the mental images that may accompany the thought are irrelevant to its truth. This, however, demonstrates their irrelevance to the thought *tout court* only so long as one thinks solely of thoughts as types rather than as tokens. Token thoughts are thought by individuals in particular circumstances. The images and the 'overheard' words are necessary for the thought to have happened in and for the individual: for me to have *had* the thought. At the very least, they are like the dust in the lightbeam that makes it visible and solidly there. However abstract and 'collective' the thoughts, then, their occurrence is highly personal and particular – indeed, singular, inasmuch as they occur at a particular time, in a particular place (I had this thought while I was waiting for the train at Stockport station) and as part of a particular stretch of my personal history.

The preceding discussion has two linked purposes. The first, as I have stated, is to argue against the depressing idea that the distance we enjoy from nature is bought at the price of becoming ever more completely dissolved into a human collective. The second, which may be less apparent so far, is to emphasise the *substantiality* of the self that has unfolded from the Existential Intuition. Each self is in many ways the product of the collective effort: the world I address and internalise has been constructed by many millions of human beings. Even so, in its existence in and for me, it is 'personalised' at every level. Selves are not merely inlets from the collective. The world that is realised in me is unique and, what is more, it is *actively* realised. Growth and development, learning and training, are active processes of the realisation of a unique part of a collective world in a unique self. While the material out of which the self is constructed may seem to be general, to belong to society as a whole, it is profoundly parochialised because I, inescapably, am a parish of the collective. While society prevents our being the prisoners of nature, our individual embodiment, which places us on a unique trajectory, prevents us from being prisoners of society. We can have a fat, multilayered self comprised of seemingly general materials without losing ourselves to them, without trading physical determinism for psycho-social determinism. This 'solid' self is necessary to ensure the the possibility of bounce-back: the active inquiry into the world that we discussed in the previous chapter; and the active control of it that we shall examine in this one.[7]

8.2 ACTING FOR REASONS

We do not merely have, that is to say, 'general human agency' but are individual human agents. The notion of the self-agent as a point of origin is captured by Aristotle:

> The stick moves the stone and is moved by the hand; in the man, however, we have reached a mover that is not so in virtue of being moved by something else. (*Physics* VIII 256a6–8)[8]

Or, as Richard Taylor (quoted in Kane, p. 120) said, 'some … causal chains … have beginnings, and they begin with agents themselves'. It is important, however, not to allow the notion of the agent as cause to commit us to nonoccurrent causation:

> the causation of action by a *thing* or *substance* (the self or agent) that cannot be explained as the causation of occurrences or events *by other occurrences or events* (i.e. by 'states' or 'changes'). (Kane, p. 120)

To this end it must be emphasised that our notion of the agent-self is not of a thing or substance.[9] For such an idea – of the agent as an unchanging substance or entity – runs into trouble. Its problem is that it is smooth, undifferentiated; it therefore provides no reason why it should cause this event to occur at this place in this time rather than another event or the same event at another time. The agent understood as an entity would have no reason for doing one thing rather than another because as a true beginning it would be severed from any history; most importantly, from the history that makes sense of a particular action and explains why we should do one thing (rationally and voluntarily) here and now rather than another thing. The notion of the Existential Intuition as the basis of the beginning is that it allows the agent to be a true point of origin without losing its contact with the history necessary to make sense of the fact that it does one thing rather than another at any given time.

The relevant kind of 'substantiveness' or 'depth' of a real human agent may be captured by considering the difference between an ordinary free, appetite-related human action and an item of animal behaviour. The animal is thirsty and, encountering water, or following the stimuli associated with water, it drinks. I am thirsty and decide that I will later go out to the pub, having worked out that this would fit with my other engagements. My choice of pub – on the grounds of the kind of additional experiences it might offer me, the people I might meet or its proximity (I don't want to drink and drive) – taps into quite a lot of what makes up Raymond Tallis: his knowledge, his predilections, and so on. The way I order my priorities, so that, for example, I skimp a bit of work in order to reach the pub by a certain time, reaches into yet more of me. Most importantly, the action, or series of actions, is steeped in propositional awareness: beliefs, thoughts, desires, reasons. For the present, I will focus largely on reasons, though reasons interact with desires, beliefs, goals.

The discussion of agency in *I Am* was concerned with the roots of agency. The emphasis was on establishing *a new point of origin* of events in the material universe. This point of origin was sketched rather thinly. It grew out of the Existential Intuition 'That I am this ...' , where 'this' was, in the first instance, the body engaged in activities relevant to its survival. Ownership of certain bodily events was established: some of *its* happenings could be appropriated as *my* doings. Selfhood and agency were equiprimordial manifestations of the Existential Intuition. As agency and selfhood developed, they also differentiated. The self became the explicit origin or owner of the actions.

We briefly described the process by which agency was gradually extended. The tool-like hand inspired tools that extended actual agency. The latter also extended the sense of possible agency. The tool, enabling action at a distance, extended the scope of the ownership of events and raised the possibility of further extension: a reach that exceeded current grasp eventually brought about a grasp that inspired yet further reach. The growth of human agency was by means of a reality-producing illusion.[10] The illusion could be fulfilled because it did not require breaking any (by definition) unbreakable laws of nature, only choosing between the several laws that are operating at any given time, a choice that is possible because of the 'outside of nature' opened up by the Existential Intuition.

This account of agency sees the Existential Intuition as 'planting the flag of here and now' in a universe that is entirely anindexical. 'Am', first-person being, brings indexicality to birth. I have the explicit sense of being at the centre of a world encircling me. This story does not, of course, encompass much human action as we know it now. While we operate on objects in our immediate vicinity – walking down stairs, eating food, typing, catching a bus, talking to someone – the frame of reference (or the multiple frames of reference) that make sense of our operations are not located in the vicinity, nor strictly located at all. We are knowing agents and our actions are guided by deindexicalised awareness. We follow trails of facts, relays of conventional signs, as we act out rather abstract intentions, notwithstanding that we are guided by immediate sense experiences and our intentions in many cases ultimately serve bodily ends. (Ultimately: for much of the time we relate only tangentially to the body and its material surroundings.) The space of possibility within which we operate – which houses the goals we set ourselves, the choices we make – has wide, indefinite boundaries, is multidimensional, multilayered. It is this that is the theatre of human freedom.

As I said, I am going to focus on 'acting for reasons'. Even this narrower brief would take me into a huge field of philosophical inquiry. I am simply going to make a few points most directly relevant to my thesis about the distance between human beings and nature, as expressed in real freedom, and the genesis of that distance. To get a hold on this distance, let us first look at reason at work in an ordinary activity.

True actions are realisations of possibilities that are explicit to the agent. Since possibilities are general, actions will always be 'thicker' in concrete detail than the goals that specify them.[11] There can be many equally valid ways of realising a reason-driven, reason-mediated goal. At least part of this is due to the fact that the goals are often invisible – the target is round many corners – and, linked with this, are general. They are rooted in deindexicalised awarness. General intentions may have visible instantiations but are not themselves visible or located in space. This is self-evidently true of goals such as 'happiness' or 'improving my communications skills' or 'getting better at tennis' or 'supporting my children to ensure they achieve fulfilling lives'. But it also true even of smaller scale, seemingly highly specific goals, such as 'having dinner with friends in Bramhall', 'going to work to check out the patients on the ward'. To them there correspond physical actions that can be specified only in highly general terms; indeed, they can be captured only in words. Only verbal descriptions can capture the framework that is realised in the complex, connected series of actions that constitute pieces of ordinary behaviour.[12]

Moreover, each of the component actions can be described, or made sense of, only with respect to an interlocking series of frames of reference of increasing generality. For example, my walking along the road is part of my journey to the station: this is its rationale, the reason which informs it and shapes it. The journey to the station is part of my journey to London: this is *its* rationale. The journey to London is part of the process by which I attain my goal of getting to the Royal College of Physicians. This is one of the steps I have to take in order to attend a meeting at the College. This reason for getting to the College of Physicians is itself subsumed under another reason: my attending the meeting is the only way I can contribute to a discussion and, by this means, shape some policy document or other. This in turn is justified by my desire to influence how health care is delivered. And so on. As the frameworks become broader and broader, so they take in more and more of myself: ever more fundamental goals and ever larger portions of the self that has been committed to those goals. I have been walking along this road for five minutes, but I have been serving my wish to influence how we deliver health care to older people for the next decade.

There are several additional points of immediate relevance. First, as I describe the motors for my action, I find it more and more difficult to keep different propositional attitudes separate: reasons, belief, knowledge and desire all feed into the goals that I set myself. Second, as I trace the rationale for my actions to higher and higher abstract levels, so I reach further and further into myself. Third, as a consequence of this, it is difficult to think of one reason in isolation: the influence of a complex network of reasons, reaching into an equally complex nexus of motivations, is apparent. Actions prompted by ever higher-level reasons are ever more free because they reach into *broader and broader stretches of myself*; they seem to converge on a point where not only are agency and selfhood close to their original unity, but they recover that unity despite an expanding content. The content of agency and the content of selfhood are one. I truly own such actions because they are my own and I must own up to them. There is a point at which my actions are not so much 'whole-hearted' as 'whole-selved'. An action is mine – I can own it or own up to it – in proportion as it partakes of what I am, the deeper and wider it reaches into my world, my own place.[13]

This interpenetration of reasons with one another and their joint rootedness in my self shows why reason-occasioned behaviour cannot be seen as being driven by simply rather complex external, mechanical, impersonal, causes – psycho-social, as opposed to physical, causes; why my reasons are not mere conduits of unchosen motivations rooted in the cultural transformation of animal appetites. There are anyway obvious differences between reasons and causes. For a start, the former has to be apparent to the actor, while the latter does not. I can be driven by a cause while not being aware of it, but I cannot act according to a reason of which I am unaware.[14] Second, the causes as it were 'push' from behind while reasons 'pull' from the front: they are clearly future-oriented, goal-related. It might be argued that a thirsty animal, whose behaviour is driven 'from behind' by physiological causes (stimulation of osmoreceptors by increased concentration of electrolytes in the blood), also has goals ahead of it. That is true; but the reasons for the action are not explicit to the animal: they are visible only to the (human) observer. To clarify this distinction, we need to identify the root difference between reasons for (deliberate, free, voluntary) actions and the causes of (instinctive or conditioned) animal behaviour. The fundamental difference is captured in the fact that causes are embedded in actuality and reasons are about possibility. Reasons spring from deindexicalised awareness, they draw on knowledge and explicit belief, as well as being energised, or linked to action, by desires. Knowledge is essential to both the posing of possible goals and to choosing between them. It is the key to deliberation and makes it possible for reasons to inform genuine actions and genuinely bring things about that would not otherwise have happened in a world where tropisms couple animal behaviour with environmental conditions.

Reason-shaped, reason-inspired, reason-promoted action acts upon the world from outside the causal net. This difference is reflected in the difference between the tight determinism of the causal net (or continuum or block) and the looseness, the constrained indeterminacy, of reason-prompted action. Therein lies the significance of Leibniz's observation that 'reason may incline but does not necessitate' – indeed, the extent to which reasons introduce the indeterminacy required for freedom in a seemingly deterministic universe of which the reasoning creature (or her body) is a part is very marked.

The notion of psychological or psycho-social determinism, in accordance with which the reasons through which my will is expressed, are simply the effects of causes that lie beyond them and are themselves to be understood as causes, is doubly flawed. For willing is disconnected in two ways from necessity. First, the outcome of reasoned intentions is not guaranteed; and second, as we have already discussed, the desired outcome is specified in only the most general terms, so that *any* particular outcome (successful or otherwise) of my reason-informed endeavours is more detailed than any specification. Let us dwell on this double disassociation a little longer.

According to psychological determinism, reasons, intentions and so on fit into the causal nexus as follows:

$$\rightarrow E/C \rightarrow E/C \rightarrow E/REASON/C \rightarrow E/C \rightarrow E/C \rightarrow$$

where E/C is an effect that is also a cause and E/REASON/C is a reason that is a cause of effects that is itself a cause of other reasons. The fact that reasons incline rather than necessitate – as demonstrated by the fact that reason-shaped willings may be successful or unsuccessful – can be illustrated as follows:

$$E/C \rightarrow E/REASON/C \nwarrow^{E/C \text{ (Success)}}_{E/C \text{ (Failure)}}$$

represents indeterminacy but grossly understates it, if only because there are many outcomes that may correspond to the vague specification of success and many outcomes that may correspond to failure. In other words, there is not merely a binary fork in the deterministic chain. There are a thousand ways of failing, not quite succeeding and succeeding, because intention has itself an incomplete specification:

$$\rightarrow E/C \rightarrow E/C \rightarrow \quad \text{VAGUE INTENTION} \quad \begin{array}{l} \text{OUTCOME 1} \\ \text{OUTCOME 2} \\ \text{OUTCOME 3} \\ \text{OUTCOME 4, etc.} \end{array}$$

This is linked with the fact that, in the natural world, there are no possibilities. Forks in the path of events are human inventions. 'A' may occur and 'B' may occur but 'Either "A" or "B"' does not belong to nature. This sense of different possibilities turns naturally occurring events into possible handles. The space of possibilities is the space within which reason can operate. And this is the realm of freedom.

Many philosophers have noted that it is important that there should be more than one way of acting rationally. If there were only one rational way of behaving and every other way was totally irrational, then freedom to act rationally would seem to be freedom to act in only one way and this would seem a severe restriction. It is because there may be more than one way to act rationally that we can truly make a *choice*; a choice, moreover, that mobilises more of oneself than an isolated rational action dictated by the precise details of a particular circumstance would do. For in choosing between rational alternatives, we reach into our memories, our inclinations, and may even choose between the different values that have gained ascendancy within us over the years of being ourselves.

This looseness of prescription comes on top of the fact that any choice that is made – Choice A as opposed to Choice B (for example, going to London for a Royal College meeting rather than doing an equally appropriate ward round) – has a thousand ways of being realised. Its million components, all bespoke to the occasion, have only to fall within a very general specification. That they do so – and component actions of the correct general character are chosen – is possible only so long as the agent is aware throughout the action, including a long journey to London, of its overarching purpose. This necessitates booster doses of intention – self-reminders and external events badged as cues – to sustain a very complex action until the goal is reached. The action is not stimulus-bound or menu-driven, so the informing purpose has to be reiterated.

The overemphasis in much of the literature on free will upon the ability to choose between a small number of rational alternatives – or a discrete number of alternatives – understates the available indeterminacy too much. The looseness of the fit between reasons/intentions and the actions that satisfy them, between the general specification and the actual action, is such that indeterminacy is present not just at the highest, most narratable, level – 'I chose to save this drowning person's life rather than to keep my suit dry' – it *'goes all the way down'*. Freedom of rational action is all-pervasive: it is not just a question of being free to choose between rational course A and rational course B as single undivided entities.

Because every goal/intention is composed of many only partly specified elements, reason has to be active throughout what is often a prolonged process of execution in order that the appropriate components can be enacted. Streams of reason, in short, widen into an ocean of general wakeful awareness: of knowing what one is doing and why and of having one's actions shaped by the agentive self – the self as agent – in the many levels and layers of the what and the why.

We could put this more generally by emphasising how the answer to a human want – for example, the desire for success – is not a single outcome or solution and the path from want to satisfaction is not clearly defined.[15] For much of our lives, there is little that corresponds to the definite goals that we observe in the lives of animals. What definition there is does not boil down to a set of bodily events that can be captured on an electromyogram, corresponding to muscle activity of a certain sort which would fit neatly into the chain of material causation.

It is this open-scriptedness – arising out of the character of the goal as an incompletely specified possibility, and (connected with this) the multi-levelled interlocking frames of reference of all actions – which, more than a bare contrast between 'pushes' and 'pulls', captures the difference between causes and reasons, reactions and actions.[16] The human agent is always trying to realise possibilities that belong to that part of the space – into which beliefs and wishes reach, where knowledge and envisaged goals are located – created by pooled deindexicalised awareness into which she buys. A true understanding of the extent of our free will should take note not only of the conditions under which choices are made but the conditions in which the range of choice is established. The space of these conditions taken at its widest is the self in the world: the 'I' which I am, facing the world which is *my* world, which grew with me and will vanish when I die.

Determinism not only neglects the complexity of the teleological framework of actions and the looseness of specification of the actions that follow from reasons (and motives and goals). It also overlooks how the *meanings* of actions and the justification of the reasons that inform actions are not confined to the head of the person who performs them. They cannot be reduced, for example, to neural activity. Goals, certainly at the higher level, are socialised through and through. This is obvious in the case of such goals as wanting to be successful; but the influence of society – either permissive, constraining or supportive – is evident in nearly everything we do.

For some, this emphasis on the psycho-social dimension of willing may be the reverse of reassuring. It may reawaken the suspicion that our collective liberation from physical determinism is bought at the cost of individual cultural determinism and submission to the collective. For some the inescapable psycho-social aspect of reasons for actions translates into 'brainwashing' – either as the specific consequence of explicit propaganda, indoctrination and procedures such as drugs and torture, or as the non-specific result of more general cultural control through education and upbringing.

The worrying force of the notion of 'psychosocial determinism' derives from merging these two senses: the focal assault on the self by others for some specific purpose (for example, to achieve political obedience); and the global shaping of the self in the interactions that take place with others in the course of one's life. The former is shocking because it aims to turn a person into something she is not in order to make her the tool of a particular end she has not chosen for herself. The latter should not, however, be regarded as a mere variant or refinement of the former. Global shaping is a key part of the process of making a person what she *is* – of individuating her – not what she is not. While individual cultures may 'lock in' individuals and groups into a particular dialect of consciousness, with a few exceptions, these dialects share sufficient of universal human values and characteristics as not to constitute prisons.[17]

The education and upbringing that shapes the self also enables that self to have specific aims and wants and motives beyond the instinctual wants. Without this upbringing, the self would be shapeless and agency would not emerge: there would be no canvas upon which the script of volition could be written in any other language than that of physiological need. Distinctively human agency requires the emergence of an agentive-self that operates in a social world. If society is woven into the very tissues of the self, it is no more an *external* coercive force than the natural forces that made my body or the physiological properties that make it viable are externally coercive.

It is important to understand that the psycho-social aspect of human willing is *not* of itself an alien force because it is one of the most fundamental differences between the springs of animal behaviour and the roots of human action. While socialisation is self-evident in human actions subordinated to abstract goals – such as improving my knowledge of idiomatic German, or even something a little more concrete such as meeting someone at a pre-arranged place and time – it is a feature even of human behaviour driven by 'primitive' wants such as thirst. The difference is between a felt want and a want that is not only felt but formulated. Thirst is solitary, but formulated thirst and the intermediate goals it gives rise to is social.

The argument that socialisation reduces the scope of free will – that it is deterministic – is given superficial plausibility by presenting human social behaviour as herd behaviour. This analysis seems most plausible in the case of totalitarian societies, where individuals are, apparently, aggregated into masses whose collective behaviour is seemingly shaped by forces that lie outside of them. Citizens believe, worship and act in accordance with the moods inculcated in them by the Great Dictator and his thousand functionaries. In practice, individuals make their own decisions and, in conditions of fear, may make cowardly decisions. The amount of their lives given over to zombie-like – as opposed to prudent or opportunistic – enactment of the Dictator's prescriptions is small. Classical reflex or operant conditioning would not be sufficient to bring about the complex actions necessary to accommodate to an evil regime. Even in such cases, there is considerable margin of freedom. The person who signs up to a political party and/or its doctrines usually does so consciously – for self-protection or in the hope of self-advancement – and there is considerable inner distance from outer action. Historians have documented how many of Hitler's executioners were 'willing' while at the same time despising the Great Leader. Others admired him not because they were in a trance, but because they had access to only limited information about what he was doing, and judged him by what he was apparently doing in support of their interests. While there were moments of mass intoxication, there were many more moments when individuals made their own calculations. *The Good Soldier Schweik* – set in the mass slaughter of the First World War – captures much more of individual behaviour under such conditions than the images of human herds shaped by indoctrination. Between 1933 and 1945 in Germany and between 1917 and 1989 in the USSR there were many more sober Monday mornings than intoxicated Saturday nights. Cynical calculation and prudence dictated by terror were greater shapers of voluntary action than helpless worship or brainwashed somnambulism.

Psycho-social determinists often claim that, even in less extreme circumstances, human actions may be explained in terms of passive herd behaviour. Let us stick with politics. Psephologists note certain trends in voting patterns; for example, that in the 1980s, individuals in socio-economic class C2 consistently voted for the Conservative Party led by Mrs Thatcher. Tell me who you are and I will tell you how you will vote. This could be taken as an example of herd behaviour: the animals of a particular herd (C2 Britons) will alway behave in the same way, suggesting that they are not making individual decisions but are constrained by (psycho-social) forces beyond their control. On closer inspection it will be seen that this conclusion can be arrived at only by looking at individuals through the wrong end of a telescope, thereby making it possible to overlook what is involved in voting decisions. If we turn the telescope the right way round, we see C2 voters – while they may not be voting very intelligently and certainly not altruistically – are not voting somnambulistically. Each voter will have made her or his own assessment of the personal benefits of a particular party getting into power. When that decision has been made, it is still necessary to get out to vote and that involves making plans to be near the relevant polling station at the right time on the right day. The Yes/No decision will carry in its train numerous other decisions, just as we discovered in relation to the earlier example of my decision to attend a meeting at the Royal College of Physicians.

It is worthwhile examining why the psycho-social deterministic approach may seem convincing in this case. First of all, the final outcome of all the voters' deliberation is very simple: Yes or No for a particular party. Every vote has to be treated as equal to every other vote. The casting of the vote cannot therefore reflect the specific thoughts that lie behind it. The voting animal is faced with a simple choice of going to the left or to the right. Everyone's voting behaviour will necessarily 'conform to a pattern' – Pattern A or Pattern B – particularly as different parties fashion their promises to appeal to the interests of certain groups. If individuals do not vote for smaller parties with a greater 'niche' appeal, this is not because they are brainwashed by their class position. It is because they judge that a vote for a small party – far from the threshold of electoral success – is a wasted vote as it will not affect the outcome. Second, and for this reason, it is possible to aggregate the actions into numbers – so many votes cast for Party A and so many votes cast for Party B – which can be linked to social classes. Third, psephologists have to allocate individuals to social classes, as if that captured their essential being. In practice, this irons out huge differences; it does, however, allow clumped votes to be linked to clumped people. This in turn makes it possible for voting behaviour to be addressed statistically and for certain general, probabilistic conclusions to be drawn: if you belong to socio-economic class C2, you are more likely to vote for Mrs Thatcher than if you belong to social class D or E.

Presented thus, the individual act of voting begins to look like the expression not of a personal decision, rooted in one's own life, but the expression of a probability and this in turns seems to suggest the operation of a quasi-deterministic probabilistic pressure for an individual in a certain class to vote in a certain way. All of the highly individual deliberations that preceded her decision to vote in one way rather than another are then seen to be no more relevant or influential than – to repeat our earlier metaphor – the toy steering wheels parents place on car dashboards to amuse their children are to the direction the car takes.

Three false moves, therefore, are required to pull off this feat of rendering the casting of a vote as quasi-somnambulistic: transferring the simplicity of the binary outcome of the vote to the processes of deliberation leading up to it; reducing individuals to the social classes into which they can be packed; and turning a *post hoc* statistical pattern (and such patterns can always be found in *any* aggregated data) into a causal connection – a force or an influence. If one takes a statistical approach to aggregated phenomena, one will always come up with correlations that seem to have a quasi-deterministic force. This is not only bad philosophy but also bad science.

None of this is intended to deny the reality of brainwashing and the possibility of making people believe and do things as a result of conditioning. What it denies is the notion of universal brainwashing that makes all social behaviour unfree because it is the result of universal conditioning. Even the manifestly brainwashed act freely in some areas of their lives. Winston Smith in *1984* may have been brainwashed into believing in Big Brother, and even into loving him, but he was still free in other respects. Outside of set-piece undue influence, there is merely the global shaping of individuals by non-localised influences, which amounts to making us what we are; to shaping the self-agent who acts freely.

The notion of human beings as rational animals has often been attacked. The most benign attacks point out that behaviour is emotion-led. 'Reason is, and ought only to be, the slave of the passions, and can never pretend to any other office than to serve and obey them,' Hume famously informed his readers.[18] Less benign commentators have argued that humans are essentially irrational. They do not know how to serve their own best interests. They engage in activities – destructive score-settling, all-out war – that are in direct conflict with their own best interests. Such behaviour has lent credence to those thinkers, most notably Sigmund Freud, for whom reason is a minor player in human behaviour and its authority, on the few occasions it is asserted, weak.

These attacks on reason, on the notion that reason has a central place in human affairs and humans are rational animals, are deeply insincere: those who deny the role of reason in human affairs expect others to be reasonable, buses and pay cheques to arrive on time, public services and bureaucracies and airlines to work efficiently. More importantly, they overlook what lies in front of our noses. Those who deny the sovereignty of reason in human affairs will usually focus on the irrational impulses, motives and values that inform some of our actions. Very few critics of the notion of Rational Man, however, will be foolish enough to deny the reality of practical reason or its dominant place in ordinary – very ordinary, day-to-day, moment-to-moment – human affairs. What they overlook is that practical reason is as necessary for the successful expression of irrational motives as it is for the accomplishment of rational actions – especially in the complex world we have built for ourselves. Let us for a moment focus on the former and examine a couple of examples of presumably irrational actions, one small-scale the other large-scale.

Suppose a man has an irrational belief that his wife is having an affair with one of her colleagues at work. The belief is irrational in so far as it is unfounded and resists contrary evidence. He decides to spy on his wife's colleague. In order to do so, he takes a series of quite complicated measures. One of these may be to tap the telephone in his house, a course of action that will itself comprise many steps. It will involve finding the address of someone who can install it, going to the relevant retail outlet, arranging for the device to be installed, testing it out and then using it. Each of these steps in turn has many steps. The simplest of them – going to the relevant outlet – will require him to make sure the shop is open; choose a time during opening hours when he can leave work and visit the shop unobserved; walk to the car; ensure that it has enough petrol; carry out a vast number of manoeuvres as he drives the car to the shop; park the car; walk from the car to the shop; explain his requirements to the salesman; choose an appropriate device; learn how to use it; pay for the device (not using his credit card so that the purchase will remain concealed from his wife); walk back to the car. The list is endless. Each of these steps will in turn have a vast number of components and choosing them and connecting them together will involve some very complex chains of practical reasoning. For example, turning the car wheel to the left at a given point is linked with the overall aim of his action – to find out whether the wife is having an affair – in a very indirect way. It would be tedious to spell out all the elements in this chain of reasoning, but here are some: he turns the wheel to the left in order that the car will turn to the left; he wants the car to turn to the left in order to go down a particular road; he goes down that particular road in order to turn into another road, which links with another road, which links with yet another road, etc., which eventually leads to the outlet that he believes sells the phone-tapping equipment. He wants to go to the place in question because he believes that he will be able to buy such a device there; he wants to buy such a device because he believes that his wife and her lover communicate by telephone and because he believes that they will say incriminating things on the telephone …

In brief, this irrational action is sustained by a complex network of practical reasons, fed and watered by a large quantity of factual knowledge and expertise, which inform moment-to-moment intentions and sustain larger-scale intentions over a period of time, for much of which the actual goal is not visible or even the kind of thing that can be sensibly thought of as 'visible': it is an object of deindexicalised awareness. Moreover, the action has to be sustained in the face of other concerns, preoccupations, intentions, which typically will have to be interdigitated with it. For example, the visit to the phone outlet may be combined with a visit to the nearby supermarket. This economy of effort may have the additional advantage of providing cover for an otherwise inexplicable trip out. Another scenario is one in which he sees a friend in the car park of the relevant shop, drives away before he is spotted, and lurks in an adjacent street until he believes the friend will have gone, listening to the radio meanwhile in order to help pass the time. Describing the full complexity of the practical reasoning deployed even in this diversion would be a very lengthy business. Suffice it to note this complexity and note also how the intention to perform the action has to be sustained across a rip-tide of events and other actions that are either irrelevant to it or necessitate modifications of the way in which it has to be implemented.

Even so-called irrational actions, therefore, are composed of a vast number of elements that are requisitioned, shaped and regulated by practical reasoning. The passions that drive them are remote from the physiological tempests that possess animals: they are ductile, being led down pathways drawn by knowledge-informed reasoning. This is even more clearly true of larger-scale goals, ambitions and life-plans that are seemingly driven by passions such as 'blind ambition'. And it applies yet more to larger-scale projects that involve vast numbers of people. For example, we are often told that wars are an expression of latent animality in humans, that they represent the resurgence of primitive emotions such as 'aggression'. The persistence of this view is a remarkable tribute to the ability of simple ideas to enable one to overlook what lies in front of one's nose. Outbreaks of primitive emotions may account for spur-of-the-moment decisions – such as signing on along with one's friends when one is drunk and in an inflamed state of patriotism. (Though a close examination of the actual contents of these actions may not necessarily support that.) Such emotions, however, hardly account for, or in any way inform, most of the actions a person carries out for most of the time in most wars. Even the moments of actual fighting – firing the gun at a visible target, hand-to-hand conflict – are closely rule-governed and driven by other forces than aggression; and they are far outweighed, what is more, by hours, days, weeks and years of preparation, hanging about, running away, driving up and down, etc. that fill the lives of most contemporary warriors. The organisational feats, the command structures, the precise allocation of responsibilities, the regulations, are unimaginably complex. A modern war is far more an affair of quartermasters than of combatants in a frenzy of bloodlust; of logistics than of sadistic glee; of discomfort, fear and boredom and glumly neutral feelings than of aggression. Remote, at any rate, from anything that any conceivable animal passion or instinct could foment.

The fact that even supposedly irrational human activity entrains a huge amount of reasoning and reason- and knowledge-driven actions illustrates a point once made by G. K. Chesterton (I cannot recall where): people who go mad do not lose their reason; their problem is that they have lost everything *but* their reason. Paranoiacs, like cranks and hypochondriacs, are reasoning machines disconnected from evidence, common sense, a sense of proportion and reasonableness.

Reasoning, however, is closely connected with freedom, because it taps into so much of ourselves. Our reason-led actions are most remote from simple physical, physiological or psychological external causation. The close relationship between responsiveness to reason and freedom reflects the way in which reasons, which are things we have to generate or accept, are manifestations of our being uncoupled from material or other external circumstances. Assent may be facilitated by external pressures, undue influence, motives of which we are only partly aware; but the chain of assent to reasons in carrying out a complex action makes the action seem more and more like an action and less and less like a reaction. If we say of someone that they should not be blamed for an action they carried out, we imply that the origin of the action lay outside of themselves: we separate agency from self. With rational action, that separation is minimised.

Consider the example of someone who kills a stranger. If he carries out this act under the influence of a poison administered to him without his knowledge, which makes him think that the stranger is about to kill him and his family, it is generally accepted that he cannot be blamed for his action. We may think of the action, despite its surface gloss of reason, as *caused* to happen in the person rather than carried out by him. Self and apparent agency seem separate: the action was not carried out by the man's true self. He could justly say, with Oedipus, 'I suffered these deeds as much as I enacted them', or with Antony that 'poisoned hours had bound me up from mine own knowledge'. There are slightly less strong reasons for exculpating a murderer on the grounds that he had an abusive father who made him prone to violence. The reasons are less strong because more of his true or actual self seems to be engaged in the action.

Less powerful excuses again apply to an alcoholic who kills a stranger by accident when he is driving a car recklessly under the influence of drink. Although his addiction may seem a mitigating circumstance, inasmuch as it was difficult for him to resist drinking on the day of the accident, the fact that his addiction was the result of many voluntary acts of drinking over the years makes him more culpable, as does his voluntarily driving: we assume he is not also a car addict. His alcoholism is at least in part the product of what Robert Kane describes as 'self-forming actions' or 'self-forming willings' – actions and willings performed by the individual in the past that contribute to the person he is now.[19] We 'inveterate' ourselves for good or ill. Just as I can take credit for a skill that has become automatic because I set myself to acquire it in the past, so I must carry the blame for habits I acquired voluntarily but which now have me in their grip. I may not be fully in command of myself now, but I should be held responsible overall for the actions in the past that made me what I am today. What I did in the past to influence my present behaviour, plus what I have just done, add up to overall responsibility for the present action. Finally, a non-alcoholic who knowingly drives when under the influence of alcohol which he has taken voluntarily – perhaps out of bravado in a drinking contest – and who kills a child is even more culpable. His action seems to have issued from his undistorted self, a self not subject to undue pressure.

Two considerations seem influential in determining the allocation or withholding of praise or blame for an action. The first is the extent to which that action is or is not 'out of character'; and the second is the extent to which it originates from an aspect of an individual which they may or may not have chosen. At one extreme is the man who murders under the influence of poison he has taken unwittingly: the action is both out of character and out of his hands. At the other is the man who has developed the habit of drinking over the limit but who is not an addict and who kills a child on the road. His action is both in character and under his control.

In assessing agency and allocating blame or credit, we may imagine following a regressive line of influences to the point where the action becomes an expression not merely of some general force but of what the person is. It is clearly less my fault if I perform an action under duress – when someone has placed a gun to my head or to my child's head. I can argue the action was out of character because I did not wish to do it. I should not be blamed for it because it was not really me. I can take credit only for the actions I wanted to carry out. Someone might argue that I am still not at fault when I carry out a crime without a gun being applied to my head because I did not choose my wants: even though my actions were not implanted in me by a drug or unconscious brainwashing, they were still instilled in me by my education and upbringing. I cannot be blamed or credited for my actions because I was not responsible for the upbringing that made me what I am. An abusive childhood may have rendered me 'ethically disabled', to use Jon Jacobson's evocative phrase.[20] Whether such ethical disability can extend to every aspect of a person's life, however, is doubtful. Even wicked people must have redeeming characteristics if they are to be excused their faults and vices. There can be no global pardon for anyone who wants to be judged as a person rather than as an organism, as a mere effect of antecedent causes.

There is a point, in other words, at which we connect the action with what a person most intimately, most personally, *is*. Where we seem to have limited power over our motives it may be because our motives came from the outside but because they came from the past; and we are still agents when we act on those motives inasmuch as we *are* those motives. In either case, there is a place at which what one does and what one is merge in the notion of the self-agent as the locus of origin. To deny the existence of such a point in order to escape blame is to deny one's status not only as an agent but as a self; it is to deny one's personhood or humanity. No one does this consistently. While it is almost routine now for scoundrels to blame factors outside the control of the self – genes, upbringing, bad role models – for their wicked behaviour, very few of them deny that they are agentive selves to the point where they would accept that the recognition and rights that are due to a person should be withheld from them.

To echo the language of *I Am*, 'where there is "am" there is responsibility'. 'Am', however, is not coterminous with current volition. There is a deposit account of (dead) choice – for example, the past more or less voluntary drinking of a drinker who is now an addict. There are choices which shape the framework, the context, the range of future choices: promises, binding contracts, the taking of one path rather than another. These are enabling frameworks, the things I buy into. And there are circumstances, which I have embraced as my home, my life, my world, where my expectations and my rights lie. Finally, there are the necessary mechanisms: inherited, learned, trained. 'Am', then, has a penumbra of 'not-quite-agency': one's past, one's world (in part shaped by one's world), contingency and chance, and one's body.

These, however, are the necessary underpinnings of selfhood, not exculpating factors. Freedom – in particular the capacity for rational self-governance – cannot be based upon an absolutely unprejudiced choice of behaviour; nor can it require an impossible self-creation *ex nihilo*. Its root is a cumulative self-appropriation. Freedom and selfhood grow in parallel. Those who deny responsibility for their actions on the grounds that they did not choose their wants, desires, motives, character, etc. are hypocritical unless they wish also to give up their status as selves and the right to be treated as persons. They are also deeply confused, or at least they exploit a confusion arising out of the fallacious notion of psychosocial determinism – 'the idea that choices and actions are determined by prior motives and character, which in turn are the products are the ultimate products of birth and upbringing' (Kane, p. 6) or that 'we are always determined to act by the strongest motives or desires' – and uncritical acceptance of the notion of psychosocial 'forces' over which individuals have as little control as they do over antecedent physical causes. The significance of this is that uncovering it requires us to reach quite deeply into the notion of distinctively human agency and to consider what happens in the evolution of the human agent beyond the early stages of hominids and the early years of human babies discovering manipulative indeterminacy and working out the consequences of an explicitly instrumental relationship to the world. Which was, of course, where we began with the bodily self-appropriation of the Existential Intuition.[21]

8.3 THE CAUSE-SEEKING ANIMAL: AGENCY AND THE CAUSAL INTUITION

The one thing the Knowing Animal really knows is that there is more to be known. Knowledge is a form of awareness that is aware of its unawareness: it intuits objects that transcend, that exist independently of, awareness. The granting of independent existence to things that are located 'out there' is key to something else that is unique to human beings: causal belief which, as Wolpert has argued, is a necessary pre-condition of the development of technology.[22] For Georg Christoph Lichtenberg, causal belief was the defining characteristic of humanity: 'Man is a creature who searches for causes; he could be named the cause-searcher within the hierarchy of minds. Other minds perhaps conceive things under other categories, incomprehensible to us.'[23]

Causal belief has several subsidiary beliefs: that objects exist independently of one's self; that they interact independently of one's self; that there are patterns governing how they interact which, being fixed, have an intrinsic necessity. Causal belief is a refinement of the general intuition that comes with knowledge that there is something (yet) to be discovered: 'the way things work'. It is this that motivates the spirit of inquiry we discussed in section 7.3; in particular, the 'imaginative trial and error' (Wolpert) that, until comparatively recently, drove the advance of technology.

The belief that there is a certain way that things work – as opposed to a mere cascade of random happenings – comes initially from immediate experience of getting similar results from similar actions: a dropped stone always falls, a shaken tree usually rustles, a stick thrown into a brook always floats. It might be argued that animals can make these observations. They do not, most fundamentally because (as we pointed out in section 7.3) they do not *make observations*; their gawping, unfocused and innocent of formulated questions and hypotheses, does not amount to observation. More specifically, they do not have the sense of agency – of themselves as creatures that might bring things about – that will italicise particular events and pick them out of the background of global change. The rustling of the shaken tree becomes particularly evident as an event – and hence as an effect – when it is linked with (effortful) action. This highlighting of certain events becomes more apparent if they are mediated by more than the proto-tool of the hand. Primitive tools, which underline *doing*, also pick out the interactions between the three components: the embodied subject, the tool and the substrate upon which it operates.

The point will be clear: it takes an agent – a knowing agent who intuits independent objects – to form a causal belief. The sense that I might bring something about, placed outside of myself or made visible in the proto-tool and its descendants, is inseparable from the notion of 'how things work'. To say this is not merely to emphasise the essentially practical nature of primitive inquiry but to link the causal sense at its most fundamental with the idea of 'getting a handle' on things. The intuition of causes is initially embedded in the sense of agency. A cause is a potential mediator of a goal that cannot be achieved directly.[24] Ultimately, as agency is more remotely mediated, with the steps between where we are now and a goal towards which we are directed becoming more numerous and various, causation is progressively located further 'out there' – an interaction between objects rather than between myself and objects. Causation, that is to say, becomes deindexicalised. Ultimately, as Wolpert points out, the causal sense links events that are widely separated in time or space.[25]

The extension of general causal principles beyond the currently visible to the invisible universe, the notion of fore-ordained patterns in the space of possibility, are built on this indexical phase rooted in personal experience and bodily effort. It begins with 'trial and error', which is more sophisticated than it looks. Not only does it have to be guided by a sense of the not-yet-revealed, it is also directed by previous experience and by a sense of the generalisability of experience from one occasion to another. Given that no two experiences are exactly the same, this requires a prior, or preliminary, generalisation of experience through identification of salient features. They do not identify themselves. Often the characteristics relevant to replication of effects are inconspicuous.

The capacity for generalisation might be thought to be widely distributed in the animal kingdom. Many species seem to have the ability to transfer the response to a particular kind of stimulus to another class of quite similar stimulus. This is not, however, analogous to the generalising capacity that lies at the root of technology, of trial and error, and eventually of science and science-based technology. There is a world of difference between, say, a robin attacking a piece of brown cloth with a red spot on it as if it were a rival – generalising from the red-on-brown pattern of rivals to the red-on-brown appearance of the cloth – and the generalisation from events which appear to have causal efficacy to the notion of a whole class of events with such efficacy. For a start, the robin is not learning from observation. Second, its behaviour is not hunch- let alone hypothesis-driven. Third, a body of knowledge, based upon happy and bitter experience is not built up and passed on from robin to robin. Most importantly, the generalisation at the root of technology is not grounded in a sense of the intrinsic properties of the objects in question; for there is no sense that there are objects with intrinsic properties. The difference between generalisation through object-knowledge as opposed to pseudo-generalisation through sentience might be illustrated by an example (taken from Wolpert) of primitive causal understanding in humans, not matched in animals.

Both humans and apes see fruit falling from a tree when the wind causes it to shake. Only humans learn from this to shake the branch to get the fruit. The reason for this is that only humans have a fully developed sense of the tree and the wind as entities existing in themselves and interacting in a way that has nothing to do with the creature conscious of them. The ape's experience of a tree does not add up to the sense of it as an object; and its experience of the wind does not give birth to the notion of a *force*[26] acting upon the object. The analogy between natural events and agency – so that natural events are seen as forces (that may be used to assist or to hinder the achievement of goals) – is not evident to the ape because it has no explicit sense of itself as an agent. The belief that events can be *brought about* is a projection on to the extra-corporeal world of the sense of agency that humans alone have, and which comes from first-person identification with certain events (actions) that are linked with the fulfilment of need and the pursuit of appetite. This is a necessary precursor before the intuitive leap which enables one to see an analogy between the wind and the human being shaking the tree, can be taken and a trial embarked upon. Both ape and human see the apple drop but the penny drops only in one of them. Sense experience becomes the necessary chance observation only in the prepared (human) mind.

The notion that there are connections 'out there' is the driver for technological extension of human agency. The sense of the otherness of objects and, connected with this, the realisation that the world must be engaged on its own terms which have to be discovered drives the evolution of powers on the basis of trial and error. Trials become more sophisticated, errors more egregious, hypotheses more explicit, our capacity for surprise and disappointment becomes more elaborate. The progressive success of technology not only extends agency but also widens the causal intuition. Recurrent, predictable outcomes crystallise into a widening sense of underlying principles. Long before technology is science-driven, it is intuited-principle-driven: it is practical and homely. However, the procedural know-how that results takes technology to places where general principles become so explicit that declarative know-that starts to take over. The fundamental article of faith of the scientist – the principle of uniformity of events – was well established by the time writing started to deposit procedural knowledge in declarative knowledge stored outside the human body and the individual craftsman and science really took off.[27]

NOTES AND REFERENCES

1. John McDowell, *Mind and World* (Cambridge, MA: Harvard University Press, 2nd edition, 1994, with a New Introduction by the author), pp. xxiii and 5.
2. Presented baldly in this fashion, the hypothesis may seem almost ludicrous – the kind of idea beloved of cranks on park benches who offer you their world-pictures, honed in solitary rooms, when you would prefer to sit quietly in the sunlight. The reader who does not wish to take on trust what has already been established is advised to read Chapter 8 of *I Am*, and Chapter 10 of *The Hand. A Philosophical Inquiry into Human Being.* A shorter account of the argument regarding free will is available in Raymond Tallis, 'Human Freedom as a Reality-Producing Illusion', *The Monist* (2003), 86(2): 200–19.
3. The notion that the self dissolves into the collective has been greatly refined in recent decades. It still misses the point. I have discussed the variant strains of this way of thinking in *Enemies of Hope. A Critique of Contemporary Pessimism* (Basingstoke: Macmillan, 2nd edition, 1999).
4. I have often thought that it was at least as much his preoccupation with his painful varicose ulcer as his love for Julia that made him insoluble in the totalitarian society which wanted to negate him.
5. For a more detailed discussion of this example, see Tallis, *Enemies of Hope*, pp. 320–1.
   The deliberateness of ordinary talk is an inescapable feature of it. We need to know what we are doing (and why), as is evident from John Searle's description cited in Chapter 1 of the present volume: 'In speaking, I attempt to communicate certain things to a hearer by getting him to recognize my intention to communicate just those things' (*Speech Acts. An Essay in the Philosophy of Language* (Cambridge: Cambridge University Press, 1969), p. 43). Ordinary talk illustrates the interaction between general rules and the expression of individual freedom. In order to communicate particular things that are unique to our situation, we submit to the general

rule of meaning-factoring – rules of language, of circumstance, of our sense of what others will understand.

6. Gottlob Frege, 'The Thought. A Logical Inquiry', trans. A. M. and Marcelle Quinton, *Mind* (1956), 65: 289–311. Reprinted in *Philosophical Logic. Oxford Readings in Philosophy* (Oxford: Oxford University Press, 1967), p. 37.

7. We may think of deliberate action as the supreme expression of the bounce-back originating from the Existential Intuition. Collectively, nature shaped us and we returned the compliment. Individually, culture shaped us and, again, we return the compliment.

8. Quoted in Richard Kane, *The Significance of Free Will* (Oxford: Oxford University Press, 1996), p. 220.

9. And they remain, of course, closely linked. As Kane (ibid.) points out, 'we distinguish ourselves *as selves* distinct from the world by virtue of our ability to control some things by our wills' (p. 96) and 'we associate being a self in the full sense with imagining ourselves doing things – making, producing, creating, bringing about – as effecting changes in the world by our wills' (p. 100). Successful willing further 'thickens' our sense of our selves, though a certain minimal thickness of self-sense is a precondition of willing. Selfhood and agency co-evolve.

10. For further details, see Tallis, 'Human Freedom as a Reality-Producing Illusion'.

11. See 'A Note on Intention', in Raymond Tallis, *Not Saussure: A Critique of Post-Saussurean Literary Theory* (Basingstoke: Macmillan, 2nd edition, 1995), pp. 223–4.

12. That there is a link between the complexity of the mediation of an action and its degree of freedom is intuitively attractive: the more intermediate steps there are, the more you have to know what you are doing in order to complete it.

13. This is linked with the intuition that connects freedom and self-expression. I don't have to have been entirely self-created in order to be free. It is sufficient that my actions are expressive of my self and that that self is sufficiently developed.

14. The unconscious motives to which Freudians and others ascribe our actions are not reasons; nor (as we shall see) can they be fulfilled without reason-led behaviour.

15. The indeterminacy of our wants haunts our lives, especially when we are in the Kingdom of Ends. See Raymond Tallis, 'The Difficulty of Arrival', in *Newton's Sleep: Two Kingdoms and Two Cultures* (Basingstoke: Macmillan, 1995), pp. 126–204.

16. It might be argued that the movements comprising hunting – for example, a fox chasing a goose – are not programmed or even tightly scripted. The goal, however, is specific and, if not visible, at least scentable. In other words, the script is fairly tight but continuously modified in the light of events. A fox chasing a goose is in pursuit of a concrete actuality, not a general possibility.

17. See Tallis, *Enemies of Hope*, pp. 362–79 for the case for universal human values.

18. *A Treatise of Human Nature*, II. iii, paragraph 3.

19. See Kane, *The Significance of Free Will*, passim, but especially pp. 74–9.

20. Jon Jacobson, *Choosing Character. Responsibility for Virtue and Vice* (Ithaca and London: Cornell University Press, 2001).

21. I have considered those reasons that 'pull' actions as propositional attitudes and the latter as ingredients of consciousness. Some philosophers would disagree very strongly with this assumption. For example, Rudiger Bittner, in *Doing Things for Reasons* (Oxford: Oxford University Press, 2002) argues that the reasons for which we act are not usually psychological states but events or states of affairs in the outside world. I find it difficult to see how the latter could guide actions except in so

far as they were assimilated into my consciousness, and individuated. Reasons seem even less likely than facts to be 'things on the surface of the globe'.

And then there is Elizabeth Anscombe's famous attempt to depsychologise intentions. In *Intention* (Cambridge: Cambridge University Press, 1957) she argued that intentional acts are defined not in terms of psychological processes that precede them but in terms of the sort of questions that have an application to them – whether the question can be a reason-question or a cause-question. The difference between actions and other events is merely a matter of the kind of explanation that is sought and the kind of description that is applied to it. This grammatical difference, she argues, does not reflect a deeper underlying reality. A given action – defined as a set of movements – can be seen as intentional or non-intentional depending on the description. An action can be intentional under one description and unintenional under another: one can intend to drive to London fast but not intend to drive at an average of 82 mph. The same action may thus have an intentional and non-intentional description. From this she concludes that the intention lies not in the actor, or in the action, but in the account.

This may leave one wondering why it is that an action can be described (correctly) as intentional and why, furthermore, we have the notion of intention. Anscombe does not attempt to account for that. The truth is that one can intend an action without separately intending all the components that make it up, or all of its aspects separately. I can deliberately lift my arm without deliberately intending the contractions of the individual fibres that cause the movement. This does not make my deliberate act of lifting my arm any less deliberate or any less different from the spontaneous twitching that may occur in an epileptic fit.

22. Lewis Wolpert, 'Causal Belief and the Origins of Technology', *Philosophical Transactions of the Royal Society of London* A (2003), 361: 1709–19. My debt to this brilliant paper extends far beyond my specific acknowledgements.

23. G. C. Lichtenberg, *Lichtenberg: Aphorisms and Letters*, trans. and ed. Franz Mautner and Henry Hatfield (London: Cape Editions, 1969), p. 62.

24. The direct (as opposed to mediated) link between causation and agency is still reflected in the legal definition of liability. While many factors may have led to a crash, the event that is picked out as the cause is the event that a person could reasonably have prevented (for example, through driving carefully or appropriate car maintenance) and can therefore be blamed for allowing to happen.

Nietzsche somewhere notes the connection between the causal sense and the propensity to blame: 'the cause-seeking animal' is the blaming (and self-blaming) animal, the grudge-bearing animal. Michael Dummett also makes this link. In 'Bringing about the Past' (*Philosophical Review* (1964), 73: 338–59) he suggests that:

> the connection between something's being a cause and the possibility of using it to bring about an effect plays an essential role in the fundamental account of how we ever come to accept causal laws: that is, that we could arrive at any causal beliefs only by beginning with those in which the cause is a voluntary action of ours.

25. Wolpert, 'Causal Belief', p. 1712. Incidentally, identification of causes is to be distinguished from associative learning of patterns of co-occurrence. Hume's reduction of cause to association based upon similarity or recurrent spatio-temporal proximity elides a huge gap between man and beast. The ontological leap to objects, selves and causes (all of those things that Hume found difficult to justify) is not based upon conditioning.

26. We may suppose that, in the first instance, the notion of force is embedded in the experience of deliberate effort. Animals are familiar with push and shove but not with the notion of *bringing things about by effort*. Even less would they be able to grasp the notion of bringing things about by indirect effort.

27. This book was essentially completed before I read Daniel J. Povinelli's *Folk Physics for Apes. The Chimpanzee's Theory of How The World Works* (Oxford: Oxford University Press, reprinted with corrections, 2003). I have been greatly reassured by Povinelli's interpretation of his own and others' experimental work.

    Povinelli's observations lead him to conclude that, even where chimps modify tools – which would seem to demand their most sophisticated grasp of the world – this is not informed 'by explicit abstract causal concepts of "shape", "pliability" and "physical connection"' (pp. 295–6). They have associationist learning but no sense of hdden connections intrinsic to objects. Unlike humans, they do not postulate unobservable intermediate events (pp. 314–15). Their everyday 'physics' is not founded on an ontology that includes material objects and forces and connections which explicitly transcend sense experience. If they do operate with mental images, they do so 'on the basis of mental images that have concrete observable references' (p. 314).

    They are, in short, confined to a world of the actual and visible. This applies even more obviously to animals such as elephants which (as Ruth Willats has pointed out to me) can learn by chance how to shake fruit from trees. This trial-and-error, cue-driven learning has nothing to do with understanding casuation or other hidden intermediary principles or forces.

PART FOUR

KNOWLEDGE
ENCOUNTERS ITSELF

CHAPTER 9

Appetites and Desires

9.1 PROPOSITIONAL ATTITUDES REVISITED: THE TRANSFORMATION OF APPETITES

Little of human awareness has remained untouched by the transformative power of the Existential Intuition. The several hundred thousand generations who have lived and died since the first hominids awoke to their own existence have seen its consequences extend into every corner of human consciousness and the ubiquitous expression of that transformed consciousness in individual and collective actions, tools and other artefacts, symbolic monuments, institutions, local and long-distance trade, stratified societies, specialisation of labour, science, documents, and so forth. The journey from the 'I-less' state of 'self-poor' and 'world-poor' pongids from which we parted company so long ago has led to our present wall-to-wall propositional awareness. Anindexical or pre-indexical sentience is now momentary and background against a continuous foreground of indexical and deindexicalised consciousness. Even those appetites which we seem to have inherited rather directly from our animal forebears are utterly transformed. This is worth exploring if only because an overestimate of the similarity between the drivers to human and to animal behaviour is a major obstacle to human self-understanding.

Of course, we share many givens with animals. Like them, we are organisms. We need food, drink, shelter from the weather and protection against attack. Maintaining the constancy of the internal environment of our bodies is the condition of free life for us as much as for them. And there is the imperative to reproduce and nurture our young. Nevertheless, our desires do not map on to the appetites or instincts that guide behaviour in animals. It is becoming more difficult to point this out because, with the rise and rise of biologism, resistance to narrowing the gap between animal instincts and human desires is seen as the tender-minded denial of an uncomfortable truth. We like to deceive ourselves, aficianados of biologism point out, and it takes a fearless thinker such as W. S. Gilbert to force us to face the truth that 'man is but a monkey shaved'.

Biologisers of the human condition reinforce the apparent strength of their position by describing human behaviour in animalomorphic terms and animal behaviour anthropomorphically. By this means, identical terms can be used to designate both rather simple animal behaviour and extremely complex human behaviour. We are so familiar with writing that describes 'the courtship rituals' of herring gulls and 'the mating behaviour' of humans that we hardly notice what is happening. It even becomes acceptable to speak – as does Matt Ridley in his recent (excellent) *Nature via Nurture* – with only a little irony, of a microscopic worm *Caenorhabditis elegans* (with a total of 302 neurons) showing 'flexible learning'. Ridley describes worms growing up in a Petri dish in the company of other worms as developing different adult 'personalities' as a result of being taught at 'school' rather than at home.[1] Not all anthropomorphisation is so gross, but the way for it is prepared by the use of capacious phrases such as 'learning behaviour' which encompass both a cow bumping into an electrified fence and never going there again and a woman clearing the ground for evening classes the following year by stockpiling babysitting tokens that will ensure that she can attend regularly. Even where there are superficial similarities of behaviour, it does not follow that the underlying cognitive processes are similar.

The case for narrowing the gap between humans and animals is also seemingly strengthened by the apparent ease with which humans descend into what is described as 'bestial' behaviour. Under conditions of war or privation, it is argued, the 'veneer' of civilisation and culture disappears and the animal heart of human nature comes to the surface. War, for example, is an expression of the essential aggressiveness of humans which reflects our animal ancestry; indeed, it reveals our ape-like essence. Jared Diamond, one of evolutionary psychology's many superstars, claims that

> of all our human hallmarks – art, spoken language, drugs and the others
> – the one that has derived most straightforwardly from animal precursors
> is genocide.[2]

The fact that genocide is a uniquely horrible, and relatively rare, event in human history, should make us question how expressive it is of our true essence. The assumption that we are most ourselves when we are most badly behaved is itself open to question. There is little evidence that a committed primary school teacher working with underprivileged children is less representative of humanity than a brutal concentration camp guard. Besides, the assumption that our true nature is revealed when we are at our worst only shows how close we are to beasts if it is assumed we are most animal-like when we are most depraved. But nothing could be less animal-like than much of our worst behaviour. As we discussed in section 8.2, the horrible wars of modern times have certainly been beastly but they are not terribly beast-like. The greater part of the experience of the vast majority of participants was remote from unbridled bloodlust or the direct fang-in-flesh of animal conflict. Modern wars are more about logistics than alpha-male violence; about words (instructions, exhortation, justification) rather than teeth, claws and fists; about the processing of information rather than physical interaction. Concentration camps, while one of their chief purposes is to degrade those imprisoned in them to the status of 'bare, forked creatures', are not themselves expressions of animal behaviour. The ideological justification, the documentation, the transports, the rules and regulations, the patient elaboration of monstrous cruelty, are remote from anything seen in the animal kingdom. No animal inflicts such intense misery upon its fellow creatures, on such a scale and with such tenacity of purpose as does a concentration camp guard.

This cuts little ice with the biologisers of humanity. We are, they argue, most ourselves (that is, our animal selves) when we are most – morally or otherwise – degraded. Here is Diamond again:

> Just imagine taking some normal people, stripping off their clothes, taking away all their possessions, depriving them of the power of speech and reducing them to grunting, without changing their anatomy at all, and let the rest of us clothed and talking people visit the zoo. Those speechless caged people would be seen for what they really are: a chimp that has little hair and walks upright.[3]

As Malik comments, this is not a very profound claim: 'if we remove our marks of humanity, we no longer appear to be human'. This is as shocking as the discovery that, if we take off all our clothes, we end up naked. It is interesting for what it illustrates: the belief that when we are stripped bare our true nature is revealed; that privation is revelation.

The important point is that human behaviour, and the drivers to behaviour, are utterly unlike anything seen in animals. When humans are wicked, their wickedness, like their goodness, is uniquely human.

The suggestion that the differences are superficial and that this is betrayed when, in situations of privation or conflict, we revert to (animal) type, has no foundation. Besides, if we were truly untransformed animals and the 'veneer' of civilisation and human culture were so thin, so fragile, it is difficult to see how it came into being in the first place, nor how, having come into being, it has stayed in being.

To affirm the fundamental difference between the drivers to human behaviour and animal instincts is one thing; to characterise it is another. Observing specific differences, however numerous and striking, is not enough. We have to connect these surface differences with the profound underlying distance between human and animal consciousness. The discussion of the role of reason in human behaviour in the last chapter was a start. It showed how, while human behaviour may sometimes be directly energised by appetites, it is for the most part occasioned and guided by propositional attitudes: beliefs, thoughts, explicit intentions, and so on. Everyday behaviour is directed by goals (to a greater or lesser degree abstract) located in a complex space of possibility – fact-steered, reason-guided, and so on. None of this would be possible without the human agent having a determinate goal in mind, a clear explicit understanding of the steps necessary to reach it, and an equally clear understanding of where each step stands in relation to an overarching plan. A mere 'drive', a general, physiologically-shaped behavioural energiser, could not direct, say, my intention to meet someone at a pre-appointed time a week hence, even if my purpose in meeting him were something as basic as that he should provide me with a free meal that will address my hunger.

The fundamental difference lies in the key role of propositional attitudes as mediators of behaviour. These are cognitive, conceptual entities whose goals are abstract, though they posit a concrete realisation. And while they have to be entertained in the consciousness of embodied subjects who *are* located, they are themselve unlocalised. A key to a propositional attitude is that it has a subject–object form, as in 'I want this'. While it is not continuously formulated in this way, it is available at any time to be thus formulated. Humans are able to say what they are about and why.

A propositional attitude, unlike a physiologically rooted appetite or an instinct, is connected with the *personal history*, the individual biography, of the subject in two ways. First, one propositional attitude does not make sense except as part of a network of attitudes. I cannot want a particular goal without believing that it will bring about other goals. I cannot, for example, want to meet you without some idea of the content or consequence of our meeting. And I cannot want to meet you without in some way knowing you. Second, propositional attitudes are organised in logical space and sometimes in a hierarchical way. For example, I may want to do X because I believe it will bring me closer to goal Y. X is explicitly *subordinated to* Y – as a necessary precursor, a preliminary step, an intermediate stage.[4] This hierarchy is sustained by knowledge – general knowledge, knowledge of where I am now, knowledge of how the world operates (or how I think it operates). It is no exaggeration to say that from one propositional attitude one could unpack, as its 'implicature' (to borrow Grice's term), a good deal of the personal history, the personality, of the individual in whom it is tokenised.

This becomes apparent when we think of the degree to which emotions that are thought to be close to animal feelings, such as anger, are *narrated*. Indeed, it is often narrative that gets them started, heats them up and keeps them going. The verbalisation of emotions does not merely articulate or individuate them: it fuels them. We may get angry, as Georg Christoph Lichtenberg once said, 'on others' advice'. Who would be able to be furious for a week over a slight without endless talking to himself about it – 'chewing it over' as they say?

Recalling the central role of cognitive rumination also reminds us of another profound difference between animal drivers to activity and whatever it is that makes humans act. This is the *normative* aspect of human behaviour and its emotional drivers. We get angry because we are outraged. Our outrage is justified against a criterion of what is expected and *should be* expected. Such justification has nothing to do with physiology, which provides causes of, but not justifications for, actions.[5] We act according to general rules and respect local customs, not merely because rules and customs are constraints, preventing certain modes of behaviour which may be backed up by sanctions, but also because we want to be well thought of. In many of our emotionally-driven transactions with others, we appeal to a chorus of onlookers, to an implicit reference group. By contrast, a robin seeing off another robin is not acting out of moral outrage at infringement of its personal space. It is merely responding to a stimulus.

Which brings us to something central to human motivation: honour, self-esteem, the desire to be loved for what we are in ourselves. This reflects another profound difference between us and beasts. Much human behaviour is shaped by an appetite that is unknown to animals, one that Hegel identified: a hunger for recognition, for acknowledgement. Such an appetite is predicated upon a stable and substantive sense of self and, as a correlative of this, a stable and substantive awareness of others as selves, who are aware of one's self. We have the sense of others as in some respect equal, at least in their ontological weight if not in their standing, to ourselves. Indexical awareness locates us in our own worlds, at their centre; deindexicalised awareness displaces us from that centre and forces us to share the honours with our conspecifics. Animals, lacking both indexical and deindexicalised awareness, have neither the self-awareness nor the awareness of others' awareness of themselves necessary to underpin the hunger for recognition, for existential acknowledgement, that drives so much of human behaviour. Hegel's famous observations that 'self-consciousness achieves its satisfaction only in another self-consciousness' and 'Self-consciousness exists in itself and for itself when and by the fact that it so exists for another; that is, it exists only on being acknowledged'[6] may overstate the extent to which other selves bring the self into being, but it captures a funda-mental difference between what motivates humans in daily life and what drives animals.

Because our consciousness is in part collectivised, our appetites – when we are not actual dying of starvation, thirst or cold – are norm-sensitive, even when they seem to connect with things as apparently basic as sexual desire. We desire that which we see others – our parti-cular reference group – desire. As Spinoza said:

> If we imagine anyone to love, desire, or hate anything which we ourselves, love, hate or desire, by that very fact we shall love, hate, or desire it the more. But, on the other hand, if we imagine what we love is avoided by someone, then we undergo a wavering of the mind … From the very fact that we imagine anyone to love anything, we shall love it ourselves.[7]

Hence there are fashions in corporeal beauty as well as in clothes, in food as well as in architecture.

Evolutionary psychologists like to explain all this by appealing to the coherence necessary for the survival of social groupings. The successful functioning of social groupings promotes the survival of individuals in the group, ensuring that they will be able to reproduce successively and so ensure the continuation of the 'selfish gene'. The problem is that social rules require a good deal of understanding – we cannot obey them without grasping their purpose. And we have to assent to them, whereas we do not have to assent to extreme thirst in order to act on it and search for water. We cannot act on our (human) desires without being conscious of them and that consciousness is of something whose animal source has been transformed and further transforms it. Behind such assent is a desire not merely to survive but also to be well thought of. We defend our actions by universalising them and we do this by trying to demonstrate that they conform to rules which all ought to obey. Psychopaths, even when they are all-powerful, try to place a positive gloss on their wicked, self-centred behaviour. A blood-boltered klepto-crat like Robert Mugabe still presents his actions as being for the benefit of those Zimbabweans who are worthy of his beneficence. The simple notion of 'adaptiveness' captures little or nothing of the conscious, deliberate activity necessary to support some large-scale outcome (for example, spreading one's genes), even those actions necessary to get a promiscuous male from the bed of one mistress to another.

The role of personal narrative, and the collective, in the shaping of the very emotions that energise our behaviour – as when we get angry on principle and talk ourselves into more and more intense anger – is a manifestation of the fact that human behaviour is rooted in de-indexicalised awareness. Human appetite is assimilated into the large narrative of the individual's life and the shared narratives of her community; through being modulations of an embodied subject rather than expressions of an organism. Robert Brandom's observation that language does not merely serve certain ends but is 'a mighty engine for the envisaging and engendering of certain ends'[8] has particular appli-cation here. If there was ever a period when hominid desires could be assimilated to animal appetites, the arrival of language in human life 50,000–100,000 years ago brought that period to an end.

Our ends, large and small – honour, to be well thought of by certain people, to attract a particular member of the opposite sex, to do a good job, to earn enough money to have a house in the country, to avenge an abstract slight experienced many years ago, to find out what happens at the end of *War and Peace* – could not be envisaged by animals or engendered in the physiology of any organism. We uncoupled animals create our personal appetites, our desires rooted in our own take on 'the world' – an idealised totality of the collective of de-indexicalised awareness. There is little or no relation between the appetites of the self-poor, world-poor beast and the self-rich, world-rich human being.

9.2 CARNAL KNOWLEDGE

Anyone who subjects himself to a serious self-examination on the subject … will be sure to find that he regards the sexual act as basically something degrading, which defiles and pollutes not only the body.

The excremental is all too intimately and inseparably bound up with the sexual; the position of the genitals – *intra urinas et faeces* – remains the decisive and unchangable factor … The genitals themselves have not taken part in the development of the human body in the direction of beauty: they have remained animal, and thus love, too, has remained in essence just as animal as it ever was.[9]

While some biologists admit that most human behaviour has only a tenuous relationship to animal drives, they do not accept that *every-thing* has been transformed. Dawkins, in the passage we quoted in section 7.3, still argues that we can 'make a simple Darwinian inter-pretation of things like hunger and sex drives'.[10] In asserting that human sexual behaviour is especially amenable to a biological interpretation, he was at one with Immanuel Kant, who argued that sexuality exposes one 'to the danger of equality with beasts'.[11] And while it is sometimes difficult to pass two dogs copulating on wasteland without feeling parodied, Kant's claim seems to be point-missing on a scale that only a man of peerless intelligence could be capable of.

Of course, sexual behaviour can appear beastly and be degrading. A drunken squaddy rutting on a Saturday night with a woman forced to sell her body to fund a drug habit is hardly testimony to the spirituality of human desires. And sex may be a potent instrument of wickedness: its intimacy offers opportunities to exercise a malign power; to express the desire to hurt, to destroy, to humiliate, to violate. This does not make it any less human of course. As will be evident from our discussion in the previous section, human evil is as human as human goodness, for all that we describe wickedness as 'inhuman'. The use of rape as an instrument of war could not have occurred to animals, innocent as they are of the notion of symbolic conquest, of possession through violation. Here, as elsewhere, when humans are beastly, their beastliness is quite unlike that of any imaginable beast.

Precisely because sex is not necessary for individual survival – to paraphrase Auden, while none has lived without food and water, millions have lived with unsatisfied sexual desires – it is most susceptible to transformation. In most cases, it is separated from its biological purpose of procreation. Its primary purpose is the pleasure of at least one of the participants, though to say that is hardly to simplify things, for the nature of sexual pleasure is very complex indeed; so complex that 'pleasure' seems a desperately inadequate word.[12]

Even in the minority of cases where the primary aim is the pukka biological one of reproduction, the subjectively experienced wish is not identical to the objective purpose of the 'ten-second jump and shriek'[13] of our primate ancestors. It is transformed by being an explicit goal, linked to other explicit goals, such as the desire 'to make something that is both of us', 'to survive after my death', 'to have an heir', 'to share the joy of bringing up a child with my partner', and so on. These profoundly social, verbalised intentions are also deeply personal, reaching into a vast, unverbalised territory of the self; all in all, a long way from the impersonal, asocial procreations of beasts that, one assumes, do not even recognise a causal link between coitus and having offspring. Even in those cases, then, where people copulate in order to procreate, sexual behaviour is no nearer beastliness.[14]

Nevertheless, Kant's feeling that there is something intrinsically beastly about sex is not easily dismissed. After all, there are few of us who would like to be observed in coitus, least of all by our friends and relatives and children. Lovemaking is fundamentally private, to be performed away from the gaze of others.[15] Few of us have such qualms about eating in public. The suspicion that it is potentially degrading therefore lingers, though almost everyone participates in it, or would like to, for much of their adult lives. What is more, the shame is unequally distributed: traditionally, women are ashamed about sex and men boast about it, though it is difficult to see how the one who is entered can be more debased than the one who does the entering, especially since there are many other aspects of lovemaking that are symmetrical and reciprocated.[16] There is shame, however, on both sides. Even the youth who wants to boast about his conquests the morning after would not be happy to learn that his exertions the night before have been spied upon by his mates. Children, when they first learn about sex, find it unbelievable. It seems like a queasy reversion to infancy – which, as we shall see, it is in some respects: a retracing of the journey taken from infancy to maturity.[17]

The connection between sexual behaviour and shame – reflected in the almost universal concealment of the genitals – is so strong as to suggest something about its fundamental significance. Readers may be familiar with the old joke in which one clubman says to another: 'Do you think sex is degrading to women?' To which the other replies, 'If it's any good it is'. One might add: 'If it's any good, it's degrading to everyone involved.' In what sense is it degrading? Answering this question takes us back to the central theme of this book: the nature of knowledge, the transcendence of the body, liberation from the constraints of organic existence.

In our everyday life, we meet each other not as bodies but as people, as knowers. To see someone merely as a body is regarded as reductive, even where, as not infrequently, a strategic mixture of concealment and exposure is the chosen mode of dress, intended to broadcast the bodiliness of the person and to incite body-directed appetites. Our characteristic mode of intercourse is verbal.[18] When embodied subjects talk, they are less like organic bodies and more like socialised subjects. They remain embodied, of course, but those bodies are attenuated, particularly as they are already transformed into complex arrays of symbols that express the worlds, the lives, the biographies of the subjects within them. Garments, ornaments, accessories, tones of voice, the speaking voice itself, partly dematerialise the body into a cloud of signs and symbols. All of these in turn point to the role, the provenance, the life of the *person* and point away from the here-and-now of the *body*.

Contrast this interaction in social intercourse between complex symbol-producing clouds of symbols with sexual intercourse. There, interaction is comparatively unmediated – or seems to aim to be so. The voice is subordinated to the direct interactions of the flesh. Ultimately, even sight and hearing are displaced by touch, smell and taste – a descent out of the daylight of society pre-figured by the closed-eyed, open-mouthed kiss. Deindexicalised awareness – locationless, abstract, set in a space of possibilities – seems to reach back towards the pre-indexical sensations that characterise infancy and animal life. Such knowledge as results is directly fabricated through the interaction of sentience with sentience. The leg rubs against a leg, the hand strokes the back, the tongue is aware of the other's mouth that encloses it. Looked at coldly, even kisses (especially of the French variety) are rather extraordinary: two people communicate by means of direct contact between the apparatus of speech, the sources of all those sentences. This seems an almost direct reversal of the journey from sentience to sentences. At the climax, the social is almost entirely eclipsed as the other – so close up as to be almost invisible – vanishes under a tidal wave of incommunicable sentience.

This is a gross simplification. Lovemaking is at no stage a purely regressive journey from knowledge to sentience. Even at the climax, sentience remains striated with knowledge. And en route to the climax, caresses, negotiation and conversation interdigitate. Sexual intercourse in humans is uniquely face-to-face: tenderness, togetherness and intimacy are of the essence of a lovemaking for which there is no analogue in animals. Each is bathed in the other's awareness and in awareness of the other's awareness and so (potentially) *ad infinitum*. Even the flesh-on-flesh aspect of lovemaking is *dialogue*, where touching and being touched carry its freight, its aura, of symbolic significance. Undressing is a symbol-charged shedding of symbols, not merely the removal of social wrappings. Its landmarks measure out, and make explicit, the distance travelled from the common world of the drawing room, the street and workplace.

Certainly, physical lovemaking promises to make the other-as-world shrink to the other-as-body, and hence make him or her literally palpable; the caress unites sentience with society, bringing the social being within the scope of sense experience.[19] This is particularly true of genital caresses, where the intensity of sensation (itself a reflection of the density of sense endings) and the charge of social significance (correlating with the high density of social prohibitions) is overwhelming. Ideally, in sexual intercourse, each is drawn to the place where the other is and the distance between them, originating from the separateness of the worlds to which they belong, is erased. At any rate, the caress attempts to bring the other's self back to the body and make it literally tangible, though each becomes touchable only in so far as they give themselves to the caress. Sexual arousal, which puts bodily self-presence in italics, seems to make the object of love more explicitly present and so more directly accessible.

But this is only half the story. While lovemaking seems to be tracing knowledge back to the point at which knowledge began, what is gained is itself knowledge. The essential scandal of carnal knowledge is that this knowledge is acquired through reversing the journey each has taken from the body to a locationless world. As each directly interacts with the other as organism, feeling the warmth of flesh next to, or inside, flesh, neither quite reverts to the condition of an organism. Each remains a knowing animal, able to experience the distance between the organic body and the living person, between the organism and the world, in both themselves and in the other. Each is aware of the other as a person as well as a body. And while the lovemakers acquire privileged knowledge of the organic basis of the other's world, this doesn't quite bring the locationless person down to a particular location, tie the wandering tresses of the person's universe to a particular place that can be touched and so, in a sense, possessed.[20] Neither party is entirely resorbed into the body from which they have emerged as persons and which remains the implicit and explicit centre of their world.

Nor, of course, is the total collapse of the other into tangible flesh what lovers really want. This is the lie at the heart of the promise of sexual desire: that a person can be accessed through their body, their world possessed through their body, without their becoming pre-personal, worldless. Indeed, the intimacy of true lovemaking – as opposed to rape or the interaction between prostitute and client – is presupposed upon the joy of being accepted (in the most direct sense) by another person who remains a person; and the pleasure is enhanced by the sense of being privileged in this way. Worlds as well as bodies lie side by side and bodies become uniquely advantaged handles on the worlds. The passage from persons in dialogue to impersonal organisms locked in a frenzy of physical pleasure would be a self-frustrating goal of sexual desire. If lovemaking were based on the abdication of the person from the body and the lovers regressed to the condition of organisms, it would seem something like a shared frenzy that had little more significance than an epileptic fit *à deux*.[21] Instead, each remains a Knowing Animal, attempting to possess the other through a specially privileged state of the other's body.

The transgression, the active nakedness, the deliberate exposure, are essential to the act, to the gift each is giving the other. The intense concentration of sensory endings and social prohibitions in certain areas both contribute to the feeling of the distance travelled, into a privileged, private world from a public day. Direct access to the impersonality of the organism underlying the other's personhood can be enjoyed only through the sense that the organism is haunted by a person. In perfect lovemaking the person, the body and the sensations merge in mutual presence. And this is an incompletely attainable ideal. Sexual desire has something ultimately unsatisfiable at its heart.[22]

This is, perhaps, one source of the frantic promiscuity exhibited by some people. It is an attempt to rehearse, or recapture, the first stages of a love affair, to experience that sense of tearing through the layers of another's world to reach the bodily basis of that world. That world, however, proves elusive every time. Touch cannot reveal how the body is experienced by the person and how it relates to its world. Most of what fills the word-mediated life remains outside the bedroom door, to be discovered only by the indirect means that we employ in ordinary life. The meeting of worlds, in short, can collapse into the interaction of bodies. The first touch crosses from one world to another. The person is invested with the aura of a world. A visitor from another planet – her planet. After the first caress, there are diminishing returns. The focus may switch to secondary compensations: the gratification of conquest, intense physical sensation, the satisfaction of curiosity, the flattery of being accepted in the most literal sense; but something fundamental nevertheless remains unsatisfied.

The true object of sexual desire is locationless. Unlike appetite, which is triggered by its object and targets its object, it is propositional. While it may focus lustfully on a person as object, as organism, as parts of an organism, that object owes its significance to the fact that it is the incarnation of a person, the instantiation of a world; indeed of *the* world exemplified in another. A person to whom we are sexually attracted seems to make the world – the world refracted to a magical individual world – apprehensible through their body though. While sexual love is

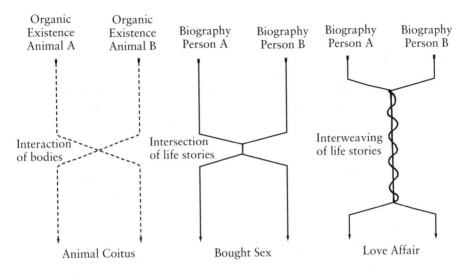

Figure 9.1 Sex in the Lives of Animals and Humans

more respectable because its object is the fathomless mystery of another person and seems to respect their person, lust owes its intensity to the fact that its objects are invested with the aura of a person.

This non-coincidence of the true object of sexual desire with the apprehensible object makes it incapable of fulfilment, even when the appetite that fuels it is satiated. For the person eludes the lover even as the loved one responds to the touch. Howsoever each wants to give themselves to the other:

> When you lift yourselves
> Up to each other's lips – drink unto drink:
> Oh, how strangely the drinker eludes his part![23]

Such complexity is remote from animal life, just as the concept of the obscene – arising out the retracing of knowledge back to its source, while retaining all the knowledge that has grown beyond that source – central to sexual desire, is absent from animal appetite.

Which links with another difference that sets human lovemaking apart from animal coitus. The lovers are not merely intertwined bodies but also interwoven stories (see Figure 9.1). Each brings a narrative to the bedroom. The most immediate narrative is the story of mutual uncovering and the negotiation, guesswork, the said and the unsaid, and risk-taking, the giving and withholding, that drives it forward. Then there is the narrative of their relationship and of their evolving ideas of each other and what they might mean to each other – of the story so far and the possible story to come. And there is the greater narrative, partly spoken, partly inferred, in the hinterland of their lives to date, that says who they are.

In some cases, the narrative may seem somewhat abbreviated and the guesswork perfunctory. Our drunken squaddy rutting with a prostitute on a Saturday night seems close to a mere body interacting with someone reduced to a mere body. But even this, however animal-seeming, expresses a desire that is still not animal; for it is interwoven with stories, based on fantasies, longings, that have a long internal pedigree. The prostitute, too, will bring her story, though it will be rather different – less about sexual pleasure than about making a living – but a story none the less. Essentially separate stories intersect for a few moments. Even the most impersonal sex – for example, the serial encounters in a gay bathhouse – is still between persons, even if the persons in question are not those who are present and the interacting bodies are haunted by ghosts imported from less immediately satisfied desires.[24]

Such encounters parasitise, by aping, sexual experiences between people who mean something to each other, otherwise the experiences would collapse to mere bodily sensation, without significance beyond sentience.[25] For at the heart of human sexuality is the fundamental need, referred to earlier, arising out of the fact that, as Hegel said, 'self-consciousness achieves its satisfaction only in another self-consciousness'. It touches on the idea of being accepted, recognised, acknowledged by another, even if that is merely simulated in commercial sex or the one-night stand that takes advantage of a drugged or drunken partner. Even some rapists fantasise that their victims 'want it' – that is to say want them. Rapists often want to be wanted by their victims; or, at the very least to *matter* to them. If they matter only through the lasting damage they cause, they will settle for that.

While tenderness, intimacy, the generosity of giving one's self and so of giving pleasure, palliate the essential obscenity of sex, arising out of its taking knowledge back along the path of its awakening to the place of its origin, obscenity remains an enduring element, as becomes evident when it is taken out of context and reduced to a spectacle or when one imagines the sexual behaviour and desires of those whom one does not oneself desire. Indeed, seeking knowledge of the other in their body, taking knowledge *beneath* its source, may become a value in its own right. The disapproval of the guardians of the collective world – God, priests, elders, parents – has, since time immemorial, added to the joy of sex. The inherently transgressive nature of carnal knowledge is intensified by social vetos compounding the epistemological scandal of interacting with a person directly through their body.

For Charles Baudelaire, the allure, the profound pleasure, of sex was inseparable from its transgressive nature, its sinfulness: 'the sole and supreme pleasure in Love lies in the absolute knowledge of doing *evil*. And man and woman know, from birth, that in Evil is to be found all voluptuousness.'[26] The essence of concupiscence is sin; or sex is most itself when it is sinful.[27] For such individuals, permission, routinisation, legitimacy, affection – even true love – all render sex insipid. They may even want to mock the profound humanity of sexuality by seasoning it with brutality – dealt or received – preferring to steal or purchase what is in essence a gift, perhaps the supreme gift from one person to another. Or by underlining its obscenity by subjecting the other to especial degradation. The use of the names of sexual acts and the erogenous zones of the body as terms of abuse – swearing in the genital case, as it were – echoes and reinforces the link between sex and degradation.

Lovemaking is profoundly immodest, because it takes knowledge to places where it should not be and this knowledge has additional allure if it is itself forbidden. The contrast between the intrinsic modesty of the Good Woman and the immodesty of the Whore or the dissipated amateur runs deep in the mythology of sexuality, in what has passed for knowledge about carnal knowledge.[28] The Good Woman gives knowledge of herself only to one whom she loves or values for some other reason. Or she 'saves herself' for a man whom others require her to value because it is her duty to do so. Until such a person has been identified, she has to keep herself 'pure' and 'spotless' and not engage in 'filthy' practices.[29] Comment on the inherent contradiction, the hypocrisy and the destructiveness of both the codes of sexual morality and the way they are applied, is not necessary.

Religious belief amplifies the significance of the knowledge sought in a regression from knowledge to sentience. The theological echoes and elaboration of the association between sex and sin have had, and are still having, an overwhelming influence on the lives of individuals, the evolution of cultures and the course of history. The story of the Fall rehearses the discovery of knowledge and connects it with the discovery of sexual desire and sexual shame. The fruit Eve gives to Adam symbolises the self-encounter of knowledge and retrospective illumination of the animal organism as an object of shame: the awakening of knowledge and the sense of sin are born together. After they had eaten from the Tree of Knowledge, Adam and Eve became aware of their nakedness and covered their genitals. 'So when the woman saw that the tree, was to be desired to make one wise, she took of its fruit and ate … Then the eyes of both were opened, and they knew that they were naked; and they sewed fig-leaves together to make themselves aprons.'[30] The Knowledge of Good and Evil may be seen as standing for knowledge *per se*, the wakening out of sentience to the possibility of error. In this case it is moral error that is in question, but the normative character of knowledge is represented: other kinds of error are possible.

The awakening of knowledge is associated with expulsion from Paradise. We may think of Paradise as standing for a state in which humankind was at one with the world, a pre-indexical consciousness when subject and object were not differentiated, before the wound in consciousness (which we shall discuss in the next chapter) was opened up. The account we have given in this book sees the awakening of sentience not as a sudden Fall but as a gradual ascent from the condition of beasts. Theology, however, turns things upside down and imagines a primordial condition in which men were angels and the primordial state of humanity an elevated, not a beastly, one. From *that* starting point, the awakening to knowledge was indeed a fall – a descent from the status of angels to one half-way to the condition of beasts: Man was a fallen angel but still placed over all the beasts, as their lord and master. This knot of intuitions captures the connection between sexuality, shame and the peculiar nature of carnal knowledge – knowledge returning to the place where knowledge began: knowledge of the other person, of one's self, as an organism.

In human lovemaking, society and the world converge on sphincters *intra urinam et faeces*, and other places where they have no right to be. Sexual desire is essentially, not accidentally, an indecent propositional attitude. Which is why literature focuses so much on adultery and other transgressive sexual passion: they bring out the transgressive nature of all sexual behaviour. Transgressive sex is sex in italics and, contrary to what bishops and mullahs may like to think, is even more, not less, remote from animal coition.[31]

9.3 DISCOVERING FINITUDE

Wanderers east, wanderers west
Know you why you cannot rest?
'Tis that every mother's son
Travails with a skeleton.[32]

Something else transforms the appetites and drives that humans have inherited from their animal ancestors. From an early age, the Knowing

Animal knows that he is going to die. The Existential Intuition, an awakening of self-consciousness, while obviously necessary for consciousnessness of death, is not sufficient to bring awareness of mortality. The passage from 'That I am this ...' to 'That I shall one day not be ...', from the sense of one's own existence to entertaining the possibility of one's non-existence, requires something more. Privation, wounds, fear of predators do not naturally extrapolate to the idea of one's extinction; on the contrary, they place one's specific existence in italics. The sense of our lives, and ourselves, as being limited, located, contingent, does not grow automatically out of these particular experiences. Even the spectacle of our fellow humans dying will awaken a sense of our own mortality only if our sense of our existence has undergone a transformation. To read the message from others' deaths, we have to see ourselves as being in some fundamental sense the same as those others. We have to step outside of our sense of being the centre of things and see ourselves as being, like others, objects in the world as well as subjects underpinning the world. Only then will we perceive the commonality of our fate so that others' extinction signals my own mortality; their immobility my future stillness; their irreversible absence my own future absence from the world. We have to be aware of ourselves as not only being objects in the world but also as being non-privilegedly located in it; as entities among entities, as instances of a type. We have to be cognitively 'precipitated' into a material world as embodied subjects located in it and displaced from the centre of it. We could not otherwise imagine the world continuing without ourselves, anticipate the state of not-being, the death, that we fear.

Thomas Nagel speaks of 'a strange sense that I both am and am not the hub of the universe'.[33] The former corresponds to the most innocent modes of indexical awareness, the awareness of the perceiving individual located in, but at the centre of, the world she perceives. But even indexical awareness can give one a feeling of being displaced from the centre: this table exists for me but also for that person over there who is seeing it from another angle. You are pointing to something I cannot see, in a region of space that does not exist for me, from which I am absent, while I am at the centre of the perceived world but I am also at the corner of a room, on the edge of a crowd, in a remote place. (As Sartre said, 'my place is exile'.) As indexical awareness is increasingly permeated by deindexicalised awareness – manifest in the beliefs, thoughts, goals, facts, and so on which guide us through our lives – so too, is there a progressive, usually implicit, displacement of ourselves from the centre of the world. This is reinforced indexically every time we are part of a crowd, stand at the edge of an occasion or join a queue, when we are reminded that we are one of many, an instance or unit of humanity. The more we learn of the world, the more we are aware of the discrepancy between our small size as embodied subjects and the vastness of the world uncovered by our growing knowledge; between what we are and what we know of. While indexical awareness may discover us as small objects in a huge canvas – as when we contemplate a landscape from a vantage-point – deindexicalised awareness discovers us yet smaller objects in an even greater cognitive landscape, upon which our warm bodies are not vantage-points.

An even more intimate assault on our sense of being at the centre of things comes from the knowledge that we have, and more importantly others have, of the objective truths about those same warm bodies.[34] The doctor who tells you that the feeling of awfulness that has transformed your world into a place of misery, and given a unique discoloration to your life, is due to processes of which you were unaware, affecting organs that you had only the haziest idea about, emphasises how even your own body, the carnal guarantor of the world of which you are centre, is simply a piece of living matter that, in many respects, has no special relationship to you.[35] The facts that determine your fate are not shaped like your direct awareness of yourself and are as hidden from you as the facts about any other object.

We do not, of course, 'grow out of' the fundamental sense of ourselves as being at the centre of things any more than we grow out of our sensations, our preoccupations, our self-interest, our emotions or our duties. We are somehow necessarily ourselves, notwithstanding that those selves are in every detail and in their very existence contingent. Our contingency hardly affects us for much of our waking lives. Paul Valery's retort to Pascal's famous assertion that 'the eternal silence of the infinite spaces' terrified him is very much to the point: 'but the hubbub in the corner reassures me'.[36] At any rate, the thoughts that dwarf us are, in the end, our own thoughts. The cognitive vastnesses in which we fear drowning are upheld by our ability to think them. If we remain child-like in our view of the world, it is because we are not merely self-centred but are selves.

Even so, the knowledge that we are not objectively the centre of the universe, that we are contingent – and that therefore the death that affects those others whose contingency is obvious to us will affect ourselves – influences everything we think and do. Our absorbing days are haunted by the shadow of the nothingness to come. That we are in line for death as we are in the queue for so many other things gives a shape to our lives. That we may die at any time only adds urgency to the projects that conceal our death from us: urgency undermined by the knowledge of ultimate pointlessness.

Life is real! life is earnest! ...
Dust thou art, to dust returnest.[37]

The discovery of contingency is often thought to be the distinctive feature of modernity.[38] In fact, it goes very deep in hominid consciousness. The Copernican revolution that displaced human beings collectively from the centre of the universe was preceded by a proto-Copernican revolution that displaced human beings from the centre of the worlds of which they are individually conscious. The acknowledgement of the positional advantage of others, suggested as the first step to deindexicalised awareness in section 4.5, already points to a polycentric world in which one is not oneself a privileged centre. In our deindexicalised awareness, we are self-marginalising; or, at any rate, our unremitting self-centredness is haunted by our sense of being an object that is not at the centre. The 'this' that I am becomes an object that is vulnerable, as are other objects, to change.

Once language enters human interaction, then this intuition can be force-fed: the fact of death, and therefore of one's mortality, is presented as an item of deindexicalised awareness that does not correspond to a uniform dawning over one's consciousness of one's vulnerability to dying. I am told of the death of others, and even that I too will die one day, before I can grasp this extraordinary truth. I encounter the most important truth about myself as a mere piece of information. This deepens the split between objective knowledge of death, which is permanent, and the intermittent terror of nothingness. The knowledge of death is a general fact which – except when one is confronted with a threat to oneself or to someone close – one has to work hard to imagine. This creates a breathing space in which death can transform us, and further transform the appetites that we have inherited from our organic ancestors. 'Death destroys a man,' E. M. Forster said, 'but the idea of death can save him.'[39]

The flight from death, the search for immortality – literally in the flesh, symbolically in the spirit or indirectly through a monument left behind in the world as a proxy for one's continuing presence – is an enduring preoccupation of the Knowing Animal. So much of human behaviour is directed to building bulwarks against the death that all animals suffer and only humans know. Burial rituals, ancestor worship, the construction of memorials, dreams of resurrection, stories of metamorphosis, are all attempts to pierce the darkness the knowing animal intuits beyond the world opened up by knowledge and to cancel mortality by creating a single community of the living and the dead.

NOTES AND REFERENCES

1. Matt Ridley, *Nature via Nurture. Genes, Environment and What Makes us Human* (London: Fourth Estate, 2003), p. 146.

2. Quoted in Kenan Malik's brilliant *Man, Beast and Zombie. What Science Can and Cannot Tell Us about Human Nature* (London: Weidenfeld & Nicolson, 2000), p. 225. The entire book, especially the chapter 'Humane Beasts and Beastly Humans', should be required reading for all biologisers of human nature.

3. Quote ibid., p. 21.

4. It might be argued that subordination of one particular step to an overall goal is evident in animal behaviour. For example, gathering the first twig of a nest makes sense only with respect to the completed nest that may be the product of many thousands of such actions. The analogy holds up only if one overlooks one or two things. First of all, my actions make sense to me only if they are plugged into my personal biography. Second, I would be able to guide and control them only if they made explicit sense. (Consider my hurried locking of my front door in order to catch a train to get me to London in time for a meeting which I hope will bring about some change in something rather abstract, such as the way we provide health care for elderly people.) The automated nest-builder requires neither of those things.

5. The relationship between the physiological and the propositional can be very complex indeed, particularly in view of the fact that we notice the physiological accompaniments of our emotional reactions and there is much objective knowledge about them. Whether or not animals observe the fast beating of their hearts when they are faced by a predator or a potential mate, humans certainly do, and this can have certain interesting consequences: the prescription of medication to damp down the activity of the nervous system when chronic anxiety causes chronic discomfort; the cultivation of emotions for their own sake; and the use of drugs to bring about the physiogical accompaniments of contentment and thus make us content.

   The tortuous relationship between the physiological and narrative components of emotional arousal is beautifully illustrated by Hans Castorp's experience when, in Thomas Mann's *The Magic Mountain*, he finds that his heart is permanently racing. This is, in fact, an effect of the high altitude of the TB sanitorium where he is visiting his cousin. He feels comfortable with it, however, only when he sets eyes on the beautiful Claudia Chauchat and 'realises' that his tachycardia is due to his passion for her.

6. G. F. W. Hegel, *The Phenomenology of Spirit*, trans. A. V. Millar (Oxford: Oxford University Press, 1977), pp. 175, 178. This fundamental feature of humanity is reflected on by Tzvetan Todorov:

   > Good and ill are 'of one substance' with human life because they are the fruits of our freedom, of our ability to choose at every point between several courses of action. Their common source is human sociability and human incompleteness, for these make us need other people to guarantee our sense of existing. But our need of others can be satisfied in two ways. We can cherish other people and seek to make them happy; or else we can subjugate and humiliate them so as to enjoy power over them. (*Hope and Memory*, trans. David Bellos (London: Atlantic Books, 2004), p. 21)

7. Benedict de Spinoza, Proposition XXXI of 'Origin and Nature of Emotions', Part III of *Ethics Proved in Geometrical Order*, trans. A. Boyle (London and New York: Everyman's Library, J. M. Dent, 1910), p. 106.

8. Quoted in Bernard Williams, *Truth and Truthfulness. An Essay in Genealogy* (New Haven, CT: Yale University Press, 2002), p. 39.

I had hoped to say more about language, both in relation to the transformation of emotions and, more generally, about its role in developing the deindexicalised awareness that has made it possible. Unfortunately, space constraints forbid. A few scattered points are, however, worth making.

Increasingly, human beings inhabit a world of possibilities instantiated in words and other symbols. It is these, rather than physical stimuli, that we have dealings with for much of our waking hours. Courtesy of language, those possibilities are more often locationless, and general (or at least specified with a precision that falls well short of the individuality of, say, a particular material object in our visual field) rather than 'over there', 'round the corner', etc. The proliferation and elaboration of possibilities can be limitless, as in the endless speculations of a jealous lover. It need not be confined to grand passion. The inner monologues of James Joyce's characters in *Ulysses* are as out of control as the analytical brooding of Marcel Proust's narrator in *Remembrance of Things Past*.

Emotion-fuelled possibilities can so expand beyond their occasions as to turn the head into an echo chamber, and the mind into an out-of-control word factory. A kind of hollow, or hollowed-out, space separates the obsessed individual from the world that actually surrounds him. At such a point, he might start to envy animals that do not entertain possibilities and have no linguistic hothouse in which to cultivate them. Beasts, which cannot cannot posit what might be the case because they do not deal in propositions, seem privileged indeed!

9. Sigmund Freud, 'On the Universal Tendency to Debasement in the Sphere of Love', in *A Critical and Cultural Theory Reader*, ed. Antony Easthope and Kate McGowan (Buckingham: Open University Press, 1992).

10. Richard Dawkins, in *Key Philosophers in Conversation. The Cogito Interviews*, ed. Andrew Pyle (London and New York: Routledge, 1991).

11. I am not sure where this comes from. It is consistent with Kant's disdainful description of marriage as an agreement between two people 'for the reciprocal use of each other's sexual organs'; quoted in Roger Scruton, *Kant* (Oxford: Oxford University Press, 1982), p. 9.

12. Even something as simple as physical pain is not simple in humans: in addition to sensory discrimination there is emotional significance and knowledge-based understanding.

13. I owe this description of primate 'lovemaking' to Dudley Young, *Origins of the Sacred. The Ecstasies of Love and War* (London: Little, Brown, 1992).

14. Indeed, for Catholics, the (biological) intent to procreate actually redeems sexual intercourse and makes it acceptable to God, the pope and the parish priest.

15. Humans are one of the few species that copulate in private. The privacy has many layers: dark places, clothes, discretion, a life that is led rather than merely lived. They also defaecate in private. The royal road to reducing individuals to the status of beasts is to make them naked, to make them defaecate and to copulate in public. This kind of exposure is routine in prison camps, as it 'demonstrates' the subhuman status of the victims.

Those who voluntarily participate in public sex – porn stars, for example – presumably count on the anonymity of being among strangers. Ditto those who indulge in group sex where all are equally exposed, so exposure, as it were, cancels out. Otherwise, lovemaking presupposes trust, that the exposure it involves will not be exploited in gossip. That is why sexual betrayal is such a fundamental abrogation of trust. It is a reminder of how close sexual intimacy is to humiliation. Its many links with laughter – cruel, nervous, affectionate – is a testimony to the incongruity of sex. Laughter, as has often been pointed out, is a response to a clash of categories. Ted Hughes even suggested, in his *Crow* poems, that sexuality was 'the great evil joke at the heart of the universe' (Elaine Feinstein, *Ted Hughes. The Life of a Poet* (London: Phoenix, 2001), p. 202), This, however, may say more about Ted Hughes than about sex.

The detailed kiss-and-tell stories that the tabloids like to run degrade both parties. For when sexual activity is removed from the sexual desire that gives it meaning, its obscenity is unredeemed. The icily clinical account of the not particularly exotic oral sex that took place in the Oval Office between Bill Clinton and Monica Lewinsky was a humiliation that the human race could have done without.

16. There are many reasons for this unequal distribution of shame, most of which have nothing to do with the thesis of this chapter. The societal regulation of female sexuality, and the loss of status that results from socially unapproved sex, is rooted in the different biological liabilities of men and women. Only recently has sex been reliably separated from pregnancy and all the social implications this has: an unattached pregnant woman is a social outcast; and a single women who engages in sex deliberately runs the risk of this social disaster. A woman who engages in sex also, by risking pregnancy, places herself at risk from losing control of her body as well as her life. Finally, the stronger sexual drive of men means that they have to overcome the woman's relative disinclination, which makes the woman's engagement a surrender and the man's a conquest. The woman can become a male trophy. A women can be cheap in the way that a man cannot, because she has a price and he does not. This, at any rate, is the historical situation.

17. The combination of nakedness, physical pleasure and loss of physical control make it seem somewhat infantile. The child's account of sexual intercourse – 'The man lies on top of the woman and is excused into her' – captures something of its curious character.

This is connected with the particular horror of child sexual abuse: apart from the physical repulsiveness of the experience, the child has to endure the sense of transgression, of reversing the path that led from sentience to knowledge, from embodiment to personhood, without the relationship that redeems it or the understanding that locates it, or the appetite that motivates it. It is hardly surprising that victims sometimes feel irreversibly besmirched. This is particularly likely to be the case when perpetrators are parents who should be the primary guarantors of the ordinary, moral, clothed world.

18. Nowadays, this is not infrequently actually disembodied or almost bodiless – as when we communicate by phone, or via e-mail. These, however, are recent developments. The disembodiment of human communication, which began with writing, is only a few thousand years old and it is only in recent centuries that more than a tiny minority of human beings has been able to read or write.

19. See also 'The Carnal Hand', *The Hand: A Philosophical Inquiry into Human Being* (Edinburgh: Edinburgh University Press, 2003), section 5.5. An unwanted caress is an invasion of one's whole world by a whole world.

20. The privilege of intimacy is to have the sense of getting to know another's body as it is experienced by that person. The special privilege of being present at the scene of another's pleasure and to be the one who brought it about is rooted in the sense that

the sexual climax is the supreme mode of bodily self-apprehension, the ultimate bodily expression of being here, now.

21. Though for some this is a relief. The utterly engrossing activity of lovemaking, with its unmediated intimacy, its regression to often quite infantile modes of being-with, its intense sensations, is an escape from the dry, airless, ever-incomplete realm of knowledge and self-consciousness.

22. The fundamental tension between the body and the person, and the paradox of trying to possess the person through the body, is played out in the notion of the substitutability of the object of love. As persons, individual humans are unique and irreplaceable; as notionally pure objects of appetite, they are neither. Christopher Hamilton, paraphrasing Roger Scruton, notes how: 'the very fact that if one is desired, one is desired as an example of one's sex ... [and] this means that one is always in principle replaceable by another as an object of desire' (*Living Philosophy. Reflections on Life, Meaning and Morality* (Edinburgh: Edinburgh University Press, 2001), p. 134).

There is, of course, much incidental joy beyond the shadow of these paradoxes: warmth, intimacy, mutual comfort, companionship, valuing the other one as special; in short, love. This is what makes sexual crimes particularly horrible: they spit on the most intimate gift one person can give to another, trample that which is most private in a person. Which is what Freud's rather cold assessment of lovemaking in the essay cited at the beginning of this section seems to overlook. Freud goes on to assert:

> There are only a very few educated people in whom the two currents of affection and sensuality have become properly fused; the man almost always feels his respect for a woman acting as a restriction on his sexual activity, and only develops full potency when he is with a debased sexual object; and this in turn is partly caused by the entrance of perverse sexual components into his sexual aims, which he does not venture to satisfy with a woman he respects ...

Poor Mrs Freud. Her husband seems to be unaware that sexual desire can be *con*cupiscient and expressive of tender concern for the other. True intimacy, far from degrading the lovers by reducing them to bodies, actually recovers the organic body for the human being. While, as Yeats said in 'Crazy Jane Talks with the Bishop',

> ... Love has pitched his mansion in
> The place of excrement

Love transfigures that place. This may be interpreted as a tension between pre- or impersonal appetites and the impulse to cherish an individual person who is irreplaceable.

23. R. M. Rilke, The Second Elegy, from 'Duino Elegies', in *Selected Works. Volume II, Poetry*, trans. J. B. Leishman (London: Hogarth Press, 1967), ll.63–5.

24. It is possible, of course, to buy a narrative as part of the package, to dress up bought sex in something that looks like a real relationship. Such narratives may range from imagined scenarios to the simulation of companionship. What remains unredeemed is the absence of care. Those who use prostitutes or who have numerous sexual partners pass at once from intimacy to indifference, and that indifference encompasses lack of interest in their partners' health and safety.

25. There is a biological dimension that cannot be overlooked. We may express it as follows: the level of testosterone may determine how little a story one is willing to settle for and how little the 'personal' needs to correspond to the person with whom one is making love. At any rate, in situations of extreme promiscuity, there is a

reversal of the more common situation: the over-direct sexual situation is elaborated by fantasies of more-than-sexual, or more-than-sphincteric, meaning.

It is necessary to recall that while sex is the most metaphysical of the appetites, it cannot cut entirely free of its biological roots. It still has its contingent features, depending for example on sexual orientation. There are the givens of sensation and appetite. So, for example, most men do not wish to possess the world, or a world, through the body of a man.

26. Charles Baudelaire, *Intimate Journals*, trans. Christopher Isherwood, with an Introduction by W. H. Auden (London: Panther, 1969), pp. 31–2.

27. This is, of course, a reflection of the religious connection between sex and sin:

> For I delight in the Law of God after the inward Man. But I see another law in my members, warring against the law of my mind, and bringing me into captivity to the law of sin which is in my members ... For to be carnally minded is death; but to be spiritually minded is life and peace. (St Paul, Letters to the Romans, 7: 22–4; 8: 6)

For St Paul, even sex legitimised by holy matrimony was only a compromise: 'It is better to marry than to burn'.

28. To develop the observations in note 16, the modesty of males is not even in question. Men are assumed to be incorrigible, to be universally immodest by inclination. They require the modesty of women to regulate their behaviour. Or immodest women to localise the expression of their immodesty. This (until quite recently) universal cultural fact was a reflection of a biological given: testosterone, which still fuels the intensity of sexual desire in males, for all that its expression is utterly transformed. Hence there are (or were) Fallen Women but not Fallen Men. The shame of sex is still to be borne by the female.

In northern Nigeria, where I worked in the 1970s, it was quite usual to subject women to complex (and often dangerous) cleansing rituals after they had given birth to their first child, to wash away the shame of the initiation into sex that having a baby implied. See Raymond Tallis, 'The Regressive Temptation', in *Hippocratic Oaths: Medicine and its Discontents* (London: Atlantic Books, 2004).

29. The 'filthiness' of sex is reinforced by the objective fact that the physical closeness its practices require are disastrous from the point of view of public health. For some, this, like degradation, becomes a secondary value. There is a *nostalgie de boue* which rejoices in a transgressive return to infancy.

30. Genesis 3: 6–7 (Revised Standard Edition). Freud argued that the assumption of the upright position was associated with the awakening of shame because this position exposed the genitals. It seems to me that they were already visible from the rear. Perhaps the upright position made hominids aware of the visibility of their genitals because they could see that they were being seen. At any rate, it is nice to think that the hand, newly liberated from locomotor duties, was available to act as an in-house fig-leaf. Of course, it is true that only a clothed creature can become naked.

31. There has been much emphasis recently in the humanities on 'transgressive' sex. There are academic posts in 'Queer Theory'. It is important, apparently, because it is a challenge to the 'hegemonic' power structures that fuel globalisation, western capitalism and other undesirable developments. This seems implausible and needs correcting. All sex is transgressive; but it is only in those cases where it cannot be assimilated into social institutions such as companionate marriage, with shared lives and responsibilities, that its transgressive nature remains evident.

32. A. E. Houseman, The Immortal Part, *A Shropshire Lad*, XLIII (London: Harrap, 1940).

33. Thomas Nagel, *The View from Nowhere* (Oxford: Oxford University Press, 1986), p. 64. It is deeply connected with the strange fact that my existence, so long as I think about it, has a *post hoc* necessity but is objectively contingent. (This was discussed in *I Am*, Chapter 2. See especially section 2.5.)
34. See *I Am*, Chapter 6.
35. This is discussed in Tallis, *Hippocratic Oaths*. There I discuss the fundamental tension within scientific medicine; namely that it is potent because it acknowledges that humans are animals and that disease is a manifestation of the dysfunction of an organism while at the same time it is itself – its knowledge, its procedures, its institutions, its ethos – is an expression of how far we have travelled from the organic state
36. I once knew where that came from, but unfortunately have mislaid the reference.
37. Henry Wadsworth Longfellow, 'A Psalm of Life', *The Complete Poetical Works of Longfellow* (Boston: Houghton Mifflin, 1983).
38. What is distinctive, perhaps, is the loss of the beliefs that clothed that sense of contingency in hope, or at least, meaning and a sense of necessity.
39. E. M. Forster, *Howards End* (London: Softback Preview, 1995).

CHAPTER 10

The Unhealing Wound

10.1 WAKING OUT OF SENTIENCE

As Knowing Animals, we are uncoupled from nature and this frees us to engage with the material world on more favourable terms. Our uncoupled state enables us to create an ever more complex outside-of-nature which further increases our leverage. The awakening out of sentience to knowledge would seem to be the key to a uniquely privileged position. There is, however, a tradition of lamenting our self-consciousness and its multitudinous consequences: the gains, it is argued, have been more than offset by the losses. Our awakening out of sentience has been a rude one. The notion that the Knowing Animal is a Sick Animal is almost as old as the history of written thought and has as many guises as Proteus.

I discussed this in *The Hand*, when I examined 'the moral and spiritual balance sheet of the hand'. And I have elsewhere examined the yearning professed by many writers for the innocence that was lost when knowledge and self-consciousness displaced the unreflective awareness of beasts or the imagined innocence of primitive cultures.[1] Leaving aside the questionable notion that there are 'more primitive' modes of being human that are not dominated by deindexicalised awareness, I concluded that, on balance, it is difficult to regret our liberation from the largely unpleasant and vulnerable life of animals unsteered by knowledge-based beliefs. We should not be prevented from appreciating the miracle of human knowledge by a vision of a cognitively primitive pre-technological paradise that has no basis in reality.

Even so, there are reasons for feeling a little sorry for the Knowing Animal. We have already examined the transformed sexual appetite, which, while making its manifestations uniquely human rather than beastly and susceptible of infinite elaboration, also opens it up to guilt, shame and dissatisfaction. And we have seen how knowing animals, uniquely among sentient creatures, live with the knowledge of their own death from their earliest years. Humans are cognitively *exposed*: they are aware of being surrounded by a world that is other than themselves, independent of themselves and indifferent to them. This is built into humans' intuition of objects as things-in-themselves that transcend their experience of them. This intuition is elaborated in a world that increasingly becomes one of facts, of bits of knowledge. The world of knowledge can seem an airless, empty, sterile place. What we know feels thinner and poorer, as well as less localised, less grounded, than our sense experiences: that the sun is a star some 93 million miles away hardly matches up to the feeling of warmth it bestows on our arms. The failure of facts to match sense experiences, and the corresponding failure of sense experiences to be fact-shaped, generalise into a feeling of being divorced from the world. Nature comes to looks like a lost home. There seems to be a wound at the heart of consciousness.

This feeling is expressed incomparably in Rilke's *Duino Elegies*, especially the Eighth:

With all its eyes the creature-world beholds
the open. But our eyes, as though reversed,
encircle it on every side, like traps
set round its unobstructed path to freedom. (ll.1–4)

We've never, no, not for a single day,
pure space before us, such as that which flowers
endlessly open into: always world,
and never nowhere without no: that pure
unsuperintended element one breathes,
endlessly knows, and never craves. A child
sometimes gets quietly lost there, to be always
jogged back again... (ll.14–21)

Always facing creation, we perceive there
only a mirroring of the free and open,
dimmed by our breath ...
For this is Destiny: being opposite,
and nothing else, and always opposite. (ll.29–33)

And we, spectators always, everywhere
looking at, never out of, everything! (ll.62–3)

Who's turned us round like this, so that we always,
do what we may, retain the attitude
of someone who's departing? (ll.66–8)[2]

Heidegger, who greatly admired Rilke, shared his vision of the forlorn relationship of mankind and the world. This unhappy relationship reached its clearest manifestation in *homo technologicus*:

> The relation between direct experience and its objectification had been characterized by Heidegger as a process of de-experiencing – the unity of the situation is dissolved, and experiencing turns into the self-perception of a subject confronted with objects.[3]

One product of de-experiencing is the reduction of space from regions of significance to boundless emptiness, susceptible of being captured in even emptier mathematical formulae.

Scientific objectivisation is a late and rather special development of deindexicalised awareness. Even so, the embodied subject, intentionally related to material objects, participates in this distance. Indeed the 'of', as when a subject is aware *of* an object, marks that gap. The division between subject and world reaches into the depths of the subject, in the division between experiences and their explicit intentional objects. It cuts ever deeper as objectivity is gathered up into a world of knowledge created out of the pooling of deindexicalised awareness. While the physical space of science does not displace the relatedness of indexical awareness or, indeed, the way we relate to things in what Dreyfus called 'absorbed coping' (see section 4.6), the nexus of facts that guides us seems to intervene between us and a world directly experienced.[4]

As Knowing Animals, we are acutely aware of our contingency. Offset from a world that has expanded as our knowledge has grown, we seem at once smaller and more particular, until we are able to see ourselves, if only momentarily, (to use Voltaire's phrase) as 'an insect on an atom of mud'. While for a merely sentient beast the theatre in which it lives is coterminous with its sensory field, the theatre of our human lives hugely outsizes us. It becomes astonishing, almost comical, at any rate, to discover one's own minute 'thisness'.[5]

We are not only fearful animals dwarfed by a world that gets larger and more complex as our knowledge and technology grow; we are also haunted by our own ignorance. Knowledge begins, as we have repeatedly emphasised, with the sense of the incompleteness of our awareness. This is inscribed in the most ordinary intuition of an object and it radiates in all directions, including inwards. The intuition that the 'This' that I am is incompletely disclosed to me is, after all, the basis of object knowledge. A knowing creature cannot know itself; even when its eyes are turned inwards, disclosure is always partial.

It is hardly surprising, then, that Arcadian dreams of a prelapsarian world when Man was at one with the world have haunted so many writers and, beyond this, have given birth to so many myths. Such dreams go beyond those pastoral idylls in which unageing, unstressed humans – most frequently shepherds who blow pipes rather slaughter sheep – make largely verbal love to unreflectively concupiscient mates in perfect climates. There are epistemological Arcadias in which the divorce at the heart of consciousness is healed. Philosophers, and artists, have dreamed of a state of consciousness in which the sensation and the idea had not separated, so that objects would be perceived without being classified or even located at a distance from the subject.[6] This would be a form of reunion, a healing of the wound in human consciousness, that would take us forward to an unprecedented phase in the collective history of mankind. It would not be simply a relapse into the sleep of sentience.

There have been less radical attempts to heal the wound opened up in human consciousness with the emergence of knowledge – a wound that becomes apparent when knowledge encounters itself, makes itself an object of inquiry, of understanding, in short, an object of knowledge. They express, in various combinations and to varying degrees, endeavours to amend different aspects of the existential predicament of the knowing animal: assuaging the uncertainty that is built into knowledge; making safer a world whose threatening character is uniquely explicit to the knowing animal; counteracting the feeling of smallness or insignificance; closing off the incompleteness of knowledge; rounding off the sense of the world. In this chapter, I shall look very briefly at some of these great projects of human consciousness: religion; the cult of the self; science; art; and, finally, philosophy.

10.2 THE NOTION OF A TRANSCENDENT OTHER

The earliest religions were animist. The gods were not readily separated from the natural phenomena that they were thought to animate. Animism

> locates the power and reality of things not in their manifest thinginess but in the invisible spirit (*anima* – wind, breath, soul) that lies beneath, behind or above them ... the animist believes that every object he encounters is alive just as he is, and hence is capable of actually *encountering* him, for good or ill.[7]

Because it locates power in the invisible sphere, it also locates the ability to control the course of events there. Animism is the globalisation of magic thinking, the projection of human consciousness back into nature. This is a manifestation of something that we alluded to in section 8.3 when we discussed the causal intuition – the universal tendency among mankind described by Hume in *Natural History of Religion*:

> to conceive all beings like themselves and to transfer to every object those qualities with which they are familiarly acquainted and which they are intimately conscious.[8]

This remains true when animist thinking is mythologised and theologised and the diffuse presence of spirits in the world is gathered up into discrete gods with distinctive personalities, powers and foibles. The more clearly delineated selves of the Titans and the Olympians, for example, as compared with the *pneuma* that sighed in the wind and the trees, corresponded to the emergence of more developed human selves. They are born of the same womb, however: the projection of the knowing self into the known world. Nietzsche (according to Rudiger Safranski) expressed it thus:

> Man invented the gods as a knowledgeable thinking creature. He saw the gods by sensing that they were looking at him. The gods are the internalized image of a nature that looks back if one looks at it.[9]

The combination of the sense of the otherness of nature (the founding intuition of a knowledge that goes beyond sentience) and of the projection of the self into nature results in an evolving theistic world picture.

The invention of the gods was, of course, a collective enterprise and reflected the awareness in each knowing animal of the collective enterprise that is knowledge.[10] To this extent Durkheim's notion of religions as 'the primitive way in which societies become conscious of themselves and their history' and his thesis that 'They are to the social order what sensation is to the individual'[11] seems consistent with this. We may think of religion, the first fruit of knowledge's global encounter with itself, as at least in part an acknowledgement of the greatness of the collectivised awareness that is expressed in the bodies of shared knowledge.

Religion is not, of course, to be understood in narrowly cognitive terms. As is implicit in Durkheim's embedding concepts in the collective, religion is a profoundly socialised, practical response to a shared existential terror. The body of beliefs, the entities it posits, are supported by, and support, social practices. There are rules, rituals, institutions and power structures that elaborate upon, express and are justified by the fundamental intuitions of the Transcendent Other that is supposed to inform, shape and uphold the world out there. Nor does religion have a single function. While it may well serve as a force of social cohesion – providing an extra-social rationale (backed up by a variety of modes of coercion) for cooperative working, requiring the subjugation of some and the elevation of others – it is also a means of rounding off the sense of the world which the awakening out of sentience has left conspicuously incomplete. Importantly, it is an attempt, in advance of science, to extend control over the world. God becomes a handle by which things that are uncontrolled might be controlled. Worship, prayer, sacrifice, obedience get a handle on that handle. This multitude of functions results in a notion of a god that, as it becomes elaborated in ever more precise formulations (and there is a passage from mythology with its narrative logic to theology with its formal logic), becomes increasingly problematic. The notion of God as creator, upholding the universe, does not sit very well with His narrower function as moral judge in human matters great and small. The Big Bang and the Wise Teacher make an odd chimera. As God evolves from a free-floating presence in the wind and in the grass and in the trees that it makes move, to ever more elaborate sentences with semi-colons and abstract ideas, so it seems more difficult to think of Him as both the Origin of All Things and an individual who makes pronouncements, intervenes in the world and hearkens to individual petitions.[12] What is more, the evidence is that he doesn't. Fatally, he attracts apologists who have an increasingly uphill task in reconciling His omnipotence and His benevolence with the appalling suffering of innocents.

Even so, the notion of God upholding 'all that fall' has an enduring appeal. Rilke captured this:

We are all falling. This hand's falling too –
all have this falling-sickness none withstands.

And yet there's One whose gently-holding hands
this universal falling can't fall through.[13]

This brings another kind of consolation that survives the undeniability of our individual vulnerability: that there is One upon Whom nothing is lost and in Whose Eternal Memory nothing is forgotten. This palliates the contingency of his own existence revealed to the Knowing Animal and the uncertainty made explicit in the ignorance that shadows knowledge. It seems possible to believe that the world into which we are cast cares for us, is made for us, is watching over us.

The personification of the collective in the enduring person of God itself brought another consolation. The Knowing Animal's justified sense of being (at least in part) other than the natural world is extended to the notion of being entirely outside the material world of the body. The animist projection of knowledge into nature is stabilised by its further projection into a god. Knowledge is connected with a hidden world separate from nature, above the destructive natural order of things. This gives existential credence to the notion that we – our thoughts, our consciousness – are not confined to our bodies and that we will not necessarily share the fate of those bodies. The divorce between the body and knowledge in the Knowing Animal opens the possibility of an after-life, of 'death as simply an unseen part of life, as it were the dark side of the moon'.[14]

It is hardly surprising, therefore, that the first fruit of the encounter of knowledge with itself would be religion rather than science. Religion not only binds society together,[15] it also offers the promise of safety from and control over nature ahead of any kind of technological achievement. It offers instant, potent, profound hope to an animal that has to live with the certainty of death. It offers survival beyond death – though that offer brings with it a new uncertainty and a new source of anxiety, as to the nature of that survival: in Heaven or Hell, as angel or insect. Religion, what is more, is self-preserving. For its truth is grounded in a sense of tradition – the authority of the past and the feeling of solidarity. There is nothing like the appearance of a rival religion to intensify the convictions of believers. The particular dialect of collective consciousness that is expressed and sacralised and celebrated in religion is resistant to the demonstration of its errors precisely because (as Peter Munz has pointed out) our errors, by being our own, are more closely related to us: 'the more absurd and invention, the more likely its usefulness as a social bond'.[16] As Anthony O'Hear expresses it:

> if a society is defined through a system of commonly held beliefs, it would be much more effective if these beliefs were peculiar and idiosyncratic, by which one could thereby distinguish one's own group from all other groups.[17]

Fitting more completely into the society of one's fellow beings – being more completely immersed in the pooled consciousness that is acknowledged to be greater than each of us swimmers in it – is, when that society is linked with the Author of the World to which one is exposed, an effective way of being insulated from the sense of being offset from the world, such

> that we don't feel very securely at home
> in this interpreted world.[18]

10.3 THE TRANSCENDENTAL SELF

The earliest sense of the collective past is mythological. In a mythological account of the past, what happened and why, the events that took place and the meaning of those events, are inseparable. The story and the framework within which it makes sense go hand in glove. However frightening the actual content of myths, they nevertheless provide an existential comfort – addressing a fundamental hunger of the Knowing Animal – of extending, even rounding off, the sense of things.

The rise of historiography created an increasingly widening gulf between events and their ultimate meaning. Attempts to restore the connection in teleological histories and various assertions of an historical world order by interested parties did not close the gap: once the presupposed has to be asserted, it is a question of 'never glad confident morning again'. The key element of historiography is not accuracy, but the idea, or the ideal, of accuracy. This separates the shape of the story that is told from any meaning that answers to a demand for fundamental sense. While this divorce was a long time being settled, there was an entering wedge that became wider. This was what Bernard Williams has called 'an "objective" conception of the past, according to which every past event had a fixed place in a temporal order'.[19] Williams argues that this conception itself had an historical origin and he locates it 'at a specific point in the development of Greek thought in the fifth century BC', and identifies Thucydides as the key figure in this momentous transformation in human self-awareness. Myths interact with one another and make mutually supporting sense: mythological time is eternal, a kind of space. All ages are equidistant from it. The past it depicts does not recede or lose any of its relevance to the present. An historical account of the past, by contrast, is in danger of seeming like one damn thing after another and the events taking place in it dwindle in size and significance with the passage of time. Non-mythological events are liable to have characteristics that do not tap into deep intuitions.

The most important feature of an historical order is that there are purely contingent time tags attached to the individual events. There is no reason why the war between Sparta and Athens that Thucydides wrote about should have begun in 431 BC and ended in 404 BC. These time tags are the start of a divorce between narration of the past and the meaning for the readers. While the writing of history might be a patriotic act, the significance is manifestly parochial. Williams' seemingly extravagant claim that 'Once the structure of historical time is in place, the gods will eventually bow out'[20] seems entirely justified.

The divorce between narrative and meaning is evident even within the realm of religion in a post-mythological age. There is a divergence between the stories and the arguments, between the humble priests and the theologians, the people and the Jesuits. God is increasingly in danger of being reduced to abstract characteristics remote from the stories that bring specific sense to lives from a mythological past. The story of Christ's birth, teaching, crucifixion and resurrection may be seen as an attempt to bring together the theological abstraction of a monotheistic God with the reality of human life. The Christian 'Word made flesh' is the reunion of myth and argument, or a *ménage à trois* of Platonic abstractions and the Judaic Hidden God with narrative. Located in historical time and recounted by individuals, it was ultimately doomed. The endless arguments and heresies surrounding the exact status of Christ – purely God, divinely appointed man, or a combination of the two? – were expressions by proxy of the inability to turn back the clock to a point where there was no clock.

The exit of the gods had two phases: first Williams' 'bowing out' and then being kicked out. The rise of alternative sources of hope and power – prefigured in the Promethean myth – gnawed at the roots of the world-picture first created when, in terror, the Knowing Animal collectively confronted what his knowledge collectively revealed about himself and the world. Once technology penetrated every aspect of life and the model of rationality that it exemplified entered human and social relations, the 'disenchantment of the world' (to use Max Weber's famous phrase) was inevitable. Of course, piety, superstition, social hierarchies with trans-cendental underpinnings continued side by side with secular practices. Human self-help displaced sacrifice, burnt offerings, prayer. The fruits of reason filled the landscape, labour became tethered to, and shaped by, those fruits and secular modes of thought became instinctive.[21]

There are limits, of course, to human self-help. The appointment in Samarra can be postponed, but not cancelled; pain can be avoided or mitigated, but only temporarily; bereavement can be delayed, but remains inevitable. Melioristic *Homo technologicus* has sooner or later to acknowledge the tragic truth that knowledge has revealed. There is another point of repair for the Knowing Animal in a demythologised world: the idea of the self as an unassailable interior, somehow separate or insulated from the fate of the body.

In some of its manifestations, it is difficult to separate the secular notion of the transcendental self from the religious idea of, say, the soul that is in the keeping of God or the gods. From the imperishable intellect postulated by Plato to Descartes' thinking substance, we have conceptions of the human being as a creature whose true essence lies beyond the reach of bodily decay and the unhappy accidents that befall living creatures. The unassailable self becomes increasingly secularised. The naturalistic world-view of the Enlightenment thinkers threatened to dissolve it completely: if the self was not merely a manifestation of the man-machine (and therefore immersed in the very forces that knowledge fears), it was dissipated into moments of consciousness, 'fugitive impressions' as Hume called them. The transcendental self of Kant, while it was an attempt to solve a particular philosophical problem posed by Hume about the self, also promised more. It looked like something within us that was both distant from nature (being a precondition of there being a revealed nature) and internally coherent. Even so, it was almost empty of substance: the transcendental self was close to being a mere 'logical subject'. The endeavours of his successors to capitalise on his breaking down of the gap between the subject and its objects led eventually (via detours such as *Naturphilosophie* and phenomenology) to a reaffirmed materialism that simply embedded humans in the natural world from which, therefore, there was no place of refuge.

There were other paths to salvation, or at least insulation from the universal death sentence pronounced by Nature upon all things she brings to life. They combined religious origins with secular manifestations. The most striking amongst these in Europe were the profound social trends, associated with Protestantism, that Max Weber famously allied to the rise of capitalism. The remnant of the idea of salvation from above drove the Protestant work ethic. Success in this world, as measured by the accumulation of capital, would become proof of God's grace, evidence that one had been one of those chosen for salvation rather than damnation. Irrespective of the truth of the religious case for self-aggrandisement, the accumulation of goods, like the acquisition of power, increased the kingdom of the self and, by making it many-layered, seemed to insulate one self from the tragedy of extinction. This was irrational, of course, but the dissipation of the self in activity that led to accumulation was a perfect distraction from the terror of death or other disaster. The story of personal evolution and growth was a perfect foil to the sense of being helplessly swept to extinction.

The metaphor for such a strategy might be that of a creature obsessed with danger who digs a more and more complex burrow for himself, sealing off that entrance, setting up this baffle, creating longer and longer channels, all to ward off invaders. Eventually, he digs to the centre of the earth and is immolated in the molten magma. In order to avoid that fate, the Knowing Animal concerns himself not only with increasing fortifications against danger, but also with his own health. He avoids the enemy from within. Ronald W. Dworkin has commented on the epidemic of obsession with mental and physical 'wellness' in contemporary United States.[22] The notion that ill health is entirely down to 'lifestyle factors' implies that the means to avoid ill health – and hence, presumably, to live forever – lies within one's grasp. This doctrine, associated with that of perpetual self-betterment, empowerment, and so on, is widespread in the West, providing a secular equivalent of the comfort provided by those hands 'this universal falling can't fall through'. This is a poor substitute, and the predictable consequence is that anxiety rises and rises and that preoccupations with health and more general concerns with safety come to dominate the lives of many.[23]

10.4 COMPLETING KNOWLEDGE: SCIENTISM DREAMS OF A FINAL THEORY

Our experience hitherto justifies us in believing that nature is the realisation of the simplest conceivable mathematical ideas. I am convinced that we can discover by means of purely mathematical constructions the concepts and laws connecting them with each other, which furnish the key to the understanding of natural phenomena. Experience may suggest the approximate mathematical concepts, but they most certainly cannot be deduced from it. Experience, of course, remains the sole criterion of physical utility of a mathematical construction. But the creative principle resides in mathematics. In a certain sense, therefore, I hold it true that pure thought can grasp reality as the ancients dreamed.[24]

The more the universe seems comprehensible, the more it also seems pointless.[25]

The Knowing Animal feels unsafe because he is aware of his own existence and knows that his existence, like that of any object in the world, is contingent. The flight into an inner fortress, reinforced by a many-layered CV, by possessions, offices, the narratives of ambition and child-rearing, connections, occupations and avocations, and so on, is, of course, only a distraction. The world, however, is objectively safer for some and this is largely the result of the development of science-based technology, along with the legally reinforced application of rational approaches to safety in everyday life, in a political context that favours justice and respect for human rights. For some, however, science seems to promise more: to bring us closer to a completion of the sense that awakening out of sentience has made both explicit and incomplete. When the work of scientists is finished, they believe, science will bring not only unlimited control over our world but complete understanding of it. Our knowledge shall be equivalent to knowing the mind of the God that science has caused to evaporate in the coldest light of the final cognitive dawning. This is what is implicit in scientism, the conviction that science is, as Mary Midgley puts it, 'omnicompetent'.[26] It is worth examining this notion and identifying why, in the end, science – notwithstanding that its value in keeping at bay the anti-meanings of cold, pain, gruelling labour, etc. cannot be overestimated – will not heal the wound in the consciousness of the Knowing Animal. For the misrepresentation of humankind through one brand of scientism, biologism, is one of the main triggers for writing this book.

There are obvious reasons why science, however well developed, cannot or will not deliver the kind of cognitive closure the Knowing Animal is seeking. Science describes the what but it does not explain, except in the narrow causal sense, the why. It cannot explain why there is something rather than nothing and why that nothing unfolds according to certain laws. In trying to explain how those laws – which seem inexplicably hospitable to the carbon atoms that are necessary for life – we have to fall back on the non-explanation of chance.[27] This is a rather abstract or general failure and it is anyway not clear what form an explanation of why there is something rather than nothing, why it unfolds according to laws, and why those laws take a certain form, would take. Only slightly less abstract is the failure of physics to give a comprehensible account of material forces (quantum mechanics, all physicists agree, is incomprehensible, though very powerful) and is quite unable to explain how psychological, tensed time can arise out of cosmological time which has neither past, present nor future. This last is an example of the mystery perspectival experience arising in a world that intrinsically has no perspective. It connects in turn with the failure of physical science to give any kind of satisfactory account of consciousness or to explain why matter matters – the nature or origin of meaning and value. This is, of course, not an accidental deficiency: science proceeds by removing precisely those things.[28] Its pursuit of the aperspectival 'view from nowhere' unbiased by interest, uprooted from occasions, eliminates consciousness, meaning and value from the outset. The image of nature as (to use Whitehead's famous description) 'merely the hurrying of material, endlessly, meaninglessly' was a forgone outcome. Steven Weinberg's observation in the epigraph to this section that as (scientific) understanding extends, so the universe seems more pointless, is hardly a surprise. This result was built into the starting premises.

There are, however, yet more ubiquitous deficiencies. Science removes not only tertiary qualities[29] but also, as we discussed in Chapter 3, secondary qualities: colours, sounds, smells, tastes, and so on. As was pointed out in that chapter, the key step in the pursuit of aperspectival objectivity is measurement – the reduction of what is there to numbers. 'Measurement began our might', as Yeats said,[30] but there is a price to pay. As we pass from the comparative sense that something is bigger than something else, or that one of its edges is longer than another, to ordering according to magnitude, to the ultimately deperspectivalisation of cardinal numbers of units, the object is at the same time generalised and emptied, shorn of significance and drained of phenomenal content. This is entirely within the tradition that begins with the Pythagorean dream of discovering the underlying reality of nature in numbers. (Pythagoras is said to have taught that mathematical entities, such as numbers and shapes, were the ultimate stuff out of which the real entities of our perceptual experience are constructed.) It was, of course, most influentially reiterated by Galileo for whom the Book of Nature was 'written in the language of mathematics'.[31] The final output of the scientific account of the world is thus an equation, describing in outline the way events cohere and how they would unfold over time. At the most, it gives the silhouette of silhouettes. The equations do not even give existence: they describe the most abstracted form of possibility. And in this sense they are deficient. They are the grossest idealisations, shedding the matter of the world, the music of what happens, the scent of the real. This becomes increasingly evident as science gets closer and closer to the kind of completeness the Knowing Animal is looking for. Increasing generalisation means increasing reduction means increasing emptiness.

Nevertheless, the scientific account of the world seems so attractive to many, precisely for its deficiencies. Numbers occupy an odourless Platonic heaven, far from the sweaty armpits, the mucky misery and frustrating misunderstandings of everyday life. They are eternal, unchanging, unbespattered by events, by decay. It is this that makes the pursuit of mathematics 'a divine madness of the spirit, a refuge from the goading urgency of contingent happenings'.[32]

These virtues are, however, inseparable from their existential hollowness. Their inadequacy as a means of closing the gap in understanding. As Russell famously said, the scientific account of the world is cast in mathematical form, not because we know so much but because we know so little. The equations, as Stephen Hawking points out, do not even require the existence of those general possibilities they describe:

> Even if there is only only one possible unified theory, it is just a set of rules and equations. What is it that breathes fire into the equations and makes a universe for them to describe? The usual approach of science of constructing a mathematical model cannot answer the questions of why there should be a universe for the model to describe. Why does the universe go to all the bother of existing?[33]

One might put this by saying that, if God really were a mathematician – 'of a very high order', according to the physicist Paul Dirac – he wasn't a very pure one because he allowed existence, which eludes his equations. John Barrow makes a connected point in the final paragraph of his *Theories of Everything*:

> There is no formula that can deliver all truth, all harmony, all simplicity. No Theory of Everything can ever provide total insight. For, to see through everything, would leave us seeing nothing at all.[34]

One could not get an existential purchase on 'the set of rules and equations' that Hawking refers to. Even if there were a single equation that gathered up all the others, it would offer no dwelling place. The wound in consciousness would not be healed by a mode of knowledge which has unlimited scope only because it has unlimited non-specificity, given that the journey to it involved shedding not merely all that was held dear – secondary qualities, meaning, value – but actuality. There is no meeting place between the most general delineation of possibility and the human beings whose knowledge instantiates the possibility of possibility.

The truth is that for an equation to exist, it has to be realised in the mind of an embodied individual. And this brings us back to the start which, as Merleau-Ponty observed, science has never in fact left:

> The whole universe of science is built upon the world as it is directly experienced and if we want to subject science itself to rigorous scrutiny and arrive at a precise assessment of its meaning and scope, we must begin by reawakening the basic experience of the world of which science is a second-order expression.[35]

This must not be taken to suggest that scientific knowledge is simply heaped-up experience, compressed sentience – a view that we specifically discarded in section 5.3 and which would be entirely contrary to the thesis of this book. The point of Merleau-Ponty's argument is brought out by his citation of Ernst Cassirer, who accused empiricists of 'mutilating perception':

> mutilating perception from below, treating it immediately as knowledge and forgetting its existential content, amounts to mutilating it from above, since it involves taking for granted and passing over in silence the decisive moment in perception: the upsurge of a *true* and *accurate* world.[36]

We cannot recover, within universal science, the worldless pre-indexical sentience and the minute parishes of indexicality from which science takes its rise. At the same time, however, science cannot elude answerability to those world-less and world-poor realms. This is the crisis at the heart of science: that it cannot escape from, or recover, the places from which it takes its rise, those places where our being has its roots. No theory, however 'final', however precisely transcribing the mind of a putative god, could heal the wound opened in human consciousness with the awakening from sentience.[37]

We first tried to fill the hole in sense with gods. Now that the gods have gone, don't let us try to fill it with science, because we shall find we have simply exchanged one form of emptiness for another.

10.5 ROUNDING OFF THE SENSE OF THE WORLD: ART

My comments here will be brief because I have covered the territory at length elsewhere.[38] Let us first restate the problem. The Knowing Animal wakens out of sentience to itself as a contingent, vulnerable creature in a universe that far outsizes him. He is the implicit centre of a world in which, as his knowledge grows, he is increasingly aware of being explicitly on the margin. The Existential Intuition, which affirms 'That I am' [here and now] is in tension with dissipation into an ownerless collective world of deindexicalised awareness, which becomes increasingly abstract and multilayered. This feeling of dissipation – of an 'unbearable lightness of being'[39] – is exacerbated by the fact that the activities that fill his days are to an overwhelming degree remote from direct interaction with his surroundings. This is not just because the present is riddled with the future but also because it is less substantive: labour, for example, is more often about processing information than about moving material objects. While even information processing involves direct interaction with his surroundings, these interactions are only intermediaries of remote effects. In our daily lives what happens 'here' is hollowed out by the boundless elsewhere to which it points, for which it exists. We are never quite here and we become haunted by the sense that we may pass through our lives and never touch the sides; or touch the sides only when, through suffering, the sides close in on us.

We accept our busy lives, our hurrying to goals that recede or are replaced as we advance upon them, because this is the price of comfort, safety, pleasure and esteem. But we want to dismount from busyness. We seek to pass from the Kingdom of Means to the Kingdom of Ends; to engage in activities that contain their own meaning rather than serving some more or less distant purpose; to have experience for its own sake; to be here for the sake of being here. And when we do, we find that we cannot so easily dismount from the Kingdom of Means. Leisure becomes another form of busyness and in our free time we find other goals and quasi-duties. We cannot dismount from hurrying, or from the 'awaying' that lies at the heart of serious, ordinary life,

> so that we always,
> do what we may, retain the attitude
> of someone who's departing.[40]

and 'we live our lives, for ever taking leave'.

In part this is because we fear that the here and now, so often hollowed by the locationless goals that it serves, will prove intrinsically hollow and that its hollowness will fill us with emptiness. More importantly, it is because we find it difficult to experience our experiences – something which does not matter in the Kingdom of Means, where experience is subordinated to an external purpose, but is of supreme importance in the Kingdom of Ends where we have experience for its own sake, where we visit a place in order to look at it and we look at it only in order to see it. There are profound reasons for this incapacity: the Faustian pact, whereby the Uncoupled Animal gave up immersion for control. We cannot reimmerse ourselves. We are separate from what we would experience directly by what we know; the objects that surround us are also objects of knowledge, thinned by the absent members of the class, or the absent network of significances, to which they belong. What we know guides our sense of what it would be to experience our experiences. The present cannot be fully present because it is here as the fulfilment of an expectation, as the realisation of an *idea* belong to the realm of deindexicalised awareness. And it cannot fulfil that expectation adequately: it is too heavy with details that were not specified in the expectation. No direct experience can match the idea that has led one to seek it.

One function of art – perhaps the supreme function of art in societies in which art no longer has a religious, didactic, informative purpose or serves as a social critque – is to make existentially present that which is physically present by narrowing the gap between the idea and the experience. In literature, this is achieved within the realm of ideas by inviting the reader to imagine what is verbally expressed, to make it present through engaging the emotions – of love, hatred, sadness, anger, curiosity. In addition, what happens at any stage is linked to what happens in the future, not only through the coherence of the story but through a variety of stylistic and structural devices that internally stitch the evolving tale. In the visual arts, the observer engages with the object whose presence is unpeeled by its being presented in a way that has no connection with the way it would be presented in ordinary, busy life, where it would be either overlooked background or reduced to an instrument subordinated to some end that passes beyond it. In representational art, the scene or object is stilled, its phenomenal characters are made objects of awareness. The elements of the object – colours, the relationship between forms – are placed before the observer to be enjoyed for their own sake. In short, it is prevented from dissolving into the flow of deindexicalised consciousness. In music, the supreme art, experience and idea are united in form: at any given moment, the sounds realise part of a form that is present throughout – unmoving movement, as Aristotle described it.

One of the immemorial functions of art has been to mediate between man and nature. This does not have the purpose of increasing control over the nature – otherwise art would be merely magic thinking, inferior technology, like prayer. (Which is not to say that art hasn't served this function from time to time; just as it has served the function of mediation between between Man and the gods he has invented.) It answers to a longing to be immersed in nature in a non-threatening way; to overcome the sense of being separated from what is 'out there'. Franz Kafka's predicament:

> I am separated from all things by a hollow space, and I do not even reach to its boundaries[41]

describes the human predicament. For while, like all other animals we are born into nature, like no other animal we are born out of nature. We are part of nature and apart from it. And this separation is replicated in our relationship to society: we are part of society – it exists because of us, it penetrates to the last corner of our conscious being – and yet we are apart from it. Art is a means of enabling us to come closer to nature and society without drowning in either; to possess (more of) it in transcendence; to make the (natural and human) world our thing.

Ultimately – at least in a secular society – art is a means of mediating between human consciousness and itself; of repairing the wound opened up by knowledge in sentience.[42] This is connected with the role of art in offering the possibility of experiencing our experiences so that we might avoid the Kafkaesque feeling of disconnection; of being separated from everything 'by a hollow space'; and hence avoiding the feeling of never being, or having been, quite there. These are, however, only temporary assuagements. Indeed, there is a danger that one will simply move from one work of art to another and the experience of art will become another aspect of consumption, another mode of hurrying through the world, another addition to the ways in which one might be dissipated.[43]

The conclusion of Nietzsche's first masterpiece *The Birth of Tragedy* was that 'the creation of art is the only metaphysical activity to which life still obliges us'. Music was the supreme art: 'Without music, life would be an error'.[44] But the music has to stop sometime and we face return to a daily routine devoid of music. 'There is such a thing as life after music ... but can it be endured?'[45] This was his constant, obsessive preoccupation; according to Safranski the motor to his entire thought. The solution is not permanent background 'Music While You Work', or while you play, provided by underpaid lackeys or CD Walkmans. Sooner or later, this would reduce music, or any other art taken to excess, to boiled sweets for consciousness. Indeed, as Nietzsche himself acknowledged, even at its greatest, art is often a mere distraction from the human condition, from the truth. We create art not to reveal the truth but because we cannot bear it. What is more, music, the paradigm art, does not have any intrinsic meaning: its significance is often what is poured into it by its aroused listeners. For this reason alone, therefore, there must be other 'metaphysical activities' to which life – or the desire for wholeness – obliges us.

10.6 KNOWLEDGE ENCOUNTERS ITSELF: PHILOSOPHY

One such activity is to dig deep into the very roots of the problem, by the unyielding application of speculative reason to the most general aspects of human life and the world of which it appears to be a part. This was how philosophy, as we at present understand it, began. The first philosophy, chronologically at least, was the theory of knowledge – the encounter of knowledge with itself. In the struggles and revelations of the pre-Socratic philosophers – most notably Parmenides, of whom it was said, not without justice, that he fathered both science and metaphysics – knowledge had not only one of its earliest but also one of its mightiest self-encounters. In Parmenides' decision 'to test all things with the power of your thinking alone' humanity mounted the first critique of its 'apparatus of knowledge'.[46] It is interesting to speculate why this critique should have taken placed when it did, less than 3,000 years ago, several million years after hominids parted company from the other primates. The sociological explanation – that Greek society at the time of the pre-Socratic philosophers had become 'dialogic', in contrast with the 'monolithic' societies around it, and that as a result it 'institutionalised criticism' – doesn't seem to cut deep enough. It might explain Parmenides' confidence – 'test all thinking with the power of your thinking alone'[47] – and the level of self-awareness he seemed to have achieved. Agonistic – 'eristic', combative – pluralism raises awareness of one's self as an independent source of opinions, and of those opinions, by undermining one's distances from others in the society of which one is a part. This awakening sense of individualism – and of the coexistence of different theories – might explain why the Greeks not only developed theories but also a theory of the knowledge of things. Even so, more is required. That more may have been writing.

It was only a hundred years or so before the pre-Socratics – between 800 and 700 BC – that writing was perfected when the Greeks completed the alphabet, by creating letters for vowels.[48] The potential impact of writing on human self-awareness cannot be overstated. Written thoughts are visible, permitting more explicit encounters of knowledge with itself. Second, writing untethers thoughts from the human body: inscriptions are mouthless, breathless, objects in themselves. This is an important further step in the deindexicalisation of awareness. The written thought is a visible token of a thought-type that can be realised an indefinite number of times. Writing has a further characteristic – relevant to the massively influential Parmenidean notion of the unreality of change: its tokens on the page are unmoving and so seem to posit unchanging objects. The 'cognitive shear' between unchanging names and the changing world as revealed to the senses is increased. Writing down makes visible the stability of the putative object of knowledge.[49]

At any rate, this first head-on encounter with knowledge took the form of an encounter with the limits of knowledge.[50] Parmenides argued that the world as we experience it through our senses was unreal. Our senses present us with the image of a world that is perpetually changing. This cannot be real because change cannot be real. Change cannot be real because it involves coming-to-be and ceasing-to-be. This requires that there should be something which 'is not' before it is. But what is not, is not – and hence unreal. All that is real is what is: being. Becoming is a mixture of being and non-being – a dilution of being with non-being – but being admits of no degrees. Reality must therefore lie beyond what is evident to our senses. It cannot be sensed, it can only be thought. The thought of being, of course, is itself unthinkable (as Anaximander pointed out). For token thoughts occur: they unfold from their beginning to their end; they are therefore unreal. All that is real is Being as revealed to an eternal standing thought and that is not available to us.

This is a mighty inauguration of the sceptical tradition, and includes even the standard self-refuting account of what it is that we do not, and cannot, know. Nietzsche relates it to 'a moment of purest absolutely bloodless abstraction, unclouded by any reality' that Parmenides had 'probably at a fairly advanced age'.[51] At any rate, it can be read as an acknowledgement of the tension at the heart of knowledge. Human knowledge, as we have argued throughout this book, is unlike animal sentience in being encircled by a sense of its own incompleteness. This is not only because there is always 'more to know' but because, more profoundly, the object of knowledge – irrespective of whether it is concrete, abstract or a concrete instance of an abstract general idea – lies beyond what is sensed. It is of the very nature of knowledge that it should be 'undetermined' by what we can sense. The Parmenidean argument about the unreality of change mirrors the paradoxical intuition of an unchanging object revealed by our (changing) sense experiences; or at least of an object whose changes do not track the changes in our experiences of it, especially those very experiences that reveal it, and its 'objectness', to us. This intuition is already present in indexical awareness, where we are aware of our awareness of the object, of ourselves as embodied subjects, and aware that that awareness is merely one perspective on the object. The very notion of an object is of something that is not exhausted by our awareness of it.

The Parmenidean awakening has subsequently been contaminated with two kinds of sleep. The first was the result of identifying the nature of the realm in which reality was supposed to be, or where it was revealed, with a theological heaven, where perfect morality and complete knowledge came together. Plato located reality – the forms of which the objects we experience are mere copies (usually characterised as 'pale') – in Heaven. Partly as a result of Plato's overwhelming genius, Parmenides' successors were deflected into theologising and moralising The Way of Truth.

The second sleep came much later, when the science provoked by Parmenides' assertion of the hidden nature of reality gradually narrowed into a scientism that tried to encompass its own source. Valery has captured this history:

Do you know the first hypothesis of all science, the idea indispensable to every scientist? It's this: *the world is almost unknown* This is a fact. Yet we often think the contrary: there are moments when everything seems clear, when all is fulfilled and there are no problems. At such times, there is no more science – or if you prefer, science is complete.[52]

The second phase is characterised by the implicit or explicit claim that a Theory of Everything is at hand. Such a theory would encompass not only the known universe, but the knower in the universe.[53]

If philosophy is truly going to address the wound in consciousness, growing ever wider as the initial ontological blush of the Existential Intuition that separates objects from subjects is spun into a proliferating network of facts, then it needs to approach knowledge from the astonished distance from which Parmenides approached it in something like that 'moment of purest, absolutely bloodless abstraction, unclouded by any reality' Nietzsche spoke of. While it will not be obligated to the same conclusion, it will be forced to acknowledge that knowledge itself is an extraordinary phenomenon, one that resists full understanding. The conflict between everything we think we know (all that is made evident to us in the realm of appearing) and what, according to logical argument, must be real – the profound civil war within our intellect, which Parmenides first took to extremes – cannot be ignored. It was prefigured in the division between our senses and the world that came with knowledge, in which the individual is induced to posit objects Indeed, this is where, if we are to look at how mankind might heal the wound in consciousness opened up by the passage from sentience to knowledge, we must begin.[54]

NOTES AND REFERENCES

1. See, for example, Raymond Tallis, *Newton's Sleep: Two Cultures and Two Kingdoms* (Basingstoke: Macmillan, 1995) and *Enemies of Hope. A Critique of Contemporary Pessimism* (Basingstoke: Macmillan, 2nd edition, 1999).
2. R. M. Rilke, Eighth Elegy, from 'Duino Elegies', in *Selected Works. Volume II, Poetry*, trans. J. B. Leishman (London: Hogarth Press, 1967).
3. Rudiger Safranski, *Martin Heidegger. Between Good and Evil*, trans. Ewald Osers (Cambridge, MA: Harvard University Press, 1998), p. 103.
4. The complex relationship between sentience and abstract knowledge, and the feeling of inner disunity, is evident in the peculiarly human ability to feel scorching anger (with accompanying bodily sensations) over abstract states of affairs.
5. Safranski (*Martin Heidegger*, p. 150) cites the wonderful sentence by the German playwright Grabbe: 'Only once in the world, and of all things as a plumber in Detmold!'
6. More ambitiously, philosophers impressed by Kant – first-wave German Idealists such as Fichte, Schelling and Hegel and the second-wave neo-Kantians dominant in Germany in the late nineteenth and early twentieth centuries – embraced his denial

of the schism between the experiencing subject and the world of material objects. Indeed, this was the goal of Idealist philosophy: 'to conceive of the unity of subject and object', to bridge the gap 'between consciousness and the thing in itself, between subject and object, by the idea' (see *German Idealist Philosophy*, ed. and Introduction Rudiger Bubner (London: Penguin Books, 1997, p. xviii). Ideas, which are *of* the mind and *about* objects, link the spontaneity of the mind with the receptivity of experience. According to philosophers such as Schelling, at the highest level – the level of the absolute discoverable by reason – mind and object are not separable.

The unity between the subject and the object was reflected in the *romantische Naturphilosophie* of German Idealist philosophists. Nature, they proclaimed, was not an inert mechanism, an intricate clockwork, but an active, self-transforming organism, imbued with mind or spirit, purposeful and striving towards perfection. For Schelling, for whom transcendental idealism and *Naturphilosophie* were complementary, thought and being were unified in the 'Absolute' – which is at once 'the first presupposition of knowing and is itself the first knowledge' (Daniel Breazedale, 'Fichte and Schelling: The Jena Period', in *The Age of German Idealism*, ed. Robert C. Solomon and Kathleen M. Higgins, *Routledge History of Philosophy*, Volume 6 (London: Routledge, 1993), pp. 169–70).

7. Dudley Young, *Origins of the Sacred. The Ecstasies of Love and War* (London: Little, Brown, 1994), p. 116. This excellent book, with which I have profoundly disagreed (and at some length) in *Enemies of Hope*, is a mighty work of scholarship. Young's claim that chimpanzees discovered religion – made on the slender basis of an observation of Jane Goodall's of chimps responding to a thunderstorm 'by charging up and down a hillside … tearing off tree branches, and hooting wildly' – is of course untenable. Chimps making whoopee are not travelling on the road that led humans to, say, The Council of Trent.

8. Quoted in Sigmund Freud, *Totem and Taboo* (London: Pelican, n.d.), p. 109.

9. Rudiger Safranski, *Nietzsche. A Philosophical Biography*, trans. Shelley Frisch (London: Granta Books, 2002), p. 174.

10. The passage from animism to mythology and thence to theology clearly requires the development of language. We may suppose that religion is therefore a relative newcomer compared with the numinous sense. To make the wound in consciousness, resulting from the awakening out of sentience, crystallise into the idea of God, requires abstract language. This is possibly the unintended meaning of the seemingly paradoxical opening of the Gospel of St. John: 'In the beginning was the Word …' Until His Name was spoken, God did not exist.

11. Emile Durkheim, *Selected Writings*, ed. Anthony Giddens (Cambridge: Cambridge University Press, 1972), p. 263. For a discussion and a critique of Durkheim's prioritising society over the individual, see Tallis, *Enemies of Hope*, pp. 240–55.

12. To develop the hypothesis put forward in note 10, the word was necessary for God to be born as a specific being within the human universe. Verbalisation lifted Him out of the natural world, as a diffuse presence, and out of the frightened and ecstatic hearts of men into the realm of deindexicalised awareness. This was not good for His health. When God was written down, it would not be long before His presence was uprooted from the sense of the numinous, and even from the aura of the authority of the priest. He was fully delivered into discrete existence. Once He had become the subject of sentences, His days were numbered: His coming of age in written words was the beginning of his end.

It is hardly surprising that the numinous age lasted hundreds of thousands, perhaps millions, of years, while the theological era has lasted only thousands. Written down concepts lose their numinousness and dry up into dogma and institutionalised ritual. Renewal can come only from their connection with power, conflict and hatred of others. Nietzsche spoke of modern churches as 'the tombstones of God'. But they always have been; so too are Bibles; and concepts that are argued, rather than danced, into existence. 'In the beginning of the end was the word ...'

This adds irony to the comedy of Archbishop Ussher's famous calculation of the age of the universe. It was a foregone conclusion that he would date the Creation at about 4000 BC: the backward glance of humanity would fade at the point where writing began. Beyond this, the trail would disappear because nothing was written down. The record of God began when the means of recording were invented; and this is where the death of God – His gradual shrinkage into a just another parish of deindexicalised awareness – also began.

13. R. M. Rilke, 'Autumn', in *Selected Works. Volume II, Poetry*, trans. J. B. Leishman (London: Hogarth Press, 1967), p. 117. The notion of the gods as guarantors of the ultimate safety of the world is widespread. Belief in a personal saviour is common to Christianity, to the mystery cults of Isis and to the Persian worship of the sun-God. See Norman Davies, *Europe: A History* (London: Pimlico, 1997), p. 200.

14. Donald Prater, *A Ringing Glass. The Life of Rainer Maria Rilke* (Oxford: Clarendon Paperbacks, 1994), p. 47.

15. As Young (*Origins of the Sacred*, p. 327) points out, the very word religion (*re-ligio*, bind back) 'arises as that body of words and gestures whereby we ritually renew, by remembering, the bonds that tie us to each other and our ground'.

16. Peter Munz, *Our Knowledge of the Growth of Knowledge* (London: Routledge & Kegan Paul, 1985), p. 292.

17. Anthony O'Hear, 'The Evolution of Knowledge', review of Munz, ibid., *Critical Review* (1988), 2(1): 78–92.

18. Rilke, *First Elegy*, ll.12–13.

19. Bernard Williams, *Truth and Truthfulness. An Essay in Genealogy* (New Haven and London: Yale University Press, 2002), p. 177.

20. Ibid., p. 198.

21. Mythology did not go quietly. There were numerous attempts to re-mythologise history, and they were not confined to nationalist myths. They became more frantic as society became more secular, and bureaucratic and its tissues dried into logistical and technological networks. The historicisms of Hegel and Marx reinserted Fate and even Overall Purpose into the chapter of accidents empirical historians had increasingly revealed the past to be.

22. Ronald W. Dworkin, 'The New Gospel of Health', *The Public Interest* (2000), 141: 77–90.

23. The fashionable accessories that go with a healthy life do, however, provide a welcome distraction. For joggers running towards eternal life, Calvin Kleinism can fill in some of the gaps left by the departure of Calvinism.

24. Albert Einstein, 1933.

25. Steven Weinberg, *The First Three Minutes* (London: André Deutsch, 1977), p. 149.

26. Mary Midgley, *Science and Poetry* (London: Routledge, 2001).

27. The alternative is to invoke the circularity of the Anthropic Principle. This rests on the logical necessity for the laws observed by physicists to be compatible with the existence of physicists, otherwise the laws would not be observed.

28. Stace pointed this out:

    The founders of modern science – for instance, Galileo, Kepler, and Newton – were mostly pious men who did not doubt God's purposes. Nevertheless, they took the revolutionary step of consciously and deliberately expelling the idea of purpose as controlling nature from their new science of nature. They did this on the ground that inquiry into purposes is useless for what science aims at: namely, the prediction and control of events. To predict an eclipse, what you have to know is not its purpose but its cause. Hence science from the seventeenth century onwards became exclusively an inquiry into causes. The conception of purpose in the world was ignored and frowned on. This, though silent and unnoticed, was the greatest revolution in human history, far outweighing in importance any of the political revolutions whose thunder has reverberated through the world. (W. T. Stace, 'Man Against Darkness', *The Atlantic Monthly*, September 1948)

29. Even when it measure such qualities. The Caregiver Strain Scale, mentioned in Chapter 3 to evaluate the effectiveness of anti-dementia drugs, digitises unbearable sorrow but at the same time elides it.

30. Yeats quote. W. B. Yeats, 'Under Ben Bulben', *The Poems*, ed. Richard J. Finneran (New York: Simon & Schuster, 1997), pp. 333–6.

31. Quoted in Stillman Drake, *Discoveries and Opinions of Galileo* (New York: Doubleday, 1957) pp. 237–8. This has had some rather extreme expressions since Pythagoras first proposed that numbers were the essential substance of the universe. P. A. M. Dirac, for example, entertained this notion in a lecture given in 1937:

    Might it not be that all present events correspond to the properties of this large number [10^{39}] and, more generally, that the whole history of the universe corresponds to the properties of the whole sequence of natural numbers...? Thus there is a possibility that the ancient dream of the philosophers to connect all nature with the properties of whole numbers will some day be realised. ('Physical Science and Philosophy', *Nature Supplement* (1937), 139: 1001)

32. A. N. Whitehead, quoted in N. Rose, *Science and the Modern World* (New York: Macmillan, 1925), p. 31.

33. Stephen W. Hawking, *A Brief History of Time. From the Big Bang to Black Holes* (London: Bantam, 1988), p. 184.

34. John D. Barrow, *Theories of Everything. The Quest for Ultimate Explanation* (Oxford: Oxford University Press, 1991), p. 210.

35. Maurice Merleau-Ponty, *Phenomenology of Perception*, trans. Colin Smith (London: Routledge & Kegan Paul, 1963), p. viii. This is connected with the comfort Paul Valery noted, when he retorted to Pascal's claim that 'the eternal silence of those infinite spaces' terrified him. The eternal silences exist only so long as they are heard by a terrified individual. To be terrified in this way takes imagination. It doesn't come bundled with the equations and their figures.

36. Ibid., p. 53. We could make the same point using the distinction Wilfred Sellars put forward between the 'manifest' and the 'scientific' images of the world, in *Science, Perception and Reality* (London: Humanities Press, 1963). The manifest image corresponds to the ordinary common-sense view of the world. While the manifest image might reveal solid chairs and tables, with particular qualities, the scientific image (at least at its most reductive) shows them to be mere collections of atoms in largely empty space. Self-evidently, the scientific image is missing a trick or two – overlooking the world from which it takes its rise.

37. Indeed, in a remarkable passage, Einstein describes the necessary failure of science to redeem knowledge:

> In the distinction between concepts and sense perceptions is the metaphysical original sin for which success in formulating descriptions of the world of immediate perceptions is the only justification.

(I have lost the source of this passage but could not resist citing it none the less.)

38. Tallis, *Newton's Sleep*, and 'The Work of Art in an Age of Mechanical Reproduction', in *Theorrhoea and After* (Basingstoke: Macmillan, 1999).

39. The reader will recognise the reference to Milan Kundera's great novel. It is important, however, not to exaggerate that lightness: pain, responsibility, shame, fear, all re-socket one back into one's 'thisness'.

40. Rilke, Eighth Elegy, ll.70–2.

41. Letter (16 December 1911), quoted in Erich Heller, *The Disinherited Mind. Essays in Modern German Literature and Thought* (London: Penguin Books, 1961), p. 175.

42. There has been much talk of art and wounds; in particular of the artist's endeavour to repair through his art the wounds inflicted upon him in his formative years. Psychoanalytic interpreters of art in particular have identified wounds as sexual ones, as failures to overcome the complexes that are usually resolved on the way to maturity. I believe that art is – or perhaps should be – ultimately motivated not by specific accidental wounds, but by the wounds that arise out of the human condition. The universal appeal of some art may, however, arise out of the fact that the specific wounds that drive some artists put them more closely in touch with general wound of human consciousness.

43. See Tallis, 'Misunderstanding Art: The Myth of Enrichment' and 'Postscript: Art, Science and the Future of Human Consciousness', in *Newton's Sleep*.

44. Nietzsche, *The Twilight of the Idols*, trans. Walter Kaufman. 'Maxims and Arrows', no. 33.

45. Safranski, *Nietzsche. A Philosophical Biography*, p. 19.

46. F. Nietzsche, *Philosophy in the Tragic Age of the Greeks*, trans. and Introduction Marianne Cowan (Chicago: Gateway, 1962), p. 79. Nietzsche's account of Parmenides and the other citizens of 'the republic of creative minds between Thales and Plato' is one of the most thrilling and elevating philosophical texts I have ever read. It brilliantly captures those first shouts of amazement, terror, puzzlement and delight with which Western philosophy began. It amply justifies Bernard Williams' observation that 'The legacy of Greece to Western Philosophy was – Western Philosophy'.

47. Quoted ibid., p. 79.

48. 'H.E.B', 'Writing', in *Encyclopaedia Britannica*, Macropaedia, Vol. 18 (15th edition, 1993). The argument that the first significant critique of 'the apparatus of knowledge' was bound to occur after writing was perfected could be turned on its head: the first recorded critique of knowledge had to await writing to record it!

49. Which is perhaps why, historically, the Parmenidean response to the discrepancies between being and becoming (which concluded that becoming was unreal) triumphed over the Heraclitan response (which argued that only becoming was real).

50. It is not entirely surprising, therefore, that the philosopher who marked the transition between the pre-Socratics and the post-Socratics – Socrates himself – should have based his claim to having superior wisdom on the fact that he alone was aware

that he knew nothing. Socratic wisdom was not merely ironical, a way of disarming opponents, but a summary of the conclusions of his predecessors who knew they couldn't trust their senses but didn't know what to conclude about what lay beyond the senses.

51. Nietzsche, *Philosophy in the Tragic Age of the Greeks*, p. 69.
52. Paul Valery, *M. Teste*, trans. Jackson Mathews (London: Routledge & Kegan Paul, 1973), p. 63. While all knowledge is haunted by a sense of its own vulnerability, or at least its limits, the sense of cognitive incompleteness, lies at the very heart of science: it is its fundamental principle.
53. Of course, both of these digressions from the Parmenidean Way of Truth have been immensely fertile and enriching of human life. While the link between the Real and the Deity and between the latter and moral and political thought has been largely malign, the transformation of Parmenides' unchanging unity, the One, into a single god was a useful stimulus to science: it made the search for unifying laws, and the presumption of the uniformity of nature, an act of piety rather than blasphemy. It also informed the scientific quest with the necessarily premature hope that kept it going in the 2,000 years before it started to deliver significant benefits. The link still remains, as in, for example, the person of Einstein whose notion of the universe as an intrinsically unchanging space-time manifold is a rehearsal of the Parmenidean Block Universe and who repeatedly spoke, only semi-ironically, of 'The Old One' – God – who legislated over the world.
54. The case for that beginning is made in more detail in Raymond Tallis, *George Moore's Hands and Parmenides' Leap. A Philosophical Inquiry into the Impossibility of Philosophy* to be submitted for publication.

Epilogue

Through such evolutionary processes, man had become lord of creation –
his preeminence did not stem from a divine mission or any innate Cartesian
endowments, but because of basic physical facts: highly sensitive hands,
for instance, had permitted the development of superior powers of
volition and understanding.[1]

While the problem of knowledge was at the heart of philosophy
from the beginning, it was not explicitly foundational until
Descartes' brilliant thought experiments inaugurated modern philosophy.
For the pre-Socratics, and many such as Plato who wrote by the light of
the luminous wonder they had lit, scepticism was primarily a way of
justifying a radical revision of our ideas as to what is truly there. It was
an instrument by which thought led the thinker from the Way of
Opinion to the Way of Truth. And for many subsequent philosophers,
downgrading sense experience to the weaving of a mere veil of appearance was welcome for other reasons. It justified a more spiritual view of
the world – providing abstract arguments in favour of religious beliefs
after the profound, unquestioning intuitions arising out of the early
encounter of knowledge with itself had somewhat evaporated. What
was more, the critique of sense experience indirectly justified being
rather sniffy about the smelly human body with its gross, ungodly,
animal appetites. Plato's mighty example showed how, by casting doubt
on the truth of sense experience, one could support the notion of a place
where discarnate knowers would bask in the sunlight of truth dispensed
by a benign God.

After Descartes, who had offered a way out of universal doubt (with
a little bit of theological help), scepticism became less of an instrument
than a curse. Increasingly, philosophers were in the business, not only of

accounting for the way things looked in everyday life, but in saving the appearances: they were stuck with what F. H. Bradley famously described as 'finding bad reasons for what we believe on instinct'. Hume's lucid demonstration of the impossibility of getting from sense experience (the only source of our knowledge) to knowledge even of humble things such as objects and selves, unassisted by theological free gifts (which he declined to use), precipitated a crisis in Western philosophical thought, which has remained. Kant's solution – to invoke the spontaneous activity of the mind in combing sense experience into consciousness of objects, and making space, time and causation 'forms of sensible intuition' – has for some simply made the problem worse. Scepticism about what lies before us, the phenomenal world, has simply been parcelled off into acknowledged complete ignorance of what there is in the noumenal world of the in-itself. Kant characterised what was necessary to get from sense experience to the kind of knowledge we have but was not able, or inclined, to say whether the passage from the one to the other is justified. Neo-Kantian thought, phenomenology, positivism, generated uniformly unsatisfactory solutions. Physical objects were either inaccessible to conscious subjects or they dissolved into mental phenomena.

It is hardly surprising, then, that philosophers who rejected epistemology were so influential in the twentieth century. Heidegger and Moore argued that epistemological questions about the reality of external objects are themselves unreal inasmuch as they never trouble us when we are engaged in the serious business of ordinary life. Frege, and after him Wittgenstein, doubted whether such questions really could be asked because one could not do so without using language that seemed to presuppose the existence of those very things that were put into question. Others, such as Carnap and Quine, argued that the problem of knowledge was a matter for the sciences to solve. Carnap believed that human knowledge could be built up out of, or boiled down to, sense experiences and that all meaningful assertions were ultimately derived from observation statements, whose aggregation was the work of science. Quine saw epistemology as 'an enterprise within natural science', a branch of cognitive psychology. Alternatively, it was a branch of the philosophy of language, with specific tasks such as showing how, in the most general way, statements about sense experiences could or might relate to statements about material objects or tracing the logical geography of concepts intending mental or physical elements.

In the present inquiry, I, too, have avoided discharging the traditional epistemological duties of justifying the belief we have in an outside world and the beliefs we have about that world, such as that it contains material objects. I have given the classic problem of perception – 'to give an account of the relationship of sense-experience to material objects'[2] – very short shrift: the transition from sentience to material objects is 'underdetermined' because a material object (or indeed any other object of knowledge, such as a fact) is based upon the intuition that there is something beyond our awareness. Knowledge simply *is*, among other things, an awareness of something – itself a font of further possible awareness – that lies beyond that of which we are aware.

I have focused instead on why it is that we humans, alone among sentient creatures, enjoy (or suffer) a form of awareness, propositional awareness 'That X is the case', that has many forms including the knowledge of objects. I have forgone epistemology for epistogony. In this way, I hope to make knowledge – and therefore our distance from animals – visible, without approaching it as a problem prompting an inquiry some regard as sterile and possibly unintelligible.

As I observed repeatedly in *I Am*, the second volume of this trilogy,[3] this position is not epistemologically agnostic, however much I should like it to be. Irrespective of whether or not the intentional objects of particular acts of perception exist independently of the sense experiences that seem to reveal them, my account of the genesis of knowledge presupposes that there are animals; most particularly human animals experiencing their own bodies as both being and not being themselves – as being only partly scrutable. This rather assumes the existence of things like organic (material) bodies as normally construed. And it is difficult to conceive of the arena in which knowledge arises as other than consisting of material objects (some living, some non-living, some human and some not human) set out in the space which we envisage biological entities inhabiting.[4]

This illustrates an inescapable feature of epistemological discussion: a tendency to turn back on itself. Indeed, it takes knowledge – for example, of error – to get scepticism off the ground. And any account of the origin of knowledge presupposes not only knowledge (for example, of animal biology) but also an ontology (of, for example, material objects) to go with it, the objects of the very knowledge that may be put in question by suggesting that it has an origin. You cannot dig beneath knowledge without assuming knowledge; without, in other words, using a spade made of bits of knowledge.

This argument could be turned to the advantage of a realist ontology. Doubts about the validity of knowledge can arise only when there is an agreed, explicit ontology of objects. Scepticism-driven epistemology is consequently self-contradictory because knowledge at the most basic level can be put into question only by knowledge at the higher level; that scepticism is always a matter of the roof doubting the ground floor. One version of this assault on scepticism is the claim that the latter arises as a late, sophisticated development of knowing animals; or a very late manifestation of a complicated discourse between human beings that has been built on the assumptions that are built into everyday know-ledge, including the split between knowledge and its non-epistemic objects.

At any rate, scepticism in the present work has been seen as a kind of awakening prompted by knowledge encountering itself. To know that one is knowing may be like dreaming that one is dreaming which, as Novalis once said, is a signal that one is close to awakening. And this was perhaps what it was at the Parmenidean moment before his insights were diverted into metaphysics and, more locally, scientific inquiry. So while one is forced to the conclusion that one can neither talk one's way into, nor out of, scepticism-driven epistemological inquiry – not without self-contradiction or pragmatic self-refutation – the mystery of knowledge is a real one. But it is a *mystery*. Indeed, as Karl Popper said, a miracle – the greatest miracle in the universe.[5] It is not just a problem which one might expect to be patient of solution. It is hardly to be expected that thinkers might one day assemble a body of knowledge that would amount to a complete, transparent and satisfying account of the nature, origin, scope and limits of human knowledge. 'A mystery,' as Marcel said, 'is a problem which encroaches upon its own data and so invades them and so is transcended *qua* problem.'[6] Here, as so often in philosophy, one is reminded of an Escher staircase, where the top step seems to support all the others. The problem of knowledge – of getting clearer about the nature of knowledge – is itself manifestly a pursuit of a kind of knowledge but not of an item of knowledge.

If to approach human knowledge as a soluble problem may seem to be misguided and result only in frustration as the problems prove insoluble or equal frustration as they seem to dissolve into emptiness, it might be thought that treating knowledge as a mystery must be equally frustrating and sterile. This is not so; for there truly is a point in thinking through some problems around knowledge with the aim of recovering the mystery from the accretions that have concealed it. This is what Heidegger aimed to do – and in some measure succeeded – when he liberated the mystery of the world from traditional problems such as that of 'the reality of the external world'. This is perhaps, also, what Wittgenstein wanted to do: to dissolve the pseudo-problems of philo-sophy in order to make the true mysteries visible – something that is very apparent in his last thoughts.[7] Of course, doing philosophy while being aware that in the end soluble problems have to give way to insoluble mysteries is to run the danger not only of losing sense of direction, but of losing serious purpose.

And it is anyway difficult enough to philosophise seriously; or to philosophise at the level of seriousness implicit in, or adequate to, its questions. It is almost as difficult to notice how frivolous, outside of certain moments, the whole business of asking philosophical questions is. (As one who was a doctor for sixty or more hours a week, for over thirty years, I am particularly aware of this.) And yet philosophy is truly serious; or a potential home for that 'hunger ... to be more serious'.[8] It is serious if one is dissatisfied with going through life understanding so little of the world, life, self one has to live. At the same time it is frivolous in so far as its questions disappear as soon as one has tooth-ache or is simply busy. When we are engaged in the daily business of life we do not ask philosophical questions. So the addressing of philsophical questions seems at once a supreme expression of human consciousness and at the same time somehow a culpable luxury. For, as Heidegger pointed out, '"mindless" everyday coping skills' are 'the basis of all intelligibility'.[9]

If philosophy has one overriding and achievable – though never completable – aim, it is to make ourselves more *visible*, to see more clearly, as if from a greater distance, what we humans are. This was the view of one of the greatest of all philosophers:

> Kant argued that the domain of philosophy was defined by three questions – What can I know? What ought I to do?, and What may I hope? – and that these questions are facets of the more general question, What is man?[10]

Similar questions troubled Hume:

> Where am I, or what? From what causes do I derive my existence, and to what condition shall I return?[11]

In pursuit of this aim, we must resist allowing our idea of ourselves to be appropriated by some pre-existing conceptual scheme – theological, scientific, socio-political. The Heideggerian dream of philosophy as 'primordial thinking' may be just that, but philosophers should resist, so far as possible, pre-packaged thinking. Darwinism, yes; Darwinosis, no.

To put this another way: the important certainties of science and of everyday experience are framed within total uncertainty as to why and what we are. While it is legitimate to speculate why, of all animals, we are the ones who have made the ascent to objective knowledge, any such speculation must be haunted by the fact that we do not understand the sentience that, through the hand, turned back upon itself and ultimately awoke to knowledge. The crucial role of the nervous system cannot be doubted but we must recognise that chasing the self and free will to smaller and smaller parts of the brain is daft. The brain is a necessary but not a sufficient condition for human consciousness. The brain in a vat would be just that: a brain in a vat, not a world-figuring consciousness. It is no using hoping to find citizens in neurones; or the accumulated pooled consciousness of several hundred thousand generations of self-conscious human beings curled up in synapses. Consciousness is of, and in, the entire person in her entire life. There will be different sorts of explanations of a pain in the toe and a feeling of shame at being unsuccessful in a bid for a job. We need a critical neuro-epistemology that can recognise and deal with these very difficult facts.[12] This would take account of the scientific facts but not be enclosed within them or regard them as having a specially privileged status compared with other sources of understanding. No such account is yet forthcoming, so knowledge is as yet unspeakable in scientific terms.

So we do not know, ultimately, why there are knowledgeable beings such as ourselves who have a privileged access to some of the truths about the world and who, indeed, are the sole bearers of truth. Equally, we cannot arrive at an unassailable assessment of the status of our objective knowledge. It is a central purpose or strategy, of philosophy to exploit the conflict between our ordinary certainties and the justified uncertainty beneath them to create a new sense of what we might be – a sense that would not leave or abandon the old sense; that would build upon it and not displace or replace it. For I cannot, for example, truly doubt that there is a table in front of me.

The overall purpose of this trilogy, expressed in the attempt in the present volume to make uniquely human knowledge visible, has been to show how it is possible to liberate mankind from a religious self-interpretation without passing straight into a stunted scientistic account of what we are. Scientism not only ignores our inability to explain consciousness or fully to understand the matter of which it believes the world is made; it also overlooks the gap between the Knowing Animal (and indeed the knowledge upon which it is based) and the natural world. My aim is to encourage entirely new attempts to rethink what we are and what is possible for us. Indeed, I think of philosophy as a means of cultivating the most extended, and tingling, sense of possibility – but one informed by the strongest sense of reality, that comes from our everyday experience and from what we truly know from science. Serious philosophy must build on what we cannot unbelieve; on the things that are the cornerstones of our ordinary collective behaviour and our expectations of and beliefs about each other and the world. But it must also acknowledge the possible truth of Nietzsche's claim that

> All our so-called consciousness is a more or less fanciful commentary on an unknown, perhaps unknowable, but felt text.[13]

'Possibility rooted in reality' – and extended by abstract thought – implies that the revelations of new understanding that philosophy seeks will not be transcendent; rather, they will be immanent. They will leave nothing real behind because that reality will simply be waiting at the far end of the revelation. It is perhaps too much to expect philosophers to be able 'to withstand toothache', but it is not too much to expect them not to deny toothache or the realities that have been created around it. If philosophy is indeed 'primordial thinking', it is thinking at its most free. It will question all received ideas, including the most widely accepted ones of modern times, namely that the voice of truth necessarily speaks in the accent of despair and that the damaged have privileged access to the truth.

What, however, would philosophical thought hope to achieve? What would be the outcome of truly serious philosophising? It might change the way one perceives things on a moment-to-moment basis. It might change the hopes one has. At any rate, it should transform one's sense of what it is to be a human being, of what one is oneself. It should lead one out of the prison house of ordinariness, of the taken-for-granted, beyond everyday perception into the sunlight of amazement. Which is not to reject the ordinary. One of the deepest impulses behind this entire trilogy has been an intense awareness of the complex miracle of ordinariness. What philosophy should aim at, perhaps, is an 'internal transcendance' that doesn't jettison the beliefs of everyday but builds on them.[14] At its best, philosophy should be 'here on fire'. At some stage, philosophy has to give way to song, without going soft on concepts and arguments. At its height, it shares the dream, common to great art and sexual love, of the convergence of absolute presence and ultimate meaning; of incandescent immanence; a kind of *in-stasis* rather than *ek-stasis*.

This is not purely of esoteric interest. The greatest threat to the future of humankind comes from the ever-increasing rate of consumption of its resources and its degradation by the processes of production and the effluent in the wake of consumption. There are two drivers to this upward spiral that threatens both to leach and degrade the planet. The first is the growth of the population. This is a problem that is taken serious wherever there is honesty, and acted upon wherever there is some measure of rationality. The other is the growth of *per capita* consumption and this seems to be taken seriously in very few places and acted upon in even fewer. There is little motivation to arrest economic growth partly because there seems to be no easy way of arriving at sustainable non-growth in successful economies without precipitating decline. This is a technical issue that needs to be urgently addressed. The other reason is that the intrinsic logic of consumption is towards increase. In part this is because increased affluence and expenditure are not only measures of success but fundamental narratives of modern life. It is a model of development that is very difficult to dismount from for lack of alternative narratives and also because each act of consumption brings further consumption in its wake. This is not only because houses require furniture, cars require spare parts and computers require endless upgrades, but because material possessions rarely translate into experiences corresponding to the idea that prompted their purchase. We pass from purchase to purchase in pursuit of the elusive experience of pleasure or delight. The reasons for this go very deep, as I have discussed at length elsewhere.[15] It is connected with the divorce discussed in the previous chapter between sentience and knowledge. We need to find new ways to experience our experiences; to enjoy the lucid pleasures of daily life, otherwise, the history of mankind will be the pursuit of ever more intense delirium, ever more frantic distractions. We shall pass from the Stone Age through the Stoned Age and, if as seems likely, the fabric of the planet is irreversibly destroyed as a consequence, back to the Stone Age.

What I have written in the present book and its two predecessors falls far below the aim of pointing the way towards *in-stasis*, though the notion of the immanent revelation does justify the fact that much of what is said in it is merely descriptive rather than explanatory; and that, in common with most other philosophers, far from ironing things out I have merely shifted 'the bump in the carpet'. Somewhat dismayingly, I do not know whether the world would have been significantly poorer if I had died before writing *Handkind*. Short of this certainty, I would be satisfied if, in thinking my way through thickets that are at least in part of my own creating, rather than confining myself to well-worn laid-out paths, I have discovered some of the more interesting areas of darkness. That, at the very least, I have made the mystery more visible so that ordinariness glows with a brightness that is truly its own and rearranged problems have come to stand in a different light. That I have contributed to something Rilke characterised as the project of 'bringing forth a pure witness to the breadth of the world, its diversity and its fullness';[16] that I have helped to bring to birth the widest mind-portable

'That'; the 'That of That' which aspires to encompass all the local 'thats' the Knowing Animal brought into the world.

I have been led by the hand to all manner of places I had not antici-pated when I first started thinking about why we humans are so different from our animal kin. I have left much unfinished business in trying to understand the path taken by humans from sentience to sentences. The completion of this book is only a temporary pause in a long, unfinished journey. I feel now as if, far from reaching the end of my questions, half a million words into this investigation I am just at the beginning.

NOTES AND REFERENCES

1. Roy Porter, *Enlightenment. Britain and the Creation of the Modern World* (London: Penguin Books, 2000), p. 443. This is a summary of the thesis put forward by Erasmus Darwin in *The Temple of Nature*, Canto 3 ll.41–6, which provides one of the epigraphs to *The Hand. A Philosophical Inquiry into Human Being* (Edinburgh: Edinburgh University Press, 2003).
2. Anthony Quinton, 'The Problem of Perception', *Mind* (1955), 28–51.
3. See especially Chapter 2.
4. Which is, as Barry Stroud has pointed out, unacceptable. When
    > we want to understand how *all* knowledge of a certain kind is possible, we cannot rely on any knowledge of that kind we might think we already possess in order to explain how we know anything at all of that kind. (Introduction to *Understanding Human Knowledge. Philosophical Essays* (Oxford: Oxford University Press, 2000), p. xiv)
5. I did think of calling this book *The Greatest Miracle*, but I feared that this might mislead readers on the lookout for a devotional text.
6. Gabriel Marcel, *Being & Having* (London: Fontana Library, 1965), p. 186.
7. See the title essay in Raymond Tallis, *On the Edge of Certainty* (Basingstoke: Macmillan, 1999).
8. Philip Larkin, 'Church Going', in *The Less Deceived* (London: The Marvell Press, 1955).
9. Hubert L. Dreyfus, *Being-in-the-World. A Commentary on Heidegger's Being and Time Division I* (Cambridge, MA: MIT Press, 1991), p. 3.
10. This view is cited in Frederick A. Olafson, *What is a Human Being? A Heideggerian View* (Cambridge: Cambridge University Press, 1995), p. 1.
11. David Hume, *A Treatise of Human Nature*, Book 1, 'Of the Understanding' (New York: Dolphin, 1961), p. 239.
12. Without invoking 'supervenience' which is simply a convenient way of cancelling out the problems arising out of wilfully 'infravenient' explanations; a cure, in short, for a self-inflicted conceptual disease.
13. F. Nietzsche, *Daybreak Thoughts on the Prejudices of Morality*, trans. R. J. Hollingdale (Cambridge: Cambridge University Press, 1982), p. 76.
14. I take a rueful sidelong glance here at the contradiction between the miracle of ordinary human life and the ordinariness of what humans do and how they perceive it; between, say, the miracle of human language and the banality of what we say to each other.

15. Raymond Tallis, *Newton's Sleep: Two Cultures and Two Kingdoms* (Basingstoke: Macmillan, 1995) and 'The Work of Art in an Age of Mechanical Reproduction', in *Theorrhoea and After* (Basingstoke: Macmillan, 1999).
16. Donald Prater, *A Ringing Glass. The Life of Rainer Maria Rilke* (Oxford: Clarendon Paperbacks, 1994), p. 308.

Glossary

Because I hope this book will be read by all kinds and conditions of Knowing Animal – by 'general readers' like me as well as by professional philosophers – I offer this Glossary to assist understanding. I have not included all the technical terms used in the book, only those that are used most commonly and are crucial to the argument. Others I define as they arise.

Among these terms are a few which, while not full-blown neologisms, are part of the idiolect I have developed in my thinking to myself. Readers may benefit from having a clear statement of my 'take' on them. Finally, there are one or two idiosyncratic phrases that are central to the vision of this book.

The reader is advised against reading through this Glossary straight away as it might be rather off-putting. The definitions will make more sense as the terms are encountered in context.

Anti-psychologism
A reaction against psychologism (q.v.). Anti-psychologism attempts to exclude contents of consciousness from the philosophical investigation of the meaning of words, the nature of thought, and even from the understanding of mind itself. It paves the way for absurdities such as 'the syntactic theory of mind' – the notion that the mind is a device for manipulating symbols – and the claim that qualia (contents of consciousness, subjective experiences, such as the sensation of yellow or the taste of coffee) are illusory.

Biologism (cf. Scientism)
The assumption that everything that matters about human beings can be explained biologically. Humans are understood as organisms whose behaviour is to be explained entirely in Darwinian terms – that is to say,

as being directly or indirectly related to organic survival.

Deindexicalised awareness
One of two modes of the propositional awareness (q.v.) that is unique to human beings. Deindexicalised awareness develops out of indexical awareness (q.v.). The subject is related to an object but not physically located with respect to it. The objects of deindexicalised awareness range from things that I anticipate but cannot yet sense to the abstract and concrete, possible and actual, objects of factual knowledge.

Epistemology
The branch of philosophy concerned with the nature, the origin and the limitations of knowledge. Historically, it has been driven by a scepticism that is awoken when knowledge encounters itself and discovers that it lacks adequate foundation.

Epistogony
A rather less ambitious approach to the philosophy of knowledge than epistemology. Epistogony does not attempt to meet the challenge of scepticism but endeavours to make knowledge visible by describing the differences between knowledge and sentience and trying to account for the awakening, uniquely in humans, of knowledge out of sentience.

Existential Intuition, the
The intuition, confined to human beings, 'That I am [this] ...'. The Existential Intuition lies at the root of first-person being, of agency and of the awakening of knowledge out of sentience – in short, of everything that distinguishes the human condition from animal life.

Indexical
A term introduced by C. S. Peirce to capture the properties of words such as 'I', 'here', 'now' that, as it were, point to themselves. In this work, it is extended to modes of consciousness: since the reference of an indexical is rooted in the particular occasion of its use, it is relative to the self-consciousness of the speaker. This is the link with 'indexical awareness' (q.v.).

Indexical awareness (indexicalised awareness)
One of the two chief modes of propositional awareness (q.v.) unique to human beings. In indexical awareness, an explicit subject is in an explicit spatio-temporal relationship with an object of consciousness. The object is experienced from a particular perspective and that perspective is itself explicit – as when I see an objective from behind, or in a certain light, and see *that* I see it from behind or in a certain light. The object of indexical awareness is intuited as being other than

the subject and as exceeding what is revealed of it to the subject in sense experience. Indexical awareness is built on the Existential Intuition (q.v.) and consequent awareness of one's self as an 'embodied subject'.

Intentionality

The relation between human consciousness and its objects. Human consciousness is explicitly 'about' or 'of' something which itself is not. Intentionality is a property both of perception (as in seeing a material object before one) and of propositional attitudes (as in, for example, thinking about something). While intentionality always characterises a relation between a conscious subject and an object posited as other than the subject, the nature of this relation may vary. Intentionality is present in both indexicalised and deindexicalised awareness; indeed, in all specifically human awareness that is awoken as a result of the Existential Intuition.

Knowledge

A distinctively human form of awareness in which a subject relates to an object. The object of knowledge may be concrete and spatio-temporally related to the embodied subject (indexical awareness, q.v.) or be abstract and not so related (deindexicalised awareness, q.v.).

Neurophilosophy

A term, given wide currency following Patricia Churchland's *Neurophilosophy* (1988). Its central claim is that consciousness (the mind, etc.) is identical with certain neural activity in the brain. Neurophilosophy has many subsidiary assumptions, most notably that the brain is a computer and the mind its software, and that the passage of nerve impulses is the 'information-processing' that underpins and constitutes all levels of awareness.

Pre-indexical awareness ('Anindexical awareness')

This characterises the sentience that is animals' mode of awareness. Whether humans ever experience sentience uncontaminated with propositional awareness is unclear. (Cf. the question as to whether it is possible to have a pure aconceptual, unclassified, sensation.)

Propositional attitude

A mental state – such as a thought, a belief, a desire – that expresses an attitude towards a particular state of affairs that is proposed (or supposed) to be the case: I think, believe, wish, 'That X is the case'. Like object perceptions, propositional attitudes have intentionality (q.v.); that is to say, there is a differentiation within awareness of the conscious content and the object that the content is 'about' or 'of'. Unlike perception, the intentional object is not always, or even typically, something that is spatio-temporarily located with respect to the body of the subject. Even where the intentional object of a propositional attitude is a particular, it is first proposed as a possibility, and hence as not being spatio-temporally related to the embodied subject. Propositional attitudes belong to the realm of deindexicalised awareness. (q.v.)

Propositional awareness
The form of awareness that comes in the wake of the Existential Intuition. Its general form is 'That X is the case'. It must not be thought of as being entirely linguistic: language is at most a mere 100,000 years old, while the Existential Intuition probably goes back several million years, when hominids first parted company from pongids. The fundamental intuition, captured in the presentential 'That', is built on an uncoupling (unique to humans) between the organism and its world; that is to say, upon an at least inchoate subject–object relationship. Propositional awareness encompasses both deindexicalised propositional attitudes and indexical awareness.

Psychologism
Psychologism is the doctrine that reduces logical entities, such as propositions, universals, numbers, to mental states or mental activities. It is linked with the endeavour to treat philosophy as a branch of empirical psychology, so that the theory of the meaning of words or logical operations could be constructed out of observations of the mental images or psychological states accompanying their use or performance. It is wrong but, unfortunately, reaction against it in analytical philosophy led to the equal and opposite error of an extreme anti-psychologism (q.v.) that resulted in de-psychologised accounts of the mind and its contents.

Scientism (adj. scientistic)
In its extreme form, scientism combines a belief in the omnicompetence of science with the assumption that all true sciences in the end boil down to physics, so that human beings are entirely subsumed into the material world. Even where humans are thought to require explanation in specifically biological terms (biologism q.v.), there is a tendency to believe that biology is only a branch of chemistry and physics and to hold that the methods of the physical sciences are the only road to truth. Scientism assimilates the first-person viewpoint to the third-person (or no-person) viewpoint of physics.

Sentience
The form of awareness available to all conscious animals, including humans. It does not have intentional objects experienced by the organism as distinct and separate itself.

Index

Note: Page numbers in bold refer to diagrams; those in italic refer to the Glossary

Index